MIGRATION IN THE TIME
OF REVOLUTION

MIGRATION IN THE TIME OF REVOLUTION

CHINA, INDONESIA, AND THE COLD WAR

TAOMO ZHOU

CORNELL UNIVERSITY PRESS
Ithaca and London

Publication of this book is supported in part by the Faculty Start-up Grant at Nanyang Technological University, Singapore, and Tier 1 Grant, Ministry of Education, Singapore.

First published 2019 by Cornell University Press

Library of Congress Cataloging-in-Publication Data

Names: Zhou, Taomo, 1984– author.
Title: Migration in the time of revolution : China, Indonesia, and the Cold War / Taomo Zhou.
Description: Ithaca : Cornell University Press, 2019. | Includes bibliographical references and index.
Identifiers: LCCN 2019015735 (print) | LCCN 2019016179 (ebook) | ISBN 9781501739941 (pdf) | ISBN 9781501739958 (epub/mobi) | ISBN 9781501739934 | ISBN 9781501739934 (cloth ; alk. paper)
Subjects: LCSH: China—Foreign relations—Indonesia. | Indonesia—Foreign relations—China. | Chinese—Indonesia—Politics and government. | Cold War.
Classification: LCC DS740.5.I56 (ebook) | LCC DS740.5.I56 Z47 2019 (print) | DDC 327.51059809/045—dc23
LC record available at https://lccn.loc.gov/2019015735

ISBN 978-1-5017-8144-5 (pbk.)

To my mother, Tao Yitao

Contents

Acknowledgments

I appreciate the financial support I received from the Faculty Start-up Grant and the Center for Liberal Arts and Social Sciences (CLASS) Postdoctoral Fellowship at Nanyang Technological University in Singapore, the Henry Luce Foundation/American Council of Learned Societies (ACLS) Pre-dissertation Grant for Research in China, the Lee-Teng-hui Fellowship, and the Knight Biggerstaff Fellowship at Cornell University.

I thank Liang Yingming, Niu Jun, Niu Ke, and Yu Tiejun at Peking University for the unwavering support they have given me for over a decade. Arne Westad has offered warm encouragement as well as incisive critiques throughout the years. At Cornell University, Chen Jian, Sherman Cochran, Eric Tagliacozzo, and Andrew Mertha have spent countless hours helping me conceptualize this project. I am grateful to inspirations from Jeff Petersen, T. J. Hinrichs, Durba Ghosh, Thomas Pepinsky, Fredrik Logevall, Chiara Formichi, Victor Seow, and Liren Zheng. *Terima kasih banyak* to my Indonesian language teacher, Jolanda Pandin.

For their contributions during my fieldwork, I owe a debt of gratitude to Kong Zhiyuan, Wang Yifu, Wang Keping, Huang Huilan, Guo Jingren, Zhao Meiling, Johan Purnama, Jona Widhagdo Putri, A. Dahana, Johannes Herlijanto, Didi Kwartanada, Annas Bentari, Dede Oetomo, Kathleen Azali, Nancy Latour, Marinus van den Berg, Maghiel van Crevel, Klaas Stutje, Ding Lixing, Jiang Zhenpeng, Zhang Changhong, Zhang Maorong, Shi Xueqin, Nie Dening, Cai Renlong, Gao Yanjie, and Mona Lohanda. I have run out of words to express my appreciation for their kindness.

The preparation of the manuscript has benefited greatly from stimulating conversations with my colleagues in Singapore, particularly Hallam Stevens, Goh Geok Yian, Fengshi Wu, Scott Anthony, Els van Dongen, Jess Hinchy, Seng Guo Quan, Koh Keng We, Wen-Qing Ngoei, Ang Cheng Guan, and Daniel Chua. I thank Liu Hong for his generous support and guidance. Evelyn Hu-DeHart read earlier drafts with meticulous attention to detail and offered extremely useful advice. I am immensely grateful to Ben Anderson,

Greg Brazinsky, Sayaka Chatani, Jack Meng-Tat Chia, David Chandler, Audrey Kahin, Charles Kraus, Mary Somers Heidhues, Julia Lovell, Hajimu Masuda, Glen Peterson, Josh Stenberg, Asui Warman Adam, Charlotte Setijadi, Leo Suryadinata, and anonymous reviewers for their thoughtful feedback. Bernadette Guthrie and Karen Carroll have edited my writing with patience and great care. At Cornell University Press, I thank Roger Haydon for his savvy advice and Susan Specter for her timely help. Portions of Chapters 3, 6, 7, and 8 appeared in "Ambivalent Alliance: Chinese Policy towards Indonesia, 1960–1965," *China Quarterly* 221 (March 2015). Chapter 8 is a revised and condensed version of "China and the Thirtieth of September Movement," *Indonesia* 98 (October 2014). I thank Cambridge University Press and Cornell University's Southeast Asia Program for their permission to reproduce them.

My friends—particularly Catherine Biba, Shiau-yun Chen, Priyamvada Jadaun, Lin Fu, Diego Fossati, Hong Haolan, Jo Ling Kent, Anto Mohsin and family, Yooumi Lee and family, Kong Tao and Torsten Juelich, Karla Ruth Orozco Toledano, Oiyan Liu and Tom Patton, Sai Pooja Mahajan, Arina Rotaru and Noriaki Hoshino, Yuanchong Wang, Xue Linyan, Genie Yoo, and Bishan Yang and family—have cheered me on through the years. My aunt, uncle, and cousin, Maggie, Doug, and Zoe Anderson, made me feel at home even when I was studying far away. My daughter Paulina slowed down my writing in the right way. I thank my father Zhou Luming and husband Andreas Brandl for their love and good humor. They understand why I dedicate this book to my mother, Tao Yitao, who has instilled a passion for research in me and has witnessed the evolution of this book every step of the way.

Abbreviations

Baperki	Badan Permusjawaratan Kewarganegaraan Indonesia (Consultative Body for Indonesian Citizenship)
BATAN	Badan Tenaga Atom Nasional (Indonesian Nuclear Agency)
CCP	Chinese Communist Party
Comintern	Communist International
CONEFO	Conference of the New Emerging Forces
CPSU	Communist Party of the Soviet Union
DPR	Dewan Perwakilan Rakyat (People's Representative Council of Indonesia)
GANEFO	Game of the New Emerging Forces
IOC	International Olympic Committee
KAMI	Kesatuan Aksi Mahasiswa Indonesia (Indonesian University Students' Action Front)
KAPPI	Kesatuan Aksi Pemuda Pelajar Indonesia (Indonesian Youth and Students' Action Front)
Masyumi	Majelis Syuro Muslimin Indonesia (Consultative Council for Indonesian Muslims)
MCP	Malayan Communist Party
MPAJA	Malayan People's Anti-Japanese Army
NCNA	New China News Agency (Xinhua tongxun she)
NU	Nahdlatul Ulama (Awakening of Religious Scholars)
OCAC	Overseas Chinese Affairs Commission (qiaowu weiyuanhui)
Permesta	Piagam Perjuangan Rakyat Semesta (Universal Struggle Charter)
PGRS	Pasukan Gerilya Rakyat Sarawak (Sarawak People's Guerilla Force)
PKI	Partai Komunis Indonesia (Indonesian Communist Party)
PLA	People's Liberation Army
PNI	Partai Nasional Indonesia (Indonesian National Party)
PRC	People's Republic of China

PRRI	Pemerintah Revolusioner Republik Indonesia (Revolutionary Government of the Republic of Indonesia)
RI	Republik Indonesia (Republic of Indonesia)
ROC	Republic of China
SOBSI	Sentral Organisasi Buruh Seluruh Indonesia (All Indonesia Center of Labor Organizations)
TNI	Tentara Negara Indonesia (Indonesian National Armed Forces)

A Note on Language

The Chinese names and terms used in this book are generally written according to the pinyin system of romanization, but there are some exceptions. Generally, I have used alternative romanizations of historical figures' names only when the alternative romanization is widely used, such as Sun Yat-sen and Chiang Kai-shek. In addition, romanization other than pinyin has been used for names of cities such as Hong Kong and Taipei as well as for Chinese Indonesian names such as Siauw Giok Tjhan and terms such as "Pao An Tui."

Except for direct quotations from historical documents, the spelling of Indonesian words follows the New Spelling adopted in 1972.

Unless otherwise noted, the English translations of texts are my own.

In the footnotes and bibliography, I have provided English translations for Chinese sources but not the Indonesian sources because *bahasa Indonesia* uses the same roman script as English.

To avoid confusion, the glossary at the end of this book lists each name and term first in pinyin, then in other romanizations (if available), and finally in Chinese characters.

MIGRATION IN THE TIME OF REVOLUTION

Introduction
Revolutionary Diplomacy and Diasporic Politics

On a day in June, 1955, at the Tanjung Priok harbor in Jakarta, twenty-four-year-old Liang Yingming, a second-generation ethnic Chinese from a Cantonese family in Solo, Central Java, was about to leave Indonesia for the People's Republic of China (PRC). Before his departure, by signing the back of his Indonesian birth certificate, he agreed never to return to Indonesia. This pledge was required by the Indonesian government, which imposed strict restrictions on the reentry of the ethnic Chinese who had been to the PRC due to fears that they would disseminate Communist ideology.[1] Liang then boarded the ship, where there were over a thousand Indonesian-born Chinese high school graduates ready to travel to the PRC for higher education. The scene was merry, cheerful, and even celebratory. Waving to his father, who came to send him off, Liang happily exclaimed: "See you in Beijing!" The passengers threw colorful paper streamers toward the shore, which were caught by friends and family. These colorful paper strips, with one end held by those onboard and the other by those on the land, tightened and finally broke as the ship started to move.[2]

Fifty-seven years later, on a midsummer afternoon in Beijing, Liang, a professor emeritus of international studies at Peking University, recounted this scene to me with sparkling eyes. That life-defining moment was as fresh in his memory as if it had happened just yesterday.

Although born and raised in Indonesia, from his early years Liang had been an avid participant in politics oriented toward the PRC among the overseas Chinese. A star student at the Bacheng High School (Bacheng Zhongxue, Sekolah Pah Tsung in *bahasa Indonesia*) of Jakarta, a Chinese-language educational institution sympathetic to the PRC, he joined the underground movement of the Chinese Communist Party (CCP).[3] After his graduation in 1950, he taught the Marxist interpretation of modern Chinese history to high school students. Shortly before his departure in 1955, he had worked with the PRC embassy in Indonesia to protect Premier Zhou Enlai against potential sabotage by the Chinese Nationalists at the Afro-Asian Conference in Bandung. After his return to China, part of his dream was realized: he received a college education and later had a successful academic career. Yet history and his personal life took unexpected turns. China embarked on several political campaigns and endured a great famine, which was followed

FIGURE 0.1.   Liang Yingming at his graduation from Bacheng High School in 1950. Personal collection of Liang Yingming.

FIGURE 0.2. Liang Yingming as the master of ceremonies at the 1952 sports meeting in Jakarta that commemorated the third anniversary of the establishment of the PRC. The person behind him giving out awards is Ang Jan Goan (Hong Yuanyuan), the president of the pro-Beijing Federation of the Chinese General Associations of Jakarta and the director of the pro-Beijing *Xin Bao*. Personal collection of Liang Yingming.

by the Great Proletarian Cultural Revolution. In Indonesia, the September Thirtieth Movement (*Gerakan 30 September*, hereafter referred to as "the movement") of 1965 resulted in a regime change and institutionalized discrimination against the ethnic Chinese.[4] As economic conditions worsened in China and its relations with Indonesia deteriorated, his family's original plan to join him in Beijing fell apart. The day at Tanjung Priok harbor turned out to be Liang's final farewell to his father, who passed away from a heart attack in 1963.

Liang's account gives us a glimpse of what it was like to live through the intertwined histories of two nations. During the Cold War, the PRC and Indonesia were connected by two kinds of ties. On the state-to-state level, in the early 1960s Beijing and Jakarta forged a strategic alignment built on a shared past of anticolonial struggle and an anticipated future of independence from the Cold War superpowers. On the transnational level, even though China and Indonesia do not share geographical borders, the existence of 2.5 million ethnic Chinese in Indonesia—many of whom had economic influence but an unclear citizenship status—gave rise to a porous social frontier. In this book, I interweave the evolution of diplomatic relations with the sociopolitical lives of the Chinese in Indonesia. The overseas Chinese were, and still are, an important but highly controversial resource for the PRC's advancement of political and economic interests abroad. But the precise extent of the PRC's control over the diaspora remains obscure.[5] How did the Communist revolution in Mainland China change the way that the Southeast Asian Chinese, who were stereotyped as affluent capitalists, perceived themselves and were perceived by others? What social dynamics in the diaspora's host countries enabled and limited China's transnational mobilization efforts? How did the overseas Chinese's personal experiences of assimilation, exclusion, and forced or voluntary migration affect the outcome of the PRC's diplomatic overtures?

More broadly, this book addresses the question of how formerly colonized countries that emerged after World War II interacted with one another on the global stage when citizenship was contested, political loyalty was in question, identity was fluid, and the boundaries for political mobilization were blurred. As a result, domestic ethnic conflicts became entangled with international politics and migrant disputes disrupted geostrategic collaborations. While recognizing states' powerful role in claiming and deploying the diaspora, this book also highlights the agency and autonomy of individuals like Liang, whose life experiences were shaped by but also helped shape the trajectory of bilateral diplomacy. With a wide range of political allegiances and agendas, the overseas Chinese responded to the developing events of the Cold War in diverse ways.

Focusing on the entanglement of diplomacy and migration, I will put forward three specific arguments. First, I will reject the widely circulated assertion that the suffering of the ethnic Chinese after the September Thirtieth Movement was a fitting retribution for Beijing's alleged sponsorship of a "Communist coup" in Indonesia. In the early 1960s, Beijing's first priority was to befriend Indonesia as part of an international united front that was independent from both the socialist bloc led by the Soviet Union and the capitalist West led by the United States. The PRC had neither the intention nor the capability to overthrow the left-leaning government led by President Sukarno. Second, despite the convergence of strategic interests between Beijing and Jakarta in the early 1960s, governmental relations inevitably intersected with communal politics and ethnic tensions. Hoping to dispel Indonesia's concern over its connection with the ethnic Chinese, Beijing dissolved the CCP's overseas branches and ceased to automatically recognize all persons with Chinese blood as PRC citizens. But these efforts failed to fully contain the political activism among the diaspora, which had a life of its own and ultimately derailed Beijing's foreign policy goals. Third, the Chinese community in Indonesia was divided along the battle lines of the Chinese Civil War, which was fought between the Communist and Nationalist Parties. This bifurcation had a profound impact on state-to-state relations between Beijing and Jakarta and on interethnic relations in Indonesia. Many ethnic Chinese actively partook in civic campaigns launched by pro-Chinese Communist and pro-Chinese Nationalist factions in Indonesia. Both sides claimed that all ethnic Chinese owed their loyalty to China's sole legitimate center: Beijing according to the Communists or Taipei according to the Nationalists. Initially incited by the Nationalist and Communist Parties, the rivalry between the pro-Taipei and pro-Beijing Chinese in Indonesia later took forms specific to the diasporic society and gained an unforeseen momentum that neither Taipei nor Beijing could control. The political enthusiasm of the ethnic Chinese aroused suspicion from the Indonesian government, aggravated ethnic tension in Indonesian society, and destabilized Sino-Indonesian relations.

Who Are the Chinese in This Book?

Scholars of Chinese migration have long debated how to define the subject of their research. While acknowledging that no term seems to be universally accepted, I use "overseas Chinese" to refer to people of Chinese birth or descent living outside of the contemporary territories of the PRC, Taiwan, Hong Kong, and Macau.[6] Since the book deals with a historical context in which citizenship was a comparatively new and unstable formation, "overseas Chinese" includes Chinese nationals (in Chinese, *huaqiao*), foreign citizens who are ethnically Chinese (*huaren*), as well as those whose citizenship status was uncertain. The term "diaspora" is used interchangeably with "overseas Chinese."[7] For centuries, maritime trade and the rise and fall of dynasties in China drove waves of migrants, primarily from Guangdong, Fujian, and Hainan Island, down to the archipelago known today as Indonesia. Earlier migrants integrated into local societies through intermarriage and the adoption of local languages and cultural practices. In my treatment of twentieth-century Indonesia, I follow G. William Skinner's proposal that people who had Chinese surnames until they were pressured to adopt Indonesian-sounding names by the Suharto regime should be assumed to be of Chinese origin.[8]

A 1930 census conducted by the Dutch colonial government showed that there were 1,233,214 Chinese living in the East Indies.[9] No official population census data regarding the ethnic Chinese is available from Indonesia for the 1950s and 1960s. Skinner estimated that in 1961 there were 2.3 to 2.6

million Chinese in the archipelago.[10] Skinner's hypothesis roughly corroborates estimations by the PRC embassy in Jakarta (2.7 million ethnic Chinese in 1956) as well as that by the Nationalist government in Taiwan (2 million ethnic Chinese in 1953).[11] A more daring estimation is made by the Chinese scholar Wu Shihuang, who calculated that, in 1952, 3 million ethnic Chinese lived in Indonesia. They constituted up to 2 percent of the overall population of Indonesia at the time (80 million) and a quarter of the total number of Chinese overseas around the world (11 million).[12] Based on these statistics, in this book I assume that, in the mid-twentieth century, ethnic Chinese in Indonesia numbered approximately 2.5 million and made up the largest percentage of foreign nationals living in Indonesia during the Cold War.

Scholars have usually differentiated between two distinct, but not mutually exclusive, subgroups of Chinese in Indonesia: the *peranakan* and the *totok*. *Peranakan* (*tusheng huaren*) refers to Indonesian-born, locally rooted ethnic Chinese who use bahasa Indonesia or a regional Indonesian language as their primary language. This group also includes descendants of mixed-race unions.[13] *Totok* (*xinke huaren*) refers to foreign-born immigrants and their descendants who continue to speak Chinese (including Mandarin and dialects such as Hokkien, Hakka, Cantonese, and Teochew). A significant number of totoks were new migrants who left China at the turn of the twentieth century due to the economic difficulties and political instability of the late Qing Empire. Many of them still maintained strong familial and emotional ties to the country. Leo Suryadinata estimated that, in the 1950s and 1960s, peranakan made up less than 40 percent of the overall Chinese population in Indonesia while totok made up more than 60 percent.[14]

More often than not, the peranakans were committed to their host country whereas the totoks tended to perceive themselves as part of a Chinese nation. I use these two categories to indicate overall tendencies, while recognizing that it would be unwise to draw a dichotomy between them. For instance, after the establishment of the PRC, many peranakans were proud of the domestic developments in socialist China but thought it might be merely a satellite state of the Soviet Union. They subsequently adopted a wait-and-see attitude, pragmatically calculating the extent to which they could look to Beijing for protection.[15] The peranakan politician Siauw Giok Tjhan (Xiao Yucan) pledged allegiance to the Republic of Indonesia and served as its minister of state for minority affairs. But he had been attracted to Marxism from an early age and was sympathetic toward socialist China. Siauw sent his children to the PRC to study and maintained cordial relations with the government in Beijing.[16] This book focuses on the diaspora who were China-oriented, the majority of whom can be considered as totoks.

The Chinese resided primarily in Java, West Kalimantan, North Sumatra, the Bangka-Belitung Islands, and the Riau Islands. At least half of the ethnic Chinese lived in Java, but they made up only 2 percent of the total number of inhabitants of this densely populated island.[17] The ethnic Chinese constituted more than 20 percent of the population of West Kalimantan, the Bangka-Belitung Islands, and the Riau Islands.[18] The Chinese in Indonesia were predominantly urban, though they were more rural in their distribution on the Outer Islands.[19] As estimated by the PRC's Overseas Chinese Affairs Commission (Zhonghua renmin gongheguo huaqiao shiwu weiyuanhui) in 1956, 67 percent of the ethnic Chinese population lived in thirty-six major cities across Indonesia.[20] The geographical scope of this book covers most of the territories in Indonesia with a high concentration of Chinese.

Intercommunal Conflict and Intracommunal Bifurcation

In the Indonesian context, "Chinese" has been a contested identity label: sometimes self-designated and sometimes prescribed or even imposed.[21] Despite Indonesia's pronounced ethnic diversity, the Chinese have frequently been referred to as a "foreign" (asing) group without territorial roots in the country and distinct from the pribumi or the so-called indigenous Indonesians.[22] Both pribumi and the Chinese are highly heterogeneous groups. Many of the peranakan Chinese were not significantly distinguishable from the pribumi in linguistic or cultural terms. But some pribumi political players deliberately overlooked internal differences within both the Chinese minority and the pribumi as well as the similarity between these two groups. As Skinner observes, right-wing pribumi were eager to perpetuate the view that, regardless of their degree of assimilation and citizenship status, all ethnic Chinese were the same in religious (non-Muslim) and moral terms (self-interested).[23] Like the proclamation "once a Jew, always a Jew," this mode of thinking essentialized a Chinese identity and denied any possibility for the incorporation of ethnic Chinese into the Indonesian nation.[24]

The image of the Chinese as an alien minority went hand in hand with the popular belief that they dominated the Indonesian economy through an impenetrable business network.[25] This perception originated in the Dutch colonial era, when the Chinese worked as mediators between the Dutch and the indigenous people.[26] During the Indonesian National Revolution (1945–1949), civilian ethnic Chinese were victims of attacks by pribumi militia, which included robbery, physical assault, and murder. Officials of the Republic of Indonesia attributed the rise of anti-Chinese violence to this ethnic minority's economic position "as middle-class shopkeepers."[27] There was no consensus among Indonesian political elites about how much control the Chinese really held over the country's economy. Though a considerable portion of the Chinese, predominantly in Java, achieved business success, throughout the Indonesian archipelago the Chinese held a broad range of occupations under varied economic conditions. Nevertheless, the stereotypical portrayal of the Chinese as a powerful trading community was widespread. Aiming to spur economic participation by the pribumi, the Indonesian government promulgated a series of policies designed to undermine Chinese influence in sectors such as commerce, transportation, and manufacturing. In 1959 the Indonesian government revoked the licenses of noncitizen Chinese to operate retail businesses in the countryside, pressuring many to leave permanently.

The political polarization of the Chinese community in Indonesia rendered them even more vulnerable. The end of World War II marked the beginning of another period of military conflicts in both China and Indonesia. Around the same time that Indonesia was struggling for national self-determination, the wartime collaboration between the Chinese Nationalists and the Communists failed, leading to a full-blown civil war. In the same year that Indonesia achieved its formal independence, the Russian-backed Communists won Mainland China from the hands of the US-backed Nationalist Party. The Communists established the PRC with its capital in Beijing. The leader of the Nationalist Party at the time, Chiang Kai-shek, evacuated his government to Taiwan and made Taipei the "temporary capital" of the Republic of China (the ROC). In 1950 the Republic of Indonesia granted diplomatic recognition to the Chinese Communist government. But under the influence of domestic anti-Communist forces, Jakarta's attitude toward the PRC was ambivalent. While technically abiding by the "One China" policy, the Indonesian government allowed organizations associated with the Nationalists to operate as a counterbalance to Beijing. Throughout the 1950s, the competition between the Chinese Communist and Nationalist Parties was carried on more openly and extensively among the Chinese in Indonesia than within Mainland China or Taiwan. The rivalry between the Red, or the pro-Beijing bloc, and the Blue, or the pro-Taipei bloc, permeated what had long been regarded as "the three pillars" of overseas Chinese societies: civic associations, Chinese-language newspapers, and Chinese-medium schools.[28] By 1958, following the Indonesian government's suppression of regional rebellions supported by Taiwan, the pro-Beijing faction became overwhelmingly dominant.[29]

The activism of the pro-Beijing Chinese alarmed the Indonesian government. In 1959, according to the American embassy in Jakarta, the Indonesian authorities were confronted with a situation where pro-Beijing elements could "remind Indonesians of their power in society by brandishing their five-starred flags."[30] To Jakarta's dismay, many totok Chinese synchronized their social life with the PRC. For instance, they celebrated holidays such as International Workers' Day and the PRC's National Day at the same time and in the same manner as socialist China. On October 1 of each year in the early 1950s, the pro-Beijing Chinese organized commemorations of the establishment of the PRC in major cities.[31] The daylong ceremonies usually started with the collective singing of the PRC national anthem, followed by a parade of young people holding a portrait of Mao Zedong side by side with that of Sukarno, and concluded with evening gala shows.[32] These rituals created spaces where individual ethnic Chinese could foster a sense of solidarity with the PRC, even though they were in Indonesia.[33] Although the majority of these celebrations were grassroots initiatives, they were construed by the pribumi elites as a Beijing-directed encroachment on Indonesian sovereignty.

When the Communal Clashes with the International

During a time when the Chinese community suffered from divisions within and discrimination from without, the PRC and Indonesian governments enjoyed remarkably cordial relations. At the Bandung Conference of 1955, the PRC pivoted toward cultivating friendship with formerly colonized countries in Asia and Africa. In the late 1950s, Beijing's relationship with Moscow deteriorated. In the early 1960s, the PRC started to regard Indonesia as a potential ally that shared its goal of replacing the bipolar world structure with a more equitable international order. During this time, the Communist Party of Indonesia (Partai Komunis Indonesia, or PKI) rose to a prominent position in Indonesian politics and grew into the largest nonruling Communist Party in the world at the time. It also sided with the CCP after the Sino-Soviet split. The Indonesian president Sukarno worked closely with the PKI, while hardening his government's attitude toward Western powers. Sukarno's theory that the "new emerging forces" (nationalism and Communism) would decimate the "old established forces" (capitalism and imperialism) through a relentless struggle echoed Beijing's international outlook. High-level official visits and cultural, educational, and economic exchanges between the two countries reached a climax in the first nine months of 1965.

The strategic alignment between Beijing and Jakarta collapsed overnight after the September Thirtieth Movement. Before dawn on October 1, army units from the Presidential Palace guard abducted and later killed six senior anti-Communist generals. The next day, General Suharto launched an effective counterattack. As he rose to power, Suharto started a nationwide purge of alleged Communists and Communist sympathizers, which escalated into one of the worst mass murders of the twentieth century.[34] It is estimated that more than 500,000 people were killed. Because the leader of the PKI, Dipa Nusantara Aidit, was a major participant in the movement, the Suharto regime made repeated, although unverified, accusations that Communist China was involved in the September Thirtieth Movement. Diplomatic relations were suspended in 1967 and remained so until the end of the Cold War. The Suharto regime's propaganda, which associated the ethnic Chinese with Communism, made this minority susceptible to violence during the mass killings of 1965–66. While the mass killings targeted PKI members, many ordinary Chinese were harassed, imprisoned, or deprived of their possessions and expelled from the archipelago by implication. Under Suharto's ensuing three-decade rule, a number of discriminatory laws were passed: for instance, the ethnic Chinese were given a special designation on their citizenship cards and Chinese-language education was banned.

Conventional wisdom holds that the public hostility against the PRC and the ethnic Chinese was a reaction to the PKI's attempt, at Beijing's instigation, to usurp state power. But newly available evidence reveals that Aidit designed the September Thirtieth Movement free from foreign intervention. Top Chinese leaders were aware of Aidit's scheme. But the swift execution of the plan took them by surprise. In his meeting with Mao Zedong on August 5, 1965, Aidit sketched out what he would do in a political scenario without Sukarno.[35] The strategies Aidit shared with Mao bear a strong resemblance to what actually happened on October 1. Mao was not the "architect of the coup," as he was portrayed by the Suharto regime and some English-language writers.[36] Meanwhile, Aidit was not a scapegoat in an internal power struggle of the Indonesian army, as he was depicted by Ben Anderson and Ruth McVey.[37] John Roosa's Pretext for Mass Murder suggests that a secret Special Bureau (Biro Khusus), which included Aidit but excluded other members of the PKI's Central Committee Political Bureau (politburo) and the rank and file of the party, was responsible for the movement. But Roosa's book does not contain solid proof of Aidit's role.[38] The Mao-Aidit conversation is probably the best evidence we have obtained so far to indicate that Aidit was a conscious actor in the movement while Beijing's influence was marginal.

Why did the Beijing-Jakarta alignment fall apart, and why were the ethnic Chinese persecuted in the aftermath of the movement even though China played no substantial role in it? Migration intricately complicated the diplomatic relations between two countries that were both pursuing a militantly anti-imperialist foreign policy. In the late 1940s, pro-Beijing and pro-Taipei factions, which ran parallel to the alignments in the Chinese Civil War, emerged among the Chinese in Indonesia. The competition between these two factions dominated the diasporic society for more than a decade. After 1949, many ethnic Chinese experienced the establishment of the PRC as a moment of national pride and a promise of protection and an elevation of social status. They carried out vigorous campaigns against their pro-Taipei rivals while overlooking the fact that pribumi civic society and the Indonesian government increasingly saw them as a threat. This was accompanied by a widespread perception among the pribumi that the Chinese minority had amassed wealth unethically. As the ancestral land of this presumably business-minded minority, the PRC was associated with both economic exploitation and political intervention. The continuous politicization of the Chinese minority contributed to the deterioration of ethnic relations and shook the Sino-Indonesian partnership to its foundations.

Bridging Diplomacy and Migration

This book treats diplomacy as a social process from the ground up. By doing so, it joins recent work by scholars such as Madeline Hsu and Meredith Oyen in bringing diplomatic history and migration studies into a single field of transnational vision.[39] Oyen has observed a division between the fields of US foreign relations and US immigration history; China scholars similarly tend to treat diplomacy and migration as two separate issues, examining the former from the angle of elite politics while approaching the latter from the perspective of social history.[40] Since the early 2000s, there has been a growing body of English-language scholarship that elucidates the People's Republic's experience during the Cold War. Works by pioneers in the field of PRC Cold War history have shown how Marxist-Leninist ideology, the ideals of equality and justice, and age-old Sinocentrism impacted Beijing's interactions with major players in the Cold War.[41] More recent studies have shed light on how the PRC expanded its influence in Asia, Africa, and Latin America.[42] Most of these discussions, however, focus on high-stakes security concerns. Nevertheless, a new generation of scholarship has broadened the concept of "Chinese foreign relations history" to encompass the domestic social protests, transnational intellectual exchanges, as well as the everyday life of people on the frontiers.[43] But the Chinese diaspora is absent in this enriched and expanded understanding of PRC diplomacy.

The themes and debates in the field of overseas Chinese studies seem quite distant from the key concerns of PRC diplomatic historians. While early works assume that the overseas Chinese had natural patriotic feelings toward the motherland, research by scholars such as Wang Gungwu, Philip Kuhn, and Leo Suryadinata has emphasized the hybridity and pluralism of their identities.[44] As the transnational turn drives scholarly attention to the movement of people, ideas, and commodities across national boundaries, an increasing number of works have reinterpreted the ties between China and the overseas Chinese from angles such as the worldwide circulation of capital, technology, and culture.[45] But how did the fluid and multidimensional connections between the diaspora and their homeland affect China's geostrategic position? This question has not yet been answered in the literature.

By drawing on vital work in both fields, I demonstrate that state-to-state diplomacy and the everyday lives of migrants were mutually constituted. In dialogue with scholarship on diplomatic history, this book complicates existing understandings of the movement for political autonomy among the Afro-Asian countries during the Cold War. It highlights the contradiction between the antiracist ideology upheld by Beijing and Jakarta and the discrimination faced by the Chinese in Indonesia. While seeking equal standing with the Western powers in world politics, newly independent countries like Indonesia were confronted with the domestic issue of renegotiating power relations among different ethnic groups. The collapse of the Sino-Indonesian partnership and the erosion of Afro-Asian solidarity reflect the tension between the participating countries' internal dilemmas and their international ambitions.

In dialogue with scholarship on Chinese migration, this book demonstrates that the overseas Chinese, who were oftentimes peripheral to nation-based bodies of knowledge, were at the center of a global battle for hearts and minds fought between the Chinese Communists and Nationalists. This conflict with domestic Chinese origins had significance far beyond the military standoffs across the Taiwan Strait. The two Chinas' contestation over the loyalty of the Chinese diaspora played out wherever there was a significant concentration of overseas Chinese. The debate over the legitimate center of China was so fundamental and essential to many overseas Chinese that there was no doubt about its importance. Research by Fujio Hara, Fredy Gonzalez, Meredith Oyen, and Charlotte Brooks sheds light on how this "Red versus Blue" struggle became a prominent feature of Chinese societies in Malaya, Mexico, and the United States.[46] Together with this excellent body of work, this book challenges a singular understanding of the Cold War as a rivalry between the socialist East and the capitalist West by revealing a specifically *Chinese* side to it.

Sources and Methodology

This book synthesizes top-down and bottom-up perspectives and incorporates both institutional history and human stories. Many of the governmental records presented here were obtained during a brief window of opportunity. Between June 2006 and November 2008, the Chinese Foreign Ministry Archives declassified thousands of documents produced between 1949 and 1965. However, this collection, including almost all the Chinese diplomatic documents used in this book, was reclassified in 2013. The most important document related to the September Thirtieth Movement, the Aidit-Mao discussion on August 5, 1965, is drawn from a collection entitled "Minutes of Meetings between Chairman Mao and Leaders of Various Communist Parties" (Mao Zhuxi yu geguo gongchandang lingdaoren tanhua), which was internally circulated among a group of senior Chinese scholars with special access to the CCP Central Archives. In addition to this body of currently inaccessible official records in Beijing, I have drawn on the National Archives of the Republic of Indonesia (Arsip Nasional Republik Indonesia or ANRI) in Jakarta; Academia Historica (Guoshi guan) and the archives of the Chinese Nationalist Party (Guomindang dangshi guan) in Taipei; and provincial and municipal archives in Guangdong, Fujian, and Hainan in China.

In both China and Indonesia, government sources have their limitations. In China, record keeping is comprehensive and rigorous but highly centralized and tightly controlled. The Indonesian official archives are less rigid but also much less systematic. The 1965 regime change led not only to the accidental or deliberate destruction of records during the chaotic transition of power but also to decades of repression of public discussion of history. Moreover, in state records from both countries, migrants appear as subjects of policies or targets of surveillance. Their life stories as told from their own perspectives are rarely documented.

To complement state archives, I consulted materials at various libraries and research centers, such as the newspaper collections at the Center for Southeast Asian Studies of Xiamen University (Xiamen daxue Dongnanya yanjiu zhongxin) and the Baptist University of Hong Kong as well as the materials on Indonesian Communist exiles at the International Institute of Social History in Amsterdam. I have also collected private documents from individuals. For instance, in Shanghai, the family of Ba Ren (which means "Common Man" in Chinese), granted me access to his unpublished manuscripts and personal letters. Ba Ren, a well-known writer in his time, lived in Sumatra for five and a half years in the late 1940s before he became the PRC's first ambassador to Indonesia.[47] In the rural regions of coastal South

China, I visited five Overseas Chinese Farms (*huaqiao nongchang*), where the ethnic Chinese who migrated to the PRC from abroad were given virgin land on which to rebuild their lives. On these farms, repatriated overseas Chinese shared material with me, including birth and marriage certificates, identification cards, school transcripts, family photos, and ferry tickets for their journeys from Indonesia to China.

In addition, I interviewed retired PRC diplomats, Indonesian Communist exiles, and members of the Chinese community in Indonesia in the 1950s and 1960s. Liang Yingming, for example, is a historian by training and a self-reflective narrator of his own past. But the economic migrants who were expelled from Indonesia in the late 1950s and 1960s tend to present their experiences with less awareness of the broader context at the time and their own position in it. As for the ethnic Chinese who remain living in Indonesia, their memories were oftentimes clouded by grievances against the Suharto regime or even residual trauma. Former diplomats are usually restrained and cautious. The PKI exiles, in contrast, tend to be eloquent speakers who frame their past in ways that validate their political beliefs. Understandably, all these memories are socially framed, revised, and restricted by the broader environment the narrator is currently situated in: the PRC, where censorship is still prevalent, or Indonesia, where the freedom of speech is gradually improving. But acknowledging the difficulties of oral history does not mean denying its value. This book weaves together public records and personal recollections, while aiming to interpret both sources with sensitivity to their pitfalls and promises.[48]

Structure of the Book

Organized chronologically, the book is divided into ten chapters. Focusing on the tumultuous times of the Japanese occupation and the Indonesian National Revolution, Chapters 1 and 2 compare and contrast the Chinese Nationalists' and Communists' ideologies and their strategies for expanding their influence among the Chinese in Indonesia. Chapter 1 argues that the Chinese Nationalist government's lack of sympathy for Indonesia's struggle for independence and its insistence on exercising jurisdiction over the Chinese in Indonesia aggravated ethnic conflicts. Claimed as citizens by both the ROC and the Republic of Indonesia but protected by neither, the ethnic Chinese in Indonesia exercised their own agency by organizing self-defense forces in collaboration with the Dutch or turning to support the Indonesian nationalists. While the Chinese Nationalists could rely on formal institutions in Indonesia, the CCP established its support base through an informal web of personal connections centered on left-leaning writers, teachers, and journalists who migrated from Mainland China. These left-wing intellectuals inspired a generation of ethnic Chinese youth and motivated them to engage in politics. Chapter 2 focuses on a representative figure, Ba Ren, who believed that a working-class alliance between the Chinese and the pribumi could fundamentally resolve ethnic conflicts. The Chinese Nationalists' and Communists' different patterns of overseas development and their opposing attitudes toward citizenship and ethnic relations set the stage for the competition that followed.

Moving to the 1950s and 1960s, Chapters 3 and 4 depict the full-blown rivalry between Beijing and Taipei among the Chinese in Indonesia. Chapter 3 unveils the fact that, with the PRC winning Mainland China and the diplomatic recognition of Indonesia, the positions of the Nationalists and Communists reversed. Having lost its diplomatic representation in Indonesia, Taipei had to challenge Beijing's legitimacy via clandestine networks in the Chinese community. Whereas Taipei proactively encouraged the ethnic Chinese to maintain their ties to the ROC, Beijing prioritized state-to-state relations with Jakarta. Starting in 1952, the PRC tempered its overseas mobilization efforts to dissipate the Indonesian government's suspicion of the Chinese diaspora as "a fifth column." Chapter 4 details how the pro-PRC bloc launched aggressive attacks against their pro-ROC rivals for control over Chinese-language media, civic associations, and Chinese-medium schools. Into the late 1950s, the pro-Beijing groups achieved a communal victory. But their activism frustrated Beijing's efforts to keep the overseas Chinese away from politics.

Chapters 5 and 6 discuss the ramifications of the Red-versus-Blue struggle. Chapter 5 demonstrates that, with the advance of the Cold War in Asia, the Indonesian authorities interpreted the ethnic Chinese's oftentimes spontaneous political activism as a systematic infiltration led by Beijing. Some anti-Communist pribumi elites saw Beijing as a strong external power intervening in Indonesian politics and ignored its waning ability to rein in the factional infighting in the Chinese community. Moreover, despite a huge variation in ideological inclinations and economic status among the ethnic Chinese, the pribumi elites tended to treat them as a monolithic group that was simultaneously Communist and capitalist. In 1959, under the pretext of reducing economic stratification, the Indonesian government suspended noncitizen Chinese retailers' business activities in rural areas and legitimized the takeover of foreign enterprises by indigenous merchants. Chapter 6 explains why Beijing adopted a moderate attitude in reaction to these discriminatory policies. Friendly, non-Communist Indonesia provided China with an unusually good chance of pulling off a major Cold War breakthrough. Therefore, the PRC was unwilling to sacrifice stable relations with Sukarno to protect the Chinese in Indonesia.

In the early 1960s, China and Indonesia joined hands to radically rebel against the bipolar international order. Chapter 7 examines Beijing's strategic collaborations with Jakarta through the second Afro-Asia Conference, the Game of the New Emerging Forces (GANEFO), and *konfrontasi*—Indonesia's campaign to block Britain's plan to merge the remains of its former Southeast Asian colonies into the Federation of Malaysia. But closer bilateral relations failed to prevent anti-Chinese riots in Indonesia. Furthermore, the two countries' common struggle against the Western imperialist presence in Southeast Asia led to new discord. Beijing and Jakarta clashed over policies toward the ethnic Chinese in Malaya, the Chinese-dominated Communist guerillas in Sarawak, and the Chinese-majority country of Singapore. The September Thirtieth Movement abruptly ended the Sino-Indonesian honeymoon. Chapter 8 clarifies that Beijing did not, as the Suharto regime charged, instruct Aidit to topple Sukarno or supply weapons to the PKI. The Suharto regime manufactured these claims to justify its anti-Communist purges.

The 1965 regime change in Indonesia gave rise to a new round of Red-versus-Blue competition. Chapter 9 shows how Beijing used the volatile suspension of Sino-Indonesian relations for domestic mass mobilization in the early stages of the Cultural Revolution, how Taipei seized the golden opportunity provided by the anti-Communist campaign in Indonesia to reestablish its influence in the archipelago, and how both sides responded to the violence against the ethnic Chinese during the power transition in Indonesia between 1965 and 1967. Although Beijing's actual role in the movement was limited, the acrimonious disputes between Beijing and Jakarta after the movement gave the anti-Communist Indonesian elites a convenient pretext for freezing diplomatic ties and inflaming ethnic hostility. At the heart of Chapter 10 are the stories of Chinese migrants who came to the PRC from Indonesia during the two-decade span of this book. These repatriated overseas Chinese carried the daily practices of capitalism and transnational investment ties with them. Ironically, their resistance against the socialist state's attempts to incorporate them helped prepare the PRC for its transition to market principles and its opening to international trade. Their tales of hope and disappointment, compromise and perseverance, conclude this story of migration in the time of revolution.

CHAPTER 1

The Chinese Nationalist Party and the Overseas Chinese

In the darkness of the night in late May 1948, a note signed "night ghost" (*hantu malam*) was attached to the door of the branch office of the pan-Chinese organization Chung Hwa Tsung Hwee (also spelled as Chung Hua Tsung Hui or Zhonghua zonghui in pinyin, the Chinese General Association) in Kedungbanteng, Central Java. Translated from bahasa Indonesia, it reads:

Look out! Beware!

Hi Chinese brothers!

You are in Indonesia.

You will die and be buried in the soil of Indonesia.

You are living a rich and peaceful life because of help from the Indonesian people.

You manage to live because you obtain water, food, and produce from Indonesia.

But what kind of contribution are you making to Indonesia?

Where is the proof that you want to unite with the Indonesian people?

I am warning you! Beware!!

Do not wait for social revolution!

Try to really understand the teachings of Dr. Sun Yat-sen![1]

A few weeks later, a similar incident happened in East Java, where the number of crimes, such as robbery and blackmail against the local Chinese community, had been increasing.[2] The years between 1945 and 1949 mark a volatile period in both China and Indonesia. In China, a full-blown civil war broke out between the ruling Chinese Nationalist Party and the oppositional Chinese Communist Party. In Indonesia, although Sukarno proclaimed the nation's independence on August 17, 1945, the Dutch did not transfer sovereignty to the newborn Republic of Indonesia until December 27, 1949. Between 1945 and 1949, Indonesian Republican military forces (Tentara Negara Indonesia or the TNI) firmly resisted the Netherlands' attempt at recolonization. During this time, ethnic relations between the Chinese and the pribumi deteriorated and the Chinese became a frequent target of violence. They faced destruction of property, forced evacuation, physical abuse, and murder at the hands of the TNI, particularly by the irregular forces loosely organized under it.[3] During a fierce battle in Bandung in March 1946, the TNI adopted a "scorched-earth policy" and burned down much of the southern half of the city, including six hundred houses owned by local Chinese. The ROC consul general publicly condemned the TNI for "a deliberate assault on the Chinese."[4] In June 1946, due to the country's descent into lawlessness, local criminal bands and mobs attacked the Chinese residents in Tangerang, twenty-five kilometers west of Jakarta.[5] The local Chinese were beaten, raped, or murdered even though they had lived in this area for centuries. Chinese community leaders counted 1,085 dead, 213 missing, and 15,300 displaced.[6]

Mary Somers Heidhues, an expert on the Chinese in Indonesia, argues that the Tangerang incident was the most notorious case of violence against this ethnic minority during the Indonesian National Revolution.[7] Attacks on the Chinese occurred in Java as well as on the Outer Islands. Some were caused by the power vacuum that emerged shortly after the Japanese surrender, others by the return of the Dutch.[8] Between 1946 and 1947, Indonesian forces attacked numerous Chinese of Bagansiapiapi, one of the world's largest fishing ports, on the Sumatran coast.[9] In January 1947, 250 ethnic Chinese died and more than 1,000 were injured during a four-day battle between the Dutch and the TNI in Palembang, South Sumatra.[10] The Chinese business quarter, 300 Chinese-owned houses, and the building of the ROC consulate were burned down.[11] In June 1947 and December 1948, the Dutch launched two major military strikes against the TNI, which were known as Dutch police actions. The Chinese were caught in the middle and were seen as enemy spies by the TNI.[12] In July 1947, in Boemiajoe, West Java, and in Tjilongok, Central Java, the TNI killed over 300 Chinese in revenge by stabbing them with sharpened bamboo sticks, burning them, or tying them up with ropes and burying them alive.[13] By the end of these two campaigns, hundreds of Chinese had been killed and thousands had gone missing.[14]

In the middle of the vortex of violence, the head of the Netherlands East Indies Visual Information Service, Niels Alexander Douwes Dekker, used his camera to capture the plight of the Chinese. His photos depict charred corpses, deserted houses, helpless refugees, and protests by the ethnic Chinese with slogans in Mandarin Chinese, bahasa Indonesia, and English such as:

> The Republic of Indonesia slaughtered the ethnic Chinese!
> Indonesians have raped Chinese women!
> The Republic of Indonesia has betrayed the Chinese!
> The Republic of Indonesia has murdered the Chinese!
> The Republic of Indonesia is the cradle of Fascism!
> We want protection from such beasts!
> We demand the surrender of the Japanese deserters and war criminals who are now directing Indonesian atrocities against the Chinese![15]

FIGURE 1.1. Ethnic Chinese protest during the Indonesian National Revolution. Undated photo from an album named "Chinese Atrocities," box 19, folder 11, Niels A. Douwes Dekker Papers, no. 3480, Division of Rare and Manuscript Collections, Cornell University Library.

Despite the great diversity within the Chinese communities and the significant variations in interethnic relations from region to region in Indonesia, overall a large number of ethnic Chinese experienced horrifying insecurity during the Indonesian National Revolution. This chapter places the issue of revolutionary violence against the Chinese in a transnational framework. It highlights the connections between the Chinese communities in Indonesia and the Chinese Nationalist government as well as the evolving structure of international relations in the Asia-Pacific after World War II. The rise of hostility against the Chinese needs to be understood in light of both the short-term general disorder and the pribumi's long-standing belief that the Chinese were collaborating with the colonizers. I argue that, in addition, the Chinese Nationalist government's condescending attitude toward Indonesia's anticolonial struggle and its strengthening of ties with the diaspora discouraged the ethnic Chinese from identifying with the Republic of Indonesia and contributed to the escalation of ethnic antagonism.

The Republic of Indonesia repeatedly protested that the ROC's persistent projection of state authority onto the ethnic Chinese interfered with its domestic affairs.[16] In a 1948 report, the Indonesian National Police accused the ROC embassy and consulates, Chinese Nationalist Party branches, and ROC-affiliated Chinese associations of functioning as "a state within a state."[17] Indonesia's 1946 nationality law opened a pathway to citizenship for the ethnic Chinese. Yet, with weak control over the perpetrators of ethnic violence, particularly the revolutionary youth (*pemuda*) who resisted military discipline, it was difficult for the Republic of Indonesia to prove that it could represent the Chinese. However, the Republic of Indonesia did not want to drive the Chinese into the arms of the ROC, as this minority was and would be crucial to the maintenance and future recovery of the Indonesian economy. Pribumi elites were disheartened by the Chinese minority's lack of faith in the Indonesian state. They complained that the Chinese, when assaulted, sought assistance from the Chung Hwa Tsung Hwee rather than the Indonesian police.[18]

Simultaneously claimed as citizens by both the ROC and the Republic of Indonesia, the ethnic Chinese received no effective state protection from either government. They used their own initiative to make varied decisions in response to violence. Some organized paramilitary self-defense forces with support from the Chinese Nationalist government and the Dutch, while others became disillusioned with the ROC and aligned themselves with the Indonesian nationalist cause. But, overall, the atrocities committed during the Indonesian National Revolution caused doubts about whether an independent Indonesia would genuinely acknowledge the membership of the ethnic Chinese.

Chinese in Indonesia in the Early Twentieth Century

A common justification for crimes against the Chinese minority was their purportedly unfair economic advantage over the pribumi during Dutch colonial rule. Dutch policy granted the Chinese the status of "Foreign Orientals," thus setting them apart from both the Europeans and the natives. As foreign orientals, the Chinese were given favored status but they also faced legal restrictions and higher taxes.[19] This distinctive treatment situated the Chinese as middlemen between Dutch-controlled modern economic sectors such as shipping and import-export trade and the indigenous population's traditional agricultural economy.[20] Commerce became the typical occupation of the Chinese in Java. Outside of Java, Chinese were more likely to be peasants, plantation coolies, mineworkers, or fishermen.[21] But, in the archipelago overall, the pribumi presence in the entrepreneurial class was much weaker than that of the ethnic Chinese. Moreover, most of the indigenous business class adhered to Islam and religious differences exacerbated the tension between the pribumi and the Chinese. One of the goals for the pribumi Muslim traders who founded the nationalist organization Sarekat Islam was to confront ethnic Chinese competition.[22] The first vice president of the Republic of Indonesia, Mohammed Hatta, was also a proponent of empowering Muslim businesses.[23] Thus, in the minds of many pribumi nationalists, Chinese economic power was part of the colonial legacy that needed to be dismantled during the revolution.

The racial politics created by the Dutch made it difficult for the ethnic Chinese to assimilate into the indigenous population. In addition, waves of immigration in the early twentieth century and subsequent demographic changes widened the chasm between the pribumi and the ethnic Chinese. During the first three decades of the twentieth century, there was, for the first time, a significant number of women among Chinese immigrants to Indonesia. As a result, new immigrants tended to marry Chinese-born wives, rather than indigenous Indonesians or local-born Chinese of mixed ancestry.[24] The Chinese scholar Zhuang Guotu has argued that, because many of these new migrants were impoverished peasants and laborers, they lacked the resources to fight against mistreatment abroad and yearned for protection from a strong motherland.[25]

The influx of migrants to the archipelago coincided with the rise of nationalism in China, which was triggered by events such as the first Sino-Japanese War in 1895 and the 1911 Revolution. Between 1912 and 1937, political activists, or what Phillip Kuhn calls "nationalist missionaries," traveled from China to Southeast Asia.[26] The idea of a modernizing homeland spread across the archipelago through overseas Chinese associations, schools, and print media. During the Dutch colonial era, the social structure of the Chinese community centered on leadership by officers or *kapitan cina*—top ethnic Chinese merchants appointed by the Dutch to govern their compatriots through their social influence, personal networks, and monetary power.[27] Kapitan cina's authority interlocked with directorships of civic groups such as surname and native-place associations.[28] Yet a growing sense of national solidarity inspired the Chinese in Indonesia to overcome divisions based on dialect, region, and kinship. In 1900 the first pan-Chinese association Tiong Hoa Hwee Koan or THHK (zhonghua huiguan) was founded in Jakarta and soon became the driving force promoting Chinese culture and national consciousness.[29]

One of the major goals of the THHK was to advance Chinese education. In 1900 the THHK established its first school, Tiong Hoa Hak Tong (zhonghua xuetang), more commonly known as Ba Hua High School (bahua zhongxue). The opening of Ba Hua reflected parents' growing desire to give their children modern instruction in Chinese. It was also a reaction against the Dutch policy of denying education to Chinese communities.[30] In the early twentieth century, there were institutions modeled after Ba Hua in almost all the major townships with large ethnic Chinese concentrations across the Dutch East Indies. Despite the high cost, the schools recruited many teachers from China to infuse their curricula with a presumably more authentic Chinese culture.[31] The Dutch later revised their policy by founding Dutch-medium schools for the Chinese (the Hollandsch-Chineesch School, or HCS), which attracted a number of peranakan elite families who believed that Dutch-language proficiency would give their children better career opportunities. However, due to the ban on Dutch and other Western schools during the Japanese occupation (1942–45), these peranakan schoolchildren had no choice but to turn to Chinese schools and became re-Sinicized through extensive exposure to Chinese language and culture. Thus, Chinese-medium education experienced substantial growth in Indonesia during the Japanese occupation.[32]

The beginning of the twentieth century witnessed a rapid expansion in the number of print media outlets in overseas Chinese communities in Southeast Asia. In the Dutch East Indies, peranakan Chinese began publishing newspapers in *bahasa Melayu* (Malay) in the early 1900s. During the 1920s and 1930s, there were around thirty peranakan newspapers, each of which belonged to one of three political camps. The first, represented by *Sin Po*, the Chinese Indonesian newspaper that enjoyed the widest circulation, promoted Chinese nationalism and denounced Dutch colonialism. For instance, *Sin Po* launched a campaign in 1919 calling upon the Chinese to reject their status as Dutch subjects. In contrast, the second camp, represented by *Siang Po*, was pro-Dutch. The third camp, represented by *Sin Jit Po* (which later changed its name to *Sin Tit Po*), advocated Indonesian nationalism.[33] A renewed identification with Chineseness among the peranakans drove them to learn and use the new Chinese lingua franca—Mandarin. The influx of totok migrants with no command of bahasa Melayu created a further demand for newspapers in Chinese. In 1921 *Sin Po*, first published in 1910 with only a bahasa Melayu edition, added a Mandarin Chinese edition, *Xin Bao*. The number of Chinese-language periodicals grew rapidly after the 1920s. But when the Japanese occupied Indonesia in 1942, all Chinese-owned newspapers in both bahasa and Mandarin were shut down except for Japan's propaganda organs.[34]

The Chinese Nationalist Party's Policy toward the Overseas Chinese

In June 1947, a Mr. Wu Qinming, an elderly totok Chinese man living in Batavia, petitioned the government of the Republic of China via its consul general Jiang Jiadong, requesting formal recognition of his son Wu Lixin's death as "a soldier's sacrifice of life for the nation."[35] Wu Lixin was born, raised, and eventually killed in Indonesia. Yet Wu Qinming firmly believed that Lixin was a martyr for the faraway motherland: the ROC. During World War II, General Zheng Jiemin, who served as the ROC's representative at the Allied Forces' headquarters in the Southeast Asian theater, established the underground Reconstruction Society (fuxing she) in Indonesia for information gathering. Before his murder, Wu Lixin was working under General Zheng's leadership as an intelligence officer for the Chinese Nationalist Party. After completing his high school education in Tegal, Central Java, Wu had returned to Guangzhou, the Wu family ancestral home, and entered the Republic of China Military Academy. In the late 1930s, Wu was recruited by the Bureau of Investigation and Statistics (juntong) and, in 1942, was dispatched back to Java for underground resistance operations against the Japanese. Wu's family believed that he was murdered by his colleague, Colonel Lin Chuan, due to interpersonal conflicts, and buried in the backyard of their secret meeting point.[36] Throughout his short life, Wu was under the ROC government's expansive system of mobilization, surveillance, and espionage among the Chinese in Indonesia.

Wu's family's story demonstrates the level of the Chinese Nationalist Party's penetration into Chinese society in the archipelago. Historically, the

Chinese Nationalist Party's own development was closely associated with the Western-educated Sun Yat-sen, the Honolulu-based Revolutionary Alliance, and the overseas Chinese who made financial contributions during the 1911 Revolution.[37] The Nationalist Party saw the overseas Chinese as its "rightful human capital," who should be managed through a systematic global network. In 1924 an Overseas Party Affairs Office (Guomindang haiwai bu) was established and placed directly under the supervision of the Chinese Nationalist Party Central Committee.[38] After the establishment of a national government in Nanjing in 1927, the Chinese Nationalist Party "embarked on an unprecedentedly ambitious and aggressive effort" to strengthen the bonds between the overseas Chinese and the homeland.[39] In 1931 the Nationalist government installed the Overseas Chinese Affairs Commission (qiaowu weiyuanhui), which took on a variety of tasks including developing and improving overseas Chinese schools and their educational materials and soliciting investment in the homeland. It usually fell to the Overseas Party Affairs Office to handle more sensitive issues and exert control over the diaspora in more covert ways, such as clandestine operations and the recruitment of Chinese Nationalist Party members abroad.[40]

The seeds of Wu Lixin's devotion to the ROC were probably planted during his early years in the Chinese-language schools in Tegal. The Chinese Nationalist government's overseas education programs succeeded, to some extent, in transforming the ethnic Chinese's existing emotional, cultural, and familial ties to China into loyalty to the Chinese Nationalist Party. Stephen Fitzgerald, a historian of the overseas Chinese, has observed that the Chinese Nationalist Party had long regarded Chinese education as the key to securing the allegiance of the overseas Chinese. Without education, "the overseas Chinese might begin to see their future in their countries of residence."[41] As early as 1920, the Nationalist Party had begun dispatching teachers to British Malaya, carrying the message of Sun Yat-sen's Three Principles of the People (sanmin zhuyi), summarized as nationalism, democracy, and the people's livelihood.[42] The Chinese Nationalist government required the Chinese-language schools overseas to follow the same curricula and management style as those inside China. In other words, overseas Chinese education in Southeast Asia modeled citizenship education programs within the Republic of China and indoctrinated its students with the same Chinese Nationalist Party ideology.[43]

Wu's participation in the underground operations of the Chinese Nationalist government also speaks to the degree of Nanjing's wartime mobilization of the overseas Chinese. Financial contributions from the overseas Chinese had been crucial to the ROC's defense against Japanese encroachment. Since the Japanese occupation of Manchuria in 1931, the Overseas Chinese Affairs Commission had sent agents to Southeast Asian countries, requesting local Chinese to redirect the focus of their attention from local issues to the crisis in the motherland.[44] From Japan's full-scale invasion of China in 1937 to the Japanese occupation of Southeast Asia, nationalist passion among the overseas Chinese in Southeast Asia surged as many individuals and organizations became engaged in the Nanyang National Salvation Movement.[45] By the end of the war, although physically devastated and politically challenged by the rising CCP, the Chinese Nationalist government was internationally recognized as one of the "Big Five" Allies and a permanent member of the UN Security Council with veto power.[46] Admiration for the ROC's status in world politics also shaped the national orientation of many Chinese in Indonesia like the Wu family.

But the Republic of Indonesia resisted the Chinese Nationalist government's effort to prolong the ROC's jurisdiction over the ethnic Chinese. In China, the 1909 nationality law upheld the jus sanguinis principle. The children of Chinese citizens would hold Chinese citizenship, no matter where they were born. A Chinese citizen's nationality would not be lost if he or she was concurrently recognized as a citizen of the Republic of Indonesia. But in April 1946, the Republic of Indonesia passed its first citizenship act, which automatically recognized any Chinese who "were born in Indonesia and who had resided there continuously for five years" as Indonesian citizens. The Indonesian legislation was designed to "minimize the number of Chinese over whom Chinese consuls could exercise jurisdiction, and through whom they might extend their influence in Indonesia."[47] The dual citizenship status of the local-born Chinese caused friction between the Chinese Nationalist and Indonesian Republican governments. In June 1946, the Republic of Indonesia's representatives in Cirebon, on the north coast of Java, required the local Chinese to invest in state bonds as one of their duties as Indonesian citizens.[48] In response, the Nationalist government urged the Chinese in Indonesia to renounce their Indonesian citizenship as soon as possible.[49] In November 1947, the ROC vice consul Niu Shu Chun (New Shu Chun) demanded that the government of the Republic of Indonesia thoroughly investigate the whereabouts of 150 Chinese from Salatiga, Central Java. The Indonesian minister of state Dr. M. Daroesman steadfastly refused this request, contending that the Chinese Nationalist government had no authority over these missing persons because the majority of them were Indonesian citizens.[50]

Many pribumi nationalists realized the importance of winning Chinese support for Indonesia's independence.[51] Though unable to substantially reduce crimes against the Chinese, the Indonesian Republican government

promised to devote more effort to safeguarding them and made political gestures to comfort the victims. After the discovery of the threatening letters
from the "night ghost" in Central and East Java in May 1948, the Indonesian National Police stated: "Because the safety of the Chinese is one of the
responsibilities of the government, our government should issue laws and
regulations to protect them. The government should take firm action and
pay special attention to the safety of all the Chinese. . . . It is not just a matter
of police control but also a matter of the Indonesian government's position
on the ethnic Chinese."[52] In March 1946, Sukarno publicly apologized to the
Chinese, "our brothers," for their losses in the fighting in Bandung.[53]

The Chinese Nationalist Government's Attitude toward the Indonesian National Revolution

As Holland's ally during World War II, the Chinese Nationalist government
was reluctant to give diplomatic recognition to the Republic of Indonesia
and urged the ethnic Chinese to stay neutral in the Dutch-Indonesian conflict.[54] In conflict zones, many Chinese households hung the national flag of
the ROC to demonstrate their neutrality, oblivious to the increasing sense of
distrust among the pribumi population.[55] The Chinese Nationalist government identified the Netherlands, the United States, and the British Commonwealth Forces as the saviors of its overseas nationals, while regarding
the armed forces of the Republic of Indonesia as the villains. A Xiamen-based
newspaper *Jiangsheng Bao* made blunt accusations: "Some Indonesian scoun-
drels took the chance to rob, rape, and kill the Chinese. The Chinese endured
indescribable cruelty."[56] Some commentators in the Republic of China even
blamed the Dutch and the British Commonwealth Forces for failing to prevent the Indonesian National Revolution. One article published in the Shang-
hai-based *Qiaosheng Bao* contended:

> After the Japanese surrender in August 1945, the Chinese, who suffered
> greatly from the Japanese occupation, looked forward to the arrival of
> the Allied Forces like the desert craves the rain. If the Allied Forces had
> deployed their troops in a speedy fashion, the Chinese would not have
> gone through such a wrenching experience. Because the Allied Forces
> were slow in restoring order, the Japanese had the time to secretly trans-
> fer their weapons into the hands of TNI soldiers. One has to remem-
> ber that when the government of the Republic of Indonesia was first
> established in 1945, there were neither well-organized military forces
> nor weapons. Now, with the Japanese military supplies, the Indonesian
> struggle for national independence is lively and widespread![57]

A Chinese journalist who returned from Medan to Xiamen in September 1946 wrote: "The Indonesian people are poorly educated and extremely immature in politics. They have an excess of political parties and factions. These parties and factions wasted all their energy and resources in internal conflicts."[58] The article reflected the mentality of the Chinese Nationalist government; while the Republic of China emerged out of World War II as a great power, Indonesia was a semicivilized nation, which would be better served by the rule of Western colonizers than national self-determination.[59]

While the ROC saw the Indonesian National Revolution as the cause of the plight of the Chinese minority, the leaders of the Republic of Indonesia tried to persuade the ROC that it was Dutch aggression that endangered the peace and security of Chinese communities. In November 1947, in an effort to win support from the Republic of China at the United Nations (UN), Sukarno wrote to the Chinese consul general: "Before the arrival and recent actions of the Dutch troops in Indonesia, there was no sign whatsoever of the Chinese population being deprived of their life and property. I am convinced that the only effective way to ensure the well-being of the Chinese in Indonesia is to support the demand of the Republic of Indonesia that the UN take effective measures to promote the withdrawal of Dutch troops from Republican territory."[60] But, contrary to Sukarno's request, the ROC used its status as a permanent member of the UN Security Council to support the Dutch. The ROC voted in favor of a resolution that empowered two Dutch allies, the United Kingdom and the United States, to mediate the conflict, granting The Hague breathing space.[61]

With a firm determination not to be conquered again by the Dutch, the Republic of Indonesia forged ahead toward independence without much regard for the cost inflicted on the Chinese or the resulting troubled relationship with the Chinese Nationalist government. In late July 1947, an hour after a radio station in Yogyakarta had announced that all property owned by foreigners would be burnt to ashes if the Dutch continued their aggression, the ROC consul general warned the TNI not to further damage Chinese property. He asserted such actions would only hurt the reputation of the Republic of Indonesia and isolate it from international support.[62] In November 1947, in a letter addressed to the Indonesian prime minister and minister of national defense, ROC's vice consul general protested the TNI's decision to place mines, dynamite, and other incendiary material in Chinese factories and houses in East Java. While ROC diplomatic representatives held that these measures caused great physical and psychological harm to the Chinese, the Indonesian side insisted that such practices were of great strategic importance.[63]

Pao An Tui and the Escalation of Ethnic Conflict

Stalemates in negotiations via government-to-government channels prompted the Chinese Nationalist government to support self-defense organizations formed by the local Chinese on their own initiative. In Java and Sumatra, these groups usually consisted of young men who patrolled the Chinese residential areas to deter crimes such as robbery, extortion, and kidnapping. In Jakarta, the Chinese Committee for Assisting in the Preservation of Law and Order (Panitya Penjagaan Keamanan Umum Tionghoa; in Chinese, Bacheng huaqiao xiezhu zhi'an weiyuanhui, or zhi'anhui) was established in October 1945. Besides preventing incidents of violence, the committee also organized refugee relief work after the catastrophe in Tangerang and acted as a liaison between the ethnic Chinese and the Republican Indonesian authorities.[64] In Sumatra, local Chinese communities organized the Pao An Tui (baoan dui) or Peace Protection Forces, which started as a group of volunteer night guards (xunye tuan) in the Chinese communities but were later enlisted by the Dutch to aid in their military advances against the forces of the Republic of Indonesia. In December 1946 in Medan, when the city was still under British military control, local Chinese formed the Pao An Tui. By the time the Dutch returned, the Pao An Tui had already developed effective strategies against Indonesian irregular forces that threatened the safety of the ethnic Chinese. They were later asked to lend support to the Royal Netherlands East Indies Army.[65] In October 1947 in Bagansiapiapi, the Indonesian government received reports that the Chinese inhabitants had "secretly organized and trained a strong Pao An Tui unit armed with tommy guns and pistols." Together with the local branch of the Three Principles of the People Youth League (sanmin zhuyi qingnian tuan), a youth organization under the Chinese Nationalist Party, the Pao An Tui blocked the TNI from entering the town.[66] The Pao An Tui was often viewed by the pribumi as an auxiliary arm of the Dutch.[67] Indonesian media accused the Pao An Tui of being "the Chinese spirit of the Dutch."[68]

The Chinese Nationalist government regarded the Pao An Tui as a necessary evil for the distraught Chinese communities during the chaos of war. The Chinese Nationalist government's deputy foreign minister George Kung-chao Yeh (Ye Gongchao) publicly announced that the Pao An Tui was "the best way so far to handle the threats faced by the Chinese in Indonesia."[69] According to Anne van der Veer's research on the Pao An Tui in Medan, Dutch sources suggest that six former soldiers of Chiang Kai-shek's National Revolutionary Army had served as drill instructors for the Pao An Tui.[70] But beyond this, the Chinese Nationalist government had little direct involvement in the development of the Pao An Tui. The Pao An Tui's affiliation with the Chinese Nationalist Party was more ideological than organizational and was forged more through local networks than contacts with China. In Medan, for example, the business elites on the advisory committee of the Pao An Tui perceived themselves as representatives of the Nationalist government who were protecting the overseas sons and daughters of China.[71] They also used this opportunity to promote the ideology of the Chinese Nationalist Party and enhance its influence abroad.

While the Chinese Nationalist government was convinced that the "Pao An Tui is the only way out," pribumi resentment against it grew.[72] The Indonesian government discerned that the "Pao An Tui is disliked by Indonesian people everywhere. . . . The Indonesian people hope that it will be disbanded soon."[73] The Pao An Tui was mainly active in Sumatra, but it amplified the overall pribumi distrust of the Chinese community during the Indonesian National Revolution. A report by the Indonesian Ministry of Information described the Chinese as an apathetic and "passive" ethnic group that cared "only about making business profits through trade" and had no interest in politics. While the Indonesian people were fighting for the freedom of their nation, the Chinese were reportedly involved in "hoarding food such as rice through the help of Dutch military forces."[74] In his letter to the ROC general Bai Chongxi, the peranakan politician Siauw Giok Tjhan wrote that some of the Chinese involved in the Pao An Tui regarded themselves as "the most loyal subjects of Queen Wilhelmina," and were unaware of the fact that their activities contradicted Sun Yat-sen's philosophy of the Three Principles of the People.[75] The Indonesian government urged the Chinese Nationalist government to recognize that the Pao An Tui's activities would "facilitate the Dutch to provoke undesirable clashes between the TNI and local Chinese inhabitants' armed forces." In his letter to the ROC consul general, Sukarno called for the abolition of the Pao An Tui because it was part of the "Dutch colonial policy in the past and in the present to stimulate feelings of suspicion, in particular between the Indonesians and the Chinese inhabitants." The Indonesian authorities asked for the Chinese Nationalist government's cooperation in eliminating "the treacherous acts of the Dutch" and "the existence of destructive misunderstanding between both of our peoples."[76]

Shifting Public Opinion among the Overseas Chinese

Existing research shows that the one-dimensional image of a helpless Chinese community waiting for rescue by the Chinese Nationalist government, the Dutch, or the Allied forces is misleading.[77] Admittedly, some of those from the upper circles, such as Westernized businessmen and the intelligentsia, were pro-Dutch. There were also a small number of opportunistic Chinese traders who profited greatly from the chaos by participating in illegal commerce, either by supplying goods to the Dutch or by smuggling contraband for the Republican forces. But the vast majority of the common people took little interest in political issues and would acquiesce to the rule of either party as long as their personal safety and economic well-being were guaranteed.[78] Last but not least, some left-leaning ethnic Chinese supported Indonesia's anticolonial struggle and envisioned themselves as citizens of the Republic of Indonesia.[79]

The predicament of the Chinese during the Indonesian National Revolution led to accusations against the ROC government for taking no action to stop the ethnic violence.[80] *Qiaosheng Bao* of Shanghai commented that the incapable ROC consul general in Batavia would probably be "too ashamed to face the overseas Chinese again."[81] While being granted the title of "the mother of revolution" in the Chinese Nationalist government's propaganda, the overseas Chinese were "orphans abroad" in reality.[82] The representatives of the ROC National Congress in the Dutch East Indies collectively submitted a petition to Chiang Kai-shek, requesting that the ROC government stop sitting idly by while "watching the sons and daughters of China being slaughtered by foreign troops in a foreign land."[83] *Nanqiao Ribao (Nan Chiau Jit Pao, Nanqiao Daily)*, based in Singapore, argued that the ROC's decision to oppose the Republic of Indonesia at the UN closed the door for reconciliation on the ethnic Chinese issue.[84] It warned that if the Chinese Nationalist government continued its unfriendly attitude toward the Indonesian Republic, ethnic relations would deteriorate further:

> The overseas Chinese will see the Indonesians as their enemies and the Dutch as their friends. And the Indonesians will definitely regard the overseas Chinese as the "fifth column" of the Dutch. By that time, the Dutch will capitalize on the anti-Chinese mentality of the Indonesians by recruiting Chinese soldiers and using the Chinese to attack the Indonesians. Consequently, the Indonesians are going to slaughter the Chinese in retaliation. Can you imagine what a miserable scenario this would be? The Chinese would become as powerless as a piece of meat on the chopping block.[85]

In addition, the Chinese Nationalist government's promotion of the Pao An Tui stoked discontent among the overseas Chinese. A Chinese newspaper published in Hui'an, South Fujian Province, one of the major native regions of the overseas Chinese communities in Indonesia, criticized the

Pao An Tui for worsening the misfortune of the Chinese in Indonesia and for sowing the seeds of ethnic hatred. The newspaper pointed out that the one thousand firearms provided by the Dutch to the Pao An Tui "were not enough to protect two million Chinese, but enough to arouse fear among the barbarians (turen)."[86] An article published in Qiaosheng Bao noted that a few narrow-minded Chinese-language newspapers in Southeast Asia used an ultranationalist and racist tone in an attempt to cater to the tastes of their poorly educated and backward readers. As a result, a portion of the Chinese population in Indonesia became dangerously biased and treated all Indonesians as a violent threat.[87] The pro-Chinese Communist Party Da Gong Bao reminded its readers that, while the establishment of the Pao An Tui was the "first time when the ethnic Chinese had their own military forces abroad," it should not be a point of pride because the Pao An Tui put the ethnic Chinese in an even more difficult social position, where they had to "look for survival through a narrow crack."[88]

Beyond criticism of the Chinese Nationalist government's inability to protect its overseas nationals, the overseas Chinese began to reflect upon their own attitudes toward the Indonesian National Revolution. Some Chinese associations made resolutions in left-wing Indonesian newspapers and magazines such as Madjallah Buruh Jogja, Madjallah Nasional Jogja, and Kedaulatan Rakjat Djokja to demonstrate their support for the Republic of Indonesia while denouncing Pao An Tui and calling for its abolition. In their statements, these Chinese associations made loyalty pledges such as "Where there is the TNI, there is safety for the Chinese people"; "Without the strength of the government of the Republic of Indonesia, there will not be any peace for the Chinese"; "World opinion is siding with the Republic of Indonesia"; and "The ROC consul general should make an official announcement that the safety of the Chinese is guaranteed by the Republic of Indonesia."[89] Some ethnic Chinese businessmen with an anticolonial ideology helped finance the Indonesian National Revolution.[90] Siauw Giok Tjhan, the minister of minority affairs of the Republic of Indonesia, helped organize the Chinese Youth Force (Angkatan Muda Tionghoa) and the Chinese Volunteer Force (Pasukan Sukarela Tionghoa), both of which joined Indonesia's struggle for independence against the Dutch. In opposition to the members of Pao An Tui, leaders of these groups believed that "peace will not arrive in Indonesia until Indonesia achieves its independence; and enmity will not disappear in Indonesia until the Dutch forces leave."[91] In Malang, East Java, local ethnic Chinese organized medical support teams to assist the TNI.[92]

Furthermore, some progressive leaders in the Chinese community took a completely different approach from the Chinese Nationalist government toward the citizenship issue. Siauw formulated the idea that the Chinese should be integrated into a multiethnic Indonesian nation-state. "Chinese" as a racial category should be separated from one's national orientation. Wen Jingduo (also known as Tony Wen), a Chinese Indonesian politician active in the government of the Republic of Indonesia, was one of the leaders of the Chinese Volunteer Force in Solo. In 1947, Wen met with a British officer from the headquarters of the Allied forces in Southeast Asia. The British officer asked Wen if he carried a Chinese passport himself and whether the Chinese Volunteer Forces would fight for Indonesia's independence even if some of its members remained Chinese citizens. Wen replied: "Of course I am a Chinese person, but under the Indonesian citizenship law, I will become an Indonesian citizen . . . at least 80 percent of the Chinese in Indonesia will become Indonesian citizens just like me."[93]

In January 2013 in Medan, North Sumatra, I met a leader of the local Chinese community, Mr. Liao Zhangran. Along with his many other titles, he is the president and founder of the Asia International Friendship College, a trilingual (Chinese, English, and bahasa Indonesia) college that has close ties to the PRC. A second-generation Chinese who has a native-level command of Mandarin, he is Chinese culturally but committed to Indonesia politically. As a nine-year-old whose family members participated in the Pao An Tui in 1947, Mr. Liao witnessed how infighting broke out between Chinese groups that supported the Indonesian National Revolution and those that opposed it. He also saw how the scorched-earth policy rendered thousands of Chinese homeless. As a little boy, Mr. Liao was resentful toward the troops of the Republic of Indonesia. However, he now believes that the Chinese Nationalist government, rather than the Indonesian Revolutionary government in Yogyakarta, was responsible for the suffering of the Chinese. "All revolutions involve sacrifices," he said, "and the Chinese suffered during the Indonesian National Revolution not because of the cruelty of the Indonesian troops but because of the nature of war itself." Mr. Liao believed that quite a number of ethnic Chinese openly supported Indonesia's struggle for independence even though their contributions had been expunged from official narratives. According to Mr. Liao, such unfair treatment of the Chinese was a result of the ROC's policies: "The leaders of China at the time could not tell right from wrong."[94]

By focusing his critique on the Chinese Nationalist government alone, Mr. Liao was eager to validate the political allegiance of the Indonesian Chinese and to deny any narrative about the past that would essentialize the antipathy between the Chinese and the pribumi. Although the ROC was not the sole wrongdoer as Mr. Liao suggested, its diplomacy and migration policy in the late 1940s failed to defuse ethnic tension and improve conditions for the Chinese in Indonesia. Committed to its Western allies and proud of its own elevated status after the Allied victory of World War II, the ROC was unsympathetic toward Indonesia's anticolonial struggle, unwilling to grant diplomatic recognition to the Republic of Indonesia, and unready to treat it as an equal partner in the post–World War II Asia-Pacific. Meanwhile, committed to the principle of the right of blood, the Chinese Nationalist regime insisted on exercising jurisdiction over and maintaining productive ties with the ethnic Chinese in Indonesia, even though the Republic of Indonesia had offered them access to full citizenship. In the face of rampant ethnic violence, the Chinese Nationalist government became even more inflexible, antagonizing the Indonesian government at the UN while pulling the ethnic Chinese further away from integration into the emerging Indonesian nation. Besides showing state-to-state communications and conflicts over the Chinese issue, this chapter also uncovers the mosaic of national orientations among individuals. While some pro-Chinese Nationalist groups followed the ROC's logic and established self-defense corps that challenged the authority of the Republic of Indonesia, others started to formulate a more sophisticated and progressive understanding of citizenship, as they foresaw the coming of a new age of nation building.

The Indonesia-oriented ethnic Chinese were not the only Chinese who were critical of the Chinese Nationalist Party's approach to citizenship. Ba Ren, a Chinese writer seeking refuge in the jungles of Sumatra, also had opinions on the nature of the Indonesian National Revolution and the issue of ethnic relations that were different from the Nationalist government's. Ba Ren was an undercover member of the Chinese Communist Party who later became the PRC's first ambassador to Indonesia. Together with a group of Chinese left-wing intellectuals, he relocated to North Sumatra during the Japanese occupation of Southeast Asia, where he was involved in the underground resistance against the Japanese. After the Japanese surrender, he went on to become an important activist in diasporic politics. In July 1947, Ba Ren was arrested by the Dutch for supporting Indonesia's struggle for independence. He reflected on his arrest in his memoir: "I am prepared to go to a Dutch jail, so that the pribumi of Indonesia will understand that the Chinese people are also making sacrifices for the Indonesian Revolution."[95] Chapter 2 will reconstruct the process through which the Chinese Communist Party, driven by similar motivations but different ideologies than its Nationalist rivals, built its networks in Chinese communities in Indonesia during the 1940s.

CHAPTER 2

The Chinese Communist Party and the Overseas Chinese

In April 1945, in a small village called Surabeia, located in the middle of the rainforests of Sumatra, Ba Ren, an undercover member of the CCP and a writer, had just recovered from a typhoid infection. While convalescing, Ba Ren spent most of his time reading books on Indonesian history in English, Japanese, and bahasa Indonesia. He wrote in his memoir: "While working, I immersed myself in the fragrance of the Indonesian earth, feeling like I could tap the pulse and hear the cries of the souls of the Indonesian people. When I got tired with reading, I composed my long poem in praise of Indonesia in my 4 by 5 square meter bedroom."[1] The poem, completed in 1952, was entitled *The Song of Indonesia (Yindunixiya zhi ge)*. In more than two thousand lines of verse, an economically and politically independent Indonesia emerges in Ba Ren's vision, with the ethnic Chinese as part of this new multiethnic nation:

> There are five million of my countrymen living all across your country,
> They are as diligent as bulls and horses, as savvy as foxes,
> They are as conservative as the black earth, as tough as ironstone,
> They are all vagrants from an ancient empire.
> They look for food on your land; and they also aspire to settle here;
> To them, the motherland is a distant dream.[2]

The Cold War generation of scholars assumed that the CCP came to power with little knowledge or experience concerning the overseas Chinese. According to Stephen Fitzgerald, the CCP "had not thought very deeply" about and were not "very much concerned with the overseas Chinese" before coming to power in 1949.[3] However, Ba Ren's special connection with Indonesia supports Glen Peterson's more recent assertion that the CCP "had already developed significant interest" in rallying political and economic support from Chinese overseas in the 1920s and 1930s.[4] Admittedly, the Nationalists had a longer history of development abroad and had accumulated more human and social capital in the Chinese community in Indonesia. Through a study of memoirs, diaries, poems, and theater scripts written by Ba Ren and those who used to work with him in the 1940s, I contend that the CCP was better able than its Nationalist rival to capture the hearts and minds of young overseas Chinese by expanding its political networks and promoting cross-ethnic alliances among the working class.

In the 1940s, the CCP built its support base among the overseas Chinese through the education and publishing efforts of left-wing intellectuals like Ba Ren who traveled from Mainland China to Southeast Asia and worked as teachers and journalists in overseas Chinese communities. The subsequent rise of literacy and increasing availability of left-wing publications created a generation of revolutionary-minded ethnic Chinese youth. Through supplies, information, and refuge provided by these young people during the Japanese occupation, the CCP established underground offices in Sumatra, which were hidden behind the counters of pastry shops, Chinese medicine companies, soap factories, and wineries. It was the enthusiasm of these left-leaning youth that allowed openly active pro-CCP civic associations and political organizations to blossom during the Indonesian National Revolution.

Ba Ren's personal skill in youth mobilization as well as the appeal of his ideas on interethnic solidarity also played an important role in the rapid growth of the CCP's influence in Sumatra in the 1940s. Ba Ren believed that "class struggle will break down the stone wall between different ethnic groups."[5] He tried to facilitate dialogue with pribumi revolutionaries. During the Japanese occupation, Ba Ren held that the antifascist struggle could not succeed unless the Chinese joined hands with the pribumi. During the Indonesian National Revolution, Ba Ren contended that the tension between the Chinese and the pribumi was a class issue rather than an ethnic one. Using a Marxist analytical framework, Ba Ren concluded that incidents of violence were the working-class pribumi's rebellion against the Chinese capitalists, rather than an explosion of the pribumi's primordial racial hostility against the ethnic Chinese as a whole.[6] From Ba Ren's point of view, Indonesia was on the frontier of the global anticolonial movement. Beyond the defeat of the Dutch, he expected a more thorough social revolution led by a multiethnic coalition of the proletariat. Ba Ren believed that the shared grievances and aspirations of the oppressed working class would help the ethnic Chinese and the pribumi overcome racial prejudice. The ultimate solution to the ethnic problem was for the ethnic Chinese to devote themselves, politically and economically, to Indonesia's struggle for national self-determination. Ba Ren's thought had a profound impact on the political consciousness of Chinese youth and contributed to their continuous activism after Indonesia's independence.

The Chinese Communist Party's Policy toward Overseas Chinese

The CCP's endeavor to attract support from overseas Chinese communities began with the First United Front of the Nationalist and Communist Parties. In February 1924, one month after the Nationalist-Communist alliance was formalized, the Nationalist Party established its Overseas Party Affairs Office.[7] In January 1926, Xu Suhun, an overseas Chinese from Kuala Lumpur and a CCP member since the party's founding in 1921, was elected chief secretary of the Overseas Party Affairs Office. For the purpose of training overseas Chinese cadres, the Overseas Party Affairs Office set up an Overseas Chinese Movement Training Institute (huaqiao yundong jiangxisuo) modeled after the famous Peasant Movement Training Institute (nongmin yundong jiangxisuo) in Guangzhou organized by Mao Zedong and Peng Pai. The institute's inaugural class of eighty students commenced a three-month course in November 1926.[8]

The Japanese invasion of China gave rise to the Nanyang National Salvation Movement and offered the CCP an opportunity to increase its influence among the diaspora. Moreover, in 1936, the Communist International (Comintern) encouraged the CCP to form a "united front" with bourgeois forces, including overseas Chinese merchants. In 1938, with permission from British authorities, the CCP created the Eighth Route Army liaison office in Hong Kong (Xianggang balujun banshichu). This office was headed by Liao Chengzhi, who later rose to be the chair of the Overseas Chinese Affairs Commission (OCAC) of the PRC. Liao worked closely with the Hong Kong–based China Defense League (Baowei Zhongguo tongmeng) headed by Sun Yat-sen's widow, Song Qingling.[9] In addition to channeling financial and material resources from the overseas Chinese communities back to China, the Eighth Route Army liaison office in Hong Kong established a significant media presence for the CCP in this "in-between place" of the global Chinese migration network.[10] A series of CCP-controlled news agencies and publishing houses enabled the Communists to reach out to Chinese in Hong Kong and beyond, thereby strengthening their stance in the emerging propaganda war against the Chinese Nationalist Party.[11] In 1939 the newly founded Southern Bureau of the CCP Central Committee (Zhonggong zhongyang nanfangjun) in Chongqing became the highest policy-making agency in overseas Chinese affairs, supervised by CCP leaders Zhou Enlai and Ye Jianying.

The CCP's construction of a united front with the overseas Chinese relied heavily on the flow of CCP members and sympathizers from Mainland China to Southeast Asia. Some fled southward to escape purges by the Nationalists or the Japanese, whereas others were dispatched by the party to promote its ideology abroad. Before its fall to the Japanese in February 1942, Singapore was a hub for left-wing writers and journalists from China. In 1940 the party sent Hu Yuzhi—the journalist, critic, and translator of Edgar Snow's *Red Star over China*—to Singapore to serve as the editor of *Nanyang Siang Pau* (*Nanyang Shangbao*, *Nanyang Business Daily*), a left-wing Chinese-language daily owned by Tan Kah Kee. In December 1941, following the outbreak of the Pacific War, Hu set up the Wartime Mission of Chinese Intellectuals in Singapore (Xingzhou huaqiao wenhuajie zhanshi gongzuotuan). The renowned Chinese writer and poet Yu Dafu, who arrived in Singapore in 1938 to work as a literary editor for *Xingzhou Ribao* (*Sin Chew Jit Poh*, *Sin Chew Daily*), became the head of the Wartime Mission.[12] Ba Ren, who was teaching at the Nanyang Overseas Chinese Normal College (Nanyang huaqiao shifan xuexiao) in Singapore at the time, was in charge of antifascist propaganda among the Southeast Asian Chinese. He had become an underground CCP member in 1925; in his initial intelligence work, he had infiltrated the Chinese Nationalist Party office in Guangzhou. After his true identity was exposed, he left for Shanghai and took up a leading role in the League of Left-Wing Writers (Zhongguo zuoyi zuojia lianmeng). In March 1941, Zhou Enlai instructed him to leave Shanghai for Hong Kong and to prepare for further travel to the US, where he would be responsible for the development of pro-CCP Chinese-language print media. However, due to difficulties in obtaining travel documents, Ba Ren was reassigned to Singapore and thus began his six-year journey through war and revolution in "the land below the wind."[13]

The CCP and Political Mobilization of the Chinese during the Japanese Occupation

In the early hours of February 4, 1942, Ba Ren and Lei Derong,[14] his comrade and traveling companion, boarded an old motor sampan bound for the Riau Islands of Indonesia to escape the Japanese invasion of Singapore. On the sampan were twenty-eight writers and journalists, including Hu Yuzhi, Yu Dafu, and Wang Jiyuan, one of the founders of *Sheng Huo Bao*, a CCP-affiliated Chinese-language newspaper headquartered in Jakarta.[15] The overcrowded vessel crossed the sea despite "ear-shattering bombardment from planes and cannons."[16] Yet, soon after this nerve-racking voyage, Indonesia met the same fate as Singapore and fell under Japanese control. Hu Yuzhi and Yu Dafu led an expedition team to explore a possible detour back to China via Sumatra, Java, and India. The frail Ba Ren was unable to join them. Instead, he and Lei Derong moved to a remote village on the Bengkalis Island, where they sought shelter with the family of a local Chinese peasant, Ren Sheng.

In this village isolated from politics and the ongoing war, Ba Ren observed the status of the ethnic Chinese with the eyes of an anthropologist and recorded them in the language of a poet. Since the middle of the nineteenth-century, the plantations and tin mines in Sumatra had attracted Chinese coolie migrants. Among the local Chinese, in the 1930s new arrivals outnumbered the locally born and the majority were Chinese-speaking. Compared with Java, there was also a higher portion of Chinese, like the Ren Sheng family, who settled in rural areas.[17] From Ba Ren's writings, vivid images emerge: the "primitive fire" radiating from the eyes of the young pribumi wife of an elderly Chinese husband; Ba Ren, himself, singing nationalist songs from Northeast China while learning to grow crops in the jungles; and the almost static life of Chinese peasants and their apathetic attitude toward the distant motherland.[18] Ba Ren wrote: "Between wild rivers and deserted harbors, between deep mountains and grand lakes, you will always come across these seeds from outside—our fellow countrymen—growing stately. They are burdened with destinies as dark as coal. But through the darkness, a fire of life is burning, as vibrantly as that from the black coal."[19]

Four months of village life with Ren Sheng and his family inspired Ba Ren to help change the fate of the working-class Chinese in Indonesia. In August 1942, Ba Ren and Lei Derong reunited with Hu Yuzhi and Yu Dafu in Payakumbuh, West Sumatra, where the latter two had settled temporarily after their unproductive search for a route back to China. Using "Zhao Lian" as an alias, Yu Dafu started a brewery with the help of locals; Ba Ren disguised himself as one of "Boss Zhao's" employees.[20] In October and November 1942,

FIGURE 2.1.   Ba Ren (second from the right) with other Chinese left-wing intellectuals who worked in Indonesia in the late 1940s. Hu Yuzhi is the fourth from the left in the front row. In the back row are the key figures of *Sheng Huo Bao*. From left to right: Wang Jiyuan, Shao Zonghan, Huang Zhougui, and Zheng Chuyun. Beijing, October 1, 1959. Personal collection of Wang Keping.

Ba Ren and Lei Derong relocated again to Siantar and Medan. In these two major cities of North Sumatra, both with large concentrations of ethnic Chinese, they had extensive interactions with local anti-Japanese organizations. Before their arrival, under the influence of the Nanyang National Salvation Movement, left-wing youth formed two underground societies: the Antifascist Alliance of the Chinese in Sumatra (Sumendala huaqiao fanfanxisi tongmeng) and the Chinese Association against Enemies (Huaqiao kangdi xiehui). Meanwhile, a "Good Earth Bookstore" (Dadi shudian), with a rare supply of smuggled classical Marxist works and CCP pamphlets, became the base camp for these organizations' underground activities.[21] Ba Ren was invited to mentor these young people, who were ardent but lacked experience.

Ba Ren was keenly aware of the contrasting attitudes of the Chinese and the pribumi toward the coming of the Japanese. Most Chinese were implacably against Japanese occupation of Indonesia, largely because of the atrocities committed by the Japanese in Mainland China. The pribumi tended to take a much softer position, possibly under the influence of the "Joyoboyo

Prophecy." This Javanese myth predicted that after a long period of subjec-
tion by a white race, a yellow race from the north would drive out the whites
and free Indonesia.[22] Ba Ren also noticed that in Indonesia the Chinese population was concentrated in the cities. Therefore, he decided that it would be
impossible for the Chinese in Indonesia to follow the steps of the Chinese in
Malaya and start a guerrilla war based in the countryside all by themselves.
He concluded: "It is imperative for the Chinese to cooperate with the indigenous people during and after the antifascist war."[23]

To attract more pribumi participants, the Antifascist Alliance of the Chinese in Sumatra, following a suggestion by Ba Ren, changed its name to the
more ethnically inclusive People's Antifascist Alliance in Sumatra (Sumendala renmin fanfanxisi tongmeng).[24] Meanwhile, Ba Ren encouraged the
Chinese youth to become proficient in bahasa Indonesia and to familiarize
themselves with the social, political, economic, and historical conditions of
the country. While serving as a senior adviser to an underground news bulletin affiliated with the People's Antifascist Alliance, the *Progressive Weekly*
(*Qianjin Zhoubao*), Ba Ren requested that the Chinese youth communicate
information and ideas from the news bulletin in local languages to the
pribumi working class.[25] Ba Ren also urged the Chinese youth to look for the
underground organizations of the PKI. However, after a yearlong search, no
connections could be made with the PKI or any of its peripheral groups.[26] As
a result, the People's Antifascist Alliance turned instead to the Malaya Communist Party (MCP) and Malayan People's Anti-Japanese Army (MPAJA) and
sent a batch of cadres to Malaya for the first time in early 1943.[27]

For many young Chinese, their encounters and engagement with Ba Ren
and Lei Derong marked a moment of political awakening. Ba Ren and Lei
played important roles in organizations such as a newspaper reading group,
a household management reading group,[28] and a fitness and book club.[29]
They regarded the members of these civic associations as "seeds of the anti-
Japanese struggle" who were dedicated but immature. At their meetings,
Ba Ren gave informal lectures on the Marxist theory of social development
and analyzed current politics. He also led discussions of left-wing literary
works such as *How the Steel Was Tempered* by Nikolai Ostrovsky, *Corrosion*
(*Shi*) by Mao Dun, and *The Family* (*Jia*) by Ba Jin. One former activist recalled:
"Ba Ren used the stories drawn from progressive literature to encourage
the youth to make the right choices in their own personal lives. At the same
time, Ba Ren also boosted the young people's confidence in victory against
the Japanese through his in-depth analysis of world affairs."[30] During these
meetings, Ba Ren was often "speaking with a strong Zhejiang accent about
the progress of the War of Resistance back in China or providing historical

FIGURE 2.2.   Ba Ren (fifth from the right in the front row) and the teachers from the Zhonghua High School of Siantar, North Sumatra, 1946. Personal collection of Wang Keping.

anecdotes in a cheerful and humorous tone." Lei, with a warm smile on her face, would "serve the young people tea and coffee and gently add a few comments at the end." Another former activist remembered: "They had a great impact on our ways of thinking and our emotional state, leading us to a more practical way to carry out the anti-Japanese struggle."[31]

The underground political activities of the Chinese in Sumatra came to a sudden halt when the Japanese initiated a heavy-handed crackdown in September 1943. With information obtained from a defector, the Japanese arrested and executed many members of both the People's Antifascist Alliance and the Chinese Association against Enemies. Ba Ren, Lei Derong, and other leaders of these organizations fled to the countryside with logistical support from a well-connected underground network.[32] To shelter its remaining members, the People's Antifascist Alliance secretly built a number of hiding places inside a chain of soap factories scattered across North Sumatra. Soap production required neither advanced technology nor a large start-up investment and so could be easily set up. Moreover, most of these factories were located in suburban areas, far out of the scope of Japanese surveillance.[33] They formed a transportation network through which funds, print materials, and secret documents could be circulated. In the words of a former member, "this transportation network was like a web of blood vessels, through which the activities of the People's Antifascist Alliance flowed smoothly."[34]

After several layovers at soap factories, Ba Ren and Lei Derong finally resettled in the village of Surabeia, where "orangutans were a hundred times more [populous] than humans."[35] Ba Ren adopted a new fake identity as an unsuccessful Chinese businessman who decided to return to farming due to the chaos of war. In his memoir, he jokingly called himself "the commander-in-chief of cats, dogs and chickens," as the flimsy bamboo hut in which he and Lei stayed was overflowing with all these animals.[36] Despite the remoteness of their location and the absence of any modern transportation or communication tools, the underground network was able to send resources such as financial aid, stationery, books, pamphlets, and the typhoid medication that saved Ba Ren's life.[37]

These two years in the village of Surabeia had a transformative impact on Ba Ren's thinking. He described himself as "a small fish that sneaked out from a hole in the fishing net, wandering in the rural areas of East Sumatra to see the bottom of Indonesian society."[38] Through everyday socialization, he developed close interpersonal relationships with his pribumi neighbors and a deeper understanding of interethnic relations in Indonesia. In his memoir, Ba Ren wrote about the gradual disappearance of ethnic divisions after rubbing shoulders with the pribumi residents in Surabeia on a day-to-day basis:

> It was as if I had forgotten my own nationality, as if I had no idea which country I originally came from. I was like an invader in this village where the Chinese, Javanese, and Malay peacefully coexisted. I saw how diligent the Chinese were, and how idle the Javanese were. Almost all the Chinese were comparatively well-off, whereas the Javanese and Malays had always been struggling to make ends meet. So the Javanese and Malays often used some seemingly witty schemes to take advantage of a Chinese newcomer like me. But their attempts were childlike, adorably awkward and naive. I felt like I could reach out my hands and touch their warm hearts. But I always felt like there was some distance between me and the diligent Chinese peasants, the smart Chinese businessmen, and the intellectuals, no matter how friendly they were to me.[39]

Ba Ren's affinity for the pribumi peasants around him translated into a passion to liberate them. In his long poem *The Song of Indonesia*, a product of his Surabeia days, Ba Ren described himself as "a pawn of revolution" and "a third-class poet" who would embrace Indonesia in his arms together with China:

> Besides my own motherland, my worker brothers,
> I care the most about your destiny.
> I used to farm in your land,
> And I smelled the fragrance of the soil of my motherland when
>   I was hoeing.[40]

The extreme contrast of wealth and poverty Ba Ren witnessed in Surabeia infuriated him. While the village itself was in decay with huts trapped in rotten foliage and half-naked residents in shabby clothes, the nearby Dutch-owned plantation was a paradise with meticulously maintained gardens and majestic mansions. He castigated Western capitalists for stealing land from the locals and enslaving thousands of foreign laborers under abhorrent conditions. As a result, his neighbors in Surabeia were "living on the margins of their own land forcibly occupied by foreigners," and they were "at their last gasp . . . awaiting their doom."[41] He was confident that, in the near future, "the flame of nationalist revolutionary struggles is going to light up" in Indonesia. In his imagination, he saw "the pictures of proletarian leaders on the walls of coolie laborers' dormitories all over Sumatra."[42] In *The Song of Indonesia*, he predicted:

> Social revolution formed a new network across the boundaries of
>   capitalist empires;
> We, as the oppressed nation and class, are connected to and echoed
>   in this web;
> We have to fight this battle to disassemble the old system;
> So as to establish a new network that is coherent, clear, free and equal.
> Leaning toward the left will not be your fatal wound,
> Why are you afraid? Why are you hesitating?
> Only an assembly of the revolutionary masses is the solution to your
>   disease that is beyond cure.[43]

Before Ba Ren finished his *Song of Indonesia*, the news of Japanese surrender arrived in Surabeia. Having already foreseen that the end of World War II would give the Dutch an opportunity to reclaim colonial rule, he soon left Surabeia for Medan and Siantar to aid Indonesia's struggle for national independence. Lei Derong stayed for a little longer in Surabeia to host a farewell banquet for the whole village. She killed and cooked all the chickens that she and Ba Ren had raised together. Over food and drinks, she revealed the couple's true identities and told the villagers about their involvement in the underground resistance movement against the Japanese. Shocked at first, their pribumi neighbors were quick to connect the dots. Ba Ren was impressed by the words of one of the neighbors as told to him by Lei: "The *bapak* does not look like a peasant, and *nyonya* seems very well-educated.[44] The Japanese invasion united the Indonesians and the Chinese. We became brothers."[45]

The CCP and Political Mobilization of the Chinese during the Indonesian National Revolution

The beginning of the Indonesian National Revolution coincided with the outbreak of a full-scale political and military confrontation between the Chinese Nationalist and Communist Parties. This rivalry also fractured the Chinese communities in Southeast Asia. According to Ba Ren, in North Sumatra in the late 1940s the Chinese community was divided into three groups: the "democratic and progressive" (*minzhu jinbu*) elements were sympathetic and supportive of both the Chinese Communists and Indonesia's anticolonial revolution; the "reactionaries" (*fandong pai*) remained loyal to the Chinese Nationalist government and had a condescending attitude toward the Indonesian people's struggle for national independence; and, last but not least, a large number of the ethnic Chinese were apolitical and "only cared about their own economic well-being."[46] The Chinese Communist and Nationalist affiliates in Indonesia competed for the support of this last group of noncommitted ethnic Chinese through print media and civic organizations. For example, via the left-wing *Democratic Daily* (*Minzhu Ribao*), Ba Ren, as a member of its editorial board, tried to evoke sympathy and respect for the Indonesian Revolution among the Chinese in Indonesia. The Chinese Nationalists in North Sumatra accused the *Democratic Daily* of "colluding with the barbarians" (*tongfan*) and betraying the interests of the ethnic Chinese. Public accusations were followed by assassination attempts, one of which left the general manager of the *Democratic Daily* permanently disabled.[47]

As the Chinese Communist Party gradually gained the upper hand in the civil war back home, the pro-Communist faction in North Sumatra began to more proactively challenge the overseas presence of the Chinese Nationalist Party. With the freedom to carry out political activities more openly following the Japanese surrender, Ba Ren deepened the interpersonal bonds he had built with the left-leaning ethnic Chinese youth. Secretive meetings that had been held behind closed doors during the Japanese occupation were transformed into public lectures in auditoriums, where Ba Ren would offer analyses of international affairs and lectures on Marxism. In Medan and Siantar, Ba Ren and Lei Derong's activities were mostly carried out through the China Democratic League (Zhongguo minzhu tongmeng). Ba Ren was the president of its branch in Medan. The China Democratic League was established in Mainland China in 1941; at first, it tried to find a middle way between the Chinese Communists and Nationalists but later became more inclined toward the former. Its apparatus in Southeast Asia served mostly as a front organization for the CCP.[48] Ba Ren mentored youth groups such as the Collective Study Society (gong xue she) and the New China Drama Club (xin Zhongguo juyi she), while Lei Derong led the Women's Society (funv hui).[49] Ba Ren and Lei Derong founded libraries with Chinese-language left-wing literature and pro-CCP magazines published in Southeast Asia, such as *Below the Wind* (*Feng Xia*), based in Singapore. In 1946 Ba Ren became the consultant for the Hua Ch'iao Chung Hui (huaqiao zonghui, the Association of Overseas Chinese Organizations) in Medan, signifying the rising influence of left-wing forces among the Chinese in North Sumatra.

Ba Ren was sensitive to the worsening of the ethnic problem during the Indonesian Nationalist Revolution, and he strongly opposed the Chinese Nationalist Party's promotion of Pao An Tui as the solution. He noted: "The

FIGURE 2.3.   Ba Ren (front row, center) with participants and guests at the First Congregation of the Association of East Sumatran Chinese Workers and Peasants and the Association of East Sumatran Chinese Youth and Women, 1946. Personal collection of Wang Keping.

conditions have changed substantially from the Japanese colonial period. . . . While war continues, some have started to blackmail Chinese businessmen behind the scenes."[50] In the summer of 1946, with support from Allied forces, the Dutch regained control of Medan. The local Pao An Tui accepted weapons from the Dutch and assisted them in driving the military forces of the Republic of Indonesia out of the region. Ba Ren was furious about such arrangements, and he sarcastically commented: "The Pao An Tui has made its best efforts in this war: sometimes it fought side by side with the Dutch forces; other times it even went ahead of the Dutch in chasing away the remaining Indonesian revolutionary troops. Its contributions should be dutifully recorded! The Dutch were most satisfied when the Pao An Tui marched into the countryside and cracked down on all the potential guerrilla bases among the Indonesian people. The benevolent Dutch are using the bloody hand of the Pao An Tui to conquer a 'primitive nation'!"[51]

According to Ba Ren, to de-escalate the ethnic conflict the Chinese in Indonesia had to reflect on the equally vicious realities of Chinese prejudice against the pribumi. In his 1947 essay on the Indonesian National Revolution, he cited Friedrich Engels's comments on the Second Opium War. Engels criticized Western observers who denigrated the Chinese people's anti-imperialist struggles as "barbaric."[52] Drawing a comparison between China's own history "written in blood and sweat" and Indonesia's ongoing "heroic struggle," Ba Ren appealed for empathy among "all Chinese with a conscience": "How could you serve as the pawns of the Dutch who murdered our fraternal ethnic groups (*xiongdi zu*)?[53] The Dutch imperialists are the mastermind of colonial exploitation in both Indonesia and China. The Chinese people and the Indonesian people are comrades-in-arms in the same struggle."[54]

Nurturing such a sense of solidarity between the Chinese and pribumi was Ba Ren's goal during the Indonesian National Revolution. In 1947, in an interview with the Indonesian journalist Muhammad Radjab, he openly stated that the "progressive and democratic" group within Chinese society harbored no resentment when they experienced or witnessed a disturbance or any other destructive behavior by the pribumi during the revolution in Sumatra. He said: "When a nation is going through political and social revolution, it is understandable that chaos will occur."[55] Left-leaning ethnic Chinese youth organized events to demonstrate a Marxist vision of racial harmony at celebrations of political holidays in Medan and Siantar. One of Ba Ren's mentees, Wang Qianyu, a political activist and music teacher at the Siantar Chung Hua School (Xianda zhonghua xuexiao), recalled that, on International Women's Day in 1947, ethnic Chinese women sang "The Song of the

Red and White Flag" (*lagu bendera merah putih*) in support of the Indonesian National Revolution and Batak girls learned Chinese melodies. On Labor Day (May 1) in Siantar, hundreds of ethnic Chinese students sang "L'Internationale" with musical accompaniment by the Indonesian Republican military forces, followed by speeches given by representatives from different ethnic groups: the Chinese, Indians, and pribumi.[56]

The work that most powerfully embodied Ba Ren's vision of a class struggle transcending ethnic divisions was a play entitled *Temple of Five Ancestors* (*Wu Zu Miao*). It was staged for the first time in Medan by the members of the New China Drama Club.[57] Ba Ren found his inspiration in an actual historical event at a Dutch-owned tobacco plantation in Dili (today, Medan) in 1871. Five Chinese laborers started a revolt and killed the Dutch foreman, which led to death sentences for all of them in the local sultan's court. According to legend, on the day that they were executed, Medan was hit by a strong storm. Elderly Chinese believed that a god in heaven was crying for the five Chinese heroes who died alone in a foreign land. After the storm ended, the leaders of the local Chinese community buried the bodies of the five laborers and built a "temple of five ancestors" in their honor. In the foreword to the play, Ba Ren wrote: "The Gayos, Bataks, Malays, and Chinese were fighting a battle collectively. . . . No matter how primitive their means, their struggle fundamentally reflected the significance of the anti-imperialist alliance among different ethnic groups. . . . The five heroes enshrined at the 'temple of five ancestors' lit the torch of multiethnic struggle against imperialism in Dili."[58]

The play projects a Marxist analysis of historical development onto the original legend. The story is set in rural Sumatra where the land was at one time collectively owned, and the heads of villages democratically elected.[59] The encroachment of Western imperialism, the introduction of plantations, and the influx of Indian and Chinese coolie laborers derailed the region from its rightful evolution, which would have led by successive stages to Communism. Ba Ren was critical toward the ethnic Chinese who were complicit in the Western plunder of Indonesia and were indifferent to the toll of their economic success on the indigenous working class. He reprimanded them:

> The Chinese have obviously become the middle class. Under the wings of the imperialists, they infiltrated the Indonesian peasant economy via usury loans, which further deepened the gulf between the Chinese and the indigenous people. . . . After World War II, they were still dreaming of the good old days—they wanted to continue their comparatively well-off life under the protection of Western imperialists. . . .

They cannot see that if they support the Indonesian revolution with the free capital in their hands, their businesses can be transformed to light industry, which will facilitate the peaceful coexistence of the Chinese and the indigenous groups. . . . Some of them even served as pioneers for the imperialists during colonial conquest, and they did harm to the Indonesian National Revolution.[60]

In the play, Ba Ren presents the Marxist argument that, because imperialists' capital permeates the entire world, the revolution of the proletariat should also be a global phenomenon that transcends national boundaries and ethnic divides. Through the words of the characters he created, Ba Ren urged the Chinese working class to join the struggle in Indonesia. A Gayo villager named Sharon says: "Destiny is like an iron chain that connects the Malays, the Bataks, the Gayos, and the Chinese coolies. Once you pick up one end and start shaking it, the chain will move as a whole."[61] The main Chinese character, Hei Er, a smart young man who speaks fluent Malay and other local languages, reinforces this idea: "The poor all over the world share the same heart! If we combine our efforts with the barbarians (*fanren*), we will win the world over to us!" Both the Dutch plantation owner and the Chinese rebels try to win over Hei Er. But, in the end, he takes the side of the laborers, exclaiming: "We have to fight wherever we live. It does not matter if it is Dili, Malaya, Java, or China. The world belongs to us—the laborers! Fight!"[62] When hunted by the plantation overseers for organizing an uprising, Hei Er receives help from the pribumi working class. But a cunning ethnic Chinese employed by the Dutch sends Hei Er and the other four rebels to death row. Before their execution, Sjahrir, a virtuous Malay village chief, delivers a last meal to the five Chinese laborers and bids them farewell:

> You landed in my country just like beans sown in foreign soil. Mother earth is as loving in this land and as benevolent as mothers everywhere. You were supposed to grow, blossom, and bear fruit here. You were also the sons of our mother earth. But our mother earth is a victim. . . . Exhausted, she cannot give you any reward.[63]

The play, staged twenty to thirty times at more than ten different locations in North Sumatra, was well received among the local Chinese communities as well as the Indonesian Republican troops and guerrilla fighters. Its adaptation to the local linguistic environment and art traditions contributed to its success. Though it was written in Mandarin Chinese, onstage actors used Hokkien mixed with a variation of Malay spoken by ethnic Chinese peasants, which could be easily understood by the pribumi audience.[64] All

Gayo and Malay characters were removed, except for a young Malay woman who had a romantic relationship with Hei Er. Although Ba Ren was very concerned about this change, the sole pribumi character managed to win the hearts of the audience through beautifully performed *pantun* songs and *ronggeng* dances, both typical folk forms in North Sumatra. A chorus affiliated with the New China Drama Club would sing Indonesian songs before each performance to demonstrate Chinese support for the Indonesian National Revolution.

In August 1947, the Dutch arrested Ba Ren because he was suspected of aiding the Republic of Indonesia. The "weak and thin" Ba Ren was sentenced to heavy manual labor at a local train station. His mentee Wang Qianyu saw the assistance he received from Malay laborers as well as the "sly sneers" from the Chinese Nationalist affiliates standing by.[65] The left-wing Chinese intelligentsia in Indonesia and Singapore strongly protested his imprisonment. An op-ed that appeared in the left-wing magazine *Below the Wind* in 1947 remonstrated: "Sympathizing with the Indonesian people's revolutionary struggles should never be regarded as a crime. The reactionaries deviously framed Baren [*sic*] with assistance from the Dutch. And the Dutch cruelly and unjustifiably arrested one of its own antifascist allies. We cannot tolerate such brutal behavior toward an outstanding Chinese intellectual."[66] But Ba Ren saw his arrest as an opportunity to change the pribumi's perception of the ethnic Chinese as apathetic or even resentful toward the Indonesian National Revolution. He wrote: "I will prepare a basin of clean water for the bloody hands of the overseas Chinese, so that they can regain their innocence."[67]

In mid-September 1947, Ba Ren was released by the Dutch and expelled from Indonesia. With a one-way travel certificate issued by the Chinese Nationalist government's consulate in Medan, he, together with Lei Derong, boarded a ship from Sumatra to Hong Kong.[68] In his memoir, he recorded a conversation during the voyage with an "open-minded, progressive Chinese gentleman." His fellow passenger commented on ethnic relations: "How could the overseas Chinese continue to live on in Indonesia? There are 40,000 Chinese in Medan, even if 2,000–3,000 of them were able to return to China, all the rest of our fellow countrymen could only stay in Indonesia. Medan of course is not the land of the Chinese. Therefore, do we have the right to shout out slogans such as 'The troops of the Indonesian Republic should never return to East Sumatra'? How could our descendants continue to live there? . . . The Chinese will be doomed if soulless people continue to run wild in Indonesian society!" Ba Ren replied: "This is the tragedy of the Chinese. There is a big Chiang Kai-shek in the motherland; and there are countless little Chiang Kai-sheks overseas."[69]

Similar to their Nationalist rivals, the Chinese Communists believed that support from the overseas Chinese would bring material benefits and bolster the party's reputation worldwide. However, they used a different strategy to enhance influence abroad and proposed a different solution to the ethnic problem. While the Chinese Nationalist government relied upon the ROC embassy, consulates, and overseas branches of the Chinese Nationalist Party, the Chinese Communists depended on an informal web of interpersonal connections. The central figures in this network were left-wing literati from China who laid a solid foundation for the development of pro-Chinese Communist print media and schools in Indonesia. They enlivened the local cultural scene and inspired many ethnic Chinese youth. While the Chinese Nationalist government condemned the military forces of the Republic of Indonesia for violence against the Chinese, Communist affiliates represented by Ba Ren identified long-standing economic structures in Indonesian society as the root cause. Drawing from his own experience of living among the pribumi, Ba Ren believed that "ordinary Indonesian working people have always been very friendly to the Chinese, and they seem to harbor no ethnic hatred."[70] At the same time, he held that ethnic Chinese businessmen were "responsible for the corruption and chaos in Indonesia," because they had "formed an alliance with Indonesian army officers to smuggle weapons." In

FIGURE 2.4. Ba Ren (right) giving a lecture on the international situation in Siantar in 1946. Chen Lishui (left) was his interpreter. Chen was among the left-leaning youth recruited from Siantar by Ba Ren. He later returned to the PRC and was part of the first generation of Indonesian interpreters at the Foreign Ministry. Personal collection of Wang Keping.

his opinion, Indonesia could only develop its industries by nationalizing the capital of the ethnic Chinese.[71]

Ba Ren's departure from Indonesia in 1947 marked an interlude rather than a farewell. Soon after his arrival in Hong Kong, he founded the Indonesia Research Group (Yinni wenti xiaozu) under the International Liaison Department of the CCP (zhonggong zhongyang duiwai lianluo bu). Many members of this group were left-leaning ethnic Chinese youth who had worked with him in North Sumatra. They were recruited to attend the Ta Teh Institute in Hong Kong (Xianggang dade xueyuan), a tertiary institution run by the CCP. Following the Communist victory in Mainland China, they were first sent from Hong Kong to Beijing for political indoctrination at the Youth Training Camp of the United Front Work Department of the CCP Central Committee (zhonggong zhongyang tongzhanbu qingxunban) and then to work for the PRC's Foreign Ministry or the International Liaison Department of the CCP.[72] In August 1950, Ba Ren returned to Indonesia as the first PRC ambassador. The following chapter will reveal how he became embroiled in the complicated struggle against the "countless little Chiang Kai-sheks" in Indonesia.

CHAPTER 3

The Diplomatic Battle between the Two Chinas

In 1950, before Ba Ren embarked on his assignment as Beijing's first ambassador to Jakarta, his memoir of the years in the Sumatran jungle was published. In the afterword to the book, Ba Ren told the story of an impoverished ethnic Chinese peasant, Ah Lu, and his wife, who made a living by selling their own babies. Reflecting on the situation, Ba Ren wrote:

> How is their life now? The liberation of China is not the liberation of the lives of little earthworms like them on a foreign land. "When Tangshan grows stronger, what is the benefit for me Ah Lu?"[1] These words from Ah Lu were once again ringing in my ears. . . . Without the profound enlightenment that he gave me, I would not have jumped into the "sea of fire" of the Indonesian Revolution after the Japanese surrender in August 1945 and "incinerated" myself. . . . In my fifty years of life, leaving aside my early years of ignorance, almost one-sixth of my productive time has been spent in this vast "land below the winds." . . . On these islands dotted on the Pacific at the end of the world, there are millions of working people with whom I shared the same smell of sweat and earth. Ten million of them are overseas Chinese, who have been torn apart and eaten by a trapped wild animal. This is the biggest source of my sorrow.[2]

Ba Ren returned to Southeast Asia with the memory of living side by side with the pribumi and hopes of liberating the overseas Chinese from the claws of a wild beast—imperialism. But he found himself in an ever more volatile environment. In postindependence Indonesia, the integrity of the state was challenged by fierce competition between anti-Communist forces and left-wing parties as well as regional dissatisfaction with the central government. In China, the Nationalists lost the mainland but continued to challenge the legitimacy of the Communist government in international politics and their outreach to the overseas Chinese. Having switched diplomatic recognition from Taipei to Beijing, Jakarta nevertheless allowed the Chinese Nationalist Party apparatus to continue its activities until 1958.

Jakarta's ambiguous attitude induced a battle for influence between the two rival Chinese governments. As a regime in exile, the Chinese Nationalist government adjusted its past policies to fit the new circumstances resulting from its retreat to Taiwan. Having lost formal diplomatic representation, the Nationalists forged clandestine alliances with the Indonesian right-wing forces through the personal networks of the remaining Chinese Nationalist loyalists. In contrast with Taipei, Beijing prioritized state-to-state diplomacy over its connections to the overseas Chinese. By suspending the activities of the CCP among the overseas Chinese and signing the Sino-Indonesian Dual Nationality Treaty, Beijing attempted to ease Jakarta's concern that the ethnic Chinese could be used as a Communist fifth column. But Taipei denied the validity of the treaty and continued to seek financial and human resources from the overseas Chinese to help facilitate an early "recovery of the mainland."

The balance of power between Beijing and Taipei vacillated in time with the swinging pendulum of Indonesian domestic politics as well as the broader geopolitical situation of the early Cold War. The initial bilateral relations between Beijing and Jakarta were tortuous. With anti-Communist politicians occupying powerful positions in the early 1950s, Indonesia was apprehensive toward Beijing. Moreover, in the early years of the PRC, the CCP had a strong sense of obligation to spread its own revolutionary experience globally. But in the mid-1950s, Chinese leaders started to view Indonesia and a few other non-Communist countries in Asia and Africa as potential allies. The 1955 Bandung Conference, at which Beijing successfully blocked Taipei while presenting itself as a rational and reasonable player in world politics, offered the PRC the opportunity to appeal to Indonesia as well as to many other Afro-Asian states. After Indonesia's turn to the political left in the late 1950s, mutual strategic interests drew Beijing and Jakarta into a more substantial collaboration in the Asia-Pacific. The ties between Beijing and Jakarta were further strengthened in 1958, when Taipei became their common enemy because of its support for the regional rebellions in Sumatra and Sulawesi.

Backdoor Diplomacy: Taipei Reconnecting with Jakarta

After Indonesia achieved its formal independence in December 1949, the Chinese Nationalist government dispatched one of its senior politicians, Wu Tiecheng, as the special envoy to Jakarta to explore the possibility of establishing diplomatic contact.[3] However, Taipei's friendly gesture came too late. In 1950 the Republic of Indonesia became one of the first countries to grant diplomatic recognition to the PRC. Still uneasy about the Communist government in Beijing, the Indonesian government granted permission to the vice consuls general of the ROC, Niu Shuchun and Zhu Changdong, and their families to continue living in Indonesia as commoners.[4] Such arrangements allowed the Chinese Nationalist Party cadres to remain politically active in Indonesia on behalf of Taipei.

Indonesia was strategically important for the Chinese Nationalists. In 1928 the Chinese Nationalist Party established its Southeast Asian regional headquarters in Batavia. Among the branches it oversaw, nineteen were located in the Dutch East Indies.[5] By the early 1950s, with the arrival of party loyalists and ROC diplomats who had been stationed abroad during the Chinese Civil War and after the Communist takeover, there were more Chinese Nationalist organizations and party members in Indonesia than in Hong Kong and other countries in Southeast Asia.[6] The archipelago thus presented a conducive environment within which Taipei could restore the faith of the overseas Chinese in the ROC government. In 1951 the Overseas Party Affairs Office of the Chinese Nationalist Party developed a set of detailed strategies to promote an "anti-Communist, anti-Soviet, national-salvation movement among the overseas Chinese": spreading the ideology of the Chinese Nationalist Party among the younger generation, attracting them to join the Chinese Nationalist Party organizations, and encouraging business elites to invest in Taiwan.[7] In 1952 the ROC convened the Overseas Chinese Affairs Conference, which brought together 240 delegates from around the world. The chairman of the Overseas Chinese Affairs Commission, Zheng Yanfen (Cheng Yen-fen), told his audience that, given the difficult circumstances following the Chinese Civil War, their support had become even more important to the ROC government than before.[8]

In Indonesia, Taipei's gravest concern was that the ethnic Chinese who remained loyal to the Nationalist government would have no choice but to register as PRC citizens. Under the provisions of the Round Table Agreement of 1949, all Indonesian-born Chinese could automatically obtain Indonesian citizenship or they could repudiate Indonesian citizenship before December 27, 1951.[9] Shortly before the nationality selection deadline, a large number of pro-Nationalist Chinese in Indonesia communicated to Taipei their anxiety over the ambiguity of their national status. Many of these ethnic Chinese were unwilling to become Indonesian citizens because they feared that they would not be granted the same rights as the pribumi. At the same time, they were confused about the existence of two Chinese governments in both Mainland China and Taiwan.[10]

In the hope that the pro-Taipei Chinese would retain their legal status as citizens of the ROC, Taipei made a great effort to establish unofficial relations with Jakarta. The rise of the Sukiman Cabinet (April 27, 1951–February 23, 1952) dominated by Masyumi (Majelis Syuro Muslimin Indonesia, or the Consultative Council for Indonesian Muslims), a major anti-Communist force in Indonesia in the 1950s, opened up a window of opportunity for Taipei. In early 1951, the Chinese Nationalist Party branch in Jakarta reported to Taipei that the Indonesian intelligence service was interested in sharing information for anti-Communist purposes.[11] The Sukiman Cabinet later invited ROC intelligence personnel to visit Indonesia for assistance in "maintaining internal security."[12] In September of 1951, Zhu Changdong, the former vice consul general of the ROC in Indonesia, reported to Taipei that in Jakarta "a secret commission" with the code name "Liu Dexian" had been actively involved in Indonesian politics.[13] This organization was built from the bottom up. Its ten core members were all Chinese Nationalist Party loyalists and included intellectuals, businessmen, and former diplomats.[14] It stayed in direct contact with and received strong support from the Overseas Party Affairs Office of the Chinese Nationalist Party, the ROC Overseas Chinese Affairs Commission, and the Foreign Ministry in Taipei. According to Zhu, the Indonesian government frequently asked the organization Liu Dexian to help them purge the pro-Beijing ethnic Chinese and undermine the influence of the PRC embassy and consulates.[15]

From early August to late October 1951, more than fifteen thousand people, most of them alleged PKI members and sympathizers, were taken into custody without a fair and thorough investigation.[16] A sizable number of pro-Beijing ethnic Chinese were among those arrested. For instance, underground Chinese Communist Party members including Wang Jiyuan, the editor-in-chief of the pro-Beijing *Sheng Huo Bao*, and Yang Xinrong, the principal of the pro-Beijing Xinghua School (Xinhua zhongxiaoxue) in Jakarta, were detained and later deported in 1952 and 1953 respectively.[17] Zhu Changdong wrote to Taipei: "With assistance from us, the Indonesian government arrested a large number of Communists for the purpose of maintaining internal security. In the past few months, approximately 1,000 Communists have been jailed, including 216 Chinese Communists and sympathizers. Nineteen of these Chinese Communists have done all kinds of evil. The Chinese society is very glad overall."[18]

Capitalizing on the Sukiman Cabinet's repression of the left wing, Taipei sent a special envoy named Chen Kewen to Indonesia. Chen's main task was to probe into the possibility of placing the pro-Taipei Chinese under the protection of consulates of countries friendly with the ROC or UN agencies in Indonesia. Chen was a senior Nationalist politician who had held several previous important positions such as chief of the Overseas Party Affairs Office. His contacts in Indonesia included an old schoolmate Tang Liangli (Thung Liang Lee or Tubagus Pranata Tirtawidjaya), whose life experience exemplifies the intertwined nature of modern Chinese and Southeast Asian history. Born in Java, Tang was European educated and published extensively in English. After leading the Chinese Nationalist Party's Communications Office in Europe, Tang returned to China and became the chief English-language spokesman and private secretary for Wang Jingwei, a longtime rival of Chiang Kai-shek and the head of a Japanese-supported collaborative government. As Wang's trusted assistant, Tang enabled Zhou Enlai, the leader of the Communist Party who was hunted by the Nationalist authorities, to escape from Shanghai. After the collapse of Wang's regime, Tang was arrested by Chiang but soon released for reasons that remain unclear. In 1949 Tang resettled in Indonesia. He adopted Indonesian citizenship and worked as a businessman.[19] In 1951–52, Tang was the personal assistant to the foreign minister of the Sukiman Cabinet Achmad Soebardjo.

Given Tang's murky political allegiances, his motives for facilitating Taipei-Jakarta back-channel diplomacy were dubious. Tang wrote to Chen: "I understand that the real Chinese nationals are largely against Peking, but they need enlightenment. And for this, great resources are needed. Many have to be persuaded."[20] Tang probably saw this project of "enlightening" the Chinese in Indonesia as a profitable business opportunity rather than an ideological mission. During his preliminary meetings with officials from the Foreign Ministry in Taipei, Tang gave a disclaimer that he was "not acting in any official capacity."[21] In a letter to Chen, Tang inquired about a special fund from the Nationalist government, which amounted to 50,000 USD, that he claimed should be at his disposal.[22] When Chen passed Tang's request on to the Foreign Ministry in Taipei, the ministry denied the existence of such a promise and condemned Tang's behavior as "unfathomable" and "contradictory."[23]

Tang's questionable involvement in Taipei-Jakarta negotiations attests to the serious limitations the Chinese Nationalists faced in recovering their international status after 1949. Between March and May of 1952, Chen Kewen, upon Tang's invitation, took an unsuccessful trip to Indonesia. At the time, the Sukiman Cabinet had been dissolved and Achmad Soebardjo, Taipei's potential ally in the Indonesian government, had resigned as the foreign minister. The proposal that a third party take over the protection of the pro-Taipei ethnic Chinese was rejected by the newly formed Wilopo Cabinet. Chen wrote in his diary near the end of his stay in Jakarta: "I thought I would take this opportunity to see whether I could improve bilateral relations. But now my distress is rising and I can only persevere. My anxiety is beyond words."[24]

Detachment from Diasporic Politics: Beijing Makes Policy Adjustments

On August 15, 1950, at a reception attended by hundreds of ethnic Chinese in Jakarta, Ba Ren, the first PRC ambassador to Indonesia, started his address to "his beloved countrymen" by condemning the Chinese Nationalists. Jakarta municipal police observed Ba Ren's "aggressive behavior," which alarmed them. The police noted that Ba Ren spent substantial time discrediting the Chinese Nationalist government as "a traitor that dashed the overseas Chinese's hope in their nation's future." Moreover, under Ba Ren's leadership, the Chinese embassy had been circulating brochures with slogans like "Fight for the consolidation of the people's victory."[25]

In the eyes of anti-Communist pribumi elites, the PRC ambassador was living evidence of Beijing's ambition to export Communism abroad. In his 1949 publication in Mandarin Chinese, *Indonesia: A Nation of a Thousand Islands (Qiandao zhiguo—Yinni)*, Ba Ren expressed sympathy toward the failed 1948 Communist-led uprising in Madiun, Central Java.[26] Also known as "the Madiun Affair," this abortive attempt to seize political power through armed revolt convinced the PKI that taking a peaceful parliamentary route was the more suitable strategy in Indonesia.[27] But in the historical narratives constructed by the anti-Communist forces in Indonesia, the Madiun Affair was evidence of the PKI's long-standing ambition to grasp state power, which culminated in the September Thirtieth Movement. Ba Ren, however, saw the Madiun Affair as a missed opportunity to advance the Indonesian National Revolution to "an entirely new level of development."[28] Unsurprisingly, the Indonesian government banned his book.

Indonesia's sensitivity to Ba Ren's activities was a reasonable response to Beijing's foreign policy from 1949 to 1950. In July 1949, Beijing and Moscow reached an agreement about the "division of labor" in promoting world revolution: the Chinese would take more responsibility in colonial and semi-colonial countries in Asia while the Russians focused on Eastern Europe.[29] In November 1949, the Chinese leader Liu Shaoqi, in his opening remarks at the Trade Union Conference of Asian and Australasian Countries in Beijing, called upon the working class in Indochina, Burma, India, Indonesia, and Malaya to violently resist imperialism.[30] According to the Indonesian attorney general's report, the Indonesian representative at this conference, Ali Harjono, referred to the Madiun Affair as a "righteous rebellion" by armed proletariats.[31] Radio Peking urged the Indonesian people to not be complacent about the leadership of national bourgeois such as Sukarno and Hatta but to continue their progress toward Communism.[32]

Because of this history, Ba Ren's request to open PRC consulates in the major cities of Indonesia unnerved Indonesian authorities. In his speech to the Chinese community in Jakarta in August 1950, Ba Ren announced: "The overseas Chinese in Indonesia, like the Chinese people within China, have their lawful rights and are under the protection of the Chinese government."[33] The establishment of consulates, from Ba Ren's perspective, was the first step in living up to the promise to safeguard the interests of the Chinese in Indonesia. Yet the issue of PRC diplomatic representation in Indonesia was inevitably intertwined with citizenship negotiations. The Indonesian government was concerned that the PRC consulates would function beyond their capacity as a diplomatic apparatus. The two sides were deadlocked. On the one hand, the PRC embassy in Jakarta insisted that the ethnic Chinese could not freely make their citizenship choice without easy access to consular service. On the other hand, the Indonesian government believed that the expansion of the PRC diplomatic mission could only be allowed after the citizenship issue of the ethnic Chinese had been solved.[34] Ba Ren exacerbated this tension by encouraging Chinese associations across Indonesia to petition for the opening of PRC consulates.[35] Ba Ren is also reported to have asked the Indonesian foreign minister Mohammad Roem how many American and British consulates there were in Indonesia. He continued pleading his case by emphasizing that the PRC had a greater need for consulates than any other country in the world because no other country had more citizens residing in Indonesia.[36]

In January 1952, Ba Ren was dismissed for violating diplomatic protocol. During the 1951 anti-Communist raids, Ba Ren allowed Wang Jiyuan, the editor-in-chief of the pro-Beijing *Sheng Huo Bao*, to take refuge in the embassy without permission from Beijing. As a result, the Indonesian government accused the PRC of interfering in Indonesian domestic politics. After returning to Beijing, Ba Ren submitted a "self-criticism" to the Chinese

FIGURE 3.1. Ba Ren, his wife, Ma Rongsheng, and the Indonesian prime minister Mohammad Natsir, at the PRC National Day reception at the Chinese embassy in Jakarta, 1950. Personal collection of Wang Keping.

Foreign Ministry, in which he said he had made "serious political and disciplinary mistakes," which were "equal to crimes." He wrote:

> As an ambassador, I failed to fully realize that I represent my country and the head of my state. I acted as if I was first and foremost a sympathizer with the Indonesian Revolution. In addition, I have always believed that "Overseas Chinese youth are the bridge to the Indonesian Revolution." I failed to give priority to establishing formal diplomatic relations with the Indonesian government.
>
> Whenever issues regarding the overseas Chinese came up, I purely emphasized our mission of "protecting the rights of overseas Chinese." I regard whatever the overseas Chinese requested as their natural right. My thinking encouraged the already-existing Han chauvinist tendencies among the overseas Chinese. The overseas Chinese thought of themselves as the people of a strong nation and thought of us [the PRC diplomats] as the representatives of a strong nation.[37]

In policy-making circles in Beijing, many were critical not only of Ba Ren's personal working style but also the policy he embodied. In their understanding,

Ba Ren supported the continuation of dual citizenship and thus assigned two missions to the overseas Chinese—to support the revolution in China from afar and to assist the indigenous people with their struggle against imperialism in their countries of residence.[38] While acknowledging the contribution of this "dual citizenship, dual mission" principle to the Communist Party's war efforts against Japanese invasion, the CCP leadership was also acutely aware of the changes in the international politics and of its own transformation from being a revolutionary force to being the ruling party of China. These new conditions propelled Beijing to reconsider the status of the CCP's branches abroad. In 1951 the director of the International Liaison Department of the CCP, Wang Jiaxiang, made it clear that, in the post–World War II era, the fundamental principle of the international Communist movement was that there should only be one Communist Party in each country. Wang emphasized that cooperation among different Communist parties must not breach any country's sovereignty. Since Indonesia and many other Southeast Asian countries had already achieved their national independence, the CCP branches in these countries should be dissolved completely.[39]

In 1952 the CCP Central Committee ordered the shutdown of its organizations abroad, ranging from youth groups and semiunderground civic associations to underground party headquarters. The CCP Central Committee encouraged its dismissed overseas cadres to return to the PRC by promising them recognition for their achievements and reassignment to new posts.[40] This decision helped improve the PRC's relations with Southeast Asian countries and ameliorated the diplomatic isolation Beijing faced in the early Cold War. When meeting with an economic and cultural delegation from Thailand in 1955, Mao Zedong announced that the dissolution of CCP overseas branches would dispel the misgivings of their host countries.[41] During a discussion with Norodom Sihanouk in 1958, Mao promised that there were no longer any CCP organizations among the Chinese in Cambodia. He added that if the hearts of the overseas Chinese remained oriented toward China while they were residing abroad, it would be disadvantageous to collaboration between the two governments for the purpose of anticolonialism.[42]

On April 22, 1955, Zhou Enlai and the Indonesian foreign minister Sunario signed the Sino-Indonesian Dual Nationality Treaty in Bandung. In 1956, in a speech to the Chinese community in Jakarta, Zhou Enlai emphasized that if an ethnic Chinese opted for Indonesian citizenship, the PRC embassy and consulates would give him or her their unreserved support. Those who chose Indonesian citizenship should not be treated as traitors who had abandoned their Chinese heritage, but as friends. They were welcome to visit the

Chinese associations as Indonesian guests. The ethnic Chinese who opted for PRC citizenship should stay away from politics in Indonesia. Otherwise, local authorities would interpret their political activities as a direct foreign intervention, which would harm bilateral relations.[43]

Deeper into Diasporic Politics: Taipei's Response

Holding firm to the right of blood principle, Taipei vowed to protect the overseas Chinese, regardless of whether the ROC had diplomatic relations with their host countries. Zheng Yanfen, the chairman of the Overseas Chinese Affairs Commission of the Chinese Nationalist government, condemned the Sino-Indonesian Dual Nationality Treaty as "an important step in the Communist bandits' conspiracy to infiltrate Southeast Asia." He warned that by "ushering the wolf [i.e., the Chinese Communists] into its own house," the Indonesian government should be prepared for the grievous consequences of its "suicidal behavior."[44] He declared during a press conference: "The majority of the Chinese living in Indonesia are anti-Communist. They do not recognize the puppet regime in Beijing, neither are they willing to accept a status as 'stateless people' in Indonesia."[45] Taipei accused the Indonesian government of forcing the pro-Taipei Chinese to register themselves as nationals of the PRC against their will, thereby violating the Universal Declaration of Human Rights adopted by the UN General Assembly. Despite the loss of diplomatic recognition from countries such as Indonesia, the ROC kept its membership in the UN until 1971. Taipei threatened to retaliate against Jakarta at the UN.[46]

However, within the Chinese Nationalist Party, there were initially different opinions on how to end the uncertain status of the ethnic Chinese in Indonesia. The ROC representative at the UN, Jiang Tingfu (Tsiang Tingfu), wrote in a report to Taipei in 1951 that "the time had come for the Chinese in Southeast Asia to try to protect their rights as citizens of the countries where they reside." Jiang recommended "a new policy freeing the Chinese from the bonds of blood," which would "facilitate the establishment of better relations between Chinese and local people in all of Southeast Asia."[47] Jiang's proposal, although farsighted and consistent with the UN Charter, was never given serious consideration because decision-making in Taipei was dominated by conservatives such as Qiu Zheng'ou. Qiu, the editor-in-chief of the Chinese Nationalist Party organ in Indonesia, *Tian Sheng Ri Bao*, held that adopting citizenship in their country of residence would "do more harm than good to the overseas Chinese" because one would be required to "fulfill obligations such as military service and national education." Qiu suggested that the overseas Chinese retain their ROC citizenship if circumstances allowed and "firmly reject the illegitimate citizenship of the Communist bandits" no matter what.[48] But for the pro-Taipei Chinese in Indonesia, it was technically impossible to follow Qiu's advice; they would either be rendered stateless or would have to take PRC citizenship. As a temporary solution, the Nationalist Party branch in Jakarta asked them to take Indonesian citizenship as a formality, so that they would be entitled to rights unavailable to noncitizen Chinese and be able to help promote pro-Taipei education, expand pro-Taipei ethnic Chinese associations, and boycott citizenship registration at the PRC embassy and consulates.[49]

More importantly, Indonesian citizenship would enable Chinese Nationalist Party cadres to carry out clandestine operations more easily. According to PRC intelligence, Taipei infiltrated Indonesian governmental departments—such as the Office of the Attorney General, the National Intelligence Service, and the Department of National Security—with agents who had obtained Indonesian citizenship as cover.[50] Evidence from the ROC corroborates this. The secret mission called Liu Dexian declared that one of its major goals was to build close interpersonal relationships between its members and leading figures in Indonesian anti-Communist political parties, the Indonesian army—the archenemy of the Communists—and American diplomats in Indonesia and the Philippines. There was even special funding for networking with these "local friends" by providing banquets and other kinds of entertainment.[51]

The Chinese Nationalists' covert attempts to influence the direction of Indonesian politics were met with a serious backlash. In August 1953, Ali Sastroamidjojo from the Indonesian National Party (Partai Nasional Indonesia or the PNI) took office and formed a cabinet that consisted mostly of left-wing politicians and excluded those from Masyumi. Taipei, which relied on cooperation with the anti-Communists, made an audacious attempt to change this new political environment. In September 1954, four members of the organization Liu Dexian—Zhang Xunyi, Zhu Changdong, Chen Xingyan, and Qiu Yuanrong—were arrested by the Indonesian authorities on charges of having "endangered peace and order in Indonesia."[52] Although the exact details of their activities were not revealed, the PKI organ *Harian Rakyat* speculated that, at a dinner party that included Mohammed Natsir, the leader of the oppositional Masyumi, these Chinese Nationalist loyalists discussed a conspiracy to topple the Ali Sastroamidjojo Cabinet with support from the American embassy in Indonesia.[53] The Indonesian Supreme Court later convicted them of conspiring to overthrow the cabinet, accumulating financial resources to rig the general election, and manipulating governmental agencies.[54]

Beijing chose to not use the arrest of pro-Taipei cadres to aggressively undermine the Chinese Nationalists out of consideration for the other stakeholders involved: Masyumi, the anti-Communist figures in various Indonesian governmental agencies, and the US. The PRC Foreign Ministry requested its embassy in Jakarta to "practice vigilance and prudence": "The Indonesian government's decision to arrest the Chiang bandits is closely related to local political struggles. The situation is extremely complicated. Therefore, our embassy should not explicitly show our attitude. . . . The local Chinese-language newspapers should only cite from Indonesian language sources. We should avoid commenting on the recent events."[55] Another directive from Beijing warned that it was too early to be optimistic. Jakarta's harsh measures against the pro-Taipei activists did not translate into a friendly attitude toward pro-Beijing ethnic Chinese: "Usually, the Indonesian authorities would not consider the patriotic ethnic Chinese as less threatening than the US or Chiang Kai-shek's agents. We also could not take for granted that the improvement of Sino-Indonesian relations would necessarily mean fewer restrictions upon and discrimination against the patriotic ethnic Chinese by the Indonesian authorities."[56]

By adopting a cautious attitude, Beijing hoped to shore up its status as the sole legitimate center of China by extending its sovereignty over all the Chinese, regardless of their political orientation. In October 1954, the Indonesian authorities announced their decision to expel Zhang Xunyi, a member of the organization Liu Dexian and chairman of the pro-Nationalist Chinese General Association in Jakarta, from Indonesia. Since Zhang had declared himself a Chinese citizen and Indonesia only recognized the PRC, the Indonesian government indicated that Zhang must be sent back to Beijing.[57] In response, the PRC not only promised to issue an entry permit to Zhang but also repeatedly vowed that "once he arrives in New China, as long as he starts with a clean slate, the government will give him an opportunity for a new life."[58] By demonstrating leniency toward Zhang and other Chinese Nationalist cadres, Beijing sent a message to the overseas Chinese that even those who used to be loyal to Taipei or were still sitting on the fence would be supported and protected by Beijing. Furthermore, Beijing saw propaganda value in Zhang Xunyi. The PRC leaders calculated that if Zhang defected and "revealed the crimes of the US and the Chiang agents," Taipei would be more isolated in the international arena.[59] The PRC Foreign Ministry instructed that all the pro-Beijing Chinese-language newspapers in Indonesia should make it clear that anyone except Chiang Kai-shek would be welcomed in Mainland China if they were willing to "forsake darkness and to come into the light."[60] In an effort to attract all ethnic Chinese who were not openly anti-Communist and to expand the PRC's united front among the overseas Chinese, the PRC embassy in Indonesia advised the pro-Beijing ethnic Chinese to keep their activities low-key and to avoid any kind of hostility against the pro-Taipei groups.[61] In December 1954, Zhang and other Chinese Nationalist Party cadres were deported to Taiwan from Indonesia. Although the turnaround of the situation was not ideal for Beijing, it still gained an advantage from Taipei's breach of Indonesian sovereignty during the political uproar of 1954.

The Bandung Conference: Beijing's Peace Offensive

Running parallel to the under-the-table 1954 competition between Beijing and Taipei in Indonesia was the open, armed conflict between the two Chinese governments during the First Taiwan Strait Crisis. In that year, Mao and his comrades decided to shift resources to focus on the eradication of the Chinese Nationalists and the integration of Taiwan into PRC territory. In July, the state-run newspaper, the *People's Daily* (*Renmin Ribao*), published an editorial essay, emphasizing that "we the Chinese people must liberate Taiwan." In September, to demonstrate its determination, the People's Liberation Army (PLA) shelled the Nationalist-controlled Jinmen (Quemoy) off the coast of Fujian Province. In response to the escalating tension, Taiwan began talks with Washington and the two sides formally signed a treaty of mutual defense in December. However, in January 1955, before the treaty was approved by the US Congress, the PLA carried out large-scale amphibious-landing operations on Yijiangshan Island off the shore of Zhejiang Province. The dispute thus became one of the most intense confrontations of the early Cold War.[62] Yet the tensions over the Taiwan Strait subsided in April 1955 when Chinese premier Zhou Enlai made reconciliatory comments during the first large-scale Asian-African conference in Bandung, Indonesia. The Eisenhower administration responded positively upon learning that Zhou had distinguished the conflict between the mainland and Taiwan from that between China and the US. Taiwan was an internal question and linked to the Chinese Civil War, Zhou said, but the tension between China and the US was an international matter, which China was willing to discuss with Washington.[63]

Beijing's restraint in the first Taiwan Strait Crisis and its competition against the ROC in Indonesia reflected a shift in the PRC's overall foreign policy. In the early years following the establishment of the PRC, Beijing's attitude toward "bourgeois nationalist" countries in the formerly colonized world—such as Indonesia, Burma/Cambodia, and India—was characterized by harsh criticism and an intention to convert them to socialism in the long run.[64] In the early 1950s, Beijing observed that, in Indonesia, "although all the cabinets claim that they carried out an independent foreign policy, they all received economic and military aid from the United Sates, and they were unfriendly toward China and the Soviet Union. They threw themselves at the American imperialists."[65] But from 1954 to 1955, for the purpose of expanding its influence in the international arena and creating a peaceful and stable environment for domestic reconstruction, Beijing shifted its priorities and focused on constructing an international united front, particularly among Third World countries.[66] Befriending Indonesia was part of Beijing's strategy to counterbalance US influence in the Asia-Pacific in light of the creation of the Southeast Asia Treaty Organization (SEATO).

At the 1955 Bandung Conference, the PRC successfully built up a nonbelligerent image despite Taipei's persistent sabotage attempts. In the previous year, together with the Indian prime minister Jawaharlal Nehru and the Burmese prime minister U Nu, Zhou Enlai introduced the Five Principles for Peaceful Coexistence (*heping gongchu wu xiang yuanze*), which would serve as the founding philosophy of the Afro-Asian Conference.[67] At Bandung, Zhou impressed the other participants by avoiding ideological language and emphasizing the PRC delegation's desire to "seek common grounds in spite of differences."[68] The ROC tried to assassinate the charismatic Zhou but failed, further tarnishing its international reputation. Prior to the conference, the Chinese Nationalist Party's intelligence organization in Hong Kong installed an explosive in the aircraft chartered by the PRC delegation.[69] When Zhou escaped unharmed, Taipei summoned the senior Chinese Nationalist Party cadre Zhang Xunyi. He was at the center of the political turmoil in 1954 and, as a result, had been deported from Indonesia to Taiwan. According to PRC intelligence, Zhang secretly returned to Indonesia before the Bandung Conference to supervise the Chinese Nationalist terrorist organization the "Blood and Iron Group" (tiexue tuan).[70] The PRC requested tighter security measures from the Indonesian police, while mobilizing pro-Beijing ethnic Chinese to protect Zhou and the rest of the PRC delegation.[71] During a meeting with the Indonesian prime minister Ali Sastroamidjojo, Zhou Enlai said: "These incidents speak to the fact that Chiang Kai-shek and his loyalists have exhausted their path. They have no reservations about doing the most despicable things."[72] Zhou urged Ali Sastroamidjojo to talk to the US, Taiwan's main sponsor and protector: "People around the world are watching the US providing improper and unethical support to such an ugly and filthy political group."[73]

Meanwhile, Zhou tactfully framed the Taiwan issue as a matter of territorial integrity to signal solidarity with Indonesia's campaign to reclaim West

FIGURE 3.2. Sukarno and Zhou Enlai in Jakarta after the Bandung Conference, 1955. Personal collection of Liang Yingming.

Irian.[74] Due to the Dutch use of West Irian as one of its most notorious colonial prison camps, it occupied a central place in Indonesia's folklore of the anticolonial movement and became a sacred site in the national imagination.[75] In a joint statement issued on April 28, 1955, both countries "expressed deep sympathy with and support for the effort of either country to safeguard its own sovereignty and territorial integrity."[76] Zhou Enlai said to Ali Sastroamidjojo: "China and Indonesia had the same suffering. West Irianian People are Indonesian people, just like people in Taiwan are Chinese people."[77] To reciprocate China's goodwill, during his visit to Beijing, Ali Sastroamidjojo told the Chinese leaders: "West Irian is as important to Indonesia as Taiwan is to China." He also offered to act as a mediator between China and the US to de-escalate the Taiwan Strait Crisis.[78] In 1956 Sukarno visited China as the first head of state from the Republic of Indonesia. Greatly impressed by the effectiveness of China's highly centralized political system, Sukarno openly expressed his admiration for the collective leadership of the Communist Party, praising the People's Republic for "catching up with the developed world at an amazing speed."[79] This experience may have been the inspiration for his 1959 decision to replace constitutional democracy in Indonesia with the more authoritarian "Guided Democracy."[80] After Sukarno's visit, the CCP organ the *People's Daily* characterized Sino-Indonesian relations as "a friendship between two nations fighting for independence."[81]

Regional Rebellions: Taipei's Intervention Angers Jakarta

Shortly after the Bandung Conference, both China and Indonesia went through periods of domestic political instability and experienced a leftward turn in foreign affairs. In the spring of 1957, Mao, who was convinced that CCP cadres had grown attached to their privileges, launched the "democratic consolidation of spirits (*minzhu zhengfeng*) campaign." This campaign against bureaucratism (*guanliao zhuyi*), subjectivism (*zhuguan zhuyi*), and factionalism (*zongpai zhuyi*) was soon followed by the "antirightist movement" (*fan youpai yundong*), resulting in a tense domestic political atmosphere. Subsequently, the Great Leap Forward (1958–61), whose original aim was to accelerate the modernization of China's economy, resulted in three years of catastrophic economic recession. These domestic political movements had a profound impact on China's foreign relations. The pragmatic and moderate policy defined by the Five Principles for Peaceful Coexistence was interrupted. In late August 1958, when the Great Leap reached its height, Mao sparked the Second Taiwan Strait Crisis by ordering the PLA to shell Jinmen. In a demonstration of support for the ROC, the Eisenhower administration dispatched the Seventh Fleet to the Taiwan Strait.[82]

Around the same time, the regional rebellions in Sumatra and Sulawesi, supported mainly by the US and the Chinese Nationalists in Taiwan, threatened to tear Indonesia apart. These insurgences originated in the economic disparities between Java and the Outer Islands of Indonesia. Though rich in natural resources of great strategic importance, such as rubber, copra, and petroleum, the regions outside Java received a much smaller share of state revenue while producing nearly three-fourths of the nation's foreign exchange income. In 1951 and 1952, open accusations against Java for "exploiting the Outer Islands as the authoritarian center" dominated the political discourse in Sumatra and Sulawesi.[83] Meanwhile, dissenting groups led by regional commanders in the Indonesian military, such as the Banteng Council (Dewan Banteng) in Sumatra and the Universal Struggle Charter (Piagam Perjuangan Rakyat Semesta or "Permesta") in Sulawesi, smuggled rubber and dried coconuts via Singapore and Manila for barter trade. After Jakarta issued an ultimatum demanding an end to barter trade by February 1958, the regional dissatisfaction exploded into an antigovernment revolt, culminating in the establishment of the Revolutionary Government of the Republic of Indonesia (Pemerintah Revolusioner Republik Indonesia or PRRI) in opposition to the Indonesian central government in Jakarta.

In a meeting with the Chinese foreign minister Chen Yi, the Indonesian ambassador Soekardjo Wiriopranoto argued that these local autonomy movements, although they arose from long-standing regional economic stratification, were exacerbated by Western anxiety over Indonesia's drift to the left. As Ambassador Soekardjo put it, "the Dutch, American, and British imperialists had shared economic interests with the rebel government through their possession of petroleum companies and large plantations." These Western countries claimed that "the Indonesian central government is sympathetic to Communism or even Communist itself and the rebel government is anti-Communist." The Indonesian ambassador informed Chen Yi that "the Banteng Council and Permesta had direct contacts with the SEATO offices in Singapore and Manila."[84]

Ambassador Soekardjo's accusation of US intervention was well founded. The Eisenhower administration had launched in Indonesia what was then the largest US covert operation since World War II, aiming to replace the increasingly pro-Left political leadership of President Sukarno. The Central Intelligence Agency (CIA), the US Navy, and a camouflaged American air force took part in the operation.[85] Through Taiwan, Washington delivered light and heavy weapons, fighter planes, and petrol for aircraft to the rebels. Many soldiers from the rebel areas in Indonesia were sent to Taiwan for training purposes. American pilots from the Civil Air Transport (CAT), owned by the CIA and stationed in Taiwan, flew combat missions for Permesta.[86] The American use of Taiwan as a conduit to support the Indonesian regional rebels infuriated Beijing. In May 1958, the PRC issued an official statement, warning that "should the US fail to stop at once its interference in the internal affairs of Indonesia, it will certainly eat the bitter fruit of its aggression and provocation."[87]

Despite its assertive rhetoric, Beijing was extremely cautious and declined Sukarno's earlier request in February 1958 for Beijing to denounce Western meddling in Indonesian politics.[88] It was only after the Soviet Union openly protested American and Chinese Nationalist intervention in Indonesia that Beijing issued the statement.[89] Moreover, Beijing deliberately took an ambiguous position on whether or not it would enter the conflict. Many observers interpreted the PRC's May 1958 statement as an ultimatum demanding an immediate suspension of American military activity via Taiwan. Afro-Asian nations such as Afghanistan and India speculated that Beijing was threatening to dispatch volunteer troops to Indonesia, adopting the same strategy it had used during the Korean War.[90] Chinese diplomatic missions in these countries alerted Beijing that local governments "[have] wrongly accused us of interfering in Indonesian domestic politics" and recommended clarification via official channels. However, Beijing turned down these suggestions. In a telegram to the Chinese embassy in New Delhi in early June, the

Chinese leadership revealed its careful calculations: "Our side should not officially deny offering volunteer military assistance to Indonesia because the Americans are testing our boundaries."[91] The PRC seemed to harbor no intentions of direct involvement in the archipelago but wanted to use a vague statement to deter further American and Taiwanese intervention in Indonesia.

In addition to moral support, Beijing offered cotton, rice, and military equipment to Jakarta to aid its suppression of the secession movements. In March 1958, Chen Yi told Ambassador Soekardjo that the Chinese government was always willing to provide "unconditional help" whenever the Indonesian government and President Sukarno needed it.[92] In the same year, a military procurement delegation from Indonesia paid a secret visit to Beijing and delivered letters of gratitude from President Sukarno and Prime Minister Djuanda to Mao Zedong and Zhou Enlai respectively.[93] This delegation brought back an offer from Beijing of 20 million USD worth of military equipment for the Indonesian army, navy, and air force.[94] In 1960 Sukarni, the newly arrived Indonesian ambassador to China, told the Chinese leaders that "the Indonesian people would never forget" Beijing's military assistance in 1958.[95]

As the situation intensified in Sumatra and Sulawesi, the Chinese Nationalist government in Taiwan sensed an imminent threat. On May 22 Chiang Kai-shek had a meeting with the US ambassador to Taiwan, Everett F. Drumright, during which Chiang "appeared to be in dead earnest" and "spoke with emotion at times." Chiang referred to the situation of the rebel forces as "deteriorating" and proposed to send a marine regiment and an aircraft squadron to assist them. Chiang predicted that if Indonesia came under Communist control, Taiwan's strategic position in the Asia-Pacific would be precarious, the prestige of the US would be gravely affected, and the global balance of power would favor the Communists. If the Chinese Communists used the Taiwan Strait area to channel soldiers or supplies into Indonesia, Chiang would immediately order his forces to attack them.[96] On May 23 the ROC Ministry of Defense made an official statement declaring that it would "take any necessary actions" if the PLA intruded in the South China Sea.[97]

But the events in Indonesia de-escalated before the two Chinas could stage a face-off in the archipelago. On May 18, 1958, an American pilot was captured while carrying out a mission for Permesta. The incident turned Indonesian public opinion against the US and resulted in an American policy shift.[98] Washington's retraction of aid to the rebels created an opportunity for the central government in Jakarta to regain control over Sumatra and Sulawesi. In addition to protesting against regional disparity, the rebels also opposed

the growing strength of the PKI in Java. By 1960 the rebels had started to
reconcile with the Indonesian army, as both sides had a mutual interest in
curbing further Communist advances. The common anti-Communist cause
made it easier for the Indonesian army to put down the rebellion. Although
the rebellion had begun with the goal of promoting local autonomy, it ironically ended with Sukarno's strengthening of central authority through the
inauguration of Guided Democracy. At the same time, as Masyumi had been
banned by Sukarno in 1960 for its support of the rebellion, the influence
of right-wing forces decreased while that of the PKI was augmented.[99] The
left-turn in Indonesian politics drew Jakarta closer to Beijing and away from
Taipei. In 1958 the Indonesian authorities pronounced all Chinese Nationalist Party branches and affiliated organizations illegal.

The January 1951 issue of *Time* magazine includes a report on "Uncle Barhen" (Ba Ren), an ambassador who was "handicapped by a lack of diplomatic
dignity":

> At dinner parties in Chinese homes, Uncle Barhen [*sic*] sometimes
> leaped up shouting, "Down with the Kuomintang![100] Down with the
> reactionaries!" He had a disturbing habit of drinking from a bottle in
> public, shocked fellow guests at a presidential party by taking a hefty
> slug when the others were raising their glasses in a toast. He addressed
> a public meeting with a cigarette dangling from his lower lip.
>   Last week Uncle Barhen's past seemed to be catching up with him.
> Indonesians had discovered that he was the same Wang Jen-shu who
> wrote a book in 1948 advocating the overthrow of the Indonesian Gov-
> ernment on the ground that it did not represent the people. President
> Soekarno's government has been rounding up copies of the book. It is
> waiting for the ambassador to make just one more boner before asking
> Uncle Mao to recall Uncle Barhen.[101]

This report precipitated the dismissal of Ba Ren, and it reflects the path
full of twists and turns that Beijing took to adapt itself to international norms
in governmental relations. While Ba Ren personally failed to make the transition from an advocate of social revolution in Indonesia to a professional
diplomat, Beijing succeeded during the 1949–58 period in transforming itself
from a revolutionary force that pursued Communist revolution worldwide
to a promoter of the principles of noninterference and Afro-Asian solidarity.
Beijing's strategy of distancing itself from diasporic politics triumphed over
Taipei's proactive interventions in Indonesian politics through behind-the-
scenes maneuvering.

In 1952 Mao Zedong had lunch with an old schoolmate, Zhang Guoji. Zhang had left for Indonesia in the 1930s to establish Chinese language schools and to expand the Chinese Communist Party. During their meeting, Zhang explained to Mao the ferocity of the struggle between the Red, or the Communists, and the Blue, or the Nationalists, in Chinese society in Indonesia. A key element of this competition was the fight over which flag should be raised: the Five-Star Red Flag of the PRC or the Blue Sky, White Sun, and Red Earth Flag of the ROC. In response, Mao recommended that the pro-Beijing ethnic Chinese should remain low-key about their political orientation and adopt a reconciliatory attitude toward the pro-Taipei group. In Mao's words, they could just "raise the Red Flag in their hearts."[102] Yet, as I will show in the next chapter, contrary to Mao's hope, the ideological division between the Red and the Blue became the central theme of the social and political lives of the totok Chinese in Indonesia in the 1950s.

CHAPTER 4

The Communal Battle between the Red and the Blue

On December 27, 1949, the day that marked the official end of Indonesia's anticolonial war against the Dutch, a battle over national symbols began in the Chinese community in Jakarta. In the early morning hours, the editors of the pro-Beijing Chinese-language newspaper *Sheng Huo Bao* hoisted the Five-Star Red Flag of the PRC side by side with the Indonesian national flag, which enraged those who remained loyal to the ROC and recognized only its Blue Sky, White Sun, and Red Earth Flag. These supporters of the Chinese Nationalist Party rallied support from the Indonesian police.[1] A former editor of *Sheng Huo Bao* recorded this incident in his semiautobiographical novel *Underneath the Red-and-White Flag (hongbaiqi xia)*: "Around 9 a.m., four or five armed Indonesian police came, angrily requesting to see the person in charge. They demanded that the Five-Star Red Flag be taken down. The editor-in-chief of the newspaper was threatened at gunpoint. Some ethnic Chinese who sympathized with *Sheng Huo Bao*'s stance protested in bahasa Indonesia, 'Don't touch our national flag!' 'If you are going to lower the Five-Star Red Flag, you will have to lower the Red-and-White Flag!'[2] But the Indonesian police forcibly took down the Five-Star Red Flag."[3]

This flag dispute helps illustrate the complex issue of citizenship facing the ethnic Chinese as well as the raging competition between pro-Beijing and pro-Taipei factions in the diasporic community. The Chinese embassy in Jakarta identified a total of 1,020,380 ethnic Chinese as eligible for PRC citizenship in the early 1950s.[4] Among them, those who were local-born also automatically obtained Indonesian citizenship. Fearing unwanted foreign intervention, the Indonesian government was apprehensive about sharing jurisdiction over such a large number of people with the PRC.[5] By signing the 1955 Sino-Indonesian Dual Nationality Treaty, Beijing hoped to encourage the assimilation of the ethnic Chinese in Indonesia and clear the way for the future development of bilateral relations. The treaty marked two fundamental changes. First, Beijing announced that Chinese nationality could no longer be inherited indefinitely and unconditionally through the law of blood. Second, Jakarta no longer automatically recognized all local-born Chinese as Indonesian citizens. Instead, individuals had to take active legal action to acquire Indonesian citizenship if they desired to do so. Yet, due to misinformation, the shortage of legal services, and the inefficiency of Indonesian bureaucracy, hundreds of thousands of ethnic Chinese lost their Indonesian citizenship even though they planned to continue living in Indonesia. Moreover, despite Beijing calling upon the ethnic Chinese to "correct the deep-rooted feelings of racial superiority" and not to regard opting for Indonesian citizenship as "losing face," many still purposefully repudiated Indonesian citizenship.[6]

The ethnic Chinese made their citizenship choices based on pragmatic considerations such as plans for education or business ownership, but they were also influenced by the Beijing-versus-Taipei competition in the diasporic community. The patterns of political activism among the Chinese in Indonesia in the 1950s resembled the three-group model devised by Wang Gungwu. Wang divides the Malayan Chinese into three groups: "Group A" includes those who were active participants in China-oriented politics. Some returned to China with the hope of joining its reconstruction. "Group B" members were "hard-headed and realistic," rarely expressing themselves politically. And those in "Group C" were committed to their host country.[7] In Indonesia, "Group A" was mostly totoks whereas "Group C" was mostly peranakans. These characterizations are meant to indicate general trends; there are always exceptions.

There have not been accurate statistics on the percentages of the two factions, but it is safe to assume that the power balance tilted toward Beijing with regional variations throughout the 1950s. From a socioeconomic perspective, the growth of Beijing's influence vis-à-vis Taipei could be attributed to the CCP's paradoxical alliance with overseas Chinese capitalism. Meanwhile, the pro-Beijing faction, confident that history was on their side, took an aggressive approach toward the Chinese Nationalist loyalists. While the pro-PRC activists' efforts were appreciated by PRC policy makers, their dangerously ultraleftist tendencies also caused concern. Beijing chastised them for "launching nonstop attacks" on the pro-Taipei groups and for arbitrarily "rejecting everyone affiliated with the Chinese Nationalist Party."[8] Their political activism reinforced many overseas Chinese's admiration for socialist China, hindered the development of their allegiance to Indonesia, exposed them to more suspicion from the pribumi, and frustrated Beijing's hope to see as many ethnic Chinese as possible settle permanently in the archipelago. Into the late 1950s, diasporic politics became more heated, the position of the ethnic Chinese in Indonesia became more precarious, and the PRC's image in the eyes of Indonesian pribumi elites became more clouded by mistrust.

The Conundrum of Citizenship

In 1949 the Republic of Indonesia announced that all Indonesian-born Chinese had to make a decision: If they wished to keep Indonesian citizenship, no action was required; if they wished to renounce Indonesian citizenship, they would need to go through legal proceedings in Indonesian courts and register with the Chinese consular authorities before December 27, 1951. This was known as "the passive system."[9] However, the two-year nationality selection period between 1949 and 1951 did not bring the citizenship issue to a close. In early December 1951, armed with chairs, thick jackets, and "astonishing spirits," groups of ethnic Chinese camped overnight outside a court in Jakarta to make certain that they would not miss the opportunity to reject Indonesian citizenship.[10] Young students rushed to secure their PRC citizenship, as they longed for a college education in China.[11] Meanwhile, many ethnic Chinese who were engaged in commerce agonized over which option to choose and advocated for de facto dual nationality. They needed Indonesian citizenship rights for business purposes, but they insisted that "the motherland should never abandon its moral responsibilities to protect the overseas Chinese."[12]

Having barely shaken off the memories of ethnic violence during the Indonesian National Revolution, many Chinese felt uncertain about their future in the archipelago. An op-ed published in May 1950 in the *Sishui Da Gong Shang Bao* (*Tay Kong Siang Po*; *Da Gong Shang Bao* of Surabaya) captured the doubt and fear that were haunting the Chinese community: "Currently Indonesia is in a state of chaos. . . . If a fascist figure came into power, those without Indonesian citizenship would surely be alienated; those with Indonesian citizenship would still suffer. The German Jews during the Holocaust is an obvious example."[13]

Many ethnic Chinese believed that even if they unequivocally pledged allegiance to Indonesia, they would still be treated differently from the pribumi. During the Sukiman Cabinet's anti-Communist purge in 1951, a prominent peranakan Chinese journalist and community leader, Liem Koen Hian (Lin Qunxian), was arrested based on allegations of participating in Communist organizations. Despite his earlier inclination toward Chinese nationalism and his admiration for socialist China, in the early 1950s Liem became an advocate for political alliances across racial boundaries to achieve a united Indonesian nation.[14] Upon his release, Liem repudiated Indonesian citizenship. Liem spoke to the press about his grave disappointment with the Indonesian government: "Even if we [the ethnic Chinese] took Indonesian citizenship, we could still be massacred."[15]

Besides political persecution, the overseas Chinese were also discouraged by the increasingly grim economic conditions they faced. Although acquiring citizenship status would help the ethnic Chinese obtain some degree of protection against flagrant illegal discrimination, they still encountered unofficial forms of mistreatment in the disorderly economic environment in Indonesia in the 1950s and early 1960s. Under most circumstances, bribery of pribumi governmental officials was the most effective form of self-protection for the Chinese. Yet, by offering bribes, the ethnic Chinese only reinforced the pribumi stereotype of them as an opportunistic, self-interested minority that was the source of corruption in Indonesian society.[16]

According to the Chinese embassy in Jakarta, during the first nationality selection period (1949–51), 636,100 Indonesian-born Chinese—roughly 30 percent of the total population of ethnic Chinese in the country—chose PRC citizenship by renouncing their Indonesian citizenship.[17] This figure matches the survey conducted by Taipei.[18] But Indonesian authorities speculated that many more Chinese passively retained Indonesian citizenship even though they had not intended to do so.[19] They might have missed the deadline for rejecting their Indonesian citizenship due to a lack of information or easy access to court services.[20] Alarmed by the inconsistency between the national allegiance and the citizenship status of these ethnic Chinese, the Indonesian government was disposed toward ceasing to grant automatic citizenship to the local-born Chinese.[21] The Indonesian government's inclination converged with the thinking of many pro-PRC totoks, who regarded the passive system as an institution that "imposes Indonesian citizenship on the ethnic Chinese."[22]

In the Sino-Indonesia Dual Nationality Treaty, the two parties agreed to replace the passive system with an active one. All Chinese descendants who chose Indonesian citizenship had to give up their Chinese nationality through a formal procedure at a PRC consulate and register at an Indonesian governmental agency. And vice versa, those who opted for Chinese citizenship also needed to declare in a court that they rejected Indonesian citizenship and register with a PRC consulate. The treaty was approved by the Standing Committee of the PRC National People's Congress on December 30, 1957. However, the ratification process at the People's Representative Council of Indonesia (Dewan Perwakilan Rakyat or DPR) was delayed until December 1960.[23] By the end of the second selection period (1960–62), as many as 390,000 ethnic Chinese, primarily totoks, renounced their Indonesian citizenship.[24]

In Chinese communities in Indonesia, the Dual Nationality Treaty was opposed by a number of PRC-oriented totoks as well as Indonesia-oriented peranakans. Some older-generation totoks who had a strong national identification with China were dismayed by the prospect of a perpetual disconnection from their ancestral homeland. Siauw Giok Tjhan and Baperki (Badan Permusjawaratan Kewarganegaraan Indonesia or the Consultative Body for Indonesian Citizenship), which was under his leadership, also had reservations for two reasons. First, in a memorandum submitted to the Indonesian government in May 1955, Baperki stated that the active system intended to "reduce the number of Indonesian citizens among the Chinese descendants to as few people as possible" and would cause "mass denationalization."[25] Second, Baperki asserted that the Dual Nationality Treaty would cause unnecessary confusion about the national allegiance of ethnic Chinese who had long been active on the Indonesian political scene by serving as party leaders, parliamentary members, or cabinet ministers. Their political roles in the Republic of Indonesia made their citizenship status self-evident, and they should not be required to make their choice of citizenship again.[26]

Siauw's suggestion to maintain the passive system in order to protect the ethnic Chinese from losing their Indonesian citizenship rights was not accepted by the Chinese and Indonesian governments. As Siauw foresaw in the early 1950s, the active system barred many ethnic Chinese from obtaining their rightful status as Indonesian citizens, especially during the Suharto era (1966–98). Even now, the Citizenship Institute of Indonesia (Institut Kewarganegaraan Indonesia), a legal aid organization, is assisting ethnic Chinese who were denied Indonesian citizenship. In one extraordinary case, an ethnic Chinese woman named Tjhja Ay Ay, born in 1969, had been stateless for thirty-three years and was issued a PRC passport in 2002, although she had never traveled outside of Indonesia and did not speak Mandarin Chinese. She had been registered at birth by the Indonesian authorities as a WNA (*warga negara asing* or alien), because her father was born in China and maintained his PRC citizenship until his death.[27] The active system gave the

Suharto regime a pretext for denying the citizenship rights of Indonesian-born ethnic Chinese like Tjhja by deliberately conflating ethnicity with citizenship. At Indonesian governmental offices under the New Order regime, it was almost inevitable that a Chinese Indonesian would be asked the question of "orang apa" (loosely translated "Who are you? / Where are you from?"). If he or she responded "orang Cina," he or she would be marked as "alien" even though "orang Cina" could have meant "Chinese Indonesian" rather than "Chinese citizen."[28]

In retrospect, the policy-making circle in Beijing recognized that the decision to switch to the active system was made based on insufficient and biased information. The staff members from the PRC's Overseas Chinese Affairs Commission later realized that they had failed to comprehend the diversity of opinion among the ethnic Chinese. Their focus was on the "patriotic leaders of the Chinese community" (those who were strongly pro-Beijing) and the older generation who had close ties to Mainland China. In other words, they marginalized or even ignored the opinion of Indonesia-oriented ethnic Chinese, such as Siauw, and the younger generation who saw their future in Indonesia. Moreover, they failed to anticipate the technical difficulty of implementing the policy. As a former diplomat who used to work at the Chinese embassy in Jakarta reflected, it was impossible for all ethnic Chinese to go to a PRC consulate or an Indonesian governmental agency for the citizenship selection procedure. More often than not, the elderly would decide on behalf of the entire household and thereby override their children or grandchildren, who were more inclined toward adopting Indonesian citizenship.[29]

Communism as a Business Model

By the late 1950s, pro-Communist groups had gained greater control over Chinese-language media, schools, and civic organizations than their pro-Nationalist rivals. Ironically, this victory was accomplished through collaboration with local ethnic Chinese businessmen and their own engagement in the capitalist economy. *Tian Sheng Ri Bao*, the organ of the Chinese Nationalist Party in Indonesia, observed that "the so-called progressive elements are mostly factory-owners, entrepreneurs, rice and fabric merchants, as well as bankers. They usually possess large amounts of capital and should be categorized as the capitalist class . . . whereas those who run small businesses or belong to the working class usually align themselves with the righteous side [the Chinese Nationalist government]."[30]

This alliance between capitalism and Communism started during the Japanese occupation. In 1943 Yang Xinrong, one of the founding members of the CCP's underground branches in Indonesia, opened the "Big Unique Cake Factory" (dabutong dangao chang) in Jakarta, which soon expanded to other parts of the archipelago. This chain of pastry factories provided a sustainable source of income and also a safe venue for underground resistance against the Japanese.[31] The success of the Big Unique Cake Factory gave the CCP cadres in Indonesia the confidence to build more comprehensive modern corporations. Yang Xinrong, Wang Jiyuan, and Huang Zhougui together founded Big China Trade Ltd. (dazhong maoyi youxian gongsi) and made it the financial vehicle for the CCP's advancement in Indonesia. The company sold a wide range of products including pepper, rubber, cane sugar, and coffee. The company used its profits to support the development of pro-Beijing Chinese-language education and left-wing print media.[32] Yang Xinrong assumed the position of principal of the pro-Beijing Xinhua School of Jakarta (xinhua xuexiao). Wang Jiyuan and Huang Zhougui were crucial figures in *Sheng Huo Bao*. The Big China Trade Ltd. board members also used their social networks to help pro-Beijing civic associations expand their influence. During the anti-Chinese campaign of 1959–60, Big China Trade Ltd. assisted the PRC embassy and consulates in Indonesia with the repatriation of the persecuted Chinese.[33] In addition to the undercover CCP members who undertook business ventures, there were also some successful totok businessmen who voluntarily provided financial support to Beijing's cause. For instance, Wang Dajun, a prominent banker in Jakarta, was one of the major investors in *Sheng Huo Bao*.[34] Weng Fulin, a successful entrepreneur in the film industry, donated his property for use by the PRC embassy in Jakarta.[35] When arrested and interrogated during the anti-Communist purge in August 1951, Weng insisted that he was "not qualified as a Communist" but belonged to "the capitalist class."[36]

"How is it that the wealthy capitalists in Southeast Asia can support a communist government in China?"[37] This was the question that William Skinner posed in the early 1950s after completing extensive fieldwork in the Chinese community in Indonesia. Skinner quoted observations from Kwee Kek Beng, a peranakan Chinese journalist who acquired Indonesian citizenship in 1950 but remained proud of socialist China: "There is no necessary contradiction between the New Democratic Government and capitalism. . . . Communism in China does not mean that it is coming here [Indonesia], while the Chinese businessmen here welcome the support that a strong Chinese government, of whatever political coloration, can give them."[38] Ang Jan Goan, a peranakan Chinese community leader, felt that most of the Chinese in Indonesia were ready to accept any government in power in China and to embrace a united China. He used the following metaphor: The overseas Chinese were like shareholders in the Chinese government. They could not expect to achieve a voice in selecting the managers (governmental leaders) or deciding the policy of the company, but they could hope for their share of the dividends (protection from the home government).[39] Zheng Chuyun, one of the left-wing intellectuals who migrated from Mainland China to Indonesia together with Ba Ren, argued that the ethnic Chinese capitalists in Southeast Asia were also "exploited and oppressed by the Western imperialists."[40] The constraints and oppression they faced in Indonesia made them eligible members of an overseas Chinese anti-imperialist patriotic united front (*huaqiao fandi aiguo tongyi zhanxian*). This united front welcomed "anyone who had a heart loyal to the motherland" regardless of his or her past political affiliations or class background.[41]

Media Warfare

Media was a major battlefield between the pro-Beijing and pro-Taipei blocs. According to the PRC embassy in Jakarta, by 1956 the ethnic Chinese owned twenty newspapers, one-fifth of the total number of newspapers in Indonesia. The number of pro-Beijing newspapers was around the same as its pro-Taipei rivals, but the pro-Beijing newspapers enjoyed wider circulation.[42] *Sin Po / Xin Bao*, with a circulation of eighteen thousand for its bahasa Indonesia edition and twenty-five thousand for its Chinese-language edition in the 1950s, targeted both peranakan and totok Chinese who identified themselves with China. *Xin Bao* portrayed China as the protector of the overseas Chinese. It advocated for the unity of the peranakan and the totok, encouraged peranakan children to obtain a Chinese education, and favored participation by the overseas Chinese in the politics of China rather than that of the Republic of Indonesia.[43] *Xin Bao* remained neutral between the Chinese Communists and Nationalists throughout the Chinese Civil War until Communist forces crossed the Yangtze River and occupied Shanghai and Nanjing. On the day the PRC was founded, *Xin Bao* changed from the Minguo calendar to the Gregorian calendar to express its open support for the new Communist government.[44] Thereafter, *Xin Bao* became very sympathetic to Beijing in its reports and remained China-oriented on issues such as citizenship choice.

The organ of the Chinese Nationalist Party in Indonesia, *Tian Sheng Ri Bao*, had the second largest circulation after *Xin Bao*, which amounted to approximately thirteen to fifteen thousand.[45] *Tian Sheng Ri Bao* accused the CCP of tainting authentic Chinese culture with Communist ideology. It emphasized the distinction between "the motherland" and "the Communist

Table 4.1   Major ethnic Chinese-owned newspapers in Indonesia, 1950–1958

POLITICAL ORIENTATION	TITLE	BASE	DESCRIPTION
Pro-Taipei	*Tian Sheng Ri Bao* (*Tian Sheng Daily, Thien Sung Yit Po*)	Jakarta	Established in 1921 as the organ of the Chinese Nationalist Party Branch in Batavia. Its managers and editors-in-chief had always been Chinese Nationalist Party members. Its daily circulation was about 13,000–15,000.
	Ziyou Bao (*Liberty Daily*)	Jakarta	Established in 1951 by Chinese Nationalist Party members. The persons in charge included Zhang Xunyi, an anti-Communist activist who was deported by the Indonesian government in 1954. Its daily circulation was about 13,000.
	Zhonghua Shangbao (*China Business Daily*)	Jakarta	Established in 1953 by the Association of the Chinese Chamber of Commerce in Indonesia (*Yindunixiya zhonghua shanghui lianhehui*). Its manager was Ma Shuli.
	Huaqiao Xinwen (*News of the Overseas Chinese*)	Surabaya	Daily circulation 7,000.
	Qingguang Ribao (*Tsing Kwang Daily Press*)	Surabaya	Established in 1946, with a daily circulation of 3,000.
	Xin Zhonghua Bao (*New Tionghwa Po*)	Medan	Established in 1928.
	Xingzhong Ribao (*Xingzhong Daily*)	Medan	Established in 1957, with a daily circulation of 4,000.
	Qiaosheng Bao (*Voice of the Overseas Chinese Daily*)	Makassar	Established by the Chinese Nationalist Branch in Makassar in 1951, with a daily circulation of 2,000.
	Cheng Bao (*Loyalty Daily*)	Pontianak	Established in 1947, with a daily circulation of 4,000.
Pro-Beijing	*Sheng Huo Bao* (*Seng Hwo Pao, Life Daily*)	Jakarta	Established in 1945 by pro-PRC businessmen and underground CCP members in Indonesia. Daily circulation around 8,000.
	Da Gong Shang Bao (*Tay Kong Siang Po, Tay Kong Business Daily*)	Surabaya	Established in 1908, initially named *Da Gong Ribao* (Tay Kong Daily). Merged in 1922 with *Shang Bao* (Business Daily) and was renamed *Da Gong Shang Bao*. Daily circulation of 25,000.
	Minzhu Ribao (*Democracy Daily*)	Medan	Started originally as *The Progressive Weekly*, the underground publication of the resistance organization against the Japanese during the period 1942–45, the People's Anti-Fascist Alliance. After the Japanese surrender, it was renamed *Minzhu Ribao* and started open circulation of both Mandarin Chinese and *bahasa Indonesia* editions.

POLITICAL ORIENTATION	TITLE	BASE	DESCRIPTION
	Sumendala Min Bao (*Sumatra People's Daily*)	Medan	Established in 1914 by Ye Yidong, a local businessman and community leader. It supported Tan Kah Kee's pro-Chinese Communist agenda and oriented toward the PRC in 1950.
	Li Ming Bao (*Lie Ming Pao, Daybreak News*)	Pontianak	Established after the Japanese surrender in 1945, it was the rival of the pro-Taipei *Cheng Bao* in Pontianak.
	Kuanglu Ribao (*Kuanglu Daily*)	Makassar	Established in 1946, initially oriented toward the Chinese Nationalist Government but had switched its loyalty to the Chinese Communist regime by the end of 1949.
	Xin Bao (*Sin Po*)	Jakarta	Established in 1910, the persons in charge included Kwee Kek Beng and Ang Jan Goan; both were *peranakan* Chinese who adopted Indonesian citizenship but were enthusiastic supporters of socialist China. Its circulation, with Mandarin Chinese and *bahasa Indonesia* editions combined, numbered 40,000–50,000 per day.
Indonesia-oriented	*Keng Po* (*Jing Bao*)	Jakarta	Established in 1923, *Keng Po* represented the anti-PRC and anti-Communist group (not necessarily pro-Taipei) in the *peranakan* Chinese community. It was also more open to the idea of the ethnic Chinese's assimilation rather than integration into Indonesian society.
	Mingguan Sadar (*Juexing Zhoukan, Awakening Weekly*)	Jakarta	Established in 1954 by Siauw Giok Tjhan and sponsored by Baperki under his leadership, *Mingguan Sadar* promoted the idea that the ethnic Chinese should integrate into Indonesian society, but it held a favorable attitude toward the PRC.

regime": "We oppose the Communist regime in Beijing out of our love for the motherland."[46] Immediately after the establishment of the PRC, *Tian Sheng Ri Bao* published an editorial condemning the PRC as "a satellite state and a cheerleading clown of the Soviet Union." It predicted that the future of the PRC would be "dim," with "barely any prospects for sustainable development," and claimed that Beijing should not be granted diplomatic recognition by "any rational government that pursues justice in international affairs."[47] Furthermore, *Tian Sheng Ri Bao* urged the overseas Chinese to bear in mind that their own economic interests were "incompatible with those of the Communist regime."[48] One editorial argued that the business-minded ethnic Chinese in Indonesia fell into the category of capitalist "exploiters." Their land and property back home would be confiscated and their family members who remained in China would become targets for political cleansing.[49]

Tian Sheng Ri Bao warned the overseas Chinese: "It would be suicidal for you to embrace the rule of the Chinese Communist Party."[50]

However, in contrast to its harsh criticism of Beijing, *Tian Sheng Ri Bao*'s attitude toward the pro-Beijing groups in Indonesia was initially conciliatory. A *Tian Sheng Ri Bao* editorial in June 1950 called for unity among different factions in the Chinese community: "The struggle between the two blocs is like family members drawing swords on each other [*tongshi caoge*]. Most of the ethnic Chinese in Indonesia merely want to make a living. No one came overseas with the goal of promoting a political movement. The pro-Beijing and pro-Taipei factions can coexist peacefully. Either side can uphold their own political beliefs freely, which does not necessarily involve attacking those who disagree with them."[51]

Shortly after the establishment of the PRC, some prominent Chinese Nationalists in Indonesia made friendly gestures toward pro-Beijing groups. In Jakarta, Zhang Xunyi, the chairman of the pro-Nationalist Chinese General Association in Jakarta, hung the Five-Star Red Flag in the office building of his organization. Zhang, together with two other senior Chinese Nationalist leaders in Indonesia, Qiu Yuanrong and Liang Xiyou, attended the welcome ceremony for the first PRC ambassador to Indonesia, Ba Ren. Despite their anti-Communist stance, many pro-Taipei Chinese still "looked forward to the arrival of Ambassador Wang because he would help protect the interests of the overseas Chinese in general."[52] But the pro-Beijing bloc dismissed these friendly gestures as "ingratiating" and "opportunistic."[53] Similarly, in Medan, when the pro-Taipei group showed interest in the welcome ceremony for the PRC consular general Shen Yiping, the pro-Beijing ethnic Chinese insisted that the "Chiang bandits and their followers should write letters of apology before joining us."[54] The pro-Taipei Chinese criticized the noncooperative attitude of the pro-Beijing bloc: "Only a very small number of ethnic Chinese are strong believers in a particular political ideology. Most make their decisions based on pragmatic considerations. Overseas Chinese civic associations are not political parties. These associations should include people from across the political spectrum and should accommodate different political ideologies. The pro-Beijing associations are shutting their doors to many of them."[55]

In contrast to *Tian Sheng Ri Bao*'s balancing of its opposition to the CCP with its accommodation of the pro-Beijing elements in Indonesia, *Sheng Huo Bao* adopted a bellicose attitude toward both the Chinese Nationalist government and the pro-Taipei groups in Indonesia. One of *Sheng Huo Bao*'s founders, Wang Jiyuan, depicted the struggle between the Nationalists and Communists as "a war between right and wrong, good and evil." Wang urged the overseas Chinese media to take a clear position. If a journalist just sat on the fence, he or she would be "an immoral opportunist."[56] While *Tian Sheng Ri Bao* framed the Chinese Communist government as a puppet of the Soviet Union, *Sheng Huo Bao* accused the Chinese Nationalists of being "the lapdogs" of the American imperialists.[57] *Sheng Huo Bao* vowed to "debunk the shameless lies of the Chinese Nationalists" and "disseminate information on the socialist construction back in the motherland."[58]

With a circulation of approximately eight thousand, *Sheng Huo Bao*'s influence was limited to the ethnic Chinese who were supporters of the CCP and who planned to maintain their PRC citizenship. *Sheng Huo Bao* could not represent the voices of those who intended to integrate into Indonesian society and to ultimately "plant their roots in the local soil."[59] Although it supported the Indonesian National Revolution based on Lenin's theory of imperialism, *Sheng Huo Bao*'s attitude toward Indonesia had been distant, unenthusiastic, and sometimes even condescending. For instance, before the Dutch-Indonesian Roundtable Conference, *Sheng Huo Bao* urged Indonesia to "learn from more advanced cultures and ideas, not to isolate itself and stagnate by refusing to make progress."[60] *Sheng Huo Bao* treated Indonesia as an "other" while addressing China as "our country" or "the motherland."

Sheng Huo Bao focused predominantly on domestic developments within China and China's relations with the outside world. Among the 1,858 editorials published between October 1945 and November 1959, 44 percent were on domestic affairs in China, 32.9 percent on the PRC's foreign relations, and 23.1 percent on the Indonesian economy, politics, and the status of the ethnic Chinese.[61] *Sheng Huo Bao*'s overwhelmingly positive reports on the PRC parroted Beijing's propaganda line. It portrayed the PRC as a rapidly industrializing socialist country with a burgeoning economy that had huge market potential.[62] While the Great Leap Forward resulted in three years of catastrophic economic recession, *Sheng Huo Bao* promised its readers in Indonesia that "there is no need to worry about your family and relatives back home" because they enjoyed free food in the People's Commune.[63] It also tried to convince its readers that "the traditional belief that peasants are at the mercy of the forces of nature should be abandoned. In the near future, the Chinese people will have over five hundred kilograms of grain and more than fifty kilograms of pork per capita per year."[64] It even sang the praises of the mass steel campaign in which small backyard furnaces had a disastrous impact on the environment.[65]

Sheng Huo Bao also waged a propaganda war against the US. The country was "the most devious enemy of all the people who are oppressed in the world," but the overseas Chinese had not yet "thoroughly understood its vicious nature."[66] A *Sheng Huo Bao* editorial after the outbreak of the Korean War warned that the US was "in the process of taking the same old aggressive track as the Japanese imperialists did in the old days." Following the movement to "resist the US and assist Korea" (*kang Mei yuan Chao*) back in China, the pro-Beijing bloc in Indonesia started a "campaign against poison" (*judu yundong*), which called upon all those who claimed loyalty to Beijing, particularly the youth, to boycott American cultural products. One ethnic Chinese student wrote to *Sheng Huo Bao*: "Today the American imperialists are on the verge of death. Their culture is in decline, too. The films produced by the big bosses from Wall Street are serving the ruling class only. It defends the capitalist system as well as imperialism. It numbs the working class's hatred of reality with romanticism and eroticism so as to delay class struggle. It promotes a narrow version of 'America first' nationalism. All American movies are poisonous."[67]

Besides the locally based *Sheng Huo Bao*, pro-PRC print media were imported to Indonesia and enjoyed a considerable readership in the 1950s and 1960s. The most widely circulated PRC propaganda magazine was the *China Pictorial* (*Zhongguo huabao*). Many ethnic Chinese youth were devoted readers. They looked forward to its arrival every month, and some would even go to the embassy to ask for it if the latest issue was not delivered on schedule. This colorfully illustrated magazine projected an image of the PRC as a land full of babies with chubby, rosy cheeks. Similar to *Sheng Huo Bao*, the *China Pictorial* blinded many young ethnic Chinese to the grim realities of the Great Leap Forward and kindled a desire to migrate to the PRC.[68] In addition to the *China Pictorial*, magazines such as *New Observation* (*Xin guancha*) and *Learning* (*Xuexi*) as well as newspapers such as *Da Gong Bao* (*Ta Kung Pa*) of Hong Kong were made available through a chain of circulation across Southeast Asia established by pro-Beijing businessmen.[69]

Table 4.2   Terms used in the propaganda war between the pro-Chinese Communist and pro-Chinese Nationalist factions in Indonesia

	HOW THEY ADDRESSED THEMSELVES / THEIR SYMPATHIZERS IN THE DIASPORIC COMMUNITY	HOW THEY ADDRESSED THEIR OPPONENTS
Chinese Communists	Progressive	Reactionary
	Patriotic	White Chinese
		Chiang Bandits
Chinese Nationalists	Loyal	Red / Communist / Mao Bandits
	Righteous	

FIGURE 4.1.   Cover page, *China Pictorial* 3 (1964)

The pro-Beijing entrepreneur Weng Fulin played a major role in marketing PRC movies and documentaries in Indonesia. A professionally trained
artist and the owner of several art and movie studios, Weng established a
film company named South Star Pictures (Nanxing yingye gongsi) in Jakarta
with the specific purpose of importing "progressive movies" from the PRC
and the Soviet Union. South Star Pictures screened the documentary *The
Birth of New China* (*Xinzhongguo de dansheng*), a 1949 production on the Chinese Civil War from the Communist perspective, at the PRC embassy and
consulates, cinemas, and Chinese-language schools across Indonesia. Like
The Birth of New China, the majority of movies that came through South
Star Pictures in the 1950s promoted Chinese nationalism and reaffirmed the

legitimacy of the CCP. *One Million Brave Soldiers Crossing over the Southern Yangtze River (Baiwan xiongshi xia jiangnan)*, *Fighter in White (Baiyi zhanshi)*, and *Iron Soldiers (Gangtie zhanshi)* portrayed the Chinese Civil War as a battle between the brave Communist forces and the moribund and corrupt Nationalist government. *Guerrilla on the Plain (Pingyuan youjidui)* and *Concentration Camp in Shangrao (Shangrao jizhongying)* traced the rise of the CCP back to the Second Sino-Japanese War. After the outbreak of the Korean War, South Star Pictures imported *The Battle of Shang Gan Ling*, which praised the heroism of PRC volunteer soldiers in a fateful military encounter with the US. Besides war-themed movies, class-themed films like *The White-Haired Girl (Baimao nv)*, which highlighted the suffering of the oppressed peasant class in the "feudalist old society," also won instant popularity among the overseas Chinese.[70] To attract local business partners, Weng offered a share of the profits to theater owners that was significantly larger than normal while promising to reimburse unsold tickets. His demand in return was that all PRC movies had to be screened three days in a row. And if the reception was good, the screening period had to be extended to a week. With the help of Weng's shrewd business strategies, PRC films and documentaries became an important part of the cultural life of the totok Chinese in the 1950s.[71]

Embattled Civic Associations

Just as they clashed in media outlets, pro-Beijing and pro-Taipei factions fought for control of Chinese civic associations in Indonesia. After the end of World War II, industry and profession-based unions—such as those among *warung* owners, textile manufacturers, tin miners, and teachers—emerged.[72] These overseas Chinese associations transcended traditional divisions based on clans, surnames, and native places. This new development inspired the CCP cadres working in the archipelago to envision a reconfiguration of the diasporic community. Wang Jiyuan, a leader in CCP underground organizations and one of the cofounders of *Sheng Huo Bao*, advocated for the establishment of an increasing number of "new, modern, and democratic" organizations that would foster cohesion and oversee the welfare of the ethnic Chinese regardless of their dialect group or ancestral home.[73]

The structural change in Chinese society created an environment that was conducive to the CCP's export of the same social mobilization model it used back in China. The structure of the CCP operation in Indonesia was in the shape of an onion: the core—the underground CCP branches—were surrounded by layers of left-leaning "peripheral mass organizations" (*qunzhongxing waiwei zuzhi*), which took the form of book clubs, drama clubs, sports teams, and study groups. For instance, in Semarang, Zheng Manru—an undercover CCP member who had immigrated to Indonesia in the 1940s and served as editor of *Sheng Huo Bao* in the early 1950s—founded the Xin You Society (Xin you she) in December 1945. Its main goal was to prevent the traditional local Chinese associations from falling into the hands of the Chinese Nationalists after the Indonesian National Revolution. The Xin You Society offered free Chinese-language classes to the local ethnic Chinese youth and distributed popular Marxist reading materials such as Ai Siqi's *Philosophy for the Masses (Dazhong Zhexue)*, the magazine *Below the Winds*, and the pro-Beijing newspaper *Wen Hui Bao* of Hong Kong.[74]

While the Xin You Society strove to carve out a space for a CCP political presence, the Chinese Nationalists were also proactively defending their territory. In 1946–47, the Chinese Nationalist Party branch in Semarang, as well as the Three Principles of the People Youth League under it, frequently carried out militia-style parades and distributed their own propaganda material such as Chiang Kai-shek's *Destiny of China (zhongguo zhi mingyun)* across Central and East Java.[75] After the founding of the PRC, the Xin You Society started to take more aggressive steps toward squeezing the Chinese Nationalists out of Semarang. It held a grand reception to celebrate the establishment of diplomatic relations between China and Indonesia in April 1950 and organized torch parades with pro-Beijing Chinese shouting slogans such as "Support New China!" and "Down with Chiang Kai-shek!"[76] The Xin You Society rapidly expanded its influence through a coalition with other pro-Beijing Chinese organizations such as the Overseas Chinese Employees' Union (huaqiao zhigonghui) and the Teachers' Union (jiaoshi gonghui) as well as through the founding of the Xin You Elementary School and Xin You Secondary School.[77] On its seven-year anniversary, the Xin You Society put on a play entitled *Growing through Struggle (zai zhandouli chengzhang)*, which told the story of how ethnic Chinese youth were trained for the battle against the "reactionary" Chinese Nationalists.[78]

A similar turf war took place in Jakarta. There was a fierce competition, which sometimes escalated into physical violence, over who would lead Jakarta's Hakka Chinese General Association (keshu tuanti huaqiao zonghui), the Cantonese Regional Lodge (Guangzhao huiguan), and the Fujian Regional Lodge (Fujian huiguan). At the Hakka Chinese General Association, for example, the pro-Beijing and pro-Taipei blocs each dispatched over one thousand supporters to stage a face-off, which only de-escalated after Indonesian police intervened.[79] The most important goal for both sides was to dominate the pan-Chinese, all-encompassing association in the capital city. In November 1949, to counterbalance the Nationalist-controlled Chinese

General Association of Jakarta (Yajiada zhonghua zonghui), an underground CCP member Yang Xinrong founded the Working Committee for the Promotion of Establishing Diplomatic Relations between China and Indonesia (Yajiada cujin zhong yinni jianjiao gongzuo weiyuanhui), which called upon ethnic Chinese across Indonesia to recognize the PRC as the sole legitimate government of China.[80] In April 1950, with its morale boosted by Indonesia's recognition of the PRC, the organization launched a round of vigorous but unsuccessful campaigns to seize the leadership of the Chinese General Association of Jakarta from the hands of the Chinese Nationalists. In the end, the pro-Beijing bloc had to start their own opposition organization, the Federation of the Chinese General Associations of Jakarta (Yajiada zhonghua qiaotuan zonghui, hereafter referred to as "the Federation").

Although PRC decision makers shared the pro-Beijing groups' interests in weakening the influence of the Nationalists, they advised the PRC diplomatic mission in Indonesia to keep a safe distance from the Red-versus-Blue struggle. In internally circulated intelligence reports, the PRC embassy in Jakarta labeled the pro-Taipei Chinese General Association as "an organization with deceptive legitimacy" that was "occupied by the Chiang bandits."[81] But when the pro-Beijing groups requested that the Federation be officially endorsed, Beijing refused.[82] The PRC Foreign Ministry commented on the situation:

> The establishment of the Federation is beneficial to the united patriotic front among the overseas Chinese. At the same time, however, the struggle between the progressive forces and the Chiang bandits is going to be more acute. It would be premature for our embassy to publicly announce our stance. The key issue is how to do practical work through the Federation, so that we can unify and educate the overseas Chinese and isolate the illegitimate Chinese General Association. The Federation should serve as a platform through which we gradually win over neutral or backward overseas Chinese civic associations. Our embassy and consulates should not come forward publicly.[83]

Although the PRC embassy did not publicly declare its support for the Federation, the fact that PRC diplomacy in Indonesia relied heavily on this organization speaks to its unique status. Though a civic association in name, the Federation acted as a mediator between the PRC and the Chinese in Indonesia: it helped the ethnic Chinese to reconnect with relatives back in the PRC; it assisted ethnic Chinese in their negotiations with local governments when their property was expropriated in their home villages in China; and it facilitated the second nationality selection process as a semiofficial representative of the PRC embassy in Jakarta. During the 1955 Bandung Conference, the Federation functioned as a special brigade that shielded the PRC delegation headed by Zhou Enlai from threats of sabotage by Chinese Nationalist elements in Indonesia.[84] The pro-Taipei groups were critical of this entanglement of state-to-state relations and civil affairs in overseas Chinese communities.[85] From their perspective, the leaders of the Red camp seemed to have forgotten that "Indonesia obtained its own independence and was not liberated by the Communists."[86]

Between 1950 and 1958, amid the hypercompetitive atmosphere of the battle between the Red and the Blue, the number of pro-PRC civic organizations mushroomed. In major cities with a significant Chinese concentration— such as Jakarta, Surabaya, and Semarang—there were four to ten times as many pro-Beijing associations as there had been at the end of World War II. According to estimates by a former leader of the Chinese community in Jakarta, there were approximately 2,040 pro-Beijing and 680 pro-Taipei civic associations in Indonesia in 1958.[87]

Contentious Campuses

Between 1950 and 1957, Chinese-medium education developed significantly. In 1949 there were 816 Chinese-language schools with a total student population of 227,608; by 1958 the number of schools had risen to 2,000 with a total student population of 420,000.[88] The growth of Chinese-language education in postindependence Indonesia went hand in hand with the intense and sometimes violent struggle between the Red and the Blue. In schools dominated by the pro-Taipei faction, many pro-Beijing teachers were dismissed or even physically attacked.[89] In Semarang, the Chinese Nationalists took advantage of the political vacuum that appeared after the Japanese surrender and established a Chinese Education Association (Zhonghua jiaoyu xiejin hui). This umbrella organization aimed to bring all the schools that had existed before World War II under its control.[90] But left-wing students of the Overseas Chinese High School of Semarang (Sanbaolong huaqiao zhongxue) resisted the Chinese Nationalists' advances by leaving their classrooms to protest in the streets.[91] In North Sumatra, the two blocs became embroiled in a battle over control of the Siantar Chung Hua School (Xianda zhonghua xuexiao), which involved both legal prosecution and violent physical conflicts. The pro-Beijing bloc accused the pro-Taipei bloc of breaking into the school office by smashing the doors with axes and forcibly hanging the portrait of "Devil Chiang" on the office wall.[92] In Palembang, South Sumatra, pro-Beijing students participating in a parade in celebration of the

PRC's National Day were attacked by pro-Taipei groups armed with wooden sticks, knives, farming tools, glass bottles, and stones. The most dramatic moment in the confrontation was when pro-Taipei elements hidden inside a local restaurant threw dishes, forks, and spoons at pro-Beijing students who happened to be passing by. The students who carried the Five-Star Red Flag were reportedly injured and hospitalized.[93]

The ideological antagonism between ordinary teenagers who grew up in the same microenvironment was, to a large extent, the result of political indoctrination conducted at pro-Beijing and pro-Taipei schools. Skinner conducted a survey of over one thousand ethnic Chinese high school seniors in Jakarta in the 1950s and discovered that the ideological stance of a student's school had a fundamental impact on his or her political orientation.[94] According to *Tian Sheng Ri Bao*, at pro-Beijing schools, teachers would ask their students questions such as "Who is the most devious imperialist in the world?" "If a student answered that it was the United States, he or she would get full marks; if a student answered that it was the Soviet Union, he or she would lose points."[95] "The irrevocable gulf between the two Chinas," as Skinner put it, made it difficult for students to stay apolitical or neutral.[96] The children from the pro-Beijing schools were called "red butts" by the pro-Taipei students, whereas children from the pro-Taipei schools were called "blue butts" by the pro-Beijing students; they would fight in the streets.[97] Skinner concluded from his research that "by the time Chinese students in Jakarta have reached the final year of middle school, they have been directly exposed to extensive and protracted political pressures. Most of them have already made several important political decisions, while many are political activists. Only a minority are as naive politically as the average American college freshman."[98]

Although exact statistics are not available, it is safe to assume that the two blocs were neck and neck in this battle in the early 1950s. By 1957, shortly before the Indonesian government implemented the policy of restricting Chinese-medium education, the pro-Beijing bloc had gradually gained the upper hand. Immediately after Indonesia's independence, many well-established schools remained in the hands of pro-Taipei groups. In a report from September 1950, the Chinese embassy in Jakarta observed that "progressive elements" had started to make significant progress in exerting their influence.[99] The ratio of pro-Beijing to pro-Taipei schools varied from region to region. In Jakarta, for example, 27 schools were Beijing-oriented whereas approximately 15–16 schools were Taipei-oriented. In Makassar, South Sulawesi, 19 out of 24 Chinese-medium schools were pro-PRC.[100] According to statistics from the China News Service—the second largest state-owned news agency in the PRC targeted at the overseas Chinese—by 1957, in the eight major cities of Indonesia (Jakarta, Bandung, Semarang, Surabaya, Medan, Palembang, Pontianak, and Makassar), roughly 70–80 percent of the Chinese-medium schools were pro-Beijing.[101]

CCP underground branches infiltrated pro-Beijing schools through openly active civic associations as well as semisecretive and completely underground youth leagues. The openly active organizations took the form of basketball teams and drama clubs. One of the major semi-open organizations was the Young Overseas Chinese Study Society (huaqiao qingnian xuexi she), in which ethnic Chinese youth gathered together to read theoretical works on Communism such as Mao Zedong's *On New Democracy*

Table 4.3 Major Chinese-medium schools in Indonesia, 1950–1957

NAME OF THE SCHOOL	LOCATION	HISTORY	SIZE	POLITICAL ORIENTATION
Bahua Zhongxue Bahua High School	Jakarta	Established by Tiong Hoa Hwee Koan in 1901, with the original name of "Tiong Hoa Hak Tong," it pioneered Chinese education in Indonesia.	800 students and 30 teachers in 1931; 4,300 students and over 100 teachers in 1956	Non-partisan. There was less political content in the instruction. Bahua followed the Indonesian Government's recognition of Beijing as the sole legitimate government of China.
Xinhua Zhongxue Xinhua School	Jakarta	Established in 1904 as Tiong Hoa Hak Tong at Pasar Baru in Jakarta, it is the second-oldest Chinese-medium school after Bahua.	3,200 students and over 100 teachers in 1956	Pro-Beijing. Yang Xinrong, the leader of the CCP underground branch in Indonesia, was the principal of Xinhua during the period 1939–53.
Zhonghua Zhongxue Zhonghua High School	Jakarta	Founded in 1939	370 students and 15 teachers in 1939; 4,277 students and 121 teachers in 1957	Strongly pro-Beijing. The teachers oriented toward the PRC and over a quarter of its graduates every year went to the PRC for higher education.
Bacheng Zhongxue Jakarta High School	Jakarta	Established in 1945	760 students and 25 teachers in 1945; 5,102 students and 155 teachers in 1957. Bacheng was the largest Chinese-language school in Jakarta.	Moderately pro-Beijing. The principal, Soeto Tjan (Situ Zan), also served as the president of the pro-Beijing Federation of the Chinese General Associations of Jakarta. About one-fifth of its graduates in 1957 continued their studies in the PRC.

Continued

Table 4.3   Continued

NAME OF THE SCHOOL	LOCATION	HISTORY	SIZE	POLITICAL ORIENTATION
Yinni huaqiao gongli gaoji shangye xuexiao ("Yinhua Gao Shang" for short) Advanced Business Polytechnic Institute of Chinese in Indonesia	Jakarta	Established in 1949	91 students in 1949; 1,265 students in 1956	Pro-Taipei. Teachers were mostly Chinese Nationalist Party loyalists. Over one-quarter of its graduates in 1957 went to Taiwan to further their studies.
Zhongshan Zhongxue Zhongshan High School	Jakarta	Established in 1951	1,500 students and 45 teachers in 1956	Strongly pro-Taipei. Around two-fifths of its annual graduating class normally proceeded to Taiwan for advanced study.
Zhonghua Zhongxiaoxue Zhonghua Elementary and Secondary Schools	Semarang	Established in 1904	20 students in 1904; 2,300 students and 60 teachers in 1954	Pro-Beijing
Huaying Zhongxue Huaying High School	Semarang	Established in 1916	227 students and 11 teachers in 1916; 1,230 students and 38 teachers in 1956	Pro-Beijing
Huaqiao Zhongxue Overseas Chinese High School	Bandung	Established in 1947	353 students and 26 teachers in 1947; 831 students, 38 teachers in 1950; 2,700 students, 110 teachers in 1957	Pro-Beijing
Nanhua Xuexiao Nanhua School	Bandung	Established in 1946	400 students in 1946; 1,400 students in 1955	Pro-Beijing
Xinhua Zhongxue Xinhua High School	Surabaya	Established in 1934	1070 students and 35 teachers in 1953; 2,894 students and 89 teachers in 1957	Pro-Beijing
Zhonghua Zhongxue Zhonghua High School	Surabaya	Established in 1948	1,300 students and 40 teachers in 1953; 2,092 students and 59 teachers in 1957	Pro-Beijing
Sudong Zhongxue East Sumatran High School	Medan	Established in 1927	7,936 students and 254 teachers in 1957	Neutral, with influence from both sides

NAME OF THE SCHOOL	LOCATION	HISTORY	SIZE	POLITICAL ORIENTATION
Mianlan Huaqiao Zhongxue ("Mian-hua Zhongxue" for short)	Medan	Established in 1945	3,384 students and 117 teachers in 1958	Strongly pro-Beijing
Medan Overseas Chinese High School (or Mian-hua High School)				
Xianda Huaqiao Zhongxue	Siantar	Established in 1949	400 students and 15 teachers in 1949; 2,300 students and 80 teachers in 1958	Pro-Beijing
Siantar Overseas Chinese High School				
Jugang Zhongxue	Palembang	Established in 1951	519 students and 31 teachers in 1951; 2,326 students and 108 teachers in 1957	Pro-Beijing
Palembang High School				
Kundian Zhen-qiang Zhongxiao-xue	Pontianak	Established in 1907	2,653 students in 1957	Pro-Beijing
Zheng Qiang Ele-mentary and Sec-ondary Schools of Pontianak				

(*xinminzhu zhuyi lun*) and *On Coalition Government* (*lun lianhe zhengfu*). The underground organization was the New Democratic Comrades' Association (xinminzhu zhuyi tongzhihui). From the late 1940s to 1952, it recruited ethnic Chinese students with outstanding grades, organizational skills, and a strong ideological inclination toward Communism. Following the communication protocols of the CCP's clandestine operations, a member of the New Democratic Comrades' Association could only have single-line contact with his or her direct supervisor, who would pass down instructions and information about the PRC's policy toward the Indonesian government and the overseas Chinese.[102] When the CCP disbanded its overseas branches in 1952, the New Democratic Comrades' Association stopped recruiting. Most of its members later returned to the PRC to work for the Foreign Ministry, the International Liaison Department of the CCP, the Overseas Chinese Affairs Commission, and research institutes. For instance, Chen Lishui, Wen Liu, and Huang Shuhai were all Indonesian-born Chinese who later became bahasa-Chinese translators for PRC leaders.[103] Their local knowledge and language skills were valuable assets for Beijing.

FIGURE 4.2.   Picture of students and teachers who participated in the October 1952 performances at Bacheng High School commemorating the sixteenth anniversary of the death of Lu Xun. At this event, students recited excerpts from Lu Xun's writings and performed a skit based on his novella *The True Story of Ah Q*. Personal collection of Liang Yingming.

Reflecting on the Red-versus-Blue confrontation, Liang Yingming remarked: "The two sides had different political beliefs. Both sides loved China. One side loved the PRC; the other the ROC. One side believed that socialism could save China; the other believed that Sun Yat-sen's Three Principles of the People could save China. These ideological differences used to define the line between the two blocs. Now people no longer care."[104] Throughout the 1950s, the confrontation between the pro-Beijing and pro-Taipei blocs dominated the communal life of the totok Chinese in Indonesia, permeating the realms of media, civic associations, and education and taking forms ranging from debates in newspapers to street fights among teenagers. In the early 1950s, the improvement of China's domestic economic conditions reassured the overseas Chinese of the Communist government's credibility.[105] In the late 1950s, false reports on the Great Leap Forward gave them an unrealizable dream of prosperity. As a result, revolutionary nationalism oriented toward Beijing was on the rise among the totok Chinese.

In this intensely politicized atmosphere, some peranakan also hoped to maintain ties with China even though their national identification was with Indonesia. In a parliamentary speech in 1950, Siauw Giok Tjan, the leader of

Baperki and an advocate for the ethnic Chinese's integration into Indonesian society, nevertheless criticized the Indonesian government's ban on the Five-Star Red Flag. Siauw contended that "in no way could the problem be solved by forbidding Indonesian citizens from raising two national flags."[106] Ang Jan Goan, the president of the pro-Beijing Federation of the Chinese General Associations of Jakarta and the director of *Xin Bao*, believed that the diaspora could be racially and culturally Chinese while remaining good Indonesian citizens. Ang insisted that even after renouncing PRC nationality, they could still retain their Chinese identity and their connections with China.[107]

In the 1950s, the rhythm of the communal life of the pro-Beijing Chinese in Indonesia followed a political calendar synchronized with Beijing's. Under Ang's leadership, the Federation organized annual sports meetings among thousands of students from pro-Beijing schools in Jakarta for the PRC's National Day on October 1.[108] Anxious about the Communist influence, the Indonesian government would only allow amateur athletic competitions. The Xin You Society in Semarang held Children's Day celebrations on June 1 and Women's Day celebrations on March 8.[109] Ang recalled that pro-Beijing groups were not totally blind to the ethnic tension that these events might cause. In his memoir he wrote that, as part of the effort to "demonstrate

椰城愛國僑團參加慶祝第三屆國慶運動大會 1952 ★ 原子影社攝

FIGURE 4.3. The 1952 sports meeting in Jakarta commemorating the third anniversary of the establishment of the PRC. Students from pro-Beijing Chinese-medium schools were the main participants. Personal collection of Liang Yingming.

solidarity with the Indonesian people," the Federation organized similar celebrations on Indonesia's Independence Day on August 17, at which thousands of Chinese students would parade in front of the Presidential Palace
and perform Indonesian ethnic dances and songs for pribumi guests. But
these events "still aroused unpleasant feelings among Indonesian political
leaders and intellectuals," who were left with the impression that "the Chinese had lots of money to squander whereas the indigenous people were
living in poverty." Ang lamented: "It would have been better if the ethnic
Chinese celebrated in their hearts only."[110]

The following chapter will investigate how the Red-versus-Blue struggle
shaped the Indonesian government's impressions of the ethnic Chinese as
disloyal and destabilizing, culminating in its decision to impose restrictions
on Chinese-language print media, civic organizations, and education and to
declare that noncitizen ethnic Chinese were ineligible to operate retail businesses in the countryside. In the face of these discriminatory actions, the
opposed identities of "Red" and "Blue" were conflated into one category in
the eyes of the pribumi: the Chinese.

CHAPTER 5

Pribumi Perceptions of the "Chinese Problem"

In 1950, in a report to the attorney general, the Indonesian Prime Minister's Office described the conflicts between the pro-PRC and pro-Nationalist Chinese as "gradually increasing," "undesirable," and posing "threats to the peace of our society and our national security."[1] In North Sumatra, the local Office of Peranakan and Foreign Nationals Affairs (Kantor Urusan Peranakan Bangsa Asing) complained that the Red and Blue blocs were given "too much freedom." As foreign "guests" (*tamu*) of Indonesia, the Chinese needed to be strictly controlled because they disrespected the laws and regulations of their host country.[2] In 1958, the year the pro-Beijing bloc secured the dominant position in most totok Chinese communities, a pamphlet entitled *The Chinese Problem in Indonesia* was published in Jakarta. The author, A. J. Muaja, argued that the issue was not that the pribumi wanted to stubbornly hold on to their prejudice against the ethnic Chinese. Rather, such discrimination was necessary because it benefited Indonesia's economic development.[3]

In this chapter, I will examine how the Indonesian government conducted surveillance of Chinese communities. Most of the archival material analyzed here consists of communications between the attorney general, the Prime Minister's Office, and local and national police. These agencies were largely occupied by anti-Communist officials in the early 1950s. For them, the

"Chinese problem" involved domestic issues such as ethnic relations, national integration, and economic equality as well as the security threats Indonesia faced in the Asia-Pacific.

As earlier scholarship has shown, although post-independence Indonesia allowed ethnic Chinese to acquire citizenship, a large number of pribumi continued to see them as culturally distinct and unduly wealthy.[4] The majority of the Chinese involved in commerce were peddlers and small-business owners, but they were seen as capitalists who exploited resources for their own enrichment. A letter from the Indonesian attorney general to the Prime Minister's Office dated October 1958 claimed: "The socioeconomic position of the ethnic Chinese is one of the causes of the overall socioeconomic problems in Indonesia."[5] Moreover, the PRC's quest for remittance and investment from the overseas Chinese spurred new anxiety about a capital drain from Indonesia. The Indonesian government launched policies that enabled the state to confiscate property owned by the Chinese in order to undermine their business presence.[6]

The rise in anti-Chinese sentiment in Indonesia through the 1950s corresponded with the escalation of the Beijing-versus-Taipei competition. There was significant variation in ideological orientation and levels of political awareness within Chinese communities in Indonesia. But, in the eyes of many pribumi elites, the Red, the Blue, and the apolitical Chinese all threatened to convert Indonesia to Communism. In reality, most of the activities labeled by the Indonesian authorities as "foreign interference" were actually low-level communal affairs unrelated to the PRC government. The Indonesian elites' fear of Communist subversion was most prominent on the Outer Islands. West Kalimantan had a large percentage of ethnic Chinese and shared borders with Sarawak, a British Crown colony that was experiencing a Chinese-dominated Communist uprising. In West Kalimantan, pribumi officials blamed the ethnic Chinese for the challenges they encountered in frontier security and immigration control. In Sumatra and on the Bangka-Belitung Islands, the ethnic Chinese were mostly engaged in plantation cultivation, mining, and small-scale agriculture.[7] This employment pattern led to the emergence of regional peasant and labor organizations. The Indonesian authorities interpreted peasants' and workers' movements in Sumatra and Bangka-Belitung as "an extension of the PRC," even though they were triggered by local land and labor disputes.[8] Contrary to the pribumi elites' beliefs, the majority of Chinese business ventures, associational lives, and political campaigns in Indonesia were not led, driven, or sanctioned by the PRC.

A Silent War: Indonesian Surveillance of Chinese Cultural Activities and Education

In a letter to the Indonesian National Police in February 1953, the attorney general referred to a report by the pro-Beijing Chinese-language daily *Da Gong Shang Bao* of Surabaya:

> At the Chinese-language school Sin Li, the school kids put on a play entitled "Liberate Taiwan and Capture Chiang Kai-shek Alive." The audience laughed so hard that their stomachs hurt. The child who played Chiang Kai-shek was surrounded by a group of boys. When the little "Chiang Kai-shek" was finally caught, the kid who played this role was so confused and embarrassed that he was almost in tears because he felt that he had become a traitor against his country.
>
> In this silent war [*perang tersembunyi*], something interesting happened. From the very beginning to the third act, one or two audience members, who appeared to be ordinary people, secretly left the theater.[9]

Why was a lighthearted theatrical performance by schoolchildren described as a war by the Chinese print media and why did such a seemingly insignificant report catch the attention of the attorney general? The mysterious audience members who left in the middle of the performance were actually undercover Indonesian National Police. The Chinese newspaper's reference to them at the end of the story was an implicit protest against Indonesian state surveillance of Chinese cultural activities. The Indonesian state might seem paranoid in the eyes of some readers, since the Chinese Nationalist government in Taiwan, rather than the Indonesian government itself, was the target of derision in the play. But the attorney general believed that cultural products from the PRC and homegrown Chinese cultural activities "propagated Communist ideology" and posed a danger to the "public order and safety" of the Indonesian nation.[10]

The Indonesian state elevated Chinese popular culture to a national security concern in the 1950s. At the time, PRC-produced songs, films, documentaries, and plays on themes such as land reform, the struggle against the Chinese Nationalist regime in Taiwan, and the military confrontation against the US in the Korean War spread to the Chinese communities in Indonesia. Moreover, the Indonesian attorney general was alarmed by the past use of socialist "mass art" by Soviet and Chinese Communists to politically mobilize the general population. In 1950 Radio Republik Indonesia surveilled "red songs" from China, and the Indonesian National Police compiled a list of "subversive music."[11] The Indonesian authorities also considered forcing Chinese-language cinemas to cancel the screenings of the PRC documentary *The Birth of New China* and *The Red Scarves*, a Soviet film dubbed into Mandarin that targeted young audiences.[12]

The Indonesian attorney general concluded that cultural performances adapted from the PRC but put onstage by the ethnic Chinese in Indonesia were the most "important, necessary, and challenging" kind of activity to monitor.[13] Technically, these performances were more difficult to record and analyze than songs or films because of the spontaneous interactions between the actors and the audience. Low-cost theaters were also more mobile. According to information gathered by the attorney general, during school holidays, left-leaning ethnic Chinese students would organize themselves into theatrical troupes and travel to remote inland areas to spread Communist internationalism through dances and plays. The attorney general estimated that "theatrical farces" like the one at the Sin Li School were "taking place throughout Indonesia." While the Indonesian authorities required that these performances be approved beforehand, the Chinese participants "seemed to show neither reservations nor regrets about not obtaining permission from the Indonesian government" and the Chinese-language newspapers freely published advertisements or reviews of these plays. At the time, the national status of the ethnic Chinese remained unsettled, which made it difficult for the Indonesian authorities to decide who among the performers and audience were under its jurisdiction. The Indonesian authorities were embarrassed that these performances were frequented by some high-ranking pribumi politicians, who would "clap to express happiness and enjoyment over things that they did not fully understand" and be "laughed at by the ethnic Chinese."[14]

In the classrooms of the Chinese-medium schools, day-to-day conflicts between the Red and the Blue were also closely watched by the Indonesian authorities. In April 1952, the police in Singakwang, Kalimantan, investigated an incident in which the ROC flag, the Indonesian national flag, and a portrait of Sun Yat-sen were all defaced with excrement at a pro-Taipei school. The main suspect was a boy named Ngui Fa Miau, who had allegedly entered "the crime scene" the night before the incident occurred and wrote with chalk "Down with the bald Chiang [Kai-shek]" on a desk.[15] In another case, a pro-Beijing teacher used corporal punishment with students who went to see an American movie. When the teacher asked them why they went to see the film, they reportedly shouted back: "Down with Mao Zedong!" According to reports by the Indonesian police, the schoolchildren were forced to walk on the sports field nonstop for three hours and were ultimately suspended from the school.[16]

The Indonesian Ministry of Education kept a detailed inventory of textbooks imported from the PRC to the pro-Beijing schools in Indonesia. These teaching materials could be roughly divided into three categories. The first group introduced Communism to young readers. The second group, which included maps of the PRC and texts on the nation's economic achievements— such as "Building A New Tibet," "The People's New Shanghai," and "The New Atmosphere of the Countryside in Lower Yangtze"—inspired nationalistic pride in a socialist China. The last group disparaged the US and the Nationalist government in Taiwan and included texts such as "We Will Hoist the Flag of Victory in Taiwan" and "How the American Imperialists Invaded China."[17] To the dismay of the Indonesian Ministry of Education, in the early 1950s many pro-Beijing schools spent a very limited number of teaching hours on Indonesian language, history, and geography, while, at the same time, one pro-Beijing school in Bandung managed to recruit a Soviet citizen to offer Russian language classes.[18]

Also disconcerting to the Indonesian authorities was the presence of the mass youth organization the Young Pioneers (shaonian ertong xianfengdui) at many pro-Beijing schools, most visibly in Sumatra. In the PRC, the Young Pioneers were, and still are, a youth division of the CCP. According to the attorney general, Ba Ren's successful political mobilization of the Chinese youth in Sumatra in the 1940s laid the foundation for the Young Pioneers' rapid growth in the region after Indonesia's independence.[19] In the early 1950s, it was reported that the Young Pioneers had developed an impressive membership and an "almost perfect organizational structure" in cities including Banda Aceh, Medan, Siantar, and Padang. Their routine activities included patrolling the neighborhoods near their schools and overseeing public safety at night. They made public appearances at ceremonies such as the opening of the PRC consulate in Medan.[20]

The attorney general found the culture of the Young Pioneers, which put great emphasis on hierarchy and discipline for children, to be very disturbing. The Indonesian authorities noted that in classrooms, at special events, and during outdoor excursions, the Young Pioneers wore their signature uniform of "crisp white shirts and bright red scarves," which was "a sign that the students were following a certain political ideology." Leaders of different ranks were appointed among the children and they could be identified by the number of white stripes on their armbands. Members would greet each other with the Young Pioneers salute, which consisted in bending the right arm and raising the right hand above the head, with all five fingers pressed together, symbolizing the "five loves": love of the motherland, love of the people, love of physical labor, love of science, and love of socialism.[21]

In light of the CCP's 1952 decision to dissolve its overseas branches, organizations like the Young Pioneers were more likely to be led by left-leaning leaders in Sumatran Chinese communities. But the striking similarities between the Young Pioneers in the PRC and Sumatra caused the attorney general to believe that these youth were mobilized by the PRC for the purpose of the Communist infiltration of Indonesia.

To exert more control over Chinese-language education, in 1952 the Indonesian government promulgated regulations regarding the education of resident aliens and established a special department for inspection purposes. The regulations required all the Chinese-medium schools to be registered with the Ministry of Education and bahasa Indonesia to be taught as a mandatory course at each school. In 1955 a new set of regulations stipulated that a minimum of four hours per week must be dedicated to instruction in bahasa Indonesia for students in the third grade and above and that over 25 percent of class time should be devoted to Indonesian history and geography for students in the fifth grade and above. In November 1957, the Indonesian government took legal action to restrict Chinese-language education to those who had rejected their PRC citizenship. In other words, ethnic Chinese students who opted for Indonesian citizenship were no longer allowed to attend Chinese-language schools. In addition, instructors at these schools had to pass a proficiency exam in bahasa Indonesia in order to receive a teaching certificate and a working permit.[22] After the crackdown on Taipei-sponsored regional rebellions in 1958, the Indonesian government banned all pro-Chinese Nationalist schools. The decision also affected some of the neutral or pro-Beijing schools despite their opposing political orientations.

In the realm of Chinese-language print media, the Indonesian authorities were highly concerned about left-wing newspapers such as *Xin Bao* and *Sheng Huo Bao* of Jakarta, the *Democratic Daily* of Medan, and *Li Ming Bao* of Pontianak. An Indonesian government report dated November 1950 enumerated the subversive activities of these newspapers, which included "encouraging both the totoks and perenakans to take PRC citizenship," "promoting the annual PRC National Day celebrations," and "facilitating the ethnic Chinese youth's repatriation to China for educational purposes."[23] In December 1951, to maintain "the internal security of the state," the Indonesian attorney general started prosecutions against *Xin Bao*, *Sheng Huo Bao*, and the *Democratic Daily*.[24] But pro-Taipei newspapers such as *Tian Sheng Ri Bao*, which had been conducting parallel propaganda campaigns on behalf of the Chinese Nationalist government, were not charged. *Sheng Huo Bao* accused the attorney general of unequal treatment of the two blocs and discrimination against "progressive newspapers."[25] However, outright confrontation counterproductively deepened the Indonesian authorities' antipathy toward the left-wing Chinese media.

Watching Over a Volcano: Indonesian Control of the Chinese on the Frontiers

In a letter to the attorney general in January 1953, officials from the Department of Education and Culture compared inspections of Chinese-medium education in West Kalimantan to "watching over a volcano that could erupt violently at any time."[26] According to their observations, "the schools in West Kalimantan indoctrinated students with teachings on the PRC and became centers of political activities for the interests of the PRC."[27] In the 1950s, Kalimantan—the Indonesian territories on the island of Borneo—had been under the very loose control of the central government in Jakarta. As with Sumatra and Sulawesi, the central government had provided few financial resources for development there while its authority had been constantly challenged, as shown in its inability to contain rampant smuggling.[28] J. A. C. Mackie has speculated that Jakarta's control of Kalimantan was probably even less effective than in Sumatra or Sulawesi.[29]

In the eyes of political leaders in Jakarta, the Chinese in Kalimantan used their economic advantages to maintain their autonomy, while completely disregarding the authority of the Indonesian state. Twenty percent of the population in the province of West Kalimantan, or around 315,000 residents in 1961, were ethnic Chinese.[30] Historically, the Chinese who had originally arrived as gold miners in West Kalimantan had created self-governing *kong-sis* independent from both the local Sultans and the Dutch.[31] After the gold mines were exhausted, they shifted to agriculture and later became dominant in rubber production. Although there had been Chinese settlements for centuries and the greater part of the Chinese population was locally born, the Chinese in West Kalimantan remained overwhelmingly Chinese-speaking.[32] The attorney general noted that after West Kalimantan became part of the newly independent Indonesian nation, many local Chinese were still unaware of the presence of the central government in Jakarta. The attorney general observed: "They do not understand the reality of the Indonesian government's jurisdiction nor do they acknowledge it. These ethnic Chinese behave as if they were living in part of China."[33] Provincial governmental departments and leadership roles of villages were allegedly "dominated by the Chinese"; non-Chinese civil servants dispatched from Java to the region were unable to understand the day-to-day functioning of local politics due to their lack of "training in Chinese language and Sinology courses"; and basic national symbols, such as the portrait of the president and the Indonesian national flag, were yet to be sufficiently popularized.[34]

The Chinese problem in Kalimantan appeared more acute in light of the left-wing movement in neighboring Sarawak, in which the ethnic Chinese played a central part. As in Sumatra, left-wing intellectuals who traveled from Mainland China to the region in the 1940s promoted Chinese-language education and publishing, nurturing a generation of Chinese youth who were politically conscious and sympathetic to the PRC.[35] In the post–World War II era, restricted employment opportunities led to discontent and frustration among these educated Chinese youth, many of whom participated in strikes and protests that were inspired by Communism.[36] In 1954 the predecessor of the Sarawak Communist Party, the Sarawak Liberation League, was formed. It recognized Marxism-Leninism and Mao Zedong's thought as its guiding philosophy and accepted organizational guidance from the MCP.[37] The dominance of ethnic Chinese in the Communist movement in Sarawak and its connections to the MCP and the PRC made Jakarta concerned about the possible rise of a Chinese-majority Communist movement in Kalimantan. The geography and demography of the borderland region made Indonesia's frontiers with Sarawak vulnerable. Kuching, the capital of Sarawak, was a little more than sixty kilometers from the Indonesian border and easily accessible from Pontianak, the provincial capital of West Kalimantan. The ethnic Chinese on both sides of the border were organically connected in terms of family ties, cultural roots, and trade relations. Many Chinese in West Kalimantan were also sympathetic to the PRC.[38] The Indonesian attorney general predicted that if the Communist movement achieved success in Sarawak, "it would quickly spread to Indonesia through a region as vast and easily penetrable as West Kalimantan."[39]

Jakarta was disturbed by the use of its porous frontier by the Communist movement in Sarawak to confront the British colonial government. Since the beginning of the Malayan Emergency of 1948, London had been determined to outlaw Communism. In Sarawak, the colonial government adopted draconian laws and measures to keep a tight rein on the "Communist influence" in Chinese-medium schools.[40] In response, many left-wing students and leaders of the Sarawak Liberation League escaped to the Indonesian side of the border to avoid arrest and rally support from the Chinese in West Kalimantan. In March 1952, the police in Sanggau, West Kalimantan, detained five ethnic Chinese, aged between seventeen and twenty-one, from Kuching. In the police report, the young men identified themselves as students from the Chung Hwa Middle School, one of the major hubs of the left-wing youth movement in Sarawak. According to them, one of their teachers and two of their schoolmates had already been detained by the British for their "sympathy toward the PRC." They fled to West Kalimantan out of fear of being arrested by the British authorities based on similar accusations.[41] While these Sarawak Chinese who crossed over to Indonesia could be directly deported, the Kalimantan Chinese who joined the Communist insurgency in Sarawak posed a much more complicated issue for Jakarta.[42] In December 1952, three to five hundred Chinese from West Kalimantan secretly entered Sarawak to rescue imprisoned Sarawak Communists. They attacked the Sarawak police with small arms, which were allegedly provided by Chung Hua Chung Hui of Singkawang. But they surrendered quickly because the promised assistance from Sarawak did not materialize.[43] During the attacks, two young female ethnic Chinese from Indonesia, Yang Chun Fang and Chung Fang San, escaped back to West Kalimantan but were later arrested by the Indonesian police in Pontianak.[44]

The involvement of Indonesian elements in acts of political violence on the borderland gave the Sarawak and Indonesian governments grounds to initiate joint efforts to crack down on the radical left-wing Chinese.[45] However, the attorney general recognized that tightened security measures against the Kalimantan Chinese gave rise to an atmosphere of "shock and terror" in the region, driving the local Chinese further away from identifying with the Indonesian nation.[46] Despite these negative repercussions, Indonesian officials believed that harsh measures were necessary given "the larger backdrop of international relations." According to the attorney general, the government of the Philippines had "announced that Indonesia would be a milestone for the spread of Communism in the region." Manila allegedly claimed that, after conquering the archipelago, "Communist agents could easily break into the Philippines from Indonesia via maritime routes."[47]

Due to their fear of the spread of Communism across Southeast Asia, political elites in Jakarta misinterpreted the issue of Chinese "dark immigrations" (*imigrasi gelap*)—a term used by the attorney general to describe illegal border crossings via land and sea by ethnic Chinese of various nationalities. Many of these Chinese were economic migrants and political refugees who were apolitical or anti-Communist. For instance, in the early 1950s, the socialist revolution and economic hardship in Mainland China pressured many Chinese, especially those who had previously been affiliated with the Chinese Nationalist Party and/or were members of the land-owning class, to seek their livelihood abroad via Hong Kong. In 1951 the immigration authorities of East Kalimantan deported eighty-one Chinese from Hong Kong who had illegally entered the region and tried to settle there, rescued forty-three passengers off a Hong Kong ship bound for Australia, and arrested the snakehead who had charged each passenger 2,000 USD.[48] In the same year, the police in Sumatra detained young Chinese males from Malaya who were fleeing conscription by the British.[49] The Indonesian authorities often regarded undocumented immigrants as potential agents of Communist subversion even though these speculations were hardly substantiated.

Pribumi Perceptions of Chinese Labor and Peasant Organizations

In 1945 the Chinese Labor Association in Belitung (Wulidong zhonghua laogong zonghui), consisting mostly of ethnic Chinese tin miners, was established. In 1948 the Overseas Chinese Laborer and Peasant Association of North Sumatra (Subei huaqiao gongnong lianhe zonghui, Gabungan Perserikatan Buruh Tani Tionghoa Diseberang Lautan Sumatera Utara) held its inaugural conference in Medan.[50] From the perspective of the Indonesian authorities, these organizations were the PRC's overseas extensions that aimed to envelop another vulnerable part of Indonesian territory in the worldwide Communist revolution. In 1953 the Indonesian attorney general claimed that Sumatra was likely "the number one area for Communist China's plan for dark politics [*politik gelap*]." Jakarta should be vigilant given the region's proximity to Malaya—where there was an ongoing Chinese-dominated Communist insurgency—and its substantial distance from the central government in Java, "which would be the last stronghold against Communist actions."[51]

Jakarta traced the development of Chinese labor and peasant organizations after World War II in Sumatra to Ba Ren's wartime legacy. Ba Ren's belief in a multiethnic alliance among the working class made the Indonesian government suspect that he had helped establish relations between the CCP and the PKI as well as SOBSI (Sentral Organisasi Buruh Seluruh Indonesia, All Indonesia Center of Labor Organizations). But officials admitted that they had no clue what the exact nature of the connection between these organizations was.[52] While, in the 1940s, left-wing Chinese youth under Ba Ren's guidance made efforts to reach out to the pribumi working class, there is no evidence to suggest that the Chinese and Indonesian Communist organizations substantially collaborated. Nevertheless, the intelligence analysts in Jakarta insisted that Ba Ren was a Comintern agent during his stay in Sumatra in the 1940s. The attorney general reminded the Indonesian president that, from the standpoint of the Comintern, post-independence Indonesia remained a "semicolonial country, an accomplice of imperialism," which must be "liberated" and transformed into a Communist state, peacefully if possible or violently if not.[53] In the attorney general's opinion, Ba Ren had laid the foundations for mass mobilization among the Chinese and pribumi working class in Sumatra, which could be used to "paralyze the government of Indonesia" and foment Communist revolution.[54]

The China Democratic League's branch in North Sumatra, established by Ba Ren and his fellow left-wing Chinese intellectuals during the Japanese occupation, was seen by Jakarta as the vehicle through which the Comintern and the PRC advanced their influence. The attorney general believed that, due to its history of serving as the intermediary between the Chinese Nationalists and Communists in Mainland China and the high percentage of intellectuals in its membership, the China Democratic League seemed "more liberal" and was thus able to "unify the petite bourgeoisie." But this appearance was a sly disguise, which "made it difficult to control." In reality, the China Democratic League was a "cover-organization of the CCP," whose orders it dutifully followed. It spread Communist ideology among the youth, and it achieved great success with its "red propaganda" that "changed people's spirits." According to intelligence gathered by the attorney general, although in the early 1950s Ba Ren was no longer its direct leader, the China Democratic League continued to expand from Medan and Palembang to Bagansiapiapi, Pulau Halang, Sinaboi, and Ujung Simbur. The attorney general was convinced that the China Democratic League had "deeply infiltrated" the pribumi labor and peasants' unions in Sumatra and that the two sides had been "working closely together."[55]

Similarly, the attorney general was concerned that the Overseas Chinese Laborer and Peasant Association of North Sumatra (hereafter referred to as "the Association") would allow the Chinese working class to forge interethnic and transnational alliances. Large portions of the Association's membership were coolie laborers on tobacco plantations while the rest cultivated farmland. At its first congregation in 1948 in Medan, the conference venue was said to be "decorated with the portraits of Sun Yat-sen, Karl Marx, and Mao Zedong."[56] The Association even requested permission from the North Sumatra government to allow its members to "wear hammer-and-sickle badges." It attempted, although unsuccessfully, to establish a collaborative relationship with the pribumi-dominated Joint Association of Peasants (Gabungan Persatuan Tani or "Gaperta"). The Association was believed to be in contact with the Port Workers' Union in Belawan (Serikat Buruh Pelabuhan Belawan) and to have donated money and food to a strike it had organized in February 1950. The Association's openly stated commitments included "building connections with laborers and peasants and the progressive people in the independent countries of the Far East." It demonstrated its internationalist spirit by dispatching a telegram to Kim Il Sung expressing moral support at the start of the Korean War and by initiating labor strikes in Sumatra in solidarity with the automobile laborers in Hong Kong.[57]

The attorney general believed that the overseas Chinese's alleged collaboration with indigenous Communist elements was part of a larger scheme masterminded by the Comintern and the PRC. In Java, the Pemuda Rakyat (People's Youth) under the PKI was described as enjoying a cordial relationship with the pro-PRC Chinese, who assisted the former with fund-raising and the logistics of mass meetings.[58] Moreover, the PKI reportedly received instructions from the PRC diplomatic mission.[59] But the Indonesian attorney general had probably exaggerated the CCP's leverage over its Indonesian counterpart and was misinformed about the role of the ethnic Chinese in the PKI. As the first Communist Party in Asia, the PKI's history went back to 1914, when the Dutch Marxist Hendricus Sneevliet founded the Indies Social Democratic Association (Indische Sociaal-Democratische Vereeniging, ISDV). The ISDV was reorganized into the Partai Komunis Indonesia (PKI), or the Indonesian Communist Party, in May 1920. Under the alias "Maring (Ma Lin)," Sneevliet later served as a Comintern representative in China and attended the first congress of the CCP, held in July 1921 in Shanghai.[60] In the 1920s and 1930s, some high-ranking PKI leaders, such as Alimin bin Prawirodirdjo, studied for brief periods in China, including the Red Capital, Yan'an.[61] Despite transnational connections to China and its participation in the Comintern's Asian activities since its early days, the PKI held firmly to its own understanding of the proper path to power in postcolonial Indonesia. The party was committed to working within the existing political system, a stark contrast with the Maoist practice of seizing power by force. Moreover, after D. N. Aidit purged Tan Ling Djie (Chen Linru), ethnic Chinese were excluded from the leading cohort of the PKI, which could be interpreted as part of the PKI's strategy to present itself as a nationalist party rather than a proxy of "red China."

The Indonesian authorities seemed to be blind to the difference in goals between the Indonesian Communists and the PRC. Whereas the PKI aimed to increase its political power via peaceful participation in parliamentary politics, Beijing's mission in Indonesia was to consolidate its status as the sole legitimate representative of China. According to the testimony of a former underground CCP member, the CCP's undercover operations in Indonesia focused mainly on opposing the Chinese Nationalists and barely overlapped with the core agenda of the PKI.[62] The CCP's clandestine organizations in Jakarta had no connection with the PKI or PKI-affiliated organizations such as SOBSI or Pemuda Rakyat.[63] Similarly, the China Democratic League's branches in Southeast Asia were established mainly to counter the Chinese Nationalist influence.[64] In 1953, on orders from Beijing, the China Democratic League closed all its branches in the archipelago to quell the Indonesian government's suspicions and smooth the way for the improvement of bilateral relations.[65]

Moreover, the Indonesian authorities wrongly believed that Beijing intended to transplant its own approach of gaining power through the mass mobilization of peasants and workers to Indonesia. According to the Indonesian attorney general, in January 1953, the Overseas Chinese Laborer and Peasant Association of North Sumatra organized a large-scale protest involving hundreds of ethnic Chinese peasants in Binjai (also spelled Bindjei), a town near Medan.[66] The attorney general described the protest organizers as "agents and agitators of Communist China" who had received "instructions from the PRC government in Beijing." Their activities were "dangerous" and "beyond the control of the Indonesian government."[67] The peasants involved were reacting against the provincial government's decision to forcefully relocate them to make space for an agricultural experiment.[68] More than half of them were unable to provide documents to validate their legal residence in Indonesia and thereby could not be recognized as Indonesian citizens. The local authorities thus denied them land ownership and accused them of farming "illegally."[69] The attorney general admitted that the affected ethnic Chinese peasants, eager to protect their land from confiscation, turned to the Association for support even though they were "not necessarily attracted by the ideologies of the PRC." The leaders of the Association, who neither farmed themselves nor cared about the interests of the peasants, "exploited" the situation to transform these peasants "into people of the PRC who were loyal to their homeland."[70]

Similarly, the Indonesian authorities found that the advocacy of the Chinese Labor Association in Belitung, where the majority of Chinese worked in tin mines, resembled the mobilization of the proletariat during the Chinese Communist Revolution. According to the attorney general, this association's monthly Chinese-language publication, the *Voice of the Workers* (*Gongsheng* or *Kung Sheng*), encouraged its readers to "engage in the great struggle against the capitalists."[71] In early 1951, the *Voice of the Workers* published an article on the Marxist theory of the creation of man by human labor. The publication attracted criticism from local Christian groups, who later filed a lawsuit against the *Voice of the Workers* for its "disrespect for other people's religious beliefs by insulting God" and its "ill intention against and disdain for the Indonesian government."[72] Under pressure from the local Chinese, the Belitung court ultimately abandoned the case. In his commentary on this incident a year later, the editor-in-chief of the *Voice of the Workers*, Zou Fangjin, scorned his prosecutors by calling them "the so-called sons and daughters of god" and "accomplices and lapdogs of the imperialists who were involved in all kinds of wicked deeds." He ridiculed the lawsuit by naming it "the Monkey Litigation" (*yuanhou susong*), a term meant to mock the religious group for their unwillingness to acknowledge Darwin's theory of evolution. In his writing, Zou quoted an editorial in the CCP's *Liberation Daily* (*Jiefang Ribao*): "Once blind faith in god is shaken, the blind faith in the exploitative ruling class will be shattered as well."[73] In 1953 the Belitung police requested that the central government in Jakarta "expel the PRC editors and agitators" of the *Voice of the Workers* from Indonesia.[74]

While the Indonesian authorities' concerns were justified, the political elites in Jakarta were probably mistaken about the PRC government's direct involvement in ethnic Chinese peasant and labor organizations in Indonesia. In its early years, under the influence of a radical foreign policy, the PRC mobilized the overseas Chinese against the Chinese Nationalists. In her speech to the overseas Chinese worldwide on the third anniversary of the establishment of the People's Republic, He Xiangning, the chairwoman of the Overseas Chinese Affairs Commission, called upon all ethnic Chinese to get rid of the influence of the "Chiang bandits," who were "the most devious enemies" and the "cause of suffering" for the overseas Chinese.[75] Yet, with a shift toward a peaceful stance in foreign affairs in 1952, the PRC government reversed this policy. Although Beijing still wanted to decrease the pro-Taipei groups' influence, it ceased to support the political campaigns of pro-Beijing groups in Indonesia in order to maintain stable state-to-state relations with Jakarta. Therefore, it is unlikely that the activism of either the Overseas Chinese Laborer and Peasant Association of North Sumatra or the Chinese Labor Association in Belitung was under the supervision of Beijing. These organizations seem to have been an organic outgrowth of the PRC's earlier strategy of proactively expanding influence vis-à-vis Taipei. Local pro-Beijing individuals continued to make aggressive advances while the PRC adopted a pragmatic and moderate attitude toward overseas Chinese affairs between 1952 and 1955.

Pribumi Perceptions of Chinese Traders and Business Owners

At the Round Table Conference of August 1949, Jakarta formally declared that its economic policy was to favor "economically weaker groups." In post-independence Indonesia, ethnic Chinese faced state-led policy initiatives designed to weaken their economic influence in sectors such as trade, transportation, finance, and manufacturing. The Indonesian government believed that undermining the ethnic Chinese would spur participation by the "indigenous Indonesians" (*bangsa Indonesia asli*) and accelerate the "Indonesian-ization" of the economy.[76] Against this backdrop, a series of discriminatory measures were implemented in the early 1950s. The Benteng System (*sistem Benteng*) was introduced in 1950 to protect pribumi importers. A second regulation, launched in 1954, required all rice mills owned by individuals with foreign citizenship to be transferred to pribumi. Since Indonesian citizens of Chinese descent were still technically dual nationals, the regulation also affected them.[77] Additionally, according to the PRC embassy in Jakarta, there were at least fifty cases of expulsion of ethnic Chinese from Indonesia in 1954. Before forcing the ethnic Chinese out of Indonesia, the Indonesian government deliberately detained them under grim physical circumstances.[78] However, these regulations failed to create a viable indigenous entrepreneurial class due to the pribumis' lack of preparation, opposition from the Chinese, continuing inflation, and corruption.[79] In many cases, the indigenization only benefited officials from the Indonesian government or the military, who enhanced their personal wealth through the confiscation of Chinese businesses.[80]

The limited success of Indonesianization gave rise to frustration among the indigenous business class and led to more severe discrimination against the Chinese.[81] In the mid-1950s, some pribumi political elites started disseminating racist messages to the general public by accusing the Chinese of being "an exclusive group that only looked after its own interests in an egotistical and materialistic manner."[82] In July 1956, Assaat Datuk Mudo, a businessman and politician, urged the government to protect the economic position of the pribumi through preferential treatment. He said: "Native Indonesian citizens must receive special protection in all their endeavors in the economic field, from competition by foreigners in general and the Chinese in particular."[83] At the time, Taipei's support for regional rebellions in Sumatra and Sulawesi provided the Indonesian authorities with a perfect opportunity to unleash systematic anti-Chinese actions. The policies of National Vigilance (*Kewaspadaan Nasional*) and Guided Economy (*Ekonomi Terpimpin*), both promulgated in 1958, empowered the Indonesian state to seize the wealth and property of Chinese Nationalists and to curb the Chinese presence in fields such as light industry, import and export, and retail.[84] Officially, the two policies could only be applied to property related to "the subversive activities of the Chinese Nationalists." But the measures taken against the pro-Taipei Chinese soon expanded into a full-fledged campaign against the entire Chinese community.

Although Beijing's official propaganda blamed the Chinese National-ist government and the pro-Taipei Chinese in Indonesia for all improper economic behavior, the pro-Beijing Chinese merchants in Indonesia also engaged in smuggling in collaboration with the largely anti-Communist Indonesian army. In August 1958, the Ministry of Foreign Trade in Beijing issued a strongly worded warning to some "patriotic" or pro-PRC Chinese businessmen involved in the large-scale smuggling of arms as well as con-sumer goods such as silk, mosquito nets, porcelain, and canned food from Singapore.[85] The PRC commercial attaché in Jakarta believed that this was extremely risky: "The Indonesian people will strongly oppose such secret dealings once they are exposed to the public. In that case, the ethnic Chi-nese businessmen will become the scapegoat and our government will suf-fer tremendous political damage."[86] As noted in previous studies, during the Indonesian National Revolution, Chinese traders used to work with Indone-sian army officers to smuggle in goods and currency from Singapore across blockade lines imposed by the Dutch.[87] This partnership may have continued into the 1950s. Like in the past, the pro-Beijing businessmen probably sought the army's protection by sharing their smuggling profits. Their pragmatism allowed them to flexibly move back and forth across ideological divides. Bei-jing's concern about potential political repercussions suggests that the PRC diplomatic mission had limited control over the economic behavior of even the PRC-oriented Chinese.

But, for the Indonesian authorities, the ethnic Chinese in Indonesia were not diverse and autonomous entities but pawns used by Beijing to fulfill its own economic needs. They saw the PRC's Overseas Chinese Affairs Com-mission as being responsible for extracting money from the overseas Chi-nese.[88] According to the attorney general, some of the commission's major goals included selling " 'victory bonds' via the Bank of China," attracting overseas Chinese investment by organizing "homecoming tourist groups," and strengthening the financial connections between the overseas Chinese and their native places."[89] Into the late 1950s, the attorney general insisted that, in light of the economic difficulties caused by the Great Leap Forward, the Second Taiwan Strait Crisis, and the intensification of the situation in Indochina, the PRC was "looking for ways to increase remittances from overseas Chinese communities all around the world, especially in Southeast Asia."[90] Although the Indonesian government had already imposed restric-tions on the outflow of remittances from ethnic Chinese, Jakarta received intelligence reports suggesting that money was being transferred to the PRC via illegal channels and exchanged from Indonesian rupiah to Hong Kong dollars on the black market.[91] Moreover, the PRC government was reported to have told the Chinese in Indonesia about methods to quickly and safely transfer their capital out of Indonesia in order to prevent financial loss if the Indonesian government took further anti-Chinese measures.[92] The anti-Communist Indonesian political elites recognized that the capital owned by the ethnic Chinese, which had been critical to the well-being of the Indonesian economy, was "hot money" with remarkable international mobility.[93] Their concern with Chinese economic power took on more urgency given the possibility of Chinese capital being drained by the PRC.

In December 1951, an anonymous letter, handwritten in Mandarin Chinese, was sent to President Sukarno:

> Your Excellency President Sukarno,
> I do not know for sure if Indonesia remains a semicolonial country or is still formally colonized by the Dutch. I'm saying this because Indonesian Customs and all other governmental agencies are still using Dutch in their official communications, as if this country is still ruled by the Dutch. Why wouldn't they use the written language of their own country? This is difficult for people to comprehend. Does Your Excellency think so? Please explain the reasons in detail in the newspapers for me. Please forgive me for bluntly raising these questions.[94]

This letter, signed by "a citizen of the People's Republic of China," could have struck Indonesian authorities as an echo of Ba Ren's characterization of post-independence Indonesia as a "semicolonial country" that had only achieved an incomplete social revolution. The Indonesian political elites may have been led to think that many ethnic Chinese, like this writer, had been indoctrinated by Beijing with the Marxist theory of social development and believed that they were obligated to facilitate Indonesia's progress toward a Communist society. This letter—together with interactive Chinese-language theaters, a plethora of left-wing print media, revolutionary songs and textbooks from the PRC, and Chinese peasant and labor movements—perturbed the Indonesian authorities. The pribumi elites in Jakarta sensed that the ethnic Chinese posed a threat of systematic Communist infiltration by Beijing, even though the Chinese participation in the PKI was limited and the CCP had no substantial influence over its Indonesian counterpart.

The Cold War heavily influenced how the pribumi elites conceptualized "the Chinese problem." With Chinese-dominated Communist insurgencies unfolding in neighboring Malaya and Sarawak, pribumi policy makers feared that Indonesia would be the next domino to fall in Southeast Asia. Their heightened sensitivity distorted their perceptions. The Indonesian authorities saw all the spontaneous activism of the Chinese in Indonesia as part of Beijing's transnational mobilization. After its policy shift in 1952, Beijing likely disapproved of local activists' political engagement in Indonesia because it jeopardized both bilateral relations and the already precariously positioned ethnic Chinese. But all ethnic Chinese, from both the Left and the Right, educated and illiterate, were equally regarded by the pribumi elites as agents of a Communist state.

This conflation of different groups of ethnic Chinese produced a paradoxical image of them as simultaneously devout Communists and shrewd businessmen who had caused the poverty of the pribumi and impeded the growth of the Indonesian national economy. In May 1959, two Indonesian government decrees precipitated a turbulent time for the Chinese minority. The first was a Ministry of Trade regulation, which announced that the trading licenses of alien residents in rural areas would be revoked by December 1959. The second was a decree enabling regional military commanders to remove aliens from their place of residence for "security reasons."[95] Six months later, Sukarno promulgated Presidential Decree No. 10, which required the suspension of all Chinese retailers' business activities in rural areas by January 1, 1960, and legitimized the takeover of foreign enterprises by indigenous merchants.[96] The next chapter, which shifts to the perspective of Chinese foreign policy decision makers and practitioners, examines Beijing's response to the 1959–60 anti-Chinese crisis in Indonesia.

CHAPTER 6

The 1959–1960 Anti-Chinese Crisis

Presidential Decree No. 10, launched by Sukarno in 1959, marked the beginning of large-scale, government-led economic actions against the Chinese minority in Indonesia. The New China News Agency or NCNA (xinhua tongxunshe) quoted Siauw Giok Tjhan's estimate that at least three hundred thousand ethnic Chinese would be forcibly removed from their homes.[1] By January 1960, 83,793 Chinese-owned businesses in rural areas had been shut down and taken over by the indigenous people.[2] In December 1959, Beijing began to call the ethnic Chinese in Indonesia back to China. By the summer of 1960, around sixty thousand ethnic Chinese had left the country; their repatriation cost the PRC government approximately 40 million USD.[3] When Beijing suspended the repatriation program due to the heavy financial burden it imposed, some deeply disappointed ethnic Chinese menaced PRC diplomats in Indonesia with big wooden sticks and threats of collective suicide by jumping into the sea. An ethnic Chinese who "either pretended to be insane or genuinely suffered from mental illness" had an emotional outburst at the PRC consulate in Jakarta and refused to leave.[4] In Beijing, Foreign Minister Chen Yi berated the Indonesian ambassador Soekardjo Wiriopranoto, saying: "In the entire world, only Indonesia uses its military against the ethnic Chinese. Even the US has not done such a deed."[5] By the end of the crisis, at least 102,000 ethnic Chinese had left Indonesia for the PRC.[6]

During this migration crisis, high politics on both the national and international levels intersected with the lives of the Chinese in Indonesia. The Indonesian government's anti-Chinese acts had their origin in long-standing ethnic tensions but were directly triggered by Taipei's aid to regional rebellions against the central government in Jakarta. Although the Chinese Nationalists were the main targets, all the ethnic Chinese were subject to discriminatory policies. Additionally, the PKI gained popularity. Its success led to retaliation against the PRC, the Indonesian Communists' perceived foreign patron, and the ethnic Chinese, their alleged domestic sponsors.

Beijing's response to the 1959–60 crisis in Indonesia was restrained.[7] Indonesia under Sukarno's leadership was crucial to the PRC's "intermediate zone" strategy, which focused on cultivating solidarity with Asian and African countries. In a series of meetings with Indonesian diplomats in late 1959 and early 1960, Chen Yi emphasized that the Chinese Communist leadership did not prioritize the interests of the overseas Chinese over its diplomatic ties with Jakarta. Instead, the PRC's primary goal was to advance friendly relations between Beijing and Jakarta while assisting Indonesia with its economic development.[8] Underneath its reconciliatory attitude, however, Beijing was profoundly dissatisfied that the Indonesian government had singled out the ethnic Chinese while condoning Western exploitation.

During the crisis the boundaries between the domestic and the international became highly permeable, which created both opportunities and challenges for Beijing. In 1959 the Sino-Indonesian Dual Nationality Treaty was not yet in effect due to a delay in legislative procedures in Indonesia. The unresolved national status of many ethnic Chinese and the close ties between the PRC embassy and consulates and the pro-Beijing Chinese community made it difficult for PRC diplomats to approach the crisis from a detached position and solely via governmental channels. On the one hand, the PRC diplomatic mission in Indonesia used the economic power and collective action of the pro-Beijing Chinese to influence Indonesian policy makers. On the other hand, the PRC diplomats faced pressure from the persecuted ethnic Chinese, who looked to them for protection and repatriation. But the Chinese government would admit only a limited number of refugees due to the country's destitute economic situation after the Great Leap Forward. To avoid an eruption of anti-PRC feeling, Beijing instructed its diplomats in Indonesia to "channel the dissatisfaction of the ethnic Chinese toward the Indonesian government" through careful "persuasion by cadres." But emotional protests continued; in Sulawesi, ethnic Chinese congregated at the Port of Makassar even though they knew that the ship bound for the PRC had already been cancelled by the Chinese consulate.[9]

The PRC's mobilization of the diaspora advanced its national interests but made the ethnic Chinese more vulnerable. Ultimately, PRC foreign policy decision makers and practitioners took advantage of shifts in Indonesian domestic politics to de-escalate the tension.

Beijing's Strategic Considerations

The period from the early to mid-1960s was a time of domestic tumult and international challenges for the PRC. As part of their critical reevaluation of domestic and international policies after the Great Leap Forward, the Chinese leadership established a principle of "actively opening up a new horizon in foreign relations" (*nuli zhudong di zai waijiaoshang kaituo xin de jvmian*).[10] This moderate approach to foreign affairs set the tone for China's cautious handling of the 1959–60 anti-Chinese crisis. Furthermore, as the Sino-Soviet alliance was coming to an end, Beijing began to shift its attention to Afro-Asian nations that could potentially be new partners in an international front against both superpowers. China's perception of the newly independent countries had its origins in Mao's concept of the "intermediate zone" (*zhongjian didai*), a buffer between the two superpowers, which included many capitalist, colonial, and semicolonial countries in Europe, Asia, and Africa.[11] Indonesia played an important role in the PRC's strategy in the intermediate zone in the early 1960s. Sukarno's vigorous campaigns challenging the existing international order made him a highly desirable candidate in China's anti-imperialist united front. Using the standard Marxist analytical lens, the Chinese Foreign Ministry categorized Indonesia as a "bourgeois nationalist" country, whose socioeconomic system was different from the PRC's.[12] But the Chinese leadership openly stated that Sukarno's socialist plans were of the same nature and quality as China's development model. As Chen Yi said to Subandrio, the Indonesian foreign minister and first deputy prime minister: "Ask the Soviets: What is socialism? Should it be the British Labor Party's socialism? Or the Vatican's socialism? Or Khrushchev's socialism? Or Lenin and Stalin's socialism? Or Mao Zedong's socialism? Which is it? President Sukarno firmly opposes imperialism and colonialism. Anti-imperialism and anticolonialism will become socialism in the future! If one wants to build socialism, learn from Sukarno's socialism."[13]

For policy makers in Beijing, the overseas Chinese issue was "only a small problem" in comparison to the importance of maintaining friendly relations with Indonesia, a sizable and populous country strategically located in the Asia-Pacific. Its international status was also on the rise after the Afro-Asian Conference of 1955.[14] While meeting with Ambassador Soekardjo

Wiriopranoto for a discussion on Indonesia's anti-Chinese measures and newspaper reports that "humiliated the respectful leaders of China," Chen Yi expressed a sense of disappointment instead of making outright accusations. If anti-Chinese actions had taken place in the US or in US-allied countries in the Third World, the Chinese leadership would not be surprised. "But a friendly country like Indonesia, which shares the same fate with us, is now carrying out an anti-China agenda. We are inevitably concerned and worried."[15] When receiving the diplomatic credentials of Soekardjo's successor Sukarni, the PRC president Liu Shaoqi downplayed the anti-Chinese crisis as a temporary situation that would not have a long-term impact on the friendship between the two countries.[16]

To demonstrate goodwill and facilitate reconciliation, PRC leaders exonerated the Indonesian government from any blame for discriminatory acts by putting the responsibility squarely on the US. Chen Yi declared to Ambassador Soekardjo Wiriopranoto: "Southeast Asian and Afro-Asian countries are not our enemies. Our enemies are mainly the US and the reviving Japanese militarism that is assisted by the US."[17] Chen Yi contended that rising antagonism toward the PRC in countries such as Indonesia, India, and Burma could be understood as a cover (*huangzi*) for the American plot to spread the Cold War in Asia by driving a wedge between formerly colonized countries. During a meeting with the Indonesian ambassador in December 1959, Chen Yi asked Soekardjo to pass on the following words to Sukarno: "Vigilance against the imperialists' conspiracy to impair Afro-Asian unity is very important."[18] According to Chinese policy makers, the most powerful weapon for crushing the American imperialists' virulent scheme was the further strengthening of Third World unity.

Beijing's Understanding of the Anti-Chinese Crisis: Three Sources of Tension

The anti-Chinese crisis began with the Indonesian government's 1958 ban on Chinese Nationalist Party organizations and affiliations in retaliation for Taipei's support for secession movements in Sumatra and Sulawesi. China, hoping that this would be a narrowly focused campaign targeting only the pro-Taipei elements, initially announced its full support. While visiting Beijing in October 1959, Subandrio requested an exchange of intelligence with Beijing regarding the economic, political, and military activities of the "Chiang bandits."[19] In early 1960, while speaking with Ambassador Soekardjo, Chen Yi announced: "There is an extremely small group of people among the overseas Chinese who oppose the Indonesian government while supporting the rebels. They also oppose China. We have no issue with you outlawing these people. We only wish that you would impose the ban on them more powerfully and more thoroughly."[20] However, the anti-Taipei campaign soon developed into a nationwide anti-Chinese action that affected the pro-Beijing factions as well as the ethnic Chinese who had already chosen Indonesian citizenship.

Viewed more broadly, the crisis was a reflection of the tug-of-war in Indonesian domestic politics between the Left, namely the PKI, and the Right, which included the Indonesian army and Islamic parties, such as the Nahdlatul Ulama or the NU (Awakening of Religious Scholars). According to the PRC embassy in Jakarta, right-wing individuals in the army were the ones who used the "anti–Chiang Kai-shek slogan" against all the ethnic Chinese in Indonesia in the name of safeguarding "national and social security" (minzu shehui zhi'an).[21] Quite a number of senior army officers had benefited personally from the nationalization of enterprises and property owned by the Chinese Nationalists, and they wanted to further profit by taking over more Chinese assets.[22] Moreover, under Guided Democracy, Sukarno had to maintain a delicate balance between his relationship with the PKI on the left and with the army and Islamic groups such as the NU on the right.[23] The army accused the PKI, whose growth infringed on its own power base, of being a Trojan horse of the PRC.[24] Together with right-wing Islamic forces, the army intended to use the anti-Chinese crisis to pressure Sukarno into distancing himself from the PKI and China.[25]

The PKI leadership understood that if the party failed to respond to right-wing provocations, it would completely lose its ground in Indonesian politics. Njoto, the PKI leader, once said: "The reactionaries and treacherous elements thought relations between the PKI and the masses were loose. They believed that the masses suffered from chauvinistic thinking and could be easily manipulated. But what is the result now? The relations between the PKI and the masses did not, at any rate, become more distant. We can proudly announce: Not a single PKI member quit the party due to the issue related to the overseas Chinese problem."[26] Although the PKI supported the implementation of Presidential Decree No. 10 in principle, it insisted that the ethnic Chinese issue should be understood from the perspective of class rather than race. It suggested to the Indonesian government that the Chinese problem could be solved by granting equal rights to every Indonesian citizen regardless of racial origin. Harian Rakjat, the PKI's organ, also published several editorials condemning the Indonesian army's use of violence when enforcing the regulation in Chinese communities.[27] Beijing was satisfied with the PKI's response to the anti-Chinese crisis, affirming that it had "proactively supported our resistance against anti-Chinese movements."[28] In Beijing's propaganda, the PKI was presented as a faithful ally. The *People's Daily* reported that the PKI had criticized the army for not treating the Chinese with PRC citizenship as guests from a friendly foreign nation.[29] Aidit sarcastically enumerated the benefits of the expulsion of the ethnic Chinese: the PRC won manpower for its domestic economic construction and the popularity of the PKI increased due to the brutality of the Indonesian army's racist campaigns.[30]

From Beijing's perspective, the ethnic Chinese, a majority of whom were working class, were like "small fish" when compared with the Western enterprises that controlled Indonesia's economic destiny.[31] Borrowing the PKI chairman Aidit's metaphor, Beijing denounced the Indonesian government for "targeting the cats while avoiding the tigers."[32] In Sukarno's economic blueprint, the construction of a socialist economy would require the complete elimination of foreign control over Indonesian resources. Ambassador Soekardjo once told PRC leaders that the ethnic Chinese still regarded the politically independent Indonesia as the old colonial Dutch East Indies, where they could accumulate wealth through exploitative economic behavior.[33] Their businesses, therefore, represented a residue of colonial influence and needed to be taken over by the pribumi. Soekardjo denied that Presidential Decree No. 10 was inherently anti-Chinese. He claimed: "There is no anti-Chinese movement. But there are indeed anti-Chinese sentiments."[34] But an analysis by the Chinese Foreign Ministry argued the opposite: "Indonesia's anti-Chinese activities were carried out under the pretext of nationalization and the construction of an Indonesian-style guided economy with socialist characteristics. . . . The economic activity of the overseas Chinese is accused of being colonialist while the Chinese government's protection of the overseas Chinese's lawful rights and interests is accused of protecting capitalists and conglomerates. . . . Although Indonesia verbally announced that it was determined to fight for socialism, it was actually turning toward capitalist countries."[35]

Beijing estimated that, in Indonesia, residents of European descent, who at most made up 0.4 percent of the entire population, controlled 65 percent of the Indonesian GDP and would thus effectively determine the economic future of Indonesia. Residents of Asian descent, mostly ethnic Chinese, made up 2.2 percent of the population and controlled approximately 20 percent of the Indonesian GDP.[36] Beijing predicted that "sharp conflicts" would arise between the emerging "indigenous comprador bourgeois class" and the ethnic Chinese who were well-established in commerce and trade. These newly empowered pribumi businessmen "did not dare to touch the imperialist enterprises that were controlling the destiny of the Indonesian economy" but had no misgivings about taking over the property owned by the Chinese.[37] Chen Yi openly said to Soekardjo: "There are indigenous Indonesian capitalists who are involved in speculative activities and landlords who commit usury. There are Dutch, British, and American imperialist forces. Why is the Indonesian government only targeting the overseas Chinese?"[38] At a meeting with Ambassador Sukarni, the PRC president Liu Shaoqi protested Indonesian media reports that labeled the ethnic Chinese as "colonialists" and "imperialists."[39] Chen Yi said to the ambassador: "One cannot think of the overseas Chinese economy as the remnants of economic colonialism. Neither the Dutch nor the Japanese colonialists would encourage their nationals residing overseas to adapt to Indonesian society because these countries want to use their overseas population as a tool of invasion. But we will never do this. We want the ethnic Chinese to assimilate."[40] Chen Yi reprimanded Indonesia for being a bully that preyed on the weak Chinese minority while being meek toward Western powers.[41]

The Chinese leadership admitted that some ethnic Chinese "lived a better life than the indigenous people," "causing discontent" among the latter.[42] Beijing supported Jakarta's actions against a small number of "Chinese capitalists involved in speculative activities." As Chen Yi told Ambassador Sukarni: "In China, we also ban these people. We support the development of an independent economy in your country. . . . If you think some of them are not suitable to continue living in Indonesia, you can send them back to China for reeducation. We have already reeducated twenty million landlords and five million capitalists."[43] But a class analysis conducted by the PRC Foreign Ministry's research office concluded that "the majority of the overseas Chinese in Indonesia are working people [laodong renmin]." Some were laborers at oil refineries, rubber plantations, and tin mines, while others were peasants. The bourgeoisie constituted a mere 10 percent of the over two million ethnic Chinese in Indonesia.[44] Besides a small number of industrialists, the vast majority of this bourgeois class engaged in trade, such as large-scale import and export businesses. The report conceded that there was Chinese dominance of retail business in certain regions, particularly in the form of warung ownership and mastery of trade in rubber, tea, spices, coffee, sugar, forestry, rice mills, cigarettes, soda, soy sauce, soap, coconut oil, and textiles; the PRC analysts also acknowledged that the Chinese bourgeoisie "exploited the indigenous people to a minor degree." But "their labor and small businesses play a positive role in meeting the needs of indigenous people and stimulating the circulation of commodities in their localities."[45]

Petty traders and shopkeepers, rather than business tycoons, suffered the most during the anti-Chinese crisis.⁴⁶ In addition, laborers and peasants were also affected. On the Bangka-Belitung Islands, the Indonesian region with the largest amount of tin production and a long history of labor migration from China, mine owners took advantage of Presidential Decree No. 10 to dismiss elderly miners. This action angered the younger miners, who left for China in protest, triggering a precipitous drop in tin production.⁴⁷ Additionally, amid the chaos created by anti-Chinese legislation, some ethnic Chinese peasants, who were involved in coffee production in rural Bali, lost their land.⁴⁸

The Chinese minority residing in rural Indonesia were forced to abandon their homes and move to urban areas. The Indonesian military frequently resorted to violence during mass evictions.⁴⁹ In East Nusa Tenggara, the southernmost province of Indonesia, PRC diplomats reported that Presidential Decree No. 10 had caused a massive influx of impoverished rural ethnic Chinese to the provincial capital city, Kupang.⁵⁰ In Bogor, West Java, the local authorities used abandoned storage units at carpet factories, old rice mills, and the run-down offices of overseas Chinese societies to house the displaced and dispossessed ethnic Chinese. At one shelter in Bogor, ten families totaling seventy-seven people were assigned to one 17 by 8 square meter living room with a leaky roof, and no running water, toilets, or bathing or cooking facilities.⁵¹ The sudden influx of rural Chinese to the cities strained urban infrastructure and resources and escalated ethnic tensions. In the East Javanese port city of Surabaya, for instance, graffiti with slogans such as "Expel the Chinese" appeared soon after the arrival of ethnic Chinese from the countryside. Mobs yelled at the homeless ethnic Chinese: "You Chinese have protruding pig tails!"⁵²

When defending Presidential Decree No.10, Soekardjo explained that the suffering of the Chinese minority was a necessary sacrifice for Indonesia's economic reform. He told Chinese leaders that Indonesia could not embark on the path to independence and development unless the economic role of the ethnic Chinese was transformed from that of merchants to industrialists.⁵³ Chinese small-business owners could put their capital into government-led cooperatives to gain an annual interest of 9 percent. Yet, despite these attractive investment schemes, the ethnic Chinese's attitude was allegedly tepid due to their "mental obstacles" as they felt disappointed about "not being able to make exorbitant profits any longer." The ambassador predicted that "if the ethnic Chinese gradually switch from business to industry, after twenty to thirty years, the ethnic Chinese problem will disappear."⁵⁴

Yet, from Beijing's standpoint, the core issue underneath the 1959–60 crisis was not "mental obstacles" on the part of the Chinese, but Indonesian governmental policies that aimed to eliminate the economic presence of this ethnic minority all at once.[55] Beijing noted with disapproval that Jakarta had been "playing a two-faced game." On the one hand, Sukarno promised that he would create new opportunities for the ethnic Chinese through participation in Indonesia's industrialization. On the other hand, the Indonesian government "crashed the ethnic Chinese economy and wantonly infringed upon the freedom and safety of the overseas Chinese."[56] Both Zhou Enlai and Liu Shaoqi emphasized to the Indonesian ambassadors that most ethnic Chinese were small business owners with limited access to financial and technological resources and raw material. They could not make a steady transition from commerce to industry without assistance from the Indonesian government.[57] During an interview with journalists from the Antara News Agency, Chen Yi asserted that the measures the Indonesian government was using against the ethnic Chinese—outright confiscation—should only be applied to imperialist and colonial profits. These actions would not only cause damage to the ethnic Chinese but also lead to economic stagnation across Indonesia. Commodity circulation in rural Indonesia largely depended on Chinese traders and would be paralyzed in their absence. Chen Yi urged the Indonesian government to gradually integrate Chinese capital instead.[58]

PRC Diplomacy during the Anti-Chinese Crisis

In mid-1959, to "expand the momentum of our struggle," the Chinese Foreign Ministry instructed the PRC embassy in Jakarta to use the "politically reliable" and "left-leaning leaders of the Chinese community" to stage a popular resistance against the enforcement of Presidential Decree No. 10. Beijing recommended that the embassy and consulates encourage representatives from the Chinese business associations "to persistently appeal to Indonesian governmental agencies, expressing their anxiety and concerns." "In areas with favorable conditions," the peddlers and traders affected by Presidential Decree No. 10 should be organized by trustworthy cadres of the pro-Beijing bloc to make direct petitions to local economic authorities. If the Indonesian government still refused to give in, the PRC embassy and consulates could consider launching shopkeepers' strikes by urging ethnic Chinese traders to deliberately slow down their business.[59] Beyond the realm of commerce, the Foreign Ministry also urged its embassy in Jakarta to mobilize the pro-Beijing bloc for protests against the Indonesian Ministry of Education's decision to reduce the number of Chinese-medium schools as well as against the Jakarta municipal government's ban on signboards written in Mandarin Chinese. The Foreign Ministry demanded that this collective action be effective but, at the same time, remain low-key. While aiming to pressure Jakarta into ending the anti-Chinese campaign, Beijing hoped that the strikes and protests would not cause bloodshed or jeopardize the pro-Beijing cadres in the Chinese community.[60]

But Beijing's strategy backfired. Jakarta angrily accused PRC diplomats of stoking the ethnic Chinese's anger against the Indonesian state. In November 1959, West Java military authorities announced that some staff members from the Chinese embassy in Jakarta had traveled to the region and talked to the local residents. These "interventionist activities" by the PRC incited hostility among the local Chinese toward Indonesian law enforcement agents. As a result, the Indonesian government imposed a travel restriction on PRC diplomats.[61] The status, role, and function of the PRC diplomats in the middle of the anti-Chinese crisis had become so sensationalized in the Indonesian media that voices from the radical Right requested that the government pronounce Ambassador Huang Zhen to be a persona non grata.[62] The two sides came to an impasse. The PRC issued a strong protest, accusing the Indonesian government of violating the rights of its diplomats, which were protected by international law.[63] Meanwhile, Jakarta argued that the PRC diplomats' meddling in its domestic politics had escalated the Chinese problem.[64]

The multifaceted conflict involving the overseas Chinese, the PRC diplomatic mission, and Indonesian law enforcement culminated in the murder of two ethnic Chinese women in Cimahi, West Java, on July 3, 1960. The tragedy was described in contradictory ways by the PRC and Indonesian states. According to reports from PRC official media, the two victims were "innocent, unarmed overseas Chinese women" who were shot by Indonesian police and military personnel in the midst of a chaotic and violent eviction.[65] But a diplomatic note issued by the Indonesian Foreign Ministry to its PRC counterpart insisted that the military personnel and armed police fired out of self-defense because several ethnic Chinese women were beating, kicking, and biting them and threatening to grab their weapons.[66] The incident set off a chain of roaring conflicts. Thousands of ethnic Chinese petitioned the regional government of West Java. The Chinese embassy requested a thorough investigation. The Indonesian government turned down Beijing's plea while pointing a finger at "external incitement." A few days prior to the murders, the PRC diplomats Mao Xinyu and Huang Shuhai had visited the Chinese community in Cimahi. Moreover, a number of letters of protest put forward by the Chinese community resembled Radio Peking and pro-Beijing newspapers in terms of both content and wording. The Indonesian government was therefore convinced that "the ethnic Chinese's confrontational attitude was shaped by outside stimulation." The incident, the Indonesian Foreign Ministry concluded, was fundamentally caused by the PRC's encroachment on Indonesian sovereignty.[67]

Decision makers in Beijing had envisioned that their diplomats' interactions with the local Chinese could be carefully controlled so that the PRC's interests would be maximized while minimizing the negative impact on the ethnic Chinese. But, in reality, such a delicate balancing act was impossible to achieve during a time of international crisis. On July 12, 1960, the office of the General Association of Overseas Chinese in Medan became a mourning house. Beginning at eight o'clock in the morning, around five thousand local ethnic Chinese came to pay tribute to the spiritual tablets (lingwei) set up on behalf of the two women killed in Cimahi. Almost everyone wore black armbands and contributed flowers and incense. Many knelt down and cried aloud. Around 11 a.m., a dozen military and armed police arrived, demanding that the memorial ceremony end immediately. But the organizer refused to obey the order and more local ethnic Chinese arrived to pay respect to the dead. Infuriated by this resistance, the Indonesian military and armed police attempted to stop the event and disperse the crowd. In protest, three thousand ethnic Chinese marched to the provincial government office of North Sumatra. Communications between the Chinese Foreign Ministry and the PRC embassy in Jakarta suggest that a telegram from Beijing, which demanded that the funeral should "stop before going too far [shike erzhi]," failed to arrive before the outbreak of the incident. The Chinese Foreign Ministry and the Overseas Chinese Affairs Commission reprimanded the embassy in Jakarta: "The ethnic Chinese in Medan ignored the regulations and bans issued by the military authority of Medan and stoutly carried out mass memorial activities. The consequences were detrimental to our struggle in Indonesia."[68]

Repatriation and De-Escalation

In December 1959 Beijing started to call back displaced ethnic Chinese who could no longer make a living in Indonesia. When explaining the rationale behind this decision to Ambassador Soekardjo Wiriopranoto, Chen Yi said the PRC was not "putting on airs" (bai jiazi) but taking the initiative to "disperse the suspicions of a friendly nation." Chen Yi remarked: "The imperialists are spreading rumors that the overseas Chinese are China's fifth column planted in Afro-Asian countries. We will take the 'fifth column' back! Then this so-called obstacle to Afro-Asian friendship will no longer exist."[69] Chen Yi demanded that the ethnic Chinese be given the freedom to decide whether to stay or leave. If they chose to return to the PRC, they should be able to depart with dignity and goodwill toward Indonesia, instead of fleeing like criminals. Most importantly, they should be allowed to cash in their property in Indonesia and bring back their funds.[70] Chen Yi criticized the restrictions imposed by the Indonesian government, which prohibited the migrants from taking valuable belongings such as bicycles and watches. As a result, the ethnic Chinese were coming back to the PRC "as if they were naked." Chen Yi reprimanded the Indonesian government for "gaining little but losing a lot."[71]

On paper, Beijing claimed repatriation would be mutually beneficial to both countries, helping Indonesia solve the vexing problem of the ethnic Chinese while giving China human resources for economic construction. In reality, repatriation had complicated implications for both sides. For Beijing, the decision to call back the ethnic Chinese was both a sign of compromise and a means to put pressure on Indonesia. With the implementation of Presidential Decree No. 10, the flow of ethnic Chinese from the countryside caused chaos in Indonesian cities. While a temporary removal of the homeless Chinese would ameliorate tensions in urban Indonesia, their permanent departure would have severe consequences for the archipelago's long-term development. While Indonesia's commerce would be affected by a vacuum in the circulation of commodities in rural areas, the country's industry and agriculture, such as the tin mines in Bangka and Belitung and tropical produce farming in Kalimantan and Bali, would suffer from a labor shortage. For instance, in West Kalimantan, the provincial government feared that an exodus of ethnic Chinese peasants would cause its revenue from export products such as rubber and coffee to plummet.[72] In an attempt to prevent a loss of manpower, local authorities in Bangka and Belitung blocked a ship, which had been dispatched from the PRC, from docking. But this course of action backfired, as the infuriated miners became more convinced that "the strong motherland always has our back."[73]

Repatriation, with prohibitively high costs for refugee transportation and resettlement, was a double-edged sword that aggravated the PRC's economic difficulties during a time when widespread famine was causing tens of millions of deaths in China. Initially, Beijing tried to hold Indonesia accountable for cost sharing. In a meeting with Ambassador Soekardjo, Chen Yi insisted that the Indonesian government "should provide vessels" and the Chinese government would play a supportive role.[74] But, near the end of 1960, the Indonesian foreign minister Subandrio confessed to Ambassador Huang Zhen that using its foreign currency reserve to transport the ethnic Chinese would cause Indonesia's already frail economy to collapse.[75] In addition, while earlier groups of returnees were mostly students and professionals who could contribute to the PRC's economic growth, those forced out of Indonesia by Presidential Decree No. 10 were mostly working-class people in rural areas. The crisis pushed many of these ethnic Chinese to the verge of bankruptcy. According to the PRC embassy in Jakarta, by the end of September 1960, a total of 282,931 ethnic Chinese had registered for a one-way journey to the PRC. Among them, 89,421 had completed the necessary paperwork to depart from Indonesia and 24,161 had been waiting at Indonesian harbors for as long as four months. Many ethnic Chinese liquidated their property only to find out a few months later that they could no longer afford to purchase back their houses or stores due to skyrocketing inflation. Changes in the clothing and luggage of the returnees made PRC diplomats aware of the rapid worsening of economic conditions. Before the crisis, some well-off ethnic Chinese wore nice jackets, brought back bicycles and watches, and carried their belongings in leather suitcases. By September 1960, at the Tanjung Priok harbor of Jakarta, the diplomats saw suitcases replaced by recycled crates for transporting milk and parcels wrapped up with worn cloth.[76]

The financial burden of repatriation compelled the PRC to implement a new policy of "fewer evacuated, more staying" (shao che duo liu). Between July and October 1960, the PRC embassy and consulates in Indonesia ceased issuing passports, stopped dispatching ships, cancelled eleven commercial fleets bound for China, and dispersed the ethnic Chinese who had congregated at the harbors. The ultimate objective of the new policy was to help the ethnic Chinese regain faith in the Indonesian government and to enable them to earn their living in Indonesia. But the PRC diplomats felt as if they were trying to "crack open a heavy door tightly sealed by the Indonesian side."[77] In West Timor, Consul Zhang Yu launched a "fight to create job opportunities." The campaign failed to reverse a prevailing sense of hopelessness among the local Chinese, who saw no chance for stable employment. In the coastal town of Pemangkat, after the first batch of refugees left for the PRC, the emotions of the Chinese community in the entire province of West Kalimantan "started to boil." During a two-day registration period, over thirty thousand added their names to the list of returnees. Many ethnic Chinese peasants completely stopped agricultural production; they were ready to leave Indonesia at any moment.[78]

By the end of September 1960, over one hundred thousand Chinese had insisted on returning to the PRC despite the Chinese diplomats' continuous efforts to persuade them to stay. While a small number of ethnic Chinese with financial capabilities could arrange for their own passage, the majority had to depend on the Chinese government for transportation. But in 1960 China did not own any ocean liners nor could the Chinese government afford the exorbitant cost of renting foreign fleets. The Chinese government ultimately decided to purchase a retired British-built cruise ship for 260,000 GBP and named it *Guanghua*, which meant "to revive China."[79] The captain, comparing the ship to an elderly person, said that it was "an aged ship with lots of illnesses."[80] When the Beijing government purchased the ship, the onboard equipment, such as compasses and radio transmitters, was barely functioning. Water leaked through the cabins and the deck. Screws were loose and anchors rusted. The electrical outlets were worn out and the danger of fire loomed large. During its voyage from the Port of Constanța, Romania, to Guangzhou, the smokestack caught fire. After being refurbished in Hong Kong, the *Guanghua* started its first voyage to Jakarta in April 1961.

Yet, by the time the *Guanghua* had taken the ethnic Chinese back, tensions between Beijing and Jakarta had already started to ease. Around July 1960, Sukarno had adopted a more sympathetic stance toward the ethnic Chinese and a more reconciliatory attitude toward Beijing. The reason for this change was threefold. First, Sukarno wanted to alleviate the economic distress that anti-Chinese measures had intensified. The Indonesian economy was at a standstill as the circulation of goods was disrupted due to the lack of ethnic Chinese traders. A shortage of basic commodities necessary for daily life had overwhelmed rural Indonesia, causing popular discontent. Second, Sukarno decided to take a tougher stance toward the Indonesian army, particularly the US-supported general Adul Haris Nasution, the minister of defense. During his meeting with Ambassador Huang Zhen, Subandrio insinuated that the US would not tolerate friendly relations between Indonesia and China and would hate to see socialism realized in Indonesia under Sukarno. Subandrio revealed that Washington had been grooming Nasution in the hope that he would replace Sukarno.[81] To remain in power, Sukarno needed political support and economic aid from China. Third, in the international arena, contentious relations with China would harm Sukarno's reputation as the leader of the Afro-Asian countries and discredit his impassioned crusade against colonialism.

Beijing had long identified Sukarno as the key figure who could resolve the ethnic Chinese conflict. In an analytical report from summer 1959, the Chinese Foreign Ministry had already drawn "a clear division between the different approaches to the overseas Chinese issue among the ruling class in Indonesia":

The nationalist bourgeoisie, led by Sukarno, . . . intend to make use of the financial resources and labor of the Chinese for Indonesia's industrial development. They also care about maintaining friendly relations between the countries. Some dangerous elements in the army have aggressively attempted to create financial difficulties for the government through a series of anti-Chinese measures. They aim to gain a firmer control over the government and drive a wedge between China and Indonesia. . . . The struggle and tension between these two forces in the ruling class are still developing. Unless Sukarno steps up and intervenes directly, there will be tremendous difficulties with easing [the tension]. Our overall suggestion is that [we should] take advantage of these contradictions and treat [the two groups of forces] differently. [We should] continue to win over the forces that strive for de-escalation centered around Sukarno while exposing the localized incidents [of violence] committed by the Indonesian military.[82]

Around July 1960, Beijing detected Sukarno's intention to ameliorate bilateral tension and seized the opportunity to extricate itself from the crisis by adopting a carrot-and-stick strategy.[83] Keenly aware of Sukarno's ego, Beijing decided that, so long as Sukarno continued to "uphold the flag of anti-imperialism, anticolonialism, peace, and neutralism," it would refrain from publicly naming him as the culprit in the anti-Chinese crisis and target instead "the most reactionary Nasution group."[84] Chinese leaders frequently hailed Sukarno as an intrepid pioneer among the Afro-Asian countries and the sole leader capable of guiding Indonesia onto a healthy path to development. As Chen Yi put it: "Without the leadership of President Sukarno, chaos will engulf Indonesia."[85] The *People's Daily* cited Sukarno's speech at the inauguration ceremony of Ambassador Sukarni, in which the Indonesian president compared the ethnic Chinese controversies to "minor scratches on the skin, which would not cause any damage to the health of the body."[86] Beijing catered to the pompous Sukarno by investing hundreds of thousands RMB to print two editions of his art collections.[87] Moreover, Beijing offered a 30 million USD loan to Indonesia as well as assistance with the construction of a textile factory and the training of technicians. But, in light of the violence and discrimination against the ethnic Chinese, the Chinese government declared that it would be difficult to continue these generous gestures. Chen Yi said to the Antara News Agency: "We are in an embarrassing situation. We are providing you with economic aid whereas you are expelling the ethnic Chinese. It looks as if we are helping you to persecute the Chinese minority. How can we justify our actions to the thirteen million overseas Chinese all over the world?"[88] Yet, at the same time, in retaliation against Jakarta's accusation of Chinese diplomats' intervention in Indonesian domestic affairs during the crisis, Beijing, at the behest of Ambassador Soekardjo, arrested an Indonesian student in Tianjin on charges of espionage and later expelled him.[89]

Starting in fall 1960, the forceful relocation of the Chinese in Indonesia gradually ceased and Sukarno staged his typical charm offensive to repair relations with China. In his Independence Day speech on August 17, 1960, Sukarno emphasized that all "nonnative funds and forces" should be given proper opportunities to participate in the Indonesian economy so long as they were law-abiding and served a "progressive" purpose. No one should do harm to the "atmosphere of cooperation" that was essential to the realization of the nation's developmental goals.[90] In his speech at the UN on September 30, 1960, Sukarno demanded that the PRC's position be restored.[91] When Zhou Enlai expressed the PRC's gratitude for Sukarno's support to Ambassador Sukarni, he responded: "If anyone wants to create two Indonesias, we will staunchly oppose them as well."[92]

In summer 1961, Sukarno paid a state visit to China. During a meeting with Mao, Sukarno declared that he personally believed that "there is no 'ethnic minority' per se in Indonesia." He was opposed "not only [to] the view that considers ethnic Chinese as a minority, but also to the so-called conceptual distinction between 'aboriginal' and 'alien,' which was created by Assaat Datuk Mudo, who participated in subversive activities." Sukarno took off his hat and pointed out his black hair to Mao: "It is hard to tell whether I am an 'aboriginal' or not; perhaps I have Chinese blood in me. Who can tell?"[93] Despite Beijing's substantial investment in its relationship with Sukarno, it is likely that the Chinese leaders still saw the Indonesian president as savvy, or even manipulative. He was a "bourgeois nationalist" who used the ethnic Chinese issue as a pawn in a domestic power game and who sheltered himself from any responsibility for the anti-Chinese campaigns. "Sukarno's Ah Q mentality was quite remarkable," the PRC ambassador Huang Zhen once commented sarcastically in his report to Beijing, comparing Sukarno to the famously narcissistic character in Lu Xun's novella who chose not to face up to reality while rationalizing every one of his failures as a psychological triumph.[94]

Beijing saw Sukarno as simultaneously charismatic and unpredictable, powerful and vulnerable, friendly and untrustworthy. His pretentious aggressiveness toward Western powers in international politics was hypocritical, as he tolerated the right-wing's racist attacks on the Chinese while being too afraid to completely eradicate the Western economic presence in Indonesia. Nevertheless, the central leadership in Beijing was unwilling to sacrifice stable relations with Sukarno to protect the ethnic Chinese. In response to the Indonesian government's discriminatory policies, Beijing adopted a constrained and cautious attitude. During the crisis, PRC diplomats exhorted the ethnic Chinese to stage strikes and protests, hoping to bring pressure to bear on the Indonesian government. But these interactions between the diplomats and the diaspora touched a political nerve in Indonesia, causing the elites in Jakarta to fear the international reach of the Chinese state.

As we enter into the first half of the 1960s, China and Indonesia are experiencing a simultaneous radicalization of domestic politics and foreign policies. With fervent campaigns unfolding at home, both Beijing and Jakarta deny any possibility for long-term peace and stability in the international system. The following chapter will trace the transformation of a relationship plagued by the ethnic Chinese issue to a partnership full of passion, promise, and peril.

CHAPTER 7

The Ambivalent Alliance between Beijing and Jakarta

On October 14, 1963, at the Port of Zhanjiang in Guangdong Province, the *Guanghua*, the ship purchased by the Chinese government for refugee repatriation, was preparing for a different kind of voyage to Jakarta. Its mission was to safely transport 750 athletes from China, Vietnam, and North Korea to Indonesia to attend the first GANEFO, an alternative international sporting event set up by Sukarno in opposition to the Olympic Games.[1] Indonesia's rebellion against the International Olympic Committee (IOC) was triggered by the punishment it received for excluding Taiwan and Israel from the 1962 Asian Games in Jakarta. Affronted by the IOC's decision to suspend Indonesia from the Olympic Games for an indefinite period, Sukarno resolved to withdraw his country from the IOC altogether and start a new international sports organization that would be free from the "manipulation of the imperialists" and could "uphold the dignity of Indonesia and the Asian-African countries."[2] The PRC, who pressured Jakarta into banning Taiwan, gave its "fullest backing" to Sukarno's proposal, which would "contribute greatly to smashing the imperialist monopoly on international sports."[3] On the *Guanghua*, the PRC sent the largest delegation consisting of its top athletes, who would win the most medals at the first and only GANEFO.[4]

The *Guanghua*'s shifting role reflected the changing tenor of the relationship between Beijing and Jakarta. Between 1962 and the first half of 1965, ticket. Several days before the opening of the sports meet, despite the scorching sun, there were long queues of people waiting in front of the booking office. Those who failed to obtain a ticket lingered around the stadium hoping to pick one up there.

Brightly lit at night, the Bung Karno sports complex bustled with activity. All together, 70,000 residents of Djakarta did one sort of job or other for GANEFO. All this shows that the Indonesian people were enthusiastic and determined to make GANEFO a success. Among the huge slogans draped across Djakarta streets the most catchy and popular one was "Onward! No Retreat!" This is the slogan especially selected by President Sukarno for GANEFO.

FIGURE 7.1. "The First GANEFO." "Sportsmen from foreign countries to the first Game of New Emerging Forces warmly welcomed at Djakarta's Tandjang Priok," *China Pictorial*, Special Supplement (December 1963).

governmental relations improved dramatically after the anti-Chinese crisis of 1959–60. At the same time that the "great helmsman" Mao Zedong was steering his country toward the storms of the Cultural Revolution, Sukarno's public speeches were awash with metaphors of thunder and lighting, of volcanic fire and lava flows.[5] As the domestic and foreign policies of both countries took a sharp turn to the left, China and Indonesia forged a dangerously intimate bond. In the Asia-Pacific, Beijing was the most enthusiastic supporter of Sukarno's konfrontasi, a military campaign in Borneo to block the formation of Malaysia. Beijing envisioned that, thanks to Indonesia's opposition to Malaysia, North Vietnam's battle against the Diem regime in the South, and Thai and Filipino left-wing resistance to Western influence, the United States would soon be expelled from Southeast Asia by "a magnificent wave of anti-imperialist struggles."[6] In the broader Afro-Asian world, through a series of joint projects such as the GANEFO, the second Afro-Asia Conference (or second Bandung), and the proposal to replace the UN with the Conference of the New Emerging Forces (CONEFO), China and Indonesia joined hands to combat not only the Western imperialists but also the Soviets, who were seeking peaceful coexistence with the Americans.

Even when state-to-state relations improved, anti-Chinese movements subsided but never disappeared. In May 1963, shortly after Liu Shaoqi's historic visit to Indonesia, which was the first visit by a head of state of the PRC, a chain of anti-Chinese riots broke out in West Java. Unlike the government-led anti-Chinese acts in 1959–60, the attacks against ethnic Chinese in 1963 were eruptions of popular discontent sparked by economic conditions. Anti-Communist groups, who were anxious about the collaboration between Indonesia and China and the PKI's growing power, manipulated these public emotions and instigated the riots.[7] The PRC, mindful of the delicate position of the ethnic Chinese, encouraged them to contribute to konfrontasi financially to prove their loyalty to Indonesia and discouraged them from making themselves politically conspicuous through rallies or gatherings.[8]

Sukarno's campaign to "crush Malaysia" (ganyang Malaysia) brought the differences between the PRC and Indonesian leaders over the ethnic Chinese issue into a broader geopolitical context. Despite persistent suspicion about the ties between the PRC government and the Chinese diaspora, Jakarta hoped that Beijing would encourage the Chinese in Malaysia and Singapore to support konfrontasi. Though the Indonesian government remained concerned about Communist subversion through the ethnic Chinese, it provided arms and training to militia forces in Sarawak, which was not only dominated by the Chinese but also guided by the Communist ideology. But the majority of Indonesian army officers dispatched to the battlefields at the Sarawak-Kalimantan border harbored a racial bias against the local Chinese guerilla fighters and treated them cruelly. While the Chinese in Sarawak were regarded as menacing Communists, the Chinese of Singapore were deemed to be cunning capitalists. Singapore, the majority of whose population was Chinese, had been part of Malaysia between 1963 and 1965. On August 9, 1965, Singapore was expelled from the federation and became an independent republic. Due to frustration with smuggling between Indonesia and Singapore, which was usually operated by ethnic Chinese, Indonesian leaders held a negative view of the city-state and were unwilling to grant it diplomatic recognition.[9]

Beijing's understanding of the ethnic Chinese issue during konfrontasi was drastically different from that of Jakarta but similarly paradoxical. Lee Kuan Yew's staunch anti-Communist stance did not prevent the Chinese leadership from being friendly toward Singapore. Beijing viewed the armed struggle in Sarawak as an anticolonial, national liberation movement. Although sympathetic toward the ethnic Chinese Communist guerillas, Beijing did not directly provide them with military aid. At the same time, Beijing detected that Sukarno's motive for launching konfrontasi was not to help the local people achieve political autonomy but instead to create a "mighty Indonesia" by annexing the territories of Borneo that had been claimed by Malaysia.[10] These misgivings help explain why, despite its pugnacious rhetoric, Beijing did not mobilize the Chinese in Malaysia and Singapore to assist Indonesia. Additionally, Sukarno's opportunistic attitude toward the second Afro-Asia Conference further deepened Beijing's distrust in his "dark side and double-dealings."[11] China and Indonesia were brought together by a shared perception of threats and insecurity. But these two countries had contradictory answers to the questions of how to strategically situate the ethnic Chinese in Cold War Southeast Asia and how to define the ethos of the solidarity movement among Afro-Asian nations. Their alliance was marred by ambivalence.

Converging Strategic Interests in *Konfrontasi*

By 1962 Beijing's previously moderate strategy of creating an intermediate zone among the newly independent countries evolved into a belligerent policy that aimed to contest the bipolar structure of the Cold War. In that year, the director of the International Liaison Department of the CCP, Wang Jiaxiang, proposed that Beijing should endeavor to search for stability with major power players and, as a result, was ruthlessly attacked by Mao.[12] In 1964 Mao began to believe that a global war was imminent and a Third World alignment would bring about a decisive shift in world politics. He told a group of Indonesian visitors that "the Soviet Union emerged from the First World War, China and many other socialist countries came out of the Second World War, and imperialism will perish in a Third World War."[13]

In this context, China granted hearty support to konfrontasi. In May 1961, the anti-Communist prime minister of Malaya, Tunku Adul Rahman—or "the Tunku," as he was commonly known—proposed the creation of a Federation of Malaysia, which would encompass the already independent Malaya (Peninsular Malaysia or West Malaysia today), the Borneo territories of Brunei, Sarawak, North Borneo (Sabah today), and Singapore.[14] Indonesia did not immediately oppose the Tunku's plan for amalgamation. But in 1962, A. M. Azahari, the head of Partai Rakyat Brunei (Brunei People's Party), staged an insurrection to form an independent Federation of North Kalimantan (Negara Kesatuan Kalimantan Utara) and proclaimed himself its prime minister.[15] Sukarno declared support for the rebellion, which angered the Tunku. Despite rounds of negotiations, including discussions of the possibility of establishing "Maphilindo," a confederation of Malaya, the Philippines, and Indonesia, Sukarno announced the policy of konfrontasi in 1963, declaring Malaysia to be "fundamentally antithetical to Indonesia's revolution" and denouncing the Tunku as the British and American imperialists' "poster boy" in Southeast Asia.[16]

Sukarno regarded Malaysia as a neocolonialist project "ingeniously devised" by the British to maintain their control over Southeast Asia.[17] Through konfrontasi, Sukarno envisioned Indonesia fighting not just for itself but for the Third World as a whole. Additionally, Sukarno reasoned that the formation of Malaysia would grant the Tunku an opportunity to rekindle the PRRI rebellions, which had set up an alternative government in Sumatra in 1958 in opposition to the central government in Jakarta. Although the Tunku officially denied any intervention, he was sympathetic to the Sumatran rebels, who, by virtue of culture and ethnicity, shared stronger ties with Malaya than with Java.[18] During Liu Shaoqi's visit to Indonesia in April 1963, Sukarno went on a tirade against the Tunku: "The Tunku acknowledged that the rebels in Sumatra were Malaysia's relatives and announced that it would serve the local people's interests if Sumatra were to become a part of Malaysia. Malaysia hopes to transform itself into a magnet for the Outer Islands of Indonesia."[19] Sukarno's fear was not unfounded. In 1960 the rebels in Sumatra declared that, should the rising PKI ever seize control of Java, they were ready to secede from Indonesia and follow the Tunku's leadership.[20] In early July 1964, the PKI branch in Medan alerted the PRC diplomatic mission about a plot by local dissidents to establish a "State of Sumatra," which had allegedly received support not only from Malaysia but also from the US, Japan, General Nasution, and the former Indonesian vice president Mohammad Hatta, who was widely regarded as the principal representative of the Outer Islands in the Javanese-dominated government.[21]

Sukarno also sensed a latent danger accompanying Malaysia's inclusion of Sabah and Sarawak, from which the Tunku's forces could easily infiltrate Indonesian territory in Kalimantan. The Indonesian ambassador Sukarni once disclosed to PRC leaders that the Tunku's affiliates had tried to create chaos in Kalimantan in July 1964. The Indonesian army arrested over one hundred people from a "counterrevolutionary clique" consisting of sultans, royals, former government employees, and smugglers who pledged loyalty to the Tunku government. They planned to attack the local civilian government and the Indonesian army, set fire to grain and oil stores, and rob shops owned by the local ethnic Chinese. The group was said to have planned to escape to Sabah and Sarawak in speedboats.[22]

The Tunku's suppression of the MCP at home and his leaning toward the US and its allies naturally attracted criticism from Beijing. However, throughout 1962, Beijing remained open to reconciliation. During a layover in Hong Kong in May 1962, the Singaporean leader Lee Kuan Yew secretly initiated communications with Beijing via the NCNA office, the unofficial representative of the PRC when Hong Kong was under British colonial governance.[23] In a meeting with Qi Feng and Liang Shangwan, the two deputy branch chiefs of the NCNA Hong Kong office, Lee expressed his respect for the Tunku as a democratically elected, independent politician with a wide base of popular support. The Singaporean leader warned that Beijing's attacks on the Tunku in media outlets such as the *People's Daily* and Radio Peking would only damage its own credibility.[24]

Lee's defense of the Tunku surprised Beijing. Before the meeting, Zhou Enlai instructed his staff in Hong Kong to be circumspect: "We should indicate that we have very little knowledge about the formation of Malaysia. We support all anticolonial struggles. However, Lee Kuan Yew should carefully consider whether the formation of Malaysia would genuinely resist colonialism and whether the imperialists would take advantage of this project. If Lee exhibits any signs of hesitation, [we should] seize the opportunity and reveal to him that the Malaysia scheme is a reactionary neocolonialist project. He should be vigilant."[25] In their report after the meeting, Qi and Liang suggested that the leaders in Beijing should consider accommodating Lee's appeal. They contended that although the Tunku was indeed "a right-wing follower of the American imperialists," he had not "committed any outrageous anti-China or anti-Chinese acts." The PRC media should tamp down its crusade on the Tunku.[26]

But, starting in 1963, the PRC's attitude toward Malaysia hardened due to the collaboration between the Tunku and Taiwan. In April 1963, Sukarno informed Liu Shaoqi that the police force in Malaya had recently recruited many undercover military and intelligence personnel affiliated with the Chinese Nationalist government. Sukarno warned Liu that the Western imperialists had changed their strategy for containing China. Instead of supporting Taipei's direct confrontation against Beijing, they were now assisting pro–Chiang Kai-shek forces with their infiltration into Southeast Asian countries for anti-Communist purposes.[27] While meeting with Deng Xiaoping in March 1964, the Indonesian ambassador Sukarni reported that "over seventy thousand people from Taiwan flooded into Malaya."[28] In December 1964, upon learning that the Tunku had granted Taipei permission to open its consulate in Kuala Lumpur, Zhou ordered the *People's Daily* to publish a strongly worded letter of protest.[29]

The Tunku's partnership with the Chinese Nationalists ultimately convinced PRC leaders that Malaysia, "an artificial creation by the British and the Americans," was not only a threat to Indonesia but also a provocation against China.[30] When discussing konfrontasi with a delegation from the Provisional People's Consultative Assembly of Indonesia in June 1964, Mao promised: "My heart is with you. The hearts of the Chinese people are with you."[31] When welcoming a delegation headed by the Indonesian first deputy prime minister and foreign minister Subandrio in January 1965, Zhou Enlai announced "the Chinese people's resolute support" for Sukarno's konfrontasi. Zhou said: "It is well known that there exists a Malaya on this globe, but there is no such thing as 'Malaysia.' This so-called 'Malaysia' is a scheme the British imposed on the people of Malaya, Singapore, Sarawak, and Sabah to perpetuate their colonial rule. . . . Without Britain and the US, the ruling clique of Malaysia cannot possibly survive for a single day."[32] Beijing publicly denounced Malaysia as "a bayonet planted by the British into the chest of the Republic of Indonesia" and the Tunku as a traitor who helped the old and new colonialists implement their policy of "using Asians to defeat Asians."[33]

Beijing's stalwart support for konfrontasi stemmed from its perception that Malaysia had become a link in an anti-Communist chain in the Asia-Pacific, which was built by the United States and Britain to confine, undermine, and destabilize China. The Chinese leadership's anxiety was intensified by an increase in the US military presence in Indochina, which endangered the Southern Chinese provinces of Yunnan, Guangxi, and Guangdong. London's historically large-scale overseas deployment to Malaysia further disconcerted Beijing. According to the scenario of a domino effect among the British colonies in Asia, these deployments could foment a crisis in British-controlled Hong Kong.[34] It was in this context that the Chinese leaders started to see the uproar in Malaysia involving "not only Indonesia but also China."[35] In their meeting with Subandrio in January 1965, Zhou Enlai and Chen Yi explained the PRC's belief that "anti-imperialist movements all around the world" were closely connected and conflicts in Southeast Asia were indivisible. While Beijing focused on offsetting threats from the United States, Indonesia would sap the energy of the British through konfrontasi and thereby lessen China's burden in counterbalancing both imperialists.[36] Beijing hoped that the guerrilla war in Borneo could reach the scale of that in South Vietnam.[37]

To what degree would China assist Indonesia in konfrontasi? In January 1965, Zhou Enlai and Chen Yi assured the visiting Subandrio:

> If the British imperialists invade Indonesia, we will definitely send support. . . . If the British and American imperialists dare to wage war on the Indonesian people, the Chinese people will not stand by. We made this declaration during the Korean War. We said the same thing when the Gulf of Tonkin Incident broke out. Of course, this is the most we can say openly. . . . Some Indonesian generals might ask: If the British launch a military attack on Indonesia, to what extent will China help us? We cannot be specific about what kind of military action we would take or from which direction [we would intervene]. All these detailed decisions depend on the situation of the enemy. But if anything happens, we surely will support you. . . . How could we not support you? Otherwise, how could we be called comrades-in-arms?[38]

During a separate meeting with Subandrio, the poetic Chen Yi unveiled some of his romantic thinking: "If a war is coming, I hope it comes soon. As a sixty-five-year-old general, I can still participate. In another ten years, I can no longer fight. But at present, I have plenty of experience and can serve as a commander in Vietnam, Indonesia, and Laos."[39] Chen Yi's impassioned oratory may have occluded the PRC leaders' more careful and pragmatic considerations. Notwithstanding its display of fearlessness in the face of potential Western aggression, Beijing recommended that Jakarta should not initiate attacks on the British or the Americans, which would bring dishonor on the archipelago in the international community.[40] Though vowing to contribute his blood and sweat in the case of a full-blown war, Chen Yi predicted that the British and the Americans, acutely aware of the stakes involved in their military ventures in Indonesia, would use indirect means to unsettle Sukarno's regime rather than publicly infringe upon Indonesia's sovereignty. "Like a crazy dog that jumps off the wall when panicked," Chen Yi conjectured that the British might create a contentious atmosphere in the region through espionage and the sponsorship of sedition, assassination, sabotage, and terrorist attacks.[41]

To help Indonesia resist such surreptitious Western hostility, China offered the country its ungrudging political support and bountiful economic aid. Upon Jakarta's request, the PRC embassies in Afro-Asian nations, particularly in the Middle East, helped disseminate propaganda materials explaining Jakarta's anticolonial mission.[42] Konfrontasi helped Sukarno distract the public from a domestic economic crisis. In 1963 rice production, which was critical to Indonesia's food security and national economy, reached a standstill. In November 1963, Indonesia put forward an unexpectedly urgent request for forty thousand tons of rice from China. When consulted by the Chinese embassy in Jakarta, D. N. Aidit, the PKI leader, explained that, due to its opposition to Malaysia, the Indonesian government was under "endless pressure" from both the American imperialists and the Soviet revisionists. Sukarno was "desperate" to secure foreign aid to alleviate the country's economic plight. The Chinese aid would be like "a pill that steadies Sukarno's heartbeat" (*dingxin wan*). Beijing obliged and promptly delivered the full amount.[43] Another pressing plea came from Indonesia in December 1964, when Sukarno and Subandrio asked the visiting Chinese foreign minister Chen Yi for a loan of 50 million USD at no interest or at a very low interest rate. Eager to boost Sukarno's morale, Beijing transmitted 10 million USD in cash and the remaining amount in the form of material supplies including rice, cloth, cement, steel, medicine, and medical equipment.[44]

However, Beijing was less generous with its military assistance. In the early 1960s, the Soviet Union, seeking détente with the US, was reluctant to increase its military aid to Indonesia. As a result, Jakarta turned to China for help. Beijing assumed that Indonesia had already acquired expensive military equipment from the United States, the Soviet Union, and other Eastern European countries in the previous years. Therefore, it agreed to provide less costly items and services such as artillery, ammunition, parts for aircraft and ships, and construction materials as well as maintenance support. As for Jakarta's request to train its air force, the PRC ambassador to Indonesia, Yao Zhongming, suggested to the Foreign Ministry that it would serve China's interests to "symbolically dispatch some volunteers" to the left-leaning Indonesian air force. But the central leadership was skeptical: "It is improper for us to share our combat experience against US aircraft. We can politely turn it [Indonesia's request] down by saying that our air force is still young."[45] Beijing refused to host the Indonesian air force for study sessions in China, but nominally agreed to send instructors to the archipelago to offer on-site training. There is no available material to verify whether this promise materialized.

When an Indonesian delegation headed by Subandrio visited Beijing in January 1965, a new set of questions was put on the table: If a war erupted, would the PRC open up its seaports to Indonesian vessels and allow Indonesian aircraft to pass through its airspace? Would China send troops to Borneo as "volunteers" as it did in the Korean War? Would China share Indonesia's strategic burden by cutting off trade ties with London and taking military action in Hong Kong, the UK's strategic soft spot?[46] General Luo Ruiqing, the chief of the People's Liberation Army (PLA) General Staff, promised the Indonesian navy and air force free passage across Chinese territory and the Indonesian army an unconditional supply of light weapons in the event of war. But he tactfully stated that the PRC's navy was still "under construction" and "might not be as modernized" in some aspects as its counterpart in Indonesia. Moreover, the nascent aviation industry in China could only produce a small number of aircraft of "elementary quality" for military use. Luo clarified that the final decision on Chinese intervention rested in the hands of the top leaders. But, as a military officer who had analyzed the situation from a technical point of view, he thought "it would be difficult" for the PLA to cross the sea. Therefore, the Indonesians would have to rely on themselves. Luo also expressed the PRC's reluctance to endanger its relations with Britain: "We do not need to say loudly that if the British attack Indonesia, we will attack Hong Kong in return. We only need to say that we will support Indonesia. The British will take our words seriously." Luo also told the Indonesian visitors that China's trade with the UK would continue as usual. These economic exchanges would purportedly "strengthen the joint efforts of Indonesia and China to oppose imperialism and colonialism."[47]

The Undercurrents of the Chinese Problem

With the steady convergence of Beijing's and Jakarta's strategic interests, the state-driven anti-Chinese movement quieted down in Indonesia. But the economic decline of the early and mid-1960s led to a popular perception that the speculative behaviors of the Chinese had caused food shortages and skyrocketing inflation. Additionally, China's support for konfrontasi, while drawing Sukarno into Beijing's orbit of fierce opposition to the Western bloc, had stirred up fear and suspicion among anti-Communist elements. To them, Sukarno's cordial relations with Beijing would further strengthen the position of the PKI, rendering the other political parties relatively powerless.[48] In May 1963, a series of anti-Chinese riots broke out in West Java and Chinese property was damaged. However, the scale and geographical scope of the unrest was limited, the number of casualties was low, and the duration was short. Outbreaks of anti-Chinese sentiments ended soon after Sukarno's intervention. Sukarno identified the supporters of the banned Masyumi, the remnant rebels of the PRRI-Permesta, and "foreign subversive elements" backed by the West as the instigators of "acts of terrorism" targeting the Chinese.[49]

The 1963 riots reminded Chinese foreign policy makers of the persistently vulnerable status of the ethnic Chinese in Indonesia even during a honeymoon period in bilateral relations. In early 1965, the PRC Overseas Chinese Affairs Commission and the Foreign Ministry suggested that the Chinese diplomatic mission should encourage affluent ethnic Chinese businessmen to purchase Indonesian government bonds for konfrontasi.[50] Monetary contributions to konfrontasi by the Chinese minority would prove their loyalty to Indonesia and dispel the idea that they were to blame for Indonesia's economic difficulties. At the same time, Beijing did not want its diplomats in Indonesia to be involved in activities that would "overshadow domestic propaganda and mobilization by the Indonesian government." For instance, the PRC Foreign Ministry rejected proposals by its consulate in Medan to organize political rallies among the local ethnic Chinese. Rather, according to Beijing, the Chinese minority in Indonesia should independently express their support for konfrontasi at cultural festivals such as the Lunar New Year or Lebaran, the celebration of the end of Ramadan.[51]

In March 1964, Sukarno asked Ambassador Yao Zhongming if China's ties with the ethnic Chinese in Malaysia and Singapore could be used to help strengthen Azahari's position.[52] The Chinese Foreign Ministry replied: "It would be improper for us to mobilize the overseas Chinese in Malaysia and Singapore because most of them have switched their national allegiance to their country of residence." Beijing also rejected Sukarno's request to use the interparty linkage between the CCP and the MCP for konfrontasi.[53] Beijng had been warned by Lee Kuan Yew during the 1962 confidential meeting that its criticism of the Tunku might cause racial tensions between the ethnic Chinese and the Malays and even stir up a large-scale anti-Chinese movement. According to Lee, the Tunku had interpreted Beijing's denunciation of him as support for the ethnic Chinese–dominated MCP and as an instigation of the local Chinese to oppose the formation of Malaysia. The PRC representatives who met Lee attested to Beijing's determination to dissuade the Chinese in Malaysia from political activism.[54]

Another crack in the outwardly smooth surface of the Sino-Indonesian collaboration in konfrontasi was the two countries' differing views on Chinese-majority Singapore. On August 9, 1965, the usually stoic Lee Kuan Yew tearfully expressed his personal anguish over the collapse of his dream of forming a united sovereignty among people "connected by geography, economics, and ties of kinship."[55] After assuming office as prime minister in

1959, the one-time leftist leader of Singapore adopted an anti-Communist stance.[56] But before Lee's meeting with what he referred to as his "friends from Beijing" in Hong Kong in 1962, Zhou Enlai instructed the NCNA Hong Kong office to demonstrate goodwill via a set of carefully worded talking points: "We understand that your position is difficult. The British will not allow you to be too progressive. What you have achieved so far is admirable. We hope you will continue your anticolonial struggle."[57] At the meeting, both sides expressed a strong interest in advancing bilateral trade relations. Lee also revealed his plan to dispatch economic delegations to Beijing in the near future.[58] The PRC originally planned to grant diplomatic recognition to Singapore right away. But Sukarno urged Beijing to "wait and see." Sukarno worried that Jakarta would appear to be softening its anti-Malaysia stance if it established relations with Singapore.[59] The PKI leaders warned that if Beijing insisted on befriending Lee's government, "the imperialists" and "right-wing elements" would have a new pretext for stirring up anti-China and anti-Chinese sentiments in Indonesia.[60] The electrifying social atmosphere created by konfrontasi was beneficial to the PKI's popular mobilization. The formation of diplomatic ties between Indonesia and Malaysia would de-escalate konfrontasi and impede the PKI's growth at home and its overseas expansion to Sabah and Sarawak. But Beijing dismissed these qualms.[61]

Beijing and Jakarta also had different attitudes toward local armed struggles in Sarawak, in which the ethnic Chinese played a prominent role. The Sarawak Communist Party and its armed wing, the Sarawak People's Guerilla Force (Pasukan Gerilya Rakyat Sarawak, or PGRS), consisted mostly of ethnic Chinese, and its top leaders, such as Wen Ming Chyuan, were inspired by the experience of the Chinese Communist revolution and admired Beijing.[62] During konfrontasi, between one and two thousand young ethnic Chinese supporters of the Sarawak Communist Party crossed into Indonesia to receive guerilla training from the Indonesian army.[63] Together with PKI sympathizers in West Kalimantan and Java and the members of the North Kalimantan National Army (Tentara Negara Kalimantan Utara) led by Azahari, they formed a volunteer (sukarelawan) force. Under the command of the Indonesian army, this volunteer force received weapons from Indonesia and carried out raids into Sarawak from Kalimantan.[64] Indonesian military troops "who had been released from their army units" also participated in these operations.[65]

Beijing openly offered generous moral support, but no direct military aid, to the local resistance against Malaysia in Kalimantan. Beijing cautioned Sukarno to practice restraint and avoid outright confrontation with Malaysia and the British forces behind it. In January 1963, the Indonesian ambassador

Sukarni notified Chinese leaders that Indonesian troops were building up defenses across the border in Kalimantan. But because Sarawak was not "Indonesia's lawful territory . . . it would be difficult for official Indonesian troops to enter straight into the region."[66] In Jakarta in March 1964, Sukarno officially informed the PRC ambassador Yao Zhongming that Indonesia had dispatched volunteers to the Malaysian territories in Borneo.[67] In response, Zhou Enlai and Chen Yi urged Sukarno to discreetly avoid taking full responsibility for the volunteers in case their connection to Indonesia was exposed. Since Indonesia's military operation was "against international norms" and Jakarta had "no legitimate cause for its actions," Sukarno should prevent the conflicts from becoming a focus of the international community and keep Indonesia from becoming the target of widespread condemnation.[68] Two months later, an Indonesian delegation arrived in Beijing to learn from China's experience during the Korean War, in which it prevented an official war with the US by constituting a separate "People's Volunteer Army."[69] In January 1965, Zhou Enlai and Chen Yi told the visiting Subandrio that Indonesia had made the correct decision in eschewing open military action in the Malaysian territory. The Chinese leaders advised Subandrio that Indonesia should organize "the most politically reliable and firmly anti-imperialist masses" in Sarawak into auxiliary forces that would "function as the eyes and ears of the formal troops."[70]

While endorsing Sukarno's intervention in Sarawak, Beijing held that his motivations were "impure."[71] Emboldened by his success in expanding Indonesia's territory, Sukarno made the decision to crush Malaysia a mere two months after The Hague turned over West Irian to Jakarta. Beijing received intelligence that the Indonesian leaders had strict control over the Federation of North Kalimantan, aiming to make it Jakarta's puppet. The leaders of the Federation of North Kalimantan who were living in exile in Indonesia were under constant surveillance by Indonesian intelligence agencies and forced to accept living arrangements planned by Nasution and Subandrio. Every step they took outside of their assigned residence had to be reported to the Indonesian government beforehand. They were forbidden to contact the outside world without permission from the Indonesian authorities. Every word they said to a third party had to be approved by the Indonesian government ahead of time. Their passports were held at the Indonesian Foreign Ministry. The Indonesian government made decisions in their name without any prior discussion. They could only passively follow along. Azahari was bitterly frustrated.[72]

Beijing was also critical of the abuse of volunteers by the Indonesian army; as there was a high percentage of ethnic Chinese youth in the guerilla force, this abuse often had a racist tinge to it. According the PRC embassy in Jakarta, the "training camps" the Indonesian army had set up were in such poor condition that they qualified as "concentration camps." When the Indonesian troops were marching, the volunteers carried the heaviest equipment. With a lack of necessary weapons, they were nevertheless made to serve as on the front line and to sacrifice their lives. If critically injured, volunteers were to be denied medical treatment or be abandoned on the spot. Anyone trying to rescue them would be harshly reprimanded. The volunteers' daily ration was 0.25 kilograms of rice. To avoid starvation, they asked to grow crops, a proposal that was rejected outright by Indonesian army officials. Instead, Indonesian military personnel encouraged the ethnic Chinese volunteers to steal food from the Dayak minorities living in the borderland region between the territories of Indonesia and Malaysia, deliberately creating ethnic tensions. Furthermore, many left-leaning ethnic Chinese youth from Malaysia and Singapore recruited by Indonesian intelligence operatives for konfrontasi ended up being imprisoned and tortured. The PRC embassy reported receiving "secret letters" from these "incarcerated, interrogated, abused, and humiliated" youth, who had not expected such a horrific outcome.[73]

The Second Afro-Asian Conference and CONEFO

Territorial expansion in Borneo through konfrontasi was only part of Sukarno's plan for his country to assume a grandiose international role. The early 1960s were Sukarno's age of ambition. Envisioning the influence of Indonesia spreading across continents like Garuda, the mythical bird of Hinduism, Sukarno named the group of UN peacekeepers drawn from the Indonesian military the "Garuda Contingent" (Kontingen Garuda). The Garuda Contingent completed two missions in the Congo between 1960 and 1963. From Sukarno's standpoint, Indonesia's odyssey to Africa accelerated the archipelago's rise as a strong advocate on behalf of the Afro-Asian nations in global politics.[74]

In his arduous plan to remake Cold War political geography and rebrand Indonesia, Sukarno did not think immediately of the PRC as an ally. In the late 1950s and early 1960s, he had a greater interest in the non-aligned movement, which he cofounded with four other Third World leaders, including two of the PRC's nemeses at the time: Jawaharlal Nehru of India and Tito of Yugoslavia. China's relations with India—an important neighbor and former crucial ally in Asia—deteriorated sharply after the Tibetan uprising in 1959, the exile of the Fourteenth Dalai Lama to India, and the resulting border conflicts. During a meeting with Subandrio in 1963, Liu Shaoqi argued that India had become a "chauvinist country" and Nehru was "no longer a representative of the Afro-Asian countries."[75] Meanwhile, Beijing's fiery ideological disputes with Belgrade led to an estrangement between the two countries. Chinese propaganda portrayed Tito as a symbol of decadence and a puppet of Western imperialists.

A second Bandung was the cornerstone of Beijing's scheme to compete with India and Yugoslavia in the Third World. Beijing wanted to prevent "imperialists, reactionaries and modern revisionists" from "tying the hands and feet of the Afro-Asian people" with slogans like "peace" and "disarmament."[76] As an alternative to the non-aligned movement, Beijing aimed to organize a bloc of Afro-Asian countries that opposed both superpowers instead of carefully maneuvering between the two camps. These fiercely independent nations had the right to develop their own nuclear weapons and to conduct nuclear experiments. Zhou Enlai said to Subandrio in January 1965: "The emphasis of the first Afro-Asian Conference was on the struggle for national independence; the emphasis of the second Afro-Asian Conference will be a full realization of that independence. Today, the world should not be divided into Communist versus non-Communist camps, but into imperialist and anti-imperialist countries. Imperialist countries cannot peacefully coexist with the new emerging forces."[77] In other words, only through militant anti-imperialism could Afro-Asian nations "gain control over their own destiny."[78]

The Chinese leaders were dismayed by Sukarno's attraction to Yugoslavia's developmental model and Tito's strategy of maximizing his country's access to foreign aid by capitalizing on the antagonism between superpowers. When Djuanda Kartawidjaja, the Indonesian prime minister, paid a state visit to Yugoslavia in September 1958, China anxiously observed the Indonesian "nationalist bourgeois" leadership's growing interest in Tito's political and economic reforms.[79] The Indonesian government later announced its plan to increase the volume of its trade with Eastern Europe through ports in Yugoslavia to decrease its economic dependence on the Dutch. At Sukarno's invitation, Tito visited Indonesia in late December 1958 and spent New Year's Eve with Sukarno on the island of Bali. The two leaders seemed to have good chemistry as Tito's "bourgeois style"—"fancy clothing, massive entourage, tough-looking bodyguards, and bullet-proof vehicles flown in from Yugoslavia to Indonesia"—distinctly mirrored Sukarno's love of splendor.[80] At a state banquet in Tito's honor, Sukarno expressed his admiration for Yugoslavia as a socialist country that upheld the principle of national independence, a stance which echoed the ideals of Indonesia. Sukarno said that this was the reason why "Indonesians very much love Yugoslavia."[81]

In Belgrade in September 1961, the PRC embassy was warily watching Sukarno's participation in the first conference of the non-aligned movement. The PRC was relieved to see that Sukarno had decided to side with Beijing in its escalating conflict with New Delhi. At a dinner reception on September 3, 1961, journalists from the New China News Agency approached the PKI leader D. N. Aidit with inquiries about Sukarno's activities. Aidit informed them that Sukarno did not even give Nehru a courtesy greeting.[82] As the first speaker, Sukarno tried to set the tone of the conference by focusing on the issues of anti-imperialism and anticolonialism. But Nehru proposed instead that anticolonialism should be a secondary issue, which prompted opposition from Sukarno. The PRC diplomats in Belgrade were acutely aware of Sukarno's vanity: "He wants to be the spokesperson for the neutralist countries to increase his personal value."[83] The Chinese leaders masterfully manipulated his weakness. When Sukarno visited Mao in Beijing in June 1961, the chairman alluded to Nehru's desire "to snatch the leadership of the world anti-imperialist movement" from Sukarno.[84] In 1963 Liu Shaoqi explicitly said to the Indonesian foreign minister Subandrio that Sukarno should replace Nehru and take charge of Afro-Asian affairs.[85]

But Tito's Yugoslavia continued to entice Sukarno into a moderate form of Third World alignment that was antithetical to Beijing's vision. After Sukarno returned from Belgrade, the Yugoslavian embassy in Jakarta launched a propaganda campaign that promoted the non-aligned movement as the path to the future while disparaging the concept of "Afro-Asian" as obsolete.[86] Sukarno was swayed by these messages, and his vacillation worried Beijing. The PRC embassy in Jakarta predicted that a second Bandung had a fifty-fifty chance of success given the upcoming "complicated and strenuous struggle" against the non-aligned movement.[87] In Beijing in March 1964 Deng Xiaoping, frustrated by Sukarno's continuous dabbling in the non-aligned movement, bombarded the Indonesian ambassador Sukarni with a series of questions: "How has Indonesia's experience in the non-aligned movement been so far? Did the member states talk about anti-imperialism, anticolonialism, or national independence? Did they dare to oppose the United States? . . . Everything looks clearer in comparison. If you put the two conferences side by side, which truly represents the interests of the Afro-Asian countries? The people of the world can easily tell."[88]

But konfrontasi had already estranged the archipelago from many of its former friends who were pursuing neutralism in the Cold War. At the second non-aligned movement summit, held in September 1964 in Cairo, the anti-imperialist radicalism underlying Sukarno's speech alienated Indonesia from the majority of the participating countries, including Yugoslavia, which had once hoped to win Sukarno over to Tito's version of the middle course. Sukarno warned the non-aligned nations that colonialism was not dead but had been reincarnated as "neocolonialism." Threats of "obstruction, intervention, sabotage, and subversion from the imperialists" still lingered even though the formerly colonized nations had achieved political independence. Peaceful coexistence was an empty lie the strong had sold to the weak: only the great powers could afford to enjoy peace whereas the small and medium-sized powers had no security. The precondition for peaceful coexistence was a balance of power.[89] Sukarno's passionate crusade against colonialism and imperialism, which had successfully mesmerized the Indonesian public, failed to convince the international audience in Cairo. The Indonesian ambassador Sukarni mentioned to Deng Xiaoping: "If the non-aligned movement does not oppose imperialism or colonialism but takes the middle road, it will be nothing more than a tool of imperialism."[90] The Indonesian foreign minister Subandrio later announced to the PRC ambassador Huang Zhen: "The non-aligned movement has lost its meaning for Indonesia."[91]

Although Indonesia was no longer part of the non-aligned movement, Sukarno's opportunistic style persisted. He sought to use the second Bandung to kindle relations with the Soviet Union after having burned bridges with the West through konfrontasi. In his famous "The Year of Living Dangerously" speech delivered on Indonesia's Independence Day in 1964, Sukarno was friendly toward Moscow.[92] When consulted by the PRC diplomats in Jakarta, Oei Tjoe Ta (Huang Zida), a peranakan Chinese politician serving as minister of state (*Menteri Negara*), expressed his suspicions that Sukarno would "sail with the wind" (*jianfeng shiduo*) and invite the Soviet Union to the conference.[93] The PRC had long objected to potential interference from its ally-turned-adversary, who, as a white nation that "did not share the same emotions and experiences of anticolonial struggle" as the Third World, should never be allowed at any Afro-Asian conference.[94] In his meeting with Ambassador Sukarni, Deng Xiaoping characterized Khrushchev as narrow-minded and trapped in a self-interested way of thinking that inhibited Moscow from "granting the Afro-Asian nations the autonomy to resolve their own issues."[95] Chen Yi told Subandrio that China's opposition to a Soviet invitation was nonnegotiable.[96] Sukarno ultimately gave in.

At the beginning of 1965 Jakarta was drawing closer to China and some other aggressively anti-imperialist countries. In 1965, in his last Independence Day speech given as the Indonesian president, Sukarno declared: "We are now fostering an anti-imperialist axis—the Jakarta—Phnom Penh—Hanoi—Peking—Pyongyang axis."[97] To protest Malaysia's presence on the UN Security Council, Sukarno withdrew Indonesia from the UN. The January 1965 issue of

Knowledge about the World (*Shijie Zhishi*), the PRC's best-known popular mag-azine on international politics, called Sukarno's decision that year's "first spring thunder that awakens the world."[98] The article said: "Some say the UN is like a tiger's backside that no one dares to touch. But President Sukarno has poked the tiger's ass."[99] Since the ROC was still the representative of China at the UN, the PRC ardently supported Sukarno's proposal to replace it with CONEFO, a revolutionary international organization for the new emerging forces. Jakarta and Beijing agreed that the first CONEFO, or, in Sukarno's words, "the first congregation of all the anti-imperialist forces of the world," would be held in Indonesia in 1966.[100] The PRC promised an unconditional sum of 43,700,000 Swiss francs for the construction of the CONEFO build-ing, scheduled for completion in August 1966.[101] In light of this new devel-opment, a second Bandung gained new meaning as a warm-up session for CONEFO.

Preoccupied with konfrontasi, Indonesia was unable to host the second Bandung, even though the Chinese leaders initially insisted that the confer-ence should remain in "the birthplace of the Bandung principle and spirit."[102] Sukarno handed the organizational task to Ben Bella, the Algerian presi-dent who had also used an ultraleftist turn in foreign policy as a remedy for domestic economic disarray. The Algerian government requested a deferral of the conference so that it would have enough time to construct conference facilities. But Sukarno told Ben Bella that "a conference held in the middle of the desert, on the back of camels or inside tents" would be even "more meaningful politically." After negotiations, the second Afro-Asian Confer-ence was postponed until June.[103] To compensate for its failure to reenact the first Afro-Asian Conference in the same location, Indonesia invited sixty countries drawn from the 1955 Bandung Conference to a ten-year anniver-sary celebration. Only a handful of the invitees, including Cambodia, North Vietnam, North Korea, and China, responded to the call. Eager to win over the increasingly divided Third World, both Zhou Enlai and Chen Yi flew to Indonesia in April 1965 to demonstrate the PRC's enthusiastic endorsement of Sukarno.[104]

Sukarno's revolutionary romanticism was crushed by political upheaval in Algeria. Shortly before the scheduled opening of the second Afro-Asian Confer-ence, the Algerian armed forces chief Colonel Houari Boumédiène ousted Ben Bella in a coup on June 19, 1965. As a result, the Chinese and Indonesian leaders had to convene in Cairo. At the Egyptian capital, Zhou Enlai and Chen Yi had a brief four-party conference with Sukarno, the Egyptian president Gamal Abdel Nasser, and the Pakistani foreign minister Zulfikar Ali Bhutto. In his farewell address delivered at the Cairo airport, Zhou Enlai vowed: "China will continue to put

forth its best efforts to help the second Afro-Asian Conference succeed."[105] But
Ben Bella's fall, which Chen Yi interpreted as the result of the Algerian leader's
"lack of resolve in combating the imperialists," marked not a temporary suspension but a permanent end to discussions concerning the second Bandung.[106] The
CONEFO project subsequently evaporated. China and Indonesia were unable
to translate their passionate rhetoric into substantial action in promoting Third
World revolution. In the eyes of many Western observers, the collapse of the
second Bandung marked the beginning of the end of the internationalist movement in the Global South.[107]

When konfrontasi reached its climax, the PRC's defense policy had already
shifted from one-sided confrontation against the United States to opposing
the US and the Soviet Union simultaneously. Both China and Indonesia felt
dreadfully insecure: while China saw itself being threatened by both the
American imperialists and the Soviet revisionists, Indonesia sensed aggression from the old and new colonialists. Mirroring Sukarno's militant anti-
imperialism, Beijing perceived itself to be in the eye of a revolutionary hurri-
cane engulfing the people of Asia and Africa. As Sukarno said in 1963, China
and Indonesia were "standing shoulder to shoulder" leading the new emerging forces. Because of that, the two countries were "disturbed, threatened,
and being ferociously attacked."[108] But ten years later, China and Indonesia
failed to rally support from the wider Third World and re-create the Afro-
Asian moment of 1955. These two radical leftist countries, which demanded
armed opposition against imperialism, faced isolation in the increasingly
fragmented Afro-Asian movement because many other newly independent
countries hoped to ameliorate international tension.[109]

A mix of anxiety and excitement masked the two countries' disagree-
ment over critical issues such as the role of the ethnic Chinese in decoloniz-
ing Southeast Asia. Beijing wished to see the ethnic Chinese in Indonesia,
Malaysia, and Singapore obtain local citizenship, pledge loyalty to their
countries of residence, and settle in for the long term. Therefore, Beijing
rejected Sukarno's requests to spur political action among the ethnic Chinese
in Malaysia and Singapore, avoiding the danger that the geopolitical issue
of konfrontasi would transform into an ethnic conflict. Singapore's position
at the nexus of Asia-Pacific trade networks contributed to Beijing's affinity
for the shrewd and pragmatic Lee Kuan Yew. Despite Sukarno's objections,
Beijing had been open to granting Singapore diplomatic recognition after its
independence. Beijing hoped to see the people in Sarawak achieve national
self-determination through armed struggle. Therefore, the PRC was indig-
nant toward Sukarno's expansionist ambitions as well as the Indonesian

military's maltreatment of the ethnic Chinese guerilla fighters and its provocation of ethnic violence between the Chinese and the indigenous groups during its campaigns.

Sukarno had launched konfrontasi partially to distract the general population at home from unfulfilled promises of economic prosperity. His bravado against imperialism notwithstanding, the Indonesian president, who was trained as an architect, did not have a clear blueprint for his country. On January 18, 1965, at Istana Palace, Sukarno expressed his gratitude to Ambassador Yao Zhongming for the PRC's support for his decision to withdraw Indonesia from the UN. When Yao mentioned that ambassadors from Yugoslavia, the United Arab Republic, and Sri Lanka had tried to persuade him to change his mind, Sukarno laughed and said: "I am going to tell them to go to hell!" When asked what the next step would be, Sukarno suddenly looked confused and murmured: "We will collaborate very well."[110] The PRC ambassador concluded that Sukarno seemed unsure about what lay ahead for his country. As will be discussed in the next chapter, the fateful month of October 1965 revealed that both Sukarno's domestic political authority and the Sino-Indonesian joint efforts to reconfigure the Cold War international structure were built on an unsound foundation.

CHAPTER 8

China and the September Thirtieth Movement

In the early morning before dawn on October 1, 1965, a group of mostly middle-ranking military officers calling themselves the September Thirtieth Movement kidnapped and killed six senior anti-Communist generals. They later announced that a Revolutionary Council (dewan revolusi) composed of left-wing, right-wing, and neutral political forces had seized power. This Revolutionary Council claimed to have taken President Sukarno under its protection as part of a series of preemptive actions to thwart a planned coup by the Council of Generals, presumably a body of right-wing army generals supported by the US. The leader of the group, Lieutenant Colonel Untung Syamsuri, was in close contact with D. N. Aidit, who was present at the movement's headquarters at the Halim Air Force Base on the outskirts of Jakarta. The next day, Major General Suharto, the head of the Indonesian army's strategic reserve (Komando Cadangan Stategis Angkatan Darat, or Kostrad), launched a successful campaign against the movement and regained control of its headquarters.

Suharto and the Indonesian army under him claimed that the PKI had organized the movement with the encouragement of and support from Beijing in order to spark a national uprising. Ten days after the movement, the Indonesian army accused the Chinese government of smuggling arms to the PKI for the revolt.[1] In April 1966, the army's newspaper, *Angkatan Bersendjata*, made a more aggressive charge against Beijing, saying that it had planned an "abortive Communist coup as part of its concept of world revolution."[2] This idea was further instilled in the minds of the general Indonesian population through the film *The Betrayal of the PKI (Pengkhianatan G30S/PKI)*, a propaganda tool of the Suharto regime that was broadcast annually on the evening of September 30 and was required viewing for schoolchildren. In the film, Chinese doctors are shown practicing acupuncture with electric shock on the ailing President Sukarno, and their diagnosis of Sukarno's health condition as "critically dangerous" is presented as the trigger for the PKI's coup attempt.[3]

This claim of Beijing's alleged behind-the-scenes role in the September Thirtieth Movement fanned anti-China and anti-Chinese sentiments in Indonesia. In the months following the September Thirtieth Movement, Sino-Indonesian relations deteriorated sharply and mass demonstrations broke out across Indonesia at PRC embassies, consulates, and news agencies. The mass violence of 1965–66 was political in nature, but had an ethnic dimension.[4] Although pribumis rather than the ethnic Chinese were the primary victims of the massacres, many ethnic Chinese suffered considerably from harassment, extortion, and loss or destruction of their property.[5] The Chinese were easy targets because they were presumed to be not only rich capitalists but also accomplices of the PKI and the PRC in their joint attempt to turn Indonesia into a Communist country. These perceptions justified the popular hostility against the ethnic Chinese between 1965 and 1967 as well as the Suharto regime's systematic discrimination against this minority.

Clarifying Beijing's role in the September Thirtieth Movement is the first step toward constructing a more accurate explanation for the aggravation of ethnic tensions in 1965–67. In this chapter, I argue that Beijing was not as influential over the turn of events in 1965 as the Suharto regime had charged. New evidence discredits two of the most widely circulated assertions of the Suharto regime and some English-language writers—that Chinese doctors predicted the imminent decline in Sukarno's health and that Beijing smuggled arms to the PKI and ordered it to carry out "an attempted coup."[6] Beijing provided medical support to Sukarno and was thus able to monitor the president's health, which became highly politicized in the months before the movement. But to Beijing's knowledge, Sukarno's condition was not as critical as had been rumored. It is unlikely that the top PKI leaders, who received updates from Beijing on Sukarno's health, rushed into action against the Indonesian army due to fear of Sukarno's approaching death. Beijing supported the PKI's proposal to establish the Fifth Force, a militia group of armed peasants and workers, to augment the existing four branches of the Indonesian armed forces—the army, navy, air force, and police—and promised supplies of light weapons for this purpose. However, the precondition for Beijing's endorsement was that this additional force be firmly under the command of Sukarno rather than the PKI.[7] All the arms deals were made on a government-to-government level rather than through inter–Communist Party channels. Moreover, due to time constraints, the China-sponsored weapons had not been delivered to Indonesia prior to the outbreak of the movement.

Underneath these two factually mistaken assertions are two erroneous assumptions about the PRC's strategic goal in Indonesia and its capacity for foreign intervention. By offering military aid and even the hope of a transfer of nuclear technology, the PRC wanted to rally Sukarno's support for its efforts to weaken Western influence in Southeast Asia and the Pacific. In 1965, instead of a full-blown Communist revolution in which the PKI would take over state power from Sukarno, Beijing hoped to see the continuation of a stable alliance between the two that would steadily lead Indonesia along the lines of militant anti-imperialism. Meanwhile, the CCP did not have control over the PKI, which was a comparatively independent party. The decision to initiate the September Thirtieth Movement was made by Aidit and a clandestine Special Bureau and shared in advance with the top Chinese leaders. Despite its foreknowledge of the scheme, Beijing did not participate in its planning and was unaware of when it would be carried out. In the first twenty-four hours after the movement took place, Beijing completely lost contact with its embassy in Jakarta. The fact that the PRC suffered from a major intelligence failure at this critical time suggests that the Suharto regime and some Western observers have exaggerated Beijing's ability to project its power in Indonesia.

The PKI, Sukarno, and China

The PKI reached the height of its strength and influence during the early 1960s through a close alliance with Sukarno under Guided Democracy. During this time, Sukarno relied heavily on the PKI for organizing public support, while carefully maintaining an intricate relationship with the PKI's archenemy in domestic politics: the army.[8] In August 1960, a journalist of the PKI organ *Harian Rakyat*, who was visiting Beijing, explained the Indonesian president's conflicting attitudes toward the PKI to his Chinese counterparts at the *People's Daily*: "Sukarno had two faces: on the one hand, he restricted the development of the PKI; on the other, he protected the PKI. If the PKI collapsed, Sukarno could hardly maintain his power."[9] Faced with ongoing economic problems and the resulting social dissatisfaction, Sukarno chose to unite his countrymen around the goal of eliminating Western imperialism. The PKI took advantage of Sukarno's strategy by building an image of itself as a forerunner of a nationalist mass movement.[10]

This left turn in Indonesia's foreign policy changed the PKI's stance on the Sino-Soviet split. Throughout the 1950s and early 1960s, although the PKI invested great effort in translating the works of Chinese Communist leaders, adapted some of China's political slogans for mass mobilization, and based some of its grassroots programs on the Chinese model, it still looked to Moscow, rather than Beijing, for suggestions and advice.[11] Beijing's evaluation of its Indonesian comrades in 1959 was mixed: "On the one hand, the PKI emphasized independence, autonomy, and equality among Communist parties; on the other, it confirmed that the Communist Party of the Soviet Union (CPSU) was the vanguard of the international Communist movement."[12] However, in the 1960s, the Indonesian Communists became far more sympathetic toward Beijing. At the twenty-second congress of the CPSU, Khrushchev's keynote speech, which condemned the personality cult of Stalin and criticized Albania, was taken by Mao as an oblique indictment of China.[13] In Moscow, Aidit refrained from joining Khrushchev in attacking the Albanian Communists.[14] Later, Aidit and other members of the Indonesian delegation traveled to Beijing, where they held discussions with Mao and other CCP leaders. Mao told Aidit: "Khrushchev is so reckless that he can do anything. His tricks change from year to year. There were so many tricks at the CPSU twenty-second congress. I think Khrushchev teaches by negative example (fanmian jiaoyuan)."[15] Upon returning home, Aidit made a statement acknowledging Albania as a "genuine socialist society" and affirming Stalin's historical contributions.[16]

In 1963 the PKI declared that it aligned itself fully with the CCP "against the Soviet's 'collaborationist' relationship with the United States."[17] Aidit was invited to visit China and was hailed as "a brilliant Marxist-Leninist theoretician" and "a close friend and comrade-in-arms of the Chinese people."[18] He also became the first non-Chinese honorary member of the Chinese Academy of Social Sciences and a speaker at the CCP Central Party School. In December 1963, in his political report to the second plenum of the seventh central committee of the PKI, Aidit proposed that "the world's countryside," Asia, Africa, and Latin America, would encircle "the world's cities," Europe and North America. Two years later, his theory would be incorporated into Lin Biao's speech, "Long Live the Victory of the People's War," a seminal text for global guerrilla warfare.[19] However, even after the PKI tilted toward China in the Sino-Soviet split, it did not change its basic position on the undesirability of armed struggle. The PKI's decision to take the parliamentary road and collaborate with Sukarno was also recognized by the CCP as a "correct policy line."[20]

As ties between the Chinese and Indonesian Communists grew closer, interparty relations intermingled with governmental diplomacy. Organizationally, the Chinese Foreign Ministry oversaw state-to-state relations while the CCP's International Liaison Department managed its ties with foreign Communist parties. The setup was originally designed to establish boundaries between governmental affairs and the international Communist movement, which had become blurry starting in the late 1950s with the radicalization of Chinese foreign policy. From 1962 to early 1965, Indonesian Communist leaders became a regular source of information and advice for the Chinese diplomatic mission in Jakarta and, occasionally, were policy influencers advocating for Beijing. In 1963, concerned about Sukarno's inability to decide between the non-aligned movement and the second Bandung, the PKI suggested that PRC media should publish more reports glorifying the Indonesian president in order to feed his big but vulnerable ego.[21] When the Indian, Yugoslavian, and Egyptian leaders met at a summit in Cairo without inviting Sukarno, the PKI, following the recommendation of its Chinese comrades, reminded the president: "Nehru, Tito, and Nasser have all abandoned you. The only correct course of action is to speed up the opening of the second Afro-Asian conference and to promote the unity of the Afro-Asian people."[22] These contacts between Chinese diplomats and Indonesian Communist leaders gave Suharto the raw materials to cook up the story that the PRC orchestrated the September Thirtieth Movement.

Chinese Military Aid

Wary of the American military buildup in Indochina, Beijing assigned greater strategic importance to Southeast Asia. In late September 1963, China hosted a strategic planning meeting with Communist leaders from Vietnam, Laos, and Indonesia in Conghua, Guangdong Province. In his keynote speech, Zhou Enlai proclaimed that Southeast Asia had become the key area for the international anti-imperialist struggle.[23] Zhou announced that China, "as the reliable home front for the Southeast Asian revolutions," had "a responsibility to fully support anti-imperialist struggles in the region."[24] Beijing's perception of heightened tension led to a shift in its attitude toward granting military aid to Indonesia. By 1959 China had contributed military equipment worth 7.5 million GBP to Indonesia, including fighter jets, bombers, aircraft artillery, landing craft, command ships, gunboats, amphibious tanks, deepwater explosives, small arms, and ammunition.[25]Between 1961 and 1963, due to budgetary constraints, China had "politely refused" many of Jakarta's requests, including those for the provision of MiG-17s, submarines, and air-to-air missiles.[26] In January 1965, General Luo Ruiqing, the chief of the PLA General Staff, voluntarily made an offer to a military delegation from Indonesia: "Now we can produce light weapons in large quantities for the infantry. If you need small weapons, we can help."[27] In June 1965, the International Liaison Department of the CCP recommended a more proactive policy toward military cooperation with Indonesia: "We need to act according to our abilities and our judgment of whether the result [of Sino-Indonesian military cooperation] would benefit the Indonesian revolution."[28]

In January 1965, the PKI leader D. N. Aidit proposed the idea of the Fifth Force to Sukarno.[29] The PKI asserted that the militia would support Indonesia's anti-imperialist struggles as well as Sukarno's Nasakom (the acronym for "nasionalisme, agama, komunisme," nationalism, religion, and Communism) doctrine.[30] Under this formula, even though the PKI's members would be well represented in the soon-to-be-created militia, the nationalists (meaning, in effect, the PNI) and the religious groups (meaning, in effect, the NU) would also be included in the Fifth Force and thus would also be armed. Therefore, the creation of the Fifth Force would benefit the PKI, but not exclusively. Yet the PKI leaders envisaged that, in the long run, the Fifth Force would help the PKI gain an edge over their rivals and gradually attain state power. Understandably, the proposal was strongly opposed by the Indonesian army.

Beijing's attitude toward the Fifth Force was encouraging but cautious. In late January 1965, during a conversation with the visiting Indonesian first deputy prime minister Subandrio, Zhou Enlai endorsed the idea of the Fifth Force: "The militia can defend the motherland's territory, airspace, and territorial waters. . . . Militarized masses are invincible."[31] In late June 1965, a delegation of Indonesian volunteers was dispatched by Sukarno to visit China, North Korea, and Vietnam to learn about the militia in these three countries. In Beijing, Luo Ruiqing told the delegation: "Whether you can follow the Chinese experience is a question only you can answer for yourself based on the situation in Indonesia. Our experience is just for your reference. Every country's circumstances are different. We all have to start from the specific conditions of our own country."[32] When Zhou Enlai met with the delegation, he also emphasized that, geographically, Indonesia was very different from China. China lacked military experience in island environments. Indonesia had to work out a method that best suited its own situation.[33]

To help Sukarno solidify his leftist positions at home and abroad, China offered to supply Indonesia with a hundred thousand light arms.[34] Instead

of targeting the Fifth Force, the deal was designed with the whole country and all four services in mind. Ultimately, only the Indonesian air force
participated in the negotiations for an initial transfer of some twenty-five
thousand weapons. In late June 1965, Andoko, an air commodore, communicated to the Chinese military attaché in Jakarta that the Indonesian air force
had decided to equip "people within a fifty-kilometer range of Halim Air
Force Base" with weapons to "forestall sabotage by imperialists and domestic
subversives."[35] Andoko also stated that the Indonesian air force would send
planes to pick up the weapons directly. When the Chinese military attaché
was reluctant to support this plan, Andoko pressured him: "If one has to wait
for unanimous agreement among the four forces [the army, navy, air force,
and police], it will be too late."[36] It seems likely that the Indonesian air force
was justifying its own request for small arms, made under the auspices of
President Sukarno, by claiming that Halim Air Force Base must be protected.
Sukarno may have appointed Air Marshall Omar Dani as his envoy to attend
to the details of the deal to ensure that the air force would receive the weapons rather than the army, navy, or police. Sukarno probably wanted to build
up the air force, whose officers were considered to be more loyal to him, in
order to counterbalance the army, whose officers were less dependable.

Despite its initial concern about being approached alone by the air force,
Beijing later understood that the arms were meant to support the air force in
its struggle against the right-wingers in the army. Dani arrived in Beijing on
September 16, 1965. On the same day, the Chinese embassy in Jakarta sent a
telegram to the Foreign Ministry, recommending approval for the air force's
request for weapons.[37] On the morning of September 17, Zhou Enlai had
a three-hour meeting with Dani and the Indonesian ambassador to China,
Djawato; its minutes have not been declassified. There is no hard evidence
confirming that the Chinese leaders in Beijing took the advice of the embassy
and green-lighted the deal. However, available information does indicate that
Beijing was inclined to help the air force strengthen itself against the anti-
Communist forces in the army. In general terms, the purpose of Dani's trip
was to discuss cooperation among the air forces of China, Indonesia, and
Pakistan as well as Chinese military aid to Indonesia.[38] After Dani's return
to Indonesia, Aidit secretly told the Chinese embassy in Jakarta that the air
marshall was "very much touched by the Chinese comrades' resolution to
defend Indonesia."[39]

However, even if the leaders in Beijing did approve the Indonesian air
force's request, given the narrow window of opportunity between Dani's
visit and the outbreak of the movement, it would have been logistically difficult for the Indonesian air force to arrange the shipment. In his confession

at the extraordinary military court (Mahkamah Militer Luar Biasa), which was used by Suharto to stage sham trials of alleged conspirators of the September Thirtieth Movement, Dani purportedly said that the Chinese leaders had asked the Indonesian air force to transport small arms since China was experiencing economic difficulties.[40] I interviewed Djali Ahimsa, the former director of the Indonesian Nuclear Agency (Badan Tenaga Atom Nasional, or BATAN), in 2013. Djali had visited China between September 21 and October 6, 1965. In Beijing, he met Sri Mulyono Herlambang, from the Indonesian air force, shortly before the movement. Herlambang revealed that he had come on President Sukarno's private plane "to request that the Chinese government deliver the weapons it had promised earlier."[41] This suggests that most of the weapons in the negotiation probably had not been processed for delivery in the week prior to the September Thirtieth Movement. Although one cannot fully deny the possibility that the Indonesian air force managed to ship some of the weapons from China to Indonesia, the underarmed status of the militia groups involved in the movement at the Halim Air Force Base suggests that these weapons most likely had not arrived in Indonesia.[42]

Last but not least, Chinese military aid to Indonesia lagged far behind the aid given by the Soviet Union and the United States. According to East German sources, during his visit to Indonesia in 1960, Khrushchev generously granted the country 100 million USD in aid, which was, at the time, one of the largest grants of Soviet foreign aid to a non-Communist country.[43] A Japanese intelligence agency, the Mainland China Research Institute, estimated that "80 to 90 percent of Indonesian air force and navy equipment was supplied by the Soviet Union," a level that the Chinese were unable to match.[44] American analysts' assessment was that "the Indonesian military establishment is almost totally Soviet-supplied."[45] In an effort to outweigh Soviet influence, the US provided a comprehensive military modernization program to Indonesia that included both material supplies and strategic training. Washington had successfully cultivated a group of pro-US leaders in the army, such as Nasution, and had been encouraging them to undermine the PKI through forceful means.[46] In comparison, Chinese military aid probably did not have a significant impact on Indonesian politics in 1965.

Beijing's Knowledge of the Movement

In the period from the late stages of Guided Democracy to the movement, the CCP leadership was concerned about internal unrest in Indonesia. By 1965 the PKI's membership had grown to an estimated three to five million,

with twenty million more in affiliated mass organizations.[47] The PKI's popularity and its close relations with Sukarno had led to seething animosity from
the Indonesian army and right-leaning religious groups such as the NU. On
May 26, 1965, Jakarta became "a city immersed in a sea of red flags" when
the PKI hosted a magnificent ceremony for its forty-fifth birthday. Zhang
Haitao, an NCNA reporter stationed in Indonesia at the time, reflected in
retrospect that this extravagant celebration might have aggravated the hostility of the party's opposition.[48] As early as mid-1963, the Chinese leaders had
already perceived the situation in Indonesia to be full of tension and ripe for
a power transition. In the words of Zhou Enlai, in Indonesia the most critical
issue was that "Nasution, with support from the US and the Chiang Kai-shek
government in Taiwan, is trying by all means to topple Sukarno and replace
him. This is a life-and-death struggle, which will continue. No matter what
Sukarno's attitude is, [the Indonesian revolution] will be born. In this new
era in the history of Indonesia's struggle against imperialism and feudalism,
a new configuration of power will occur. The speed at which things evolve
depends on the relative power of the PKI and its strategies. I believe that the
PKI has foresight and will be prepared."[49]

From late October to December 1964, Chinese intelligence agencies in
Hong Kong reported on rumors surrounding plots against Sukarno by anti-
Communist forces and speculations about his deteriorating health.[50] In the
early 1960s, the PRC had been providing medical aid, principally for chronic
kidney problems, to the Indonesian president. A Chinese medical team also
treated Sukarno when he suffered a severe cerebral vasospasm attack on
August 5, 1965, which caused much commotion on the Indonesian political
scene. At the time, Aidit was visiting Beijing and was originally scheduled
to travel from Beijing to Hanoi on August 7. After being briefed by Zhou
Enlai of Sukarno's condition, Aidit decided to cancel his trip to Vietnam
and return to Indonesia on August 6.[51] But Sukarno made a speedy recovery
and appeared healthy and energetic by the time of the Independence Day
celebrations on August 17. Sukarno's life span also proved that, in 1965,
his illness was persistent but not critical. From late 1964 to August 1965,
Aidit was probably making plans to deal with a political scenario that did
not include Sukarno. But immediately before the movement, it was likely
concerns other than the impending death of Sukarno that pushed Aidit to
take action.

On August 5, 1965, Aidit, his wife, Tanti, and Jusuf Adjitorop, a Politburo member, had a meeting with Mao Zedong and other top Chinese
leaders, including Liu Shaoqi, Zhou Enlai, Deng Xiaoping, and Chen Yi.
During the meeting, Zhou reported to Mao about Sukarno's health and

Aidit's revised travel arrangements. Subsequently, both sides talked about the Indonesian army:

MAO: I think the Indonesian right wing is determined to seize power. Are you determined, too?

AIDIT: (Nods) If Sukarno dies, it would be a question of who gains the upper hand.

MAO: I suggest that you should not go abroad so often. You can let the Number Two person (i.e., your deputy) [in your party] go abroad instead.

AIDIT: The right wing could take two possible kinds of action. First, they could attack us. If they do so, we would have reason to counterattack. Second, they could adopt a more moderate method by building a Nasakom government. Without Sukarno, it would be easy for the right wing to win the support of those who are in the middle in order to isolate us. The latter scenario would be difficult for us. However, no matter what, we have to deal with them. The US advised Nasution not to initiate a coup. This is because if he initiates a coup, the left wing would also take the same course of action. The Americans told Nasution that he should wait patiently; even if Sukarno dies, he [Nasution] should be flexible rather than [initiate] a coup. He accepted the suggestion from the Americans.

MAO: That is unreliable. The current situation has changed.

AIDIT: In the first scenario, we plan to establish a military committee. The majority of that committee would be left wing, but it should also include some moderate elements. In this way, we could confuse our enemies. Our enemies would be uncertain about the nature of this committee, and therefore the military commanders who are sympathetic to the right wing will not immediately oppose us. If we show our red flag right away, they will oppose us right away. The head of this military committee would be an underground member of our party, but he would identify himself as [being] neutral. This military committee should not last for too long. Otherwise, good people will turn [into] bad people. After it has been established, we need to arm the workers and peasants in a timely fashion.[52]

The plan Aidit spelled out for Mao, particularly the establishment of a committee that would not be obviously left-leaning and would be headed by an underground PKI member in the Indonesian army, strongly resembles the events that took place on the morning of October 1, 1965. This piece of information is consistent with John Roosa's argument that Aidit and an

FIGURE 8.1. D. N. Aidit (first from the left), his wife, Tanti Aidit, and the PKI Politburo member Jusuf Adjitorop with Mao Zedong, August 5, 1965. Photo courtesy of Hersi Setiawan.

exclusive group including progressive army officers made the plan for the movement without alerting the entire party membership or even the politburo.[53] Beijing was aware of the plan and at least did not object to it. But the Chinese leaders had no direct control over Aidit. In the record of the meeting quoted above, Mao shifted the conversation to his own experience at the Chongqing Negotiations with the Chinese Nationalist Party. Given the historical background of the Chinese Civil War, Mao might have been making an oblique suggestion that Aidit should be prepared for both peace talks and armed uprising.

The September Thirtieth Movement occurred on the same day as the PRC's National Day celebrations. At the time of the movement, approximately 4,500 Indonesians were visiting China as part of political, economic, military, and cultural delegations dispatched by the Indonesian government as well as by the PKI and affiliated organizations. In Beijing alone there were twenty-eight groups totaling almost five hundred people. At the national banquet in Beijing on the evening of September 30, 1965, Indonesians made up the largest percentage of foreign guests.[54] This striking synchrony was used by *Angkatan Bersendjata* to suggest that Mao rushed Aidit into taking action on this particular date so that a future "Indonesia People's Republic of the Chinese" would share the same national day with Beijing and become subordinate to it.[55] It is unlikely that Beijing knew the exact timing of the movement or participated in its planning. It is perplexing, however, that a few hours before the outbreak of the September Thirtieth Movement, Mao had encouraged Indonesia to develop its own nuclear bomb. Mao embraced the idea of a nuclearized Indonesia during a conversation with Chairul Saleh, a cabinet minister and speaker of the Provisional People's Consultative Assembly who led a forty-five-member governmental delegation to China.

CHAIRMAN MAO: Now, the world is not peaceful, so we need military forces and, moreover, the atomic bomb. Do you want to build an atomic bomb?

CHAIRUL SALEH: We would love to.

CHAIRMAN MAO: You should build one.

CHAIRUL SALEH: We do not agree that nuclear weaponry should be dominated by a few big powers.

CHAIRMAN MAO: That's right. Two big countries in the world want to monopolize nuclear power, but we won't listen to them. We will create our own. However, we are currently at the beginning stage. The Americans sent out a message threatening to blow up our nuclear reactors. That will be the end of the world. Some people say that reactors can be blown up, but ideals cannot be blown up. Even if the first batch of nuclear reactors were blown up, people with ideals could build a second batch.

CHAIRUL SALEH: Yes, new ones could be built.

CHAIRMAN MAO: It was the secretary of defense of the United States who said that.

CHAIRUL SALEH: Modern technology can no longer be monopolized by imperialists.

CHAIRMAN MAO: Yes, there should be no monopoly. All [technologies] should be open; all [countries] should be able to communicate [freely].

CHAIRUL SALEH: Therefore, we are very happy. Chairman Mao just said that China was only at the beginning stage of nuclear technology development. But for us, China creating its own atomic bomb is an event with great significance. We are greatly encouraged by this event both spiritually and materially. This event will further encourage all the New Emerging Forces to build a new world.

CHAIRMAN MAO: You have to build up your agriculture and light industry first. And you need to find the raw material to build an atomic bomb. Is there any in your country?

CHAIRUL SALEH: I believe there is. Our current geographical survey has shown some positive signs. Now we are vigorously conducting a survey and making use of the natural resources.

CHAIRMAN MAO: Do you have iron mines or coal mines? The resources in your country are richer than those of my country. You have huge amounts of petroleum and rubber, both of which are rare in the world.

CHAIRUL SALEH: That is true. It is for this reason that we sent an economic delegation to China to learn from China and foster closer collaboration between the two countries. Developing the iron industry and heavy industry are the most important tasks for Indonesia. We don't have large-scale ironmaking and steelmaking industries. In that aspect, we would be glad to build up these industries as soon as possible, if China is willing to offer us help.

CHAIRMAN MAO: This is totally workable. We surely can help you unconditionally.[56]

Given Mao's capricious and elusive style when in dialogue with foreign dignitaries, it is unclear exactly what he meant and why he brought up such a sensitive topic at such a sensitive time. Since Mao spent much time critiquing the Western powers and Soviet Union's erroneous assumption that the Asians were incapable of mastering high-end technology, it is reasonable to understand "the nuclear bomb" in this context as a symbol for militant confrontation against both superpowers. There is ambiguity about the extent of Mao's "unconditional" support to Indonesia. Mao's offer could be interpreted narrowly, as referring solely to the steel industry, or broadly, as an offer that would include nuclear assistance. Since Mao urged the Indonesian leaders to be patient and to concentrate their efforts on agriculture and light industry, it is more likely that he was promising a continuation of general Chinese economic aid to Indonesia, which did not necessarily include nuclear technology.[57] Prior to this conversation, Beijing had raised the prospect of providing Indonesia with nuclear technology by hosting an Indonesian Atomic Energy Group that consisted of nuclear scientists, engineers, and military personnel.[58] But China was far from ready to provide concrete aid to a strategic nuclear program in Indonesia. Mao was probably using the nuclear bomb as a carrot to entice Indonesia to join China in its fierce struggle against imperialism in all forms.

The Aftermath

After receiving news of the movement from foreign media on October 1, Beijing sent a telegram to its embassy in Jakarta requesting clarification. Yet a reply did not reach Beijing until more than a day later due to a disruption in communication.[59] During his first official meeting with the Indonesian guests after the movement, Zhou Enlai said that according to the information Beijing had gathered from foreign sources, "the Council of Generals staged an abortive coup. . . . The guards of the Presidential Palace captured those involved and formed a 'Revolutionary Council' to take control of the situation."[60] On October 2, some telegrams finally went through between Beijing and Jakarta, including one from the Chinese embassy confirming the safety of Sukarno. However, radio signals from the Chinese embassy were constantly disrupted and the NCNA Jakarta office was completely blocked.

In his talk with Chairul Saleh on October 1, Zhou put forward an interpretation that the Revolutionary Council was responding to an attempted coup by the Council of Generals rather than simply launching the September Thirtieth Movement on their own initiative. In a meeting in mid-November with the North Korean prime minister Ri Ju-yeon, Chen Yi said that the leader of the movement, Untung, "was following Sukarno's instructions." He further explained: "There were supporters of Sukarno as well as spies from the army and the right wing within the PKI. Sukarno's supporters and PKI members were inside the army, too. It is difficult to understand what was going on."[61] Given that both Zhou Enlai and Chen Yi were present at Aidit's discussions with Mao on August 5, the two top Chinese leaders could have been trying to protect the PKI as well as the CCP itself by hiding the fact that Beijing was notified ahead of time. But Beijing might have been expecting a longer period of Sukarno-PKI collaboration, which would have allowed the

PKI to buy more time for full-scale militarization. Thus, Beijing was probably troubled by the speed with which the PKI had rushed into action. By October 2, the foreign policy–making circle in Beijing had already learned that the Revolutionary Council had failed and that Suharto had taken control of the situation.[62]

It seems that, in the period stretching from the immediate aftermath of the September Thirtieth Movement to late October 1965, the Chinese leaders were still hoping that a progressive, left-leaning government based on an alliance between Sukarno and the PKI would reemerge. Beijing had high expectations that Sukarno would be a game changer. On October 3, while meeting with the delegation of the staff college of the Indonesian air force, Zhou said he was relieved to hear President Sukarno's own voice in a speech broadcast on the radio in Jakarta on that day. By the end of the conversation, Zhou told the head of the delegation: "Please tell President Sukarno to take good care of his health for the sake of Indonesia's revolution."[63] On October 4, before Chairul Saleh set off for Jakarta, Zhou asked him to convey his regards to Sukarno on behalf of the Chinese leaders, including Mao Zedong, Liu Shaoqi, Zhu De, Chen Yi, Peng Zhen, and himself. Zhou said: "All of us have been listening to news about the situation in Indonesia from October 1 to October 3."[64]

Yet such friendly gestures took a sharp turn. A conflict broke out between the Chinese embassy staff and members of the Indonesian army at the PRC embassy compound in Jakarta due to the former's refusal to lower the Chinese national flag to half-mast to commemorate the army generals killed in the movement. The clash was followed by the Indonesian military's search of the dormitory used by the Chinese embassy staff and the residence of Chinese engineers at the construction site of the Beijing-sponsored CONEFO building.[65] In the eyes of the Chinese leaders, Sukarno's failure to protect China's interests during this time was a deal breaker, reflecting Sukarno's lack of both credibility and political prowess in the midst of the fast-changing political scene in Indonesia. In mid-November, Chen Yi told the visiting North Korean prime minister, Ri Ju-yeon, that Sukarno had little leeway to take control of the situation.[66] On the same occasion, Zhou Enlai said: "We believe Sukarno and Subandrio are devoted to maintaining friendly relations with China . . . but the right wing wanted to destroy bilateral relations completely. . . . Sukarno hopes that we will give him some more time. But time has passed already. He could only shake his head and sigh. . . . It is difficult to say how much Sukarno can do. I don't think he has much leverage."[67]

Deeply disappointed with Sukarno, Beijing began to expect a full-fledged Communist revolution in Indonesia beginning in mid-November 1965. As

Chen Yi bluntly put it in his conversation with Ri Ju-yeon: "Personally I think it will be a good thing if Sukarno is overthrown. . . . The future of Indonesia depends on the armed struggle of the PKI. This is the most important thing. It is definitive."[68] However, at the time Beijing was not able to receive any information directly from the PKI or indirectly from the North Korean or North Vietnamese embassy in Jakarta. There were PKI members coming to China from Jakarta, but the number seemed small and none of them had reliable information about conditions outside of the capital. The Chinese leadership knew that there was an armed force of more than ten thousand in Central Java. Beijing was confident that the PKI was building up its strength and had a good chance in the final showdown with the army because Beijing believed that the party had control over the vast countryside and mountainous regions. Chen Yi strongly endorsed the PKI's armed struggle: "The PKI was most resolute in its anti-imperialist, antirevisionist campaigns. It can definitely withstand this test. Obviously, the united front is not doing the PKI any good. The PKI should resolutely shift its policy to armed struggle. . . . An overall revolution is inevitable in Indonesia. No matter what actions the United States and the right-wing forces take, no matter what tricks Sukarno plays, the fundamental issues will need to be resolved. Indonesia is now in the eye of a storm, on the eve of a great revolution."[69]

With regard to China's response to the radical change in Indonesian domestic politics and subsequently in bilateral relations, Chen Yi and Zhou Enlai seem to have had different stances, as shown in their conversations with North Korea's prime minister in mid-November 1965. Chen Yi's position was more aggressive, as he claimed: "It would serve us best if our ambassador is expelled, which indicates that there is hope for Indonesia's revolution. I hope the conflicts between the right wing and left wing will escalate." Zhou Enlai, in contrast, was measured and diplomatic. He made a clear distinction between the two parts of the Chinese policy. In terms of state-to-state relations, Zhou said Beijing would continue to work with Sukarno as long as he was sincere, while continuing its strong protest against the army and other anti-China right-wing groups. In regard to inter–Communist Party relations, Zhou said: "We support our fraternal party [the PKI], but our support is within proper boundaries. It is the Indonesian people's revolution, led by the Indonesian left wing. We cannot surpass them. Now, the PKI has not yet made any public announcement. Therefore, we cannot speak on its behalf."[70]

The Chinese leadership's expectations were soon shattered. In late November 1965, Suharto's troops captured and executed Aidit in Central Java. In December 1965, Mao wrote a poem to commemorate the PKI leader:

Sparse branches stood in front of my windows in winter, smiling
   before hundreds of flowers
Regretfully those smiles withered when spring came
There is no need to grieve over the withered
To each flower there is a season to wither, as well a season to blossom
There will be more flowers in the coming year.[71]

The poem shows Mao's confidence in a revival of the Communist movement in Indonesia. After the September Thirtieth Movement, the PRC adopted a generous policy toward Indonesian visitors, including many PKI cadres and left-leaning students, intellectuals, and activists.[72] To those who could not or opted not to return to Indonesia—including the PKI politburo member Jusuf Adjitorop, Aidit's daughter Ibarruri, and Aidit's brother Asahan Sobron—the Chinese government offered shelter and a means of living. These Indonesian exiles enjoyed a privileged life insulated from economic difficulties. According to the playwright and PKI member Utuy Tatang Sontani, who stayed in China between 1965 and 1974, most of those who had health concerns were initially transferred to hospitals in Guangzhou and later to a sanatorium in South China.[73] Healthy exiles or those who had recovered

FIGURE 8.2.   PKI exiles Suar Soroso (middle), his wife (left), and Sukinah. Nanchang, October 9, 2013. Photo by author.

were relocated to the Nanjing Military Academy, where, according to some witnesses, they received training in guerrilla-warfare strategies.[74] However, instead of developing any concrete plan for a reunion with the PKI remnant back home, the exiles were drilled in Cultural Revolution propaganda and forced to carry on meetings for criticism and self-criticism, and to attend daily study sessions on the works of Mao Zedong.[75] By 1971 many of this group, like Ibarruri, became cognizant of the erosion of unity among the exiles and of the dim prospects for returning home to rebuild the PKI.[76]

Beginning in 1979, Deng Xiaoping started steering China away from endless political campaigns and toward economic development. Deng's reforms granted the exiles a greater sense of autonomy and a vision of a better life fostered by encounters with the outside world, encouraging many among them to leave China for Western countries. Moreover, stimulated by the dynamics of trade, both Beijing and Jakarta sought to normalize bilateral relations, which were frozen in 1967. The official status granted to the PKI exiles was downgraded from "foreign guests of the Party" (*wai bin*)—a prestigious title in China—to "residents of foreign origin" (*wai qiao*). Those who remained in China were given Chinese passports and national identity cards and were assigned to jobs in the civil sector.[77] When Qian Qichen, the Chinese foreign minister at the time, met with the Indonesian state minister Murdiono in 1989, Qian explained China's position this way: "We had noticed that Indonesia was particularly concerned about noninterference in the internal affairs of other countries. I stressed that China had no connection with the Indonesian Communist Party—we do not even know whether there is such a party today. There had once been some Indonesians living in China, but most of them had left and probably only a few dozen remained. Some of these had retired; others were employed. We did not allow Indonesians living in China to engage in political activities."[78]

From late 1964 to September 1965, Beijing used much of its political leverage to create a scenario that best suited its interests in Indonesia: a firm leftist government jointly led by Sukarno and the PKI and a right wing that had been either undermined or eliminated. Beijing intended to help pro-Sukarno forces—the PKI and the Indonesian air force—strengthen themselves against right-wing elements in the Indonesian army. Although deeply invested in Indonesian politics, Beijing's role in the political developments in Indonesia in 1965 was insubstantial. The small arms the Chinese leaders offered on a state-to-state level to Indonesia probably had not arrived prior to October 1. Evidence from China supports John Roosa's theory that Aidit and the Special Bureau designed the movement, leaving the rest of the PKI leadership in the dark.[79] Beijing was informed of the plan for the movement during Aidit's visit to China in early August 1965 and most likely acquiesced to it. But the swift execution of the plan took Beijing by surprise. The Chinese government protected the Indonesian Communist exiles after the movement and provided them with a life of material comfort during the Cultural Revolution. However, consumed with the political campaigns in China, it seems highly unlikely that anyone returned to Indonesia from the PRC to resurrect the PKI. These conclusions about Beijing's limited influence in Indonesia in 1965, which are based on Chinese materials, can also be corroborated by recently declassified US sources. These new materials reveal that in early 1966, American diplomats in Jakarta had already considered accusations of Chinese involvement to be a "hoax" manufactured to serve "the propaganda needs" of the Suharto regime.[80] Yet the US nevertheless encouraged the media in both Indonesia and abroad to link China to the September Thirtieth Movement in their reports.[81]

On October 7, 1965, the Chinese minister of defense, Lin Biao, received a message from his Indonesian counterpart Nasution congratulating him on the sixteenth anniversary of the founding of the PRC. Nasution was originally a kidnapping target during the September Thirtieth Movement but survived because his personal aide, Pierre Tandean, was mistakenly identified as him. In addition to goodwill on behalf of the Indonesian Armed Forces, Nasution expressed his hope for "the further development of the existing good relations between the armed forces of the two countries."[82] The telegram was published in the *People's Daily* on the same day (October 7, 1965) while news of the September Thirtieth Movement was withheld until late October. According to the Chinese Foreign Ministry, foreign ministers of defense had rarely sent congratulatory telegrams on the PRC's national day in the past. The sudden turn of events in Indonesia and the unclear political situation in the immediate aftermath of the movement left Beijing confused about what signals lay behind Nasution's telegram. This intriguing telegram suggests that, shortly after the September Thirtieth Movement, even right-wing figures like Nasution did not immediately identify Beijing as the mastermind and were not irrevocably anti-PRC. This open-mindedness soon disappeared as right-wing forces in Indonesia felt the need to produce rhetoric against "Red China" on an ad hoc basis to fuel their reprisals against the Communists at home.

The next chapter examines how Beijing and Taipei responded to the shifting political landscape in Indonesia after the September Thirtieth Movement. The rekindled rivalry between the Red and the Blue in the aftermath of the movement exacerbated tensions in bilateral diplomacy between Beijing and Jakarta as well as interethnic relations within Indonesian society. In particular, Beijing's lack of restraint in its anti-Suharto propaganda paradoxically lent credence to the unfounded allegations of the PRC's involvement in the movement and further jeopardized the position of the ethnic Chinese in Indonesia.

CHAPTER 9

Beijing, Taipei, and the Emerging Suharto Regime

In spring 1966, twenty-nine-year-old Kong Zhi-yuan wrote to his friends in Beijing from the Chinese embassy in Jakarta: "My head could be chopped off and my blood could be spilled. But I cannot harm the dignity of my motherland."[1] In 1964 Kong, who would later become an authority on bahasa Indonesia language and literature in China, won a government scholarship for postgraduate education at the University of Indonesia (Universitas Indonesia). After the September Thirtieth Movement, Kong's studies were interrupted and he moved into the Chinese embassy compound, working as a translator for the diplomatic mission. Between October 1965 and November 1966, Kong witnessed rounds of conflict between the PRC embassy staff and the Indonesian army and right-wing groups, particularly KAMI (Kesatuan Aksi Mahasiswa Indonesia, Indonesian University Students' Action Front), KAPPI (Kesatuan Aksi Pemuda Pelajar Indonesia, Indonesian Youth and Students' Action Front), and Pemuda Pancasila (Pancasila Youth).[2] In February 1966, over a thousand radicalized right-wing youth forced their way into the embassy and smashed the PRC national emblem. Chinese diplomats telephoned the Indonesian Foreign Ministry and police to request protection but to no avail. Confined within the battered office building and dormitory, with barely any weapons to protect themselves, Kong and other staff members invented self-defense strategies using beer bottles, light bulbs, and Chinese martial arts.[3] In order

FIGURE 9.1. Kong Zhiyuan (left) with the Five-Star Red Flag at the Chinese embassy in Jakarta, October 1966. Personal collection of Kong Zhiyuan.

to block the Indonesian army and right-wing youth from taking hold of the PRC flag—a symbol of national pride—Kong and his comrades secured it with iron chains and applied motor oil to the flagpole to make it too slippery to climb. During these days of violence and terror, Kong's spirits were high; he felt as if the entire Chinese nation was standing behind him.[4]

Suharto claimed to be the guardian of the Indonesian nation against internal subversion and external intervention by Communists. During his rise to power, attacks on the PRC diplomatic apparatus helped cement the legitimacy of his leadership. Suharto's strategy attracted a once-estranged bedfellow: Taipei. In June 1967, Xu Juqing, the former editor-in-chief of the Chinese Nationalist Party's organ in Indonesia, *Tian Sheng Ri Bao*, returned to Indonesia as the first ROC passport holder to enter the archipelago since relations between Jakarta and Taipei had turned sour in 1958. As the president of Taipei's Overseas News Agency and the special secretary of the Overseas Chinese Affairs Commission, Xu donated to Pemuda Pancasila, a paramilitary organization that played an important role in the 1965–66 mass killings. When he learned of KAMI's plan to launch a massive assault on the PRC embassy on the two-year anniversary of the September Thirtieth Movement, Xu contributed 100,000 Indonesian rupiah's worth of food, beverages, and other supplies to the group. To Xu's satisfaction, the "illegitimate embassy" suffered disastrous damage in the assault. Vehicles were smashed, a portrait of Mao Zedong burnt, the PRC national flag torn apart, documents and cash stolen, and a telegraph transmitter destroyed. Nine of its staff members were beaten "to the extent that their heads were covered with blood."[5] On October 9, 1967, pressured by KAMI, the Indonesian government announced its decision to "freeze" diplomatic relations with Beijing. The Chinese Nationalist government later invited the KAMI cadres, together with Indonesian military intelligence personnel, to Taiwan for training.[6] Xu Juqing reported to Taipei that his strategy of riding the tide of political violence perpetrated by right-wing radicals had proven to be convenient and effective. "From now on," Xu wrote, "we should establish frequent contact with the Indonesian anti-Communist youth and make good use of them."[7]

As Suharto's authoritarian rule replaced the Sukarno-PKI alliance, the cross–Taiwan Strait politics between the two Chinas became intertwined with the anti-Communist campaign and mass violence in Indonesia. The suspension of Sino-Indonesian relations reflected the paralysis of PRC diplomacy and greatly contributed to the growing sociopolitical mobilization during the early stages of the Cultural Revolution. The popular misperception in Indonesia that the PRC had sponsored a Communist coup was bolstered by the violent clashes between the PRC's Indonesian diplomatic mission and right-wing youth, the Red Guards' retaliatory attacks on the Indonesian diplomatic compound in China, the inflammatory broadcasts of Radio Peking, and the fiery tirades in the *People's Daily* against Suharto. Meanwhile, the Chinese Nationalist government in Taiwan capitalized on the golden opportunity provided by the anti-Communist fervor in Indonesia, which had been fueled by the fall of Sukarno, the demise of the Indonesian Communists, and the country's turn toward the capitalist West.

The political turmoil in Indonesia between 1965 and 1967 gave rise to a period of insecurity for most of the Chinese in Indonesia. There has been ongoing controversy over the nature of the violence against the ethnic Chinese following the September Thirtieth Movement. Robert Cribb and Charles Coppel's research refutes the Cold War journalism that portrayed the 1965–66 massacres as a genocide of the ethnic Chinese.[8] I concur with Cribb and Coppel that the majority of the victims of the 1965–66 mass killings were targeted due to their alleged political affiliation rather than their ethnicity. As a minority, the ethnic Chinese constituted a small percentage of the victims compared to the pribumi.[9] But I believe that, proportionately, the ethnic Chinese were particularly vulnerable to violence after the movement as they were collectively associated with Communism. Most anti-Communist pribumis were not inclined to draw a fine distinction between the pro-Taipei and the pro-Beijing Chinese, or between those who had taken on Indonesian citizenship and those who had chosen PRC nationality. Neither the anti-Communist stance of the pro-Taipei individuals nor the citizenship status of the naturalized Chinese shielded them from indiscriminate violence against the entire diasporic community.

The Breach of Beijing-Jakarta Relations and the Beginning of the Cultural Revolution

Shortly after the September Thirtieth Movement, the PRC's presence across the archipelago became the target of violence. While the PRC embassy in Jakarta was under siege, similar aggressions were occurring in Banjarmasin in South Kalimantan, Makassar in Sulawesi, Medan in North Sumatra, and Bandung in West Java. In Medan, for example, on November 2, 1965, more than three thousand right-wing activists ransacked the PRC consulate.[10] According to the New China News Agency, local law enforcement "made no attempt to stop the mob." The assailants even reportedly presented the PRC national flag they had stolen from the consulate as a trophy to the military commander of North Sumatra.[11] In addition, architects, technicians, and engineers dispatched from China to Indonesia for aid programs were subject to hostile treatment by the Indonesian army and police.[12] Between October and December 1965, Beijing's response to the Indonesian government's maltreatment of its diplomats and expatriates remained rational and restrained. Although the top leaders had been closely watching the political maelstrom in the archipelago, there was zero media mention of the September Thirtieth Movement until October 19.[13] In the following few days, the September Thirtieth Movement and its aftermath were the front-page story in almost all the nationwide newspapers in China. But the tone of these reports was carefully measured. Beijing narrowly targeted "a small clique" (*yixiaocuo*) of Indonesian right-wing elements, who, despite their vicious deeds instigated by the US, were incapable of ruining the enduring friendship between the two nations.[14] In a restless atmosphere that foreshadowed the Cultural Revolution, the release of this information to an already politically agitated general public caused a commotion. At the Beijing Steel and Iron Institute (Beijing Gangtie Xueyuan), enraged Chinese youth interrogated fellow students from Indonesia and sought permission from the institute's leadership to put up Big Character Posters (*dazibao*) to admonish the "Indonesian reactionaries." Similar incidents occurred in other parts of China as well. In an attempt to harness this nationalist fervor, the Foreign Affairs Office under the State Council (guowuyuan waishiban) issued the following guidelines:

1. We should differentiate between the Indonesian guests, experts, and students in China and the right-wing anti-China, anti-Chinese elements in Indonesia. Toward the former group, we should maintain the same friendly attitude as before. We aim to win their hearts and minds and to unite them.
2. When talking about the anti-China, anti-Chinese measures unleashed by the Indonesian army, we should carefully follow the diplomatic note issued by our government. . . . If any Indonesian guests, experts, or students disagree with us, we should kindly reason with them without provoking an altercation.
3. We should not allow any protest or Big Character Posters. Posters that are already up should be taken down. The work units of the poster makers should prevent them from taking further action.[15]

In Indonesia, the Chinese diplomatic mission was following the same moderate policy. When the Indonesian army forced its way into the CONEFO construction site to search for "arms smuggled to the PKI," the PRC embassy in Jakarta reported to Beijing: "The Indonesian side is pressuring us to compromise. If they do not cause significant damage to our interests, we can ignore them."[16]

However, with the unfolding of the Cultural Revolution and the radicalization of Chinese foreign policy, intemperate outbursts replaced reasoned judgments. Instead of containing the conflicts, the CCP leadership saw new value in using the Suharto regime in its preparatory propaganda for domestic political campaigns. In 1966, coerced by pro-Suharto forces in the Indonesian military, Sukarno signed the Order of March 11 (*Surat Perintah Sebelas Maret*, or *Supersmar*), giving Suharto the authority to take any action necessary to maintain national security. Suharto proceeded to speed up his anti-Communist campaign. A month later, on April 15, 1966, over one thousand right-wing activists assailed the PRC embassy in Jakarta, reportedly under the protection of armored cars dispatched by the Indonesian army. While

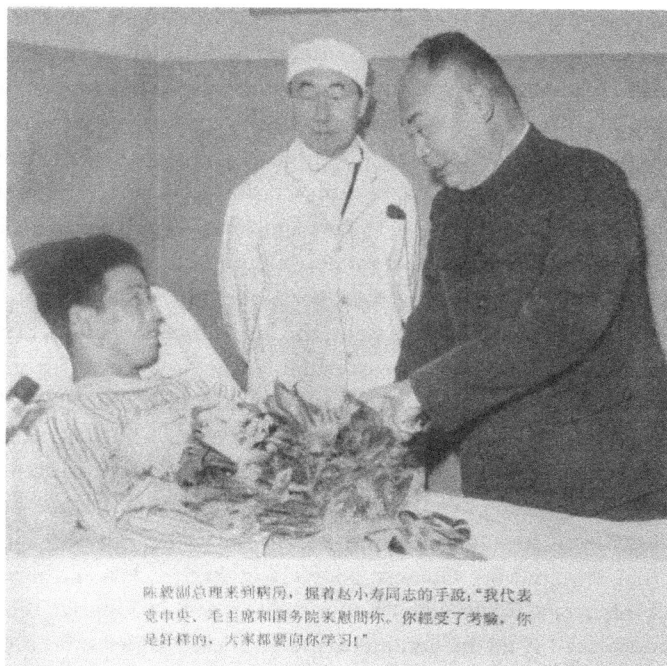

FIGURE 9.2. Vice Premier Chen Yi visiting Zhao Xiaoshou in his hospital room. *Shijie Zhishi* 9 (1966).

trying to protect the Five-Star Red Flag, a Chinese diplomat named Zhao Xiaoshou was shot in the lungs.[17] The image of an injured Zhao being carried on a stretcher toward an airplane dispatched by Beijing for medical evacuation became a media sensation in the early stages of the Cultural Revolution.[18] When visiting Zhao on behalf of the Communist Party leadership, the Chinese foreign minister Chen Yi cried out: "The imperialists and the reactionaries fired at our comrades. . . . The blood debts need to be paid back with blood!"[19] An editorial in *Knowledge about the World* warned of "a small clique of anti-China 'heroes' in Indonesia": "You cannot easily bully Chinese diplomats or the great Chinese people. You cannot easily vilify or oppose the great socialist China. If you continue on this anti-Communism, anti-China, anti-people path, your day will soon end."[20]

After this violent conflict, Beijing started to openly oppose the Suharto regime. By berating Suharto nonstop in both Mandarin Chinese and bahasa Indonesia, Radio Peking ironically gave the Indonesian army an excuse to depict the PRC as the mastermind of the September Thirtieth Movement.[21] The Indonesian Foreign Ministry issued a diplomatic note protesting Radio

Peking's "systematic verbal abuse of Indonesia worldwide" and its "rough and direct intervention in Indonesia's internal politics." In reply, the Chinese Foreign Ministry stated: "Honestly speaking, we are exposing you too little rather than too much. . . . You are frantically suppressing the Communist Party and the people, slaughtering hundreds of thousands of civilians, bathing Indonesia in blood, and implementing a cruel fascist rule. . . . Your wrongdoings are against history. People in Asia and Africa are all enraged. You can never escape the righteous condemnation of hundreds of millions of people around the world."[22] At 3 a.m. on October 1, 1967, the two-year anniversary of the September Thirtieth Movement, the PRC embassy in Jakarta suffered its forty-third and last attack. The remaining staff were cut off from access to water, electricity, and communication with the outside world.[23] They left Indonesia by the end of October 1967, after Beijing and Jakarta had suspended bilateral relations and closed their embassies and consulates.

The PRC propaganda machine depicted the turmoil in Indonesia as part of a "vicious anti-China, anti-Chinese wind all over the world" (guoji fanhua yaofeng) that required the Chinese people to further advance their revolution.[24] An important figure who dramatized the Sino-Indonesian diplomatic breach and placed it at the center of the political theater of the Cultural Revolution was Yao Dengshan.[25] A former People's Liberation Army commander, Yao became the chargé d'affaires of the PRC in Jakarta after Ambassador Yao Zhongming's recall in April 1966. In his role as a diplomat, Yao Dengshan disregarded protocol by directly quarreling with Indonesian army officers.[26] Yao, together with the PRC consul general Xu Ren, was later named a persona non grata by the Indonesian Foreign Ministry. At the Beijing airport on April 30, 1967, more than seven thousand people, including seven senior party leaders, gathered to welcome Yao and Xu, the "red diplomatic fighters" expelled from Indonesia. Zhou Enlai embraced Yao after he disembarked from the plane.[27] The next day, at the International Labor Day parade at Tian'anmen Square, Mao Zedong, Lin Biao, and Jiang Qing welcomed Yao and Xu. Holding Mao's hand, Yao said: "On behalf of all the patriotic overseas Chinese in Indonesia, all the comrades working in our embassy there, we express our warmest regards to Chairman Mao, wishing Chairman Mao boundless longevity. . . . The Indonesian people have boundless love for Chairman Mao."[28] The continuous propaganda against the "fascist" Suharto government animated the Red Guards, whose tendency toward violence during the Cultural Revolution resembled that of KAMI and KAPPI during the Indonesian mass murders. Between April 24 and 28, 1967, more than six hundred thousand of them protested in front of the Indonesian embassy in Beijing.[29] In August 1967, upon hearing that KAMI and KAPPI members had set fire to two buildings inside the Chinese diplomatic compound in Jakarta, the Red Guards stormed the Indonesian embassy in Beijing.[30]

In a twist of history, the vortex in Indonesia entered the political discourse Mao deployed for his purge of Liu Shaoqi. In 1963 Liu and his wife Wang Guangmei visited the archipelago. The trip was recorded in *Chairman Liu's Visit to Indonesia* (*Liu zhuxi fangwen Yindunixiya*), one of the rare color documentaries in China at the time. The documentary shows Wang, an elegant and articulate first lady, wearing a *qipao* dress at a state banquet in Jakarta. In 1967, after Liu was censured by Mao as the foremost "capitalist roader" within the party, the Red Guards at Tsinghua University forced Wang to put on the same dress, with a necklace made of ping-pong balls. The "red diplomatic fighters" Yao Dengshan and Zhao Xiaoshou jointly published an article in the *People's Daily* entitled "An Ugly Farce That Promotes Surrenderism (*touxiang zhuyi*) Internationally—Critiques on the Counterrevolutionary Documentary *Visit to Indonesia*." In their diatribe, Yao and Zhao wrote: "In this documentary, we can see how intoxicated the biggest capitalist roader [Liu Shaoqi] was with the decadent bourgeois life style! He and Wang . . . acted like buffoons. To please the Indonesian bourgeoisie, Wang dressed in a seductive style. . . . She even proposed to visit the lewd bedrooms of the Indonesian bourgeoisie and the biggest capitalist roader followed her. In the end, he shamelessly boasted: 'We did not have such a merry time when Wang and I got married. This trip was like a make-up wedding for us!'"[31]

Taiwan's Diplomatic Maneuvering after the "October First Coup"

In Indonesia, the naming of the incident that took place in the early morning of October 1, 1965, was heavily politicized. Sukarno suggested at a cabinet meeting on October 9 that the event be called *Gestok*, an abbreviation of *Gerakan Satu Oktober*—"the October 1 Movement." The army-controlled media ignored him and called the movement *Gestapu*, an abbreviation of *Gerakan September Tiga Puluh* (the September Thirtieth Movement), with a reference to the Gestapo, the Nazi secret police. As Suharto's anti-Communist campaign unfolded, the event became *Gestapu/PKI*, with a direct accusation of the Indonesian Communist Party. In Mandarin Chinese, Beijing used the direct translation of "September Thirtieth Movement" (*jiusanling yundong*) or "September Thirtieth Incident" (*jiusanling shijian*) whereas Taipei chose the term "The October First Coup" (*shiyi zhengbian*) to connect the political changeover in Indonesia to the PRC's National Day on October 1. The Federation of Overseas Chinese Associations (huaqiao jiuguo lianhe zonghui) in Taipei portrayed the September Thirtieth Movement as a case of the Machiavellian PKI taking advantage of a power struggle between Sukarno and the anti-Communist army generals.[32] Citing *Angkatan Bersendjata*'s fabricated account of the discovery of China-made weaponry in Jakarta and the rumor that the PKI chairman D. N. Aidit hid in the PRC embassy as "powerful evidence," the federation concluded that "the Communist bandits" were "the mastermind behind the stage." It interpreted the PRC embassy's controversial decision not to lower its national flag to half-mast as "an act of a thief who felt guilt over his crime (*zuozei xinxu*)."[33]

It remains uncertain whether the policy-making circle in Taipei genuinely believed in this version. Most likely, Taipei's attention and energy were directed toward planning ahead instead of looking back. Since their retreat in disgrace in 1958, the Chinese Nationalists had been waiting for the chance to return to Indonesia, "where the ethnic Chinese reached each and every corner of the archipelago and amounted to the largest overseas Chinese community in the world."[34] The demise of the PKI boded well for the Chinese Nationalist Party's counteroffensive against the Communists.[35] Beyond politics, Taiwan also aimed to establish trade relations with Indonesia. Progressing industrialization prompted the Chinese Nationalist government to seek overseas markets. With a population of 120 million at the time, Taipei regarded the archipelago as the export destination "every country had its eyes on."[36] To revitalize relations with Indonesia, Taipei remobilized the Chinese Nationalist Party cadres who were familiar with the country. In addition to Xu Juqing, Mah Soo Lay (Ma Shuli)—who had also been incarcerated and deported by the Indonesian government in 1959—ardently rose to the occasion. A multilingual world citizen, Mah had been educated in Japan and the Philippines before being posted to Indonesia to oversee the Chinese Nationalist Party branches. In 1965 Mah was the chief of the Third Group of the Chinese Nationalist Party's Central Committee, the organization in charge of the party's overseas expansion.

The first glimpse of hope for Mah, Xu, and other Nationalist elites with ties to Indonesia came in April 1966, when the Indonesian attorney general, Sugih Arto, announced during a visit to Bangkok that Communist China was Indonesia's biggest enemy. Taipei's expectations soared in June 1966, when Suharto dispatched his confidante, Ali Murtopo, to Taiwan to discuss a collaboration to fight Communism. The vice president of the Republic of China, Yen Chia-kan (Yan Jiakan), met with Suharto's envoy, signaling Taipei's intent to reopen backdoor diplomatic channels. In October 1966, a number of diplomats, representatives of the army, the Bank of Indonesia, and the Provisional People's Consultative Assembly (Majelis Permusyawaratan Rakyat Sementara) visited Taiwan.[37]

In May 1967, the Indonesian Foreign Ministry officially announced that Indonesian passport holders and "stateless" individuals—a category given by the Indonesian government to those who maintained ROC citizenship—were allowed to travel to Taiwan and freely reenter Indonesia. This flexible policy stood in stark contrast to the tight restrictions imposed by the Indonesian government on travel to the PRC.

But Taipei's optimism was premature. In early April 1967, Mah Soo Lay met with Adam Malik, the Indonesian foreign minister, in Tokyo. In his report to Taipei, Mah declared that Malik was "firmly anti-Communist," "friendly" toward Taiwan, and held "immense admiration" for Chiang Kai-shek. In spring 1967, Malik described the political environment in Indonesia as "stable" after the mass violence. But he thought Suharto's purge was not thorough enough: "Only 100,000 out of 3 million Communists have been eliminated. The remaining Communists have gone underground."[38] When Mah urged Indonesia to cut off relations with the "Communist bandits," Malik became circumspect and insisted that Indonesia would not initiate a breach of diplomatic ties. He tried to reassure Mah that the Communist Chinese diplomats were ready to leave at any time, even though their departure would only mark a suspension rather than a termination of Indonesia-PRC relations. He cited the existence of over one million ethnic Chinese, the majority of whom supported the PRC, as the main reason for Indonesia's decision to temporarily freeze, rather than permanently end, bilateral relations.[39]

By 1969 it was apparent to Taiwan that, given the sheer size of the PRC, even the most adamantly anti-Communist politicians in Indonesia would rationally seek "to appease the Communist bandits." The Chinese Nationalists blamed the Indonesian ruling elites for their "pathological fear of the Communist bandits" (kong fei bing) as well as their weakness in front of the "sugar-coated bullets of money" shot by the left-leaning ethnic Chinese in Indonesia.[40] Most importantly, Mainland China remained an important consumer of raw materials from Indonesia. Indonesia's foreign donors in North America and Western Europe, although part of the capitalist camp, also maintained economic and/or cultural contacts with the PRC and advised Indonesia against irrevocably breaking away from the PRC.[41] Interestingly, not long after his friendly interactions with Taipei, Malik assisted the PRC with its reentry to the UN.[42] In 1971, as president of the UN Assembly, Malik announced the UN's decision to drop its support for the Chinese Nationalist Party's claim to represent China and to give the UN seat to the PRC.

Unable to shake Beijing's powerful political status, Taipei turned to challenging the PRC's economic presence in Indonesia. The trade relations between Taipei and Jakarta warmed in 1967 with Indonesia's purchase of textiles from the ROC and a subsequent deal for cotton processing, which brought Taiwan 6.7 million USD of profit.[43] Hoping to take over the PRC's market share in Indonesia, Taipei helped the ethnic Chinese loyal to the Nationalist government organize large import-export companies that would outperform the trading firms owned by pro-Beijing Chinese. Taipei also devised a marketing strategy of employing Indonesian-born ethnic Chinese who had studied in Taiwan as the salespeople for its products. Besides the trade war, Taipei assisted the pro-Taipei ethnic Chinese with opening new banks that would break down the monopoly of financial institutions run by pro-Beijing figures.[44] The Chinese Nationalist government also set aside a budget for entertaining Indonesian officials, determined to bribe them to support Taipei.[45]

At the 1969 Jakarta Fair (*Pekan Raya Jakarta*), which lasted for a historically long period of seventy-one days and included the US president Richard Nixon among its VIP guests, the ROC paid its first public visit to Indonesia in two decades. In addition to its own exhibitions, the ROC also contributed to KAMI's anti-Communist photo gallery of the Cultural Revolution in China, which included pictures showing "floating bodies in the Pearl River," "the Communist suppression of religion," and "Maoist demonstrations against Indonesia."[46] Despite increased international exposure, Taiwan's experience on this occasion was mixed. Initially, the ROC delegates had proposed to paint the top of their pagoda-shaped exhibition hall with the pattern of the Blue Sky, White Sun, and Red Earth flag. But the director of the Jakarta Fair turned down this proposal. After mediation by Malik, the Taiwan exhibition team reluctantly accepted a compromise in which the entrance to the hall would be decorated with five Chinese characters, "Hall of the Republic of China" (*Zhonghua minguo guan*).[47] More concerning than the noncooperative attitude of their Indonesian host was the phantom of the PRC. The Taiwan delegation was deeply worried about "active attacks and passive insults from underground Chinese Communist elements and left-wing groups."[48] In the end, although the pro-Beijing Chinese did not sabotage the exhibition, they allegedly retaliated against Bong A Lok (also known as Suwandi Hamid, Ong Ah Lok, Wang Yalu), a board member of the pro-Taipei Indonesia Commerce Center (Yindunixiya shangwu zhongxin). After the exhibition, Wang found himself on the verge of bankruptcy due to the pro-Beijing group's sudden withdrawal of funds from the bank he owned. Wang ultimately lost his business in Indonesia and immigrated to Taiwan.[49]

Beijing's and Taipei's Response to Anti-Chinese Violence

During my fieldwork in 2013 in Surabaya, East Java, I met Mr. Weng Deyong. A third-generation ethnic Chinese, he had adopted the Indonesian-sounding name "Ongko," as required by the Suharto regime's anti-Chinese legislation. His father, a peranakan Chinese who worked as a bookkeeper for the Baperki, was shot dead by Indonesian army officers in 1966 during a search of his home. Pak Ongko was fifteen years old at the time. He described the macabre atmosphere during those days: "There were beheaded bodies dumped on the streets. The chopped-off heads were displayed on the bridges. More bodies were dumped into the river. The color of the river turned red because it was full of blood. The corpses were washed further into the ocean. Some people would go to the seashore for the thrill of watching the floating bodies."[50] Pak Ongko's personal tragedy echoes the story of Li Peinan, a second-generation ethnic Chinese from Segiri, Aceh. Li's elder brother, a member of the Pemuda Rakyat, was captured and murdered by the local military authority. According to Li, KAMI and KAPPI asked the pro-Beijing Association of Overseas Chinese (huaqiao zonghui) to announce that the ethnic Chinese with PRC citizenship should hang the Five-Star Red Flag outside their houses, so that they would be recognized as outsiders in Indonesian politics and would not be implicated in any campaign after the movement.[51] However, these houses were later targeted by KAMI and KAPPI. "When they saw the flag, they would shout 'ganyang' [destroy] and start attacking." Li ultimately left Aceh in 1966 and resettled on the Quanshang Overseas Chinese Farm in the Fujian Province of China.[52]

Recent research on the 1965–66 mass killings shows that when the massacres were in their later stages and all the alleged Communists and sympathizers had already been annihilated, the ethnic Chinese oftentimes became the alien scapegoats in regions such as Aceh, North Sumatra, South Sulawesi, and West Kalimantan.[53] At the beginning of the mass killings, the ethnic Chinese members of the PKI and its affiliated organizations, like Li's brother, were targeted alongside pribumi Indonesians. Baperki members and affiliates, like Pak Ongko's father, were also victims of extrajudicial arrests, beatings, and killings during this period.[54] Even though most of its members were Indonesian citizens with little command of Mandarin Chinese, Baperki was deemed to be an accomplice to the "PKI's coup" and put under pressure to dissolve itself.[55] Right-wing youth groups ransacked the Universitas Res Republik founded by Baperki in Jakarta and forced its closure, while the Indonesian army arrested and later imprisoned many student activists.[56]

These politically charged assaults later developed into indiscriminate violence against Chinese communities in provinces such as Aceh.[57] Jess Melvin's study shows that anti-Chinese violence was used as a final step in the military's consolidation of its power in April 1966.[58] The military authority in Aceh ordered all noncitizen Chinese to leave the province by August 17,

1966.[59] In Lhokseumawe, Aceh, where ethnic violence was reported to be particularly rampant, an estimated 10,000 ethnic Chinese were driven out of their homes.[60] Liao Yiping, an Aceh Chinese from Lhokseumawe, recalled that threats of violence were used by KAMI and KAPPI to force 1,000 to 1,500 local Chinese, including Liao's father, to stand in the searing tropical sun with paint poured over their heads and "RRC"—an insulting acronym that meant "Repulik Rakyat Cina" (The People's Republic of Cina)—painted on their backs.[61]

Political and economic restrictions targeting the Chinese community as well as incidents of robbery, arson, and vandalism targeting Chinese property were more widely recorded than murder. The Chinese-language press and schools were closed after the September Thirtieth Movement. In Jakarta in April 1966, approximately fifty thousand Chinese Indonesians with Indonesian citizenship were called together to pledge their loyalty to the Indonesian state.[62] The political uproar led to economic disarray. Believing that the ethnic Chinese should be held accountable, some local officials and military commanders implemented the 1959 Presidential Decree No. 10 more vigorously. For example, in East Java in late December 1966, the regional military commander issued a ban on wholesale trade by Chinese nationals across the province and on the use of the Chinese language in commerce.[63] The general lawlessness after October 1 also provided an ideal opportunity for crimes based on ethnic bias, greed, or jealousy. For instance, in March 1966 at the Port of Hong Kong, an ethnic Chinese businessman who had just sailed from Jakarta told reporters that anti-Communist pribumi mobs had been roaming the streets of Jakarta and destroying shops owned by the ethnic Chinese. He found it impossible to make a living in Indonesia.[64]

While most outbursts of public hostility against the ethnic Chinese died down in Java soon after the new Suharto regime consolidated its power, West Kalimantan witnessed the last and perhaps gravest episode of anti-Chinese violence in October and November 1967. The local situation was unique not only because of the high percentage of the Chinese population but also due to the presence of the Chinese-dominated Sarawak People's Guerilla Force (PGRS), who entered the neighboring Indonesian territory of Kalimantan for refuge and military training during konfrontasi.[65] After the September Thirtieth Movement, the hostilities between Indonesia and Malaysia ended. The PGRS regrouped in the jungles along the Indonesia-Malaysia border and fought against the armies of both countries.[66] Because it was suspected that the ethnic Chinese living in border areas were providing supplies, information, or shelter to the PGRS, the Indonesian army detained alleged Communists and Communist sympathizers in the latter half of 1966 and forced an estimated fifty thousand ethnic Chinese to move from the interior to coastal areas. Many ended up in refugee camps where they lived in dire conditions.[67] The Indonesian military also incited the Dayaks to attack the ethnic Chinese. Anti-Chinese massacres in West Kalimantan, largely triggered by the Indonesian army's provocation of an ethnic feud, resulted in two to five thousand deaths.[68]

How did the two competing Chinese governments react to the terrorizing of the ethnic Chinese by the Suharto regime? Taipei believed that the suffering of the overseas Chinese was "all bestowed by the Communist bandits."[69] The ethnic Chinese were "caught in the crossfire" and were victims of Beijing's expansionist policy toward Indonesia. One of the biggest concerns Taipei had after the movement was that newly empowered right-wing groups were not differentiating "anti-Communist" from "anti-Chinese" policies. In its opinion, only "the core elements of the Maoist gang" in Indonesia should be punished for their role in "the PKI coup," while the pro-Taipei Chinese should be seen as the Suharto regime's "indispensable" partner in its efforts to "destroy the subversive Communist conspiracy." Taipei urged the Chinese in Indonesia to separate themselves "from the Communist bandits and stand together with the Indonesian people."[70] Pledging their loyalty to the Suharto regime was the only way for the Chinese in Indonesia to guarantee their own safety.

Planning ahead, Taipei intended to reform the Chinese society in Indonesia and "enlighten" the ethnic Chinese who had been "bewitched" by the Chinese Communists.[71] In order to "expand the force of faithful overseas Chinese," Taipei aimed to replace the older generation of community leaders with young ethnic Chinese educated in Taiwan. It also hoped to revive pro–Chinese Nationalist Chinese-medium education and media as well as to resume the export of cultural products from Taiwan to Indonesia.[72] Yet Taipei faced mammoth obstacles. First and foremost, its absence since 1959 made Taipei unable to reunify the terror-stricken and deeply divided Chinese community in Indonesia under its banner. Moreover, while accepting economic aid, intelligence-analyst training, and other benefits from the ROC, the Suharto regime refused to reciprocate Taipei's goodwill by allowing the promotion of an anti-Communist version of Chinese culture. Determined to forcefully assimilate the ethnic Chinese, Suharto imposed a wholesale ban on Chinese-medium education and media.[73]

Beijing, on the other hand, condemned "the special agents from the Chiang clique" as accomplices in the Suharto regime's conspiracy of "using the Chinese to oppose the Chinese."[74] Beijing claimed that, in 1967, the head of the Indonesian military in North Sumatra "held numerous meetings with a small group from the Chiang clique, assigning them anti-Chinese tasks."[75] There has been scholarly speculation that the pro-Taipei group might have secretly supported the attacks against the pro-Beijing group, and the military, in return, might have tried to protect the pro-Taipei community.[76] But this collaborative relationship has not been substantiated by hard evidence. However, it is clear that with the Cultural Revolution looming large on the horizon, the PRC's attitude toward the Indonesian government became increasingly belligerent. In a tirade in the *People's Daily* published in June 1966, Beijing announced that it "would never give up protecting the rights of its citizens residing overseas."[77] Beijing warned Suharto: "Over one million overseas Chinese living in Indonesia will never stop their righteous struggle as long as you continue your oppression."[78]

The September Thirtieth Movement triggered another major exodus of ethnic Chinese. A minority of well-off Chinese, particularly peranakan, chose to immigrate to Western countries. A small number of the totok community moved to Taiwan.[79] The PRC opened its doors to the remaining ethnic Chinese who saw no future in Indonesia. In 1966 and 1967, Beijing sent the ship *Guanghua* on four trips to Medan and took back more than four thousand ethnic Chinese, a large portion of whom were expelled from Aceh.[80] It is likely that there were many ethnic Chinese left behind after the PRC reached the limit of its ability to transport and absorb the refugees.[81] The *Guanghua*'s voyages were suffused with tension. A safety guideline produced in 1966 assessed the repatriation project as a high-risk endeavor: "The situation on the enemies' side is complicated and the struggle is acute." Sensing threats from three enemy forces—"the American imperialists, the Indonesian reactionaries, and the Chiang bandits"—the guidelines demanded that the crew be prepared for direct bombardment, secret implantation of explosives in the passengers' luggage, and underwater attachment of magnetic torpedoes to the bottom of the ship. Other potential dangers included infiltration by spies, kidnapping of the crew at the Indonesian port, and riots at the harbor instigated by the Indonesian military and right-wing mobs.[82] The Chinese government dispatched eighty-one military personnel from the East China Sea Fleet of the PRC navy to protect the *Guanghua*'s safety.[83] The ship's time on the sea turned out to be comparatively smooth. But negotiations with Indonesian immigration and customs during each of its arrivals were grueling. In late April 1967, on its last voyage, the *Guanghua* was banned from entering the Port of Belawan in Medan by the Indonesian authorities and almost ran out of food and water supplies. After a forty-day standstill, the Indonesian authorities finally granted the *Guanghua* permission to dock.[84]

Together with the stories of "red diplomatic fighters," the transgressions suffered by the ethnic Chinese refugees entered the political discourse of the Cultural Revolution. Beijing heedfully focused its castigation solely on the Suharto regime. For instance, in a *People's Daily* editorial based on stories recounted by the repatriated ethnic Chinese, a seven months pregnant ethnic Chinese woman from Lhokseumawe was said to have been captured by a mob, pushed onto the ground, and forced to run until kindhearted pribumi passersby came to her rescue. The leader of the Overseas Chinese Association of Lhokseumawe, Rao Jucai, thanked a compassionate Indonesian military officer who intervened when a group of hooligans attempted to bury him alive.[85] The editorial concluded: "The ultimate victory belongs to the Indonesian people, who will rise up against the reactionaries!"[86] Reporting on the departure of the third batch of refugees leaving from Medan, the *People's Daily* described a scene in which "many Indonesian friends waved farewell to the passengers, exclaiming: 'Long live the friendship between the Chinese and Indonesian people!'"[87] In Beijing's media coverage, the culprit for the anti-Chinese violence was Suharto, who joined a worldwide conspiracy against the PRC. The working-class pribumi, on the other hand, were as oppressed by Suharto's tyranny as the ethnic Chinese.

PRC propaganda depicted the repatriation of the persecuted ethnic Chinese as a validation of the universality of the cult of Mao Zedong. The *Guanghua*'s voyages in 1966 and 1967 were heavily politicized. The crew onboard was instructed to "prioritize political education" and "use Chairman Mao's theory of class struggle" to "militarize" themselves. The captain required that "all security personnel must firmly uphold their proletarian principles and follow the party committee's instruction."[88] The *Guanghua* was a crash course on the sea to prepare the refugees for the Cultural Revolution through rigorous study sessions on Mao Zedong's thought.[89] According to reports from the China News Agency, when the third batch of 1,070 refugees left the Port of Belawan at Medan on January 29, 1967, passengers were shouting slogans from the deck of the *Guanghua* including "Long live the invincible Mao Zedong's thought," "Long live our dearest, dearest great leader Mao Zedong," and "Down with American imperialism!"[90] When the *Guanghua* arrived at the Zhanjiang port in Guangdong Province on May 23, 1967, after its last voyage to Indonesia, the welcoming crowd sang "The East Is Red" while waving the Little Red Book at the returned refugees. A "Maoist thought propaganda team for refugee youth" onboard reciprocated with the chorus of "Father is dear, mother is dear, but not as dear as Chairman Mao" (*Dieqin niangqin buru Mao Zhuxi qin*) and a handmade pennant with "Long Live Chairman Mao" sewn in gold-colored thread.[91]

Once they arrived in China, the refugees were immediately immersed in the Cultural Revolution. At "congregations for denunciation," the migrants were said to have angrily decried the "outrageous crimes" of the Suharto regime. "The Chinese people are not to be trifled with!," they cried out. The New China News Agency reported that the refugees had "speedily mastered the important weapon of the Cultural Revolution: the Big Character Poster" and used it against "the Indonesian reactionaries."[92] Their experience during Suharto's anti-Communist campaign was remolded into vivid propaganda material. The most widely circulated story revolved around the "forty-one young ethnic Chinese heroes," a group of pro-Beijing ethnic Chinese youth who clashed with the Indonesian military and were thus imprisoned in Medan in October 1966. Almost all were students at the Medan Overseas Chinese High School, which was transformed into a temporary shelter for displaced ethnic Chinese from Aceh and North Sumatra from the latter half of 1966 to early 1967.[93] These left-leaning youth assisted with refugee relief work by distributing food and giving lessons to the children. They also listened to Radio Peking, which started to include quotations from Chairman Mao in its special program for overseas Chinese, and then dispersed the information.[94]

The transplantation of China's Cultural Revolution into the contentious environment in Indonesia led to a conflict in October 1966 when officers from the Medan army came to inspect the refugee settlement in the Medan Overseas Chinese School. According to Adam Wong, one of the "forty-one young ethnic Chinese heroes," the visitors wanted to take pictures to prove to the world that the Indonesian government was not mistreating the Chinese minority.[95] The PRC media claimed that these photo sessions were meant to "collect deceptive propaganda materials" and "sabotage the Chinese government's efforts to repatriate the Chinese who wish to return to their motherland."[96] The students' attempts to grab the camera led to their arrest and incarceration. An editorial in the People's Daily praised them for their "boundless veneration, respect, and love for the great leader Chairman Mao," as they were reported to have written "Long live Chairman Mao!" on the prison wall with blood.[97] They were ultimately released by the Indonesian authorities and deported to the PRC.

Back in China, the "forty-one little heroes" became an icon of the Cultural Revolution. In Beijing, they were in the spotlight at a welcome ceremony attended by over ten thousand people, including top leaders such as Zhou Enlai and Chen Yi. In front of a crowd waving the Little Red Book, Zhou Enlai accepted on Mao Zedong's behalf a gift from the "forty-one little heroes": a Five-Star Red Flag they had made by hand in prison. Chen Yi warned the Indonesian government in his speech: "The Chinese people, armed with Mao Zedong's thought, cannot be humiliated; the overseas nationals of strong socialist China can never be persecuted blatantly. The 700 million Chinese people will always stand beside the Indonesian people. The savage Indonesian reactionaries will ultimately face the harsh judgment of history."[98] The "little heroes" also participated in Mao Zedong's purge of the director of the International Bureau of the CCP, Wang Jiaxiang, as well as "the biggest capitalist roader inside the party," Liu Shaoqi. By connecting the "appeasement strategies" promoted by Wang and Liu to the crisis in Indonesia, the "little heroes" announced that the overseas Chinese would not have suffered if PRC diplomacy had not been hijacked by "a survivalist philosophy that forced the revolutionary people to kowtow to the imperialists, revisionists, and reactionaries."[99] In 1967 the "little heroes" started a nationwide tour. In Shanghai, they attended the opening ceremony of the People's Commune as special guests. In Tianjin, the motivational speeches they delivered at Nankai University galvanized the revolutionary ardor of the "818 Red Rebellion Group" (Ba Yi Ba hongse zaofantuan) on campus, who wrote a public letter to Suharto: "You Indonesian reactionaries are thoroughly evil, worse than Hitler in Germany. We are the Red Guards of Chairman Mao. We do not even care about your masters—the American imperialists and Soviet revisionists. We have no fear of your despicable pawns."[100]

In August 2013, on the Yingde Overseas Chinese Farm (Yingde huaqiao nongchang) in northern Guangdong Province, a group of ethnic Chinese who had left Indonesia after the September Thirtieth Movement sang me the song they had composed in honor of the "forty-one young ethnic Chinese heroes":

> We are the overseas sons and daughters of the Chinese nation,
> We are the youth of the Mao Zedong era,
> We fought alongside the Indonesian people,
> We continued our struggle in the prison,
> Oh, my motherland, you are my biggest source of support!
> I swear to you,
> I will protect your glory and dignity,
> at the price of my beautiful youth and my blood.[101]

This revolutionary melody is a witness to the almost synchronized emergence of the Cultural Revolution in China and Suharto's dictatorship in Indonesia. These two significant and stormy processes in Cold War Asia were mutually reinforcing. Both countries used bilateral friction to develop domestic propaganda and propel mass mobilization. Whereas Suharto identified Chinese ethnicity with Communism, Beijing blurred the boundaries between the overseas Chinese with PRC citizenship and the ethnic Chinese who had adopted Indonesian citizenship. Mao's vision of China as the center of a world revolution—a core ideology of the Cultural Revolution—encouraged Beijing's reckless handling of governmental relations with Indonesia after the September Thirtieth Movement. The PRC media repeatedly deplored the "fascist" Suharto regime while denouncing the "racist terrorism" and "anti-China hysteria" perpetrated by "the Indonesian right-wing mobs."[102] In the heat of the Cultural Revolution, Beijing saw the future of Indonesia in the hands of the pribumi proletariats who would ultimately overthrow Suharto.

Meanwhile, the ROC aimed for the "normalization" of Taipei-Jakarta ties, which would "lay the foundation for long-term peace in an Asia free from the threats posed by Communism."[103] Initially, Taipei took advantage of the frenetic pace of Suharto's anti-Communist campaign to undermine the PRC's diplomatic representation in Indonesia. However, Indonesian elites used anti-China propaganda as a temporary strategy to stir up public anger. They did not want to make China their long-term geopolitical enemy. By 1969 Taipei had to face the reality that, despite the Suharto regime's vehement anti-Communist stance and its framing of the PRC as the foreign sponsor of "the PKI's coup," Indonesia continued to regard "the Communist bandits" as "China" and the Chinese Nationalist regime in exile as "Taiwan."[104]

Thousands of ethnic Chinese fled the mass violence in Indonesia and many of them came to the PRC. While this and the previous chapters have demonstrated that the ethnic Chinese's departure from the archipelago usually took place in a conflict-stricken environment, the next chapter will show that their "homecoming" to China was also a conflict-laden process. Before their departure from the archipelago, almost none of these ethnic Chinese—who were often perceived as Trojan horses of China by the pribumi right-wing forces—had any real-life experience living or working in a Communist country. The following chapter uncovers their experiences in an environment that was both strange and familiar. I will also demonstrate how the influx of migrants from overseas gave rise to both opportunities for and challenges to the PRC.

CHAPTER 10

The Overseas Chinese "Returning" to the People's Republic

Between the early 1950s and early 1960s, an estimated 60,000 ethnic Chinese students in Indonesia came to the PRC for higher education.[1] From 1959 through the first half of 1965, at least 100,000 economic migrants boarded ships heading for the PRC; most of them had lost their licenses to operate retail businesses in the countryside due to the Indonesian government's nationalist economic policy.[2] In 1966 and 1967, more than 4,000 migrants moved to China to escape the terror of the rising Suharto regime. By the late 1960s, at least 164,000 ethnic Chinese had "returned" to their ancestral homeland even though most of them were born and raised in Indonesia. The majority started their lives all over again on the overseas Chinese farms, primarily located in the mountainous regions in the Southern Chinese provinces of Fujian, Guangdong, and Hainan. Educated youth, however, might have the opportunity to pursue a college degree and ultimately land in work units in the cities. In April 1960, a CCP cadre working for the Overseas Chinese Affairs Commission of Fujian Province explained how he had escorted a batch of newly arrived migrants from Java, Sumatra, and Belitung to their new homes on an overseas Chinese farm in rural Fujian:

> Everyone speaks bahasa Indonesia. Except for the children and the
> elderly, almost all can speak Mandarin Chinese. They love arts and

sports. Many brought back radios, portable pianos, accordions, and badminton bats. Their lifestyle is more or less the same as that of the Indonesian people. . . . They spend money without making future financial plans. They want to take showers every day.

The majority of the returned overseas Chinese have pure thoughts. However, because they lived in a capitalist society for a long time, they brought back capitalist ideas. Moreover, because most of them used to engage in private business in urban areas in Indonesia, they are accustomed to high living standards. Already, seven people have requested to go back to Indonesia shortly after their arrival. One hundred and twenty-three people refused to abide by the state policy of uniform distribution. They want to live in the big cities and are unwilling to go to the farms. They are afraid that the farms will be situated in backward and isolated areas. They see no future in doing agricultural work. They are afraid of "eating bitterness" [*chiku*] and conducting heavy labor. A returnee with technical skills said: "Once settled on the farms, my whole life will be wasted."

They strongly resist the socialist economic system. They are very uncomfortable with the planned distribution of commodities. For instance, the team leader of Chinese from Sukabumi, Yan Chizhu, wanted to buy a bun at the guesthouse for returned overseas Chinese in Guangzhou [*Guangzhou huaqiao zhaodaisuo*]. When a staff member asked him to present his stay permit and food coupons, he not only refused to do so but also threatened to gather together the returnees from his region to beat up that staff member.[3]

Once marginalized as an ethnic minority in Indonesian society, the migrants found themselves at the margins of the PRC. In Indonesia, the Chinese minority were often regarded by right-leaning pribumi factions as an alien group with disproportionate economic power and dubious national allegiance. In China, where they were officially known as "returned overseas Chinese" (*guiguo huaqiao*) or "returnees" (*guiqiao*), they still stood out as foreign. For those who used to engage in commerce, their skills and talents in private business were incompatible with the planned economy. While most returnees had enjoyed being free consumers in the past, in the PRC they had to accept the fact that access to everyday commodities would be determined by the government. Whereas many returnees had taken part in Beijing-oriented activities in Indonesia, they found the logic of the political campaigns in the PRC hard to comprehend. Moreover, their unfamiliarity with manual labor, love for music and the arts, and even their habit of taking daily showers were labeled bourgeois and deemed politically incorrect. Once again, their loyalty to the state was viewed with suspicion.

While the 1950s and 1960s are commonly perceived of as a period of isolation in PRC history, the stories of domestic overseas Chinese with connections to Indonesia—including not only returnees but also their dependents (*qiaojuan*) who had not been abroad themselves but were supported by remittances from family members abroad—demonstrate how transnational influences shaped China's domestic transformation. Shortly after its establishment in 1949, the PRC central government had had weak control over the southern coastal regions with a high concentration of rural emigrant counties (*qiaoxiang*). For instance, it was almost impossible for the CCP to stop the circulation of foreign currency in these areas. Additionally, with a self-sufficiency granted by the remittances, qiaojuan and guiqiao households were usually recalcitrant in the face of the state's efforts to establish authority. In the 1950s and 1960s, the PRC saw a great opportunity for not only strengthening preexisting financial ties between the overseas Chinese and qiaoxiang but also attracting new investments. Meanwhile, the Chinese government tried to assimilate the domestic overseas Chinese into the socialist system by building centralized economic organizations on the overseas Chinese farms. The migrants adapted, while also using a variety of techniques to resist state penetration into their personal lives, including creating and circulating sarcastic slogans, participating in illegal border crossings, and circumventing the planned economy. During my fieldwork at Yingde Overseas Chinese Farm in Guangdong Province, I was introduced to "Pak Lemper." He was known for the Indonesian sticky rice cakes he had made and sold to the local community during the 1960s and early 1970s, a time when having a personal small business was a punishable offense.[4] Paradoxically, the economic autonomy of returned overseas Chinese like Pak Lemper helped prepare coastal South China for the reform that started in the late 1970s.

Little Americas and the Economic Cold War

In November 1949, Wang Hanjie, the chairperson of the Overseas Chinese Affairs Commission of Fujian Province, came to the port city of Xiamen for a survey of the region. A Fujian native, Wang was the military consultant to the Filipino Communist Party Central Committee and the leader of the Filipino Chinese Anti-Japanese Guerillas before returning to China in early 1949. A veteran of World War II, Wang faced a much more complicated battleground in post–Communist victory Fujian, where law and order were barely maintained. Armed robberies were so rampant that it was hard to

separate innocent civilians from criminals.[5] Moreover, the residents on the
Fujian coasts were frequently caught in the crossfire of the continuous conflicts between the Communists and the Nationalists.[6] In 1954, for example,
fighter jets from Taiwan carried out airstrikes in Jinjiang, which led to civilian
casualties. The specter of infiltration by Chinese Nationalist spies constantly
haunted the local Communist government.[7] Similarly, the central government's control of Hainan was weak. The PLA did not wrestle this remote
island away from the Nationalist troops until May 1950.

Besides these appalling security conditions, the connections between the
emigrant districts of South China and Chinese diasporic communities worldwide hindered Beijing's efforts to regulate the local economy. As Wang noted,
from 1937 to 1942, the overseas Chinese sent approximately 800,000 silver
dollars to Fujian from abroad, 600,000 of which came through the postal
system and banks and the remainder via private overseas agents (shuike).[8]
It was very common for people to carry a few US dollars in their pockets
because everyday commodity exchanges heavily relied on them. When the
Quanzhou municipal government officially banned the use of foreign currency in the market at the end of 1949, transactions of daily goods came to a
complete standstill.[9] Wang predicted that if the government were to confiscate the foreign currency owned by ordinary people, popular protests would
erupt all across Fujian. According to Zeng Jingbing, the party secretary of
Fujian Province, this was why the native places of the overseas Chinese were
sometimes called "Little Americas" (xiao Meiguo).[10]

Moreover, it was difficult for the CCP to cultivate political allegiance
among the domestic overseas Chinese. In 1949, in Fujian Province, there
were 1.5 to 2 million returned ethnic Chinese from abroad and families with
overseas connections. They were connected to the 3 million Chinese diaspora
through the global circulation of mail and remittances.[11] Zeng described the
political attitudes of these domestic overseas Chinese as follows: "They loved
the motherland during the Manchu rule; they loved the motherland during
the rule of the warlords; and they continued to love the motherland during the
rule of the Chiang bandits. . . . They do not care which party is good or which
party is bad. As long as their remittance is not cut off, they embrace a party's
leadership completely."[12]

The little Americas, with their distinctive social structure, economic system, and material culture shaped by emigration, posed formidable threats to
the political authority of the CCP after 1949. The physical appearances of qiaoxiang were shaped by the infrastructure sponsored by the overseas Chinese,
while local governance was managed by powerful local families and through
transnational migrant networks.[13] But control over these simultaneously

highly globalized and yet parochial societies in Guangdong and Fujian was vital to Beijing.[14] At a meeting of the Overseas Chinese Affairs Commission of Fujian Province held at the end of 1949, Zeng stressed that it was to the PRC's great advantage that the overseas Chinese's remaining family members, ancestral graves, and property all fell within its territory. Beijing thus had more leverage than Taipei to "unify the twelve million overseas Chinese by strengthening their connections to the motherland." Zeng urged the CCP cadres to mobilize qiaojuan to write "a large amount of vivid and endearing letters" that projected a vision of a rising new China to their family members abroad.[15]

Beijing courted the overseas Chinese's political loyalty as well as their economic assets. In 1950 the US initiated an embargo against the PRC due to the latter's military intervention in the Korean War. The UN followed suit.[16] The transnational Chinese financial and business networks provided important channels for the PRC to circumvent international sanctions and gain access to capital and strategic materials worldwide. Remittances were an important source of foreign exchange for China during the Cold War. The transfer of funds from the overseas Chinese to their families who stayed behind had been conducted through a system of monetary management centered on overseas Chinese remittance firms (qiaopiju) and private agents. The rise of independent nation-states in Southeast Asia after World War II and the subsequent tightening of state-led foreign exchange controls disrupted this arrangement. In the early 1950s, the Indonesian government stipulated that, after the nationality selection period ended, only those who opted for PRC citizenship were eligible to transfer money to China. As a result, the ethnic Chinese who had acquired Indonesian citizenship could only use unauthorized methods to send remittances. In May 1952, two ethnic Chinese were charged with organizing underground international money transfers.[17] During the Lunar New Year of 1955, a peak time for the overseas Chinese to send money home, Indonesian authorities dispatched undercover police to infiltrate overseas Chinese remittance firms in Semarang, Solo, and Jakarta and successfully cracked down on these services.[18] Similar operations were repeated the next year. The suspects involved were detained and tortured by the Indonesian police, causing panic across the Chinese society in Indonesia.[19]

Undeterred, Beijing encouraged underground remittance houses to continue their "righteous struggle" against the repressive Indonesian authorities. Theoretically, these institutions should be labeled as "politically backward." But the CCP held that the remittance agencies were "irreplaceable" due to their capability of ingeniously transferring funds from abroad to China "right under the eyes of the imperialists."[20] From Beijing's point of view, the crackdown in Indonesia was caused by an oversight by the practitioners of underground remittance and by greed on the part of anti-Communist political forces.[21] In order to prevent further losses, the People's Bank of China (Zhongguo renmin yinhang), China's central bank, requested that Overseas Chinese Affairs Commissions in Fujian and Guangdong go house to house among the remittance recipients, cautioning them about the language used in their communications with families abroad. Many of them tended to use the same code of "receiving a certain number of pills" to acknowledge receipt of a certain amount of remittance and the Indonesian police had begun to catch on to this code.[22] The Chinese economic attaché in Jakarta also smoothed relations with local authorities through Chinese Indonesians who had professional affiliations and personal ties with the Central Police Bureau and the Attorney General's Office.[23]

While protecting the continuous flow of remittances, Beijing also appealed to Chinese business leaders in Indonesia to devote their capital and technological know-how to the industrialization of the PRC. Back in 1949, in the final stage of the Chinese Civil War, the Beijing-oriented *Sheng Huo Bao* of Jakarta had published an editorial promoting socialist new China as the "most secure" destination for investment.[24] Wang Jiyuan, the editor-in-chief of *Sheng Huo Bao*, forecasted that after the end of the colonial era in Indonesia, the economic role of the ethnic Chinese would continue to be circumscribed by the domination of Western capitalist financial conglomerates. Therefore, Wang argued that only by transferring their capital back to Mainland China could the ethnic Chinese businessmen in Indonesia build long-lasting enterprises.[25] In 1953 the party secretary of Fujian Province, Zeng Jingbing, encouraged local cadres to seek overseas Chinese investments patiently and persistently. He emphasized that, although the overseas Chinese might make only small investments individually, the cumulative effect in the long term would be significant. In his words, the overseas Chinese would move their capital back to China incrementally in the same fashion as "rats moving from one hole to another" (*laoshu banjia*).[26] As part of its marketing strategies, the PRC invited ethnic Chinese from Indonesia and other Southeast Asian countries for sightseeing tours, which showcased investment opportunities.[27]

As shown in Glen Peterson's research, in the early and mid-1950s, the PRC sought to reserve a "special niche of state capitalism" for the overseas Chinese by linking their investments directly to the state's industrial priorities.[28] For instance, in response to the PRC's call, Huang Jie migrated from Indonesia to China in 1951 and became the chairman of the Board of Directors of the Overseas Chinese Industrial Construction Corporation and then the vice chairman of the Guangdong Overseas Chinese Investment Company. Huang had more faith in the prospects of socialist China than those of Indonesia. In the late 1940s, Huang saw "two different paths" lying ahead of him: "one is to continue my life as a Nanyang Pak (*Nanyang bo*) and make money in a foreign land, another is to contribute my humble capabilities to the economic construction of the motherland."[29] During his initial experiments in China, Huang requested governmental permission to conduct business in collaboration with state-owned industrial sectors. The Industrial Department of Guangdong Province (Guangdong sheng gongyeting) approved Huang's proposal and recognized it as "a kind of state capitalism."[30] The socialist state's welcoming policies influenced Huang's decision to completely relocate his business to the People's Republic and become "a nationalist capitalist in New China."[31]

The Chinese from Indonesia also contributed to the development of tropical agriculture on Hainan Island. Rubber, key to China's industrialization efforts and military capability, was placed high on the international embargo list by the US. Although technically the Indonesian government took a neutral stance in UN discussions of the embargo against the PRC during the Korean War, Beijing discovered that the "Sukarno-Hatta reactionary faction" was inclined toward the West in the early 1950s.[32] As a major exporter of rubber, Indonesia followed market principles and sold the majority of its annual product to the highest bidders: the United States and Western Europe. To obtain rubber, the Chinese government contemplated the possibility of smuggling it from Surabaya via Timor to Macau with ethnic Chinese merchants as the middlemen. Although the Chinese department in charge, the Committee of Transport and Commodity Circulation under the South China Ministry of Finance (Huanan caiwei diaoyun weiyuanhui), identified the ethnic Chinese businessmen in Indonesia as members of the "comprador class," it nevertheless considered them to be a useful tool and proposed luring them with monetary benefits: "With high rewards, there will surely be brave men who will take up the challenge. They could serve as our outposts. . . . Given the long history of Chinese commercial activities, it would be difficult for the Indonesian government to detect our dealings."[33] Interestingly, even returning ethnic Chinese students were recruited into the smuggling networks. Before their departure, representatives from an organization named "the Returnee Students' Association" (guiguo tongxuehui) would discreetly distribute mysterious small packages wrapped in handkerchiefs and ask them to stay quiet when passing through customs. Inside the packages were seeds of rubber and tropical produce such as coffee, coconuts, and pepper. This was part of China's strategy to break through the American-led embargo in a piecemeal fashion.[34] Taking advantage of the expertise and labor of the Chinese from Indonesia, the PRC built state-directed plantations on Hainan Island for large-scale production of these commercial crops.[35]

Positioning the Overseas Chinese in the Socialist System

For the CCP cadres without background knowledge, "overseas Chinese" was a nebulous and confusing concept: Were they an ethnic group different from the Han majority in China? Did they have their own spoken language and written characters different from Mandarin Chinese? Was there a nation of the overseas Chinese?[36] The party secretary of Fujian Province, Zeng Jingbing, corrected the "faulty understanding" that the overseas Chinese were antagonistic to the goal of socialist construction in China: "Some of our comrades think that because the overseas Chinese have been living abroad most of their lives, they probably have close relationships with the imperialists. They cannot be good people. Actually, the overseas Chinese are not all wealthy. Neither are all of them friends with the imperialists. . . . They belong to different [economic] classes: some are capitalists; some are intellectuals or freelancers; others are apprentices, workers, peasants, unemployed, and even beggars."[37]

Cadres like Zeng, who himself grew up in Bangkok, were sympathetic to the domestic overseas Chinese and were cautious in using harsh political force to accelerate their integration into the socialist system. For instance, in late 1949 and early 1950, the Chinese government conducted a nationwide survey of income level and land ownership, largely in preparation for the forthcoming land reform. Zeng openly criticized the "inflation" of the class status of residents with overseas ties. Some regional governments, he said, labeled 20–30 percent of the returned overseas Chinese as landlords and industrialists, whereas a survey by the central government classified only 2 percent of the returned overseas Chinese and qiaojuan as landlords and 7 percent as industrialists.[38] Furthermore, Zeng urged the cadres in Fujian to allow the domestic overseas Chinese to maintain their religious and popular beliefs, as well as to continue rituals such as "building houses or conducting merit ceremonies for the dead." Zeng argued that by banishing these practices as "feudalistic," the CCP would alienate itself from the domestic overseas Chinese and lose support from their families abroad. "The overseas Chinese suffered from discrimination when they were living abroad," Zeng concluded, "they should not again be discriminated against after returning to China. We should help them, educate them, and build a united front with them."[39]

Starting from the late 1950s, the intense political campaigns of the Great Leap Forward required the state to take more aggressive measures to transform the domestic overseas Chinese.[40] Fang Fang, the deputy director of the PRC Overseas Chinese Affairs Commission, used to uphold the liberal principle of "seeking common ground despite differences." But in 1958, his attitude changed as he demanded that the returnees and qiaojuan completely renounce their capitalistic customs and "erase" their "special characteristics."[41] Fang used a metaphor to explain his argument: "It is as if the families of the overseas Chinese got on the socialist train, but in fourth class. Although it is not as comfortable as the first class, they still made it onto the train." Fang warned that it would be dangerous to overstress the contribution of the domestic overseas Chinese, as they tended to fall victim to "overseas Chinese chauvinist" (*dahuaqiao zhuyi*) thinking and feel entitled to privileges.[42]

This policy reversal manifested itself most acutely in the overseas Chinese's changing position in rural class struggles. For instance, in the early 1950s in Longxi, Fujian Province, many domestic overseas Chinese were classified as feudalistic landlords and had their property expropriated.[43] But the policy makers in the Fujian provincial government instructed lower-level administrators to "correct the mistakes in class status identification," return wrongly confiscated property or offer monetary compensation for it, and avoid interfering in the lives of domestic overseas Chinese except for those of "bad and counterrevolutionary" individuals.[44] Yet, against the background of nationwide political radicalization, in 1963 in Chao'an County in Guangdong Province, two production teams proposed to relabel several domestic overseas Chinese heads of households as landlords or, in other words, to "make them wear the hats of the wealthy and land-owning class again."[45] The local authorities noted that, in the past, over 90 percent of families with overseas connections had received a moderate class label during the land reform. But now it was time to reclassify them as enemies. According to the county leaders, these returnees and qiaojuan were "subversive" elements who posed the greatest threat to public security and to collective production in local communities. They not only took advantage of the lenient state policy toward the overseas Chinese by "audaciously taking back their houses" but also "engaged in speculation and profiteering." They avoided manual labor, "continued their economic exploitation," and even tried to "use material interests to bribe the party cadres."[46]

Resettlement of New Migrants

The ship *Guanghua*, the PRC's first ocean liner, was a major vessel that took the ethnic Chinese back from Indonesia. From 1961 to 1967, the *Guanghua* made thirteen trips to major ports including Jakarta, Surabaya, and Medan. When bilateral relations were friendly, the *Guanghua* facilitated public diplomacy. At most of the harbors the *Guanghua* visited, banquets and cocktail parties were hosted on the ship with assistance from the PRC embassy and consulates as well as local Chinese community leaders. Guests at these occasions were mostly officials from Indonesian immigration offices, customs, ministries of trade and commerce, and the navy. The *Guanghua's* captain would usually give out gifts in exchange for favorable treatment through customs clearance and other procedures.[47] Moreover, following instructions from the Overseas Chinese Affairs Commission in Beijing, the staff on the *Guanghua* identified "propaganda and education" for the returnees as one of its most important tasks and designated members who specialized in mass mobilization to take charge of it. A returnee named Zhang Liukun, who relocated from Indonesia to the Xinglong Overseas Chinese Farm in Hainan, remembered how he was impressed by the youth and energy of the cadre responsible for propaganda work during his sea journey: "He was twenty-five or twenty-six years old . . . lively, generous, and vigorous. . . . He represented the spirit of New China in the eyes of many returnees onboard."[48]

Sailing on the *Guanghua*, the returnees' nationalistic passion and revolutionary romanticism rapidly grew. On the ship, political messages were inscribed on blackboards, broadcast on the radio, and presented through movies, documentaries, and even gala shows.[49] Zhang recalled attending lessons on revolutionary music on the deck of the *Guanghua* at 8 a.m. every morning: "The first song he [the cadre in charge of propaganda work] taught us was entitled 'Orphans Overseas Now Have Their Mother' [*haiwai de guer youle niang*]. This song gives voice to the feelings of the overseas Chinese from the bottom of their hearts. Everyone sang with great passion. Later, he taught us songs of the Great Leap Forward, such as 'Chairman Mao Visits Our Farm' [*Mao Zhuxi laidao zan nongzhuang*] and 'Socialism Is Good' [*Shehui zhuyihao*]. These songs accompanied the overseas Chinese for a long time during their life's journey after their return to China."[50] Yet Zhang reflected that, while spending lots of time explaining how the people became the masters of the nation after the Communist victory, the crew on the *Guanghua* avoided talking about the economic difficulties caused by the Great Leap Forward. Zhang wrote: "This might be one of the reasons why the returned overseas Chinese were confused by the food shortage in China and were reluctant to follow the state policy to settle on the farms."[51]

The end of the returnees' sea voyage marked the beginning of new journeys to different state-designated locations for resettlement. Among the returnees from the archipelago, young students could usually enter overseas

Chinese continuation schools" (*huaqiao buxi xuexiao*), which were established to meet their particular needs.[52] A small percentage who excelled in college entrance exams would be able to receive a university education. Jinan University (Jinan daxue) in Guangzhou, with historical connections to the diaspora in Southeast Asia, reserved quotas for the returned ethnic Chinese students. Among the adults, a small number of elites, usually those with either exceptional professional skills or political connections, were offered jobs in state-owned enterprises or in educational, medical, or governmental units in the cities.[53] The official policy was to relocate the vast majority of the migrants from Indonesia to the overseas Chinese farms in Guangdong, Fujian, and Hainan, where they would be given land to build homes on and to grow tropical produce such as coffee, rubber, pepper, and coconuts.

Since a significant number of the returnees had been petty traders or shopkeepers in the urban areas back in Indonesia, many resisted rural relocation, either by staying with relatives in the city or by surviving on the savings they had brought back.[54] Many of those who moved to the countryside were despondent when they saw the bleak conditions on the farms for the first time. An investigative team under the Fujian provincial government to the Changshan Overseas Chinese Farm reported in August 1960:

> The food supply is not sufficient. It is difficult to see fresh vegetables. The kitchen has not yet been built. There are not enough cooking and agricultural tools. To get food and drinkable water, people have to line up for a long time every day. There is not enough fuel. As a result, sometimes the rice served in the canteens is half-cooked. At the daycare center of the production team, children only have a simple lunch and an afternoon snack of watery porridge plus half a spoon of soy sauce or salt water. There is only one clinic on the farm, with two doctors of Western medicine and one of Chinese medicine. They have poor training and suspicious political backgrounds. One of the Western doctors used to spy for the British and to work at the Far East Intelligence Bureau of Singapore. The other is a religious person and a cadre of the Three People's Principle Youth Group of the Nationalist Party. Their thoughts are reactionary and their attitudes are horrible. The returnees do not trust these doctors. There are thirteen patients with mental illness living in the clinic. They often run away from their wards and disrupt the lives of the returnees.[55]

The gap between the returnees' high expectations and the grim realities in China gave rise to widespread disenchantment with the government. Except for a very small group, who read about the food scarcity from Western or

Chinese Nationalist Party–controlled newspapers or in letters sent back by relatives who had already been resettled in the PRC, the majority of the returnees had believed in the prosperity of new China.[56] When a batch of returnees saw their new homes—huts made out of mud and straw—on Binlinshan Overseas Chinese Farm in Hainan Province, many started crying out in despair. Some migrants went on a hunger strike and told the CCP cadres in charge: "Back in Indonesia I heard we can find everything we need in the motherland. But there is neither oil nor meat here."[57] On Changshan Overseas Chinese Farm in Fujian, monotonous meals consisted of water spinach and cabbage. The returnees sarcastically praised their dire situation with slogans such as "Long live water spinach" (Kangkung wansui) and "the motherland is great, three cabbages a day" (Zuguo henhao, shixing sanbao).[58] Some migrants said: "In the past, our country was weak and we were sold overseas as piglets;[59] now that our country is strong and is capable of buying these people back, it only uses them as piglets again."[60] On Shuangdi Overseas Chinese Farm in Fujian, "reactionary slogans" such as "I love imperialism" (wo ai diguo zhuyi) were secretly written at the entrance to the local elementary school.[61] Although disappointment was the prevailing emotion among the returnees, ethnic Chinese miners from Belitung, many of whom had lost their jobs and most of their property in Indonesia, willingly obeyed the state's resettlement arrangements and were very grateful to the Chinese government.[62] A Communist Party cadre who received 665 miners from Belitung in August 1959 reported that many of them repeatedly said "My thanks to Chairman Mao" in Hakka dialect when they received their allowance. Some said that they would go wherever the government wanted them to go and do whatever the government wanted them to do.[63]

But for many business-minded returnees, it was difficult to comprehend the logic of centralized state distribution and confusing to use coupons (piao) and certificates (zheng) to purchase goods. One returnee recalled the shock he felt when he found out that, wherever he went, there was nothing he could buy if he had only money but no state-issued coupons or certificates: "In 1961 all the adults on the Xinglong Overseas Chinese Farm received cloth coupons that were only enough for half a pair of trousers. Couples would put their quotas together and make it into one pair of long pants. But for single guys, they could only make shorts out of the quota."[64]

Many of the returnees openly rejected the planned economy. Some told the CCP cadres: "Nanyang has everything we wanted. There are not enough commodities in China. There's no free buying and selling. The black market is way too expensive. In Nanyang we don't need to wrack our brains to find supplies."[65] Another said: "We cannot depend on the collective canteens. The collective organizations cannot feed you for a lifetime."⁶⁶ A returnee named Lin Tianliang wrote in a letter from Shuangdi Farm to his brother in Shanghai: "I never dreamed that we would be sent to wastelands. . . . Here, we need coupons for rice, vegetables, biscuits, and cigarettes."⁶⁷ Rao Huihuang, who migrated from Bali and was sent to the Binlinshan Farm on Hainan Island, wrote a letter of petition to Liao Chengzhi, the chairman of the OCAC, expressing his bafflement over the fact that they even needed "coupons to buy watery porridge for breakfast."⁶⁸ Besides vocal protests, some attempted barter trade or the private exchange of coupons and certificates.⁶⁹ Many adopted a noncooperative attitude toward the collective production teams. Rather than spending the required eight-hour workday farming on the collective land, they made every attempt to sneak out so that they could tend to the crops and produce on their own private plots.⁷⁰

Among the returnees, the socialist state was particularly challenged by the rebellious youth from Indonesia: they would typically keep a "gangster hairstyle" (afei tou), wear wide-cut jeans (laba ku), sing "yellow" or pornographic songs, and date against school regulations. At the Guoguang High School in Nan'an, Fujian, the teachers reported that these "little hooligans," contaminated by the capitalist way of life they used to have back in Indonesia, would openly express counterrevolutionary opinions such as "Happiness is money; it is to eat well and dress well." They complained about the lack of freedom. Some secretly wrote slogans such as "Down with Chairman Mao, long live Chiang Kai-shek" in classrooms. They also threatened to write to newspapers overseas to "expose the worst side of the motherland" and "warn the overseas Chinese against returning to the motherland to suffer."⁷¹ At the continuation school for the returned overseas Chinese students in Guangzhou, some told their teachers: "Indonesia is a heaven of material pleasure."⁷² They further claimed: "Heaven equals the material life of Indonesia and the socialist system of the motherland."⁷³ On the overseas Chinese farms in Lufeng and Huaxian in Guangdong, the young people originally thought they would live the life of the Soviet collective farms they had seen in films: farms with electricity, modern agricultural machinery, and unlimited supplies of food. Disappointed, they complained: "We were duped into returning to the motherland" and "The motherland sent ships to Indonesia to repatriate the overseas Chinese because it needs laborers to develop the virgin lands."⁷⁴ When I visited the Yingde Overseas Chinese Farm in 2013, Chen Zhende, a former rebellious youth who had migrated from Semarang, showed me a picture taken in 1963 of the members of an organization he had founded: the Poor Boys' Club. Chen and seven of his fellow returnees gathered around a blackboard that displayed a lion logo and the slogan of

FIGURE 10.1.   Chen Zhende (standing, second from the right) with members of "the Poor Boys' Club," Yingde Overseas Chinese Farm, 1963. Personal collection of Chen Zhende.

their organization in English: "Poor Boys Club: This Boys [*sic*] No Time, No Money, and No Love."[75]

To "purify their thoughts," the Communist youth leagues in Guangdong, Fujian, and Hainan launched educational programs targeted at the returned overseas Chinese youth. At the continuation schools and on the farms, the Communist youth leagues organized study sessions and debates centered on topics such as "Which is better: Indonesia or the motherland?"; "Were we tricked into coming back to the motherland?"; "Is there enough food to eat?";[76] "Is Indonesia a paradise of material resources?"; and "Is the future of the youth brighter in Indonesia or in the motherland?"[77] At these occasions, the Communist youth league strategically arranged a few "model students" who were politically reliable to steer the direction of the discussions. The Overseas Chinese University in Fujian took its students to the countryside

FIGURE 10.2. Returned Chinese youth from Indonesia at the Jimei Overseas Chinese Continuation School, 1961. Personal collection of Chen Xiuming.

for a summer camp in 1963. Xie Aina, a freshman majoring in Chinese literature, gave a celebratory account of how her political awareness had improved
significantly during the two-week stay with the peasants. Before going down
to the rural areas, she thought the peasants were dirty and selfish. These
"bourgeois thoughts" made Xie itch all over her body when taking care of
an infant from the peasant family she stayed with. However, after she had
formed bonds with the poor peasants, Xie reported that her skin allergies
were cured automatically.[78]

Yet, for the returned overseas Chinese youth, learning to think in the
socialist way and speak the socialist language was not easy. Many complained
that the ideas of class struggle and the battle against modern revisionism
were confusing. For instance, a teacher recorded that an otherwise hard-
working and polite returned overseas Chinese student said at a political study
session: "I have never read about what 'exploitation' is or what a 'landlord'
is. In Nanyang most of the people from the bourgeois class were leaders of

the overseas Chinese communities. These landlords were important political figures. I cannot see any evil in them." Another said: "I believe that socialism is good, capitalism is bad. But I cannot tell clearly why and how capitalism is bad." Some confessed that they did not know how to hate the old feudalist society and how to love the new society. As for the critical thinkers among the young returnees, their earlier exposure to a marketplace of ideas back in Indonesia made them resistant to state efforts to unify their thinking. For instance, many students at the Overseas Chinese University did not believe in the reports by the *People's Daily*. They insisted on listening to foreign radio broadcasts every day.[79] These returned overseas Chinese students were less reserved in their criticism of socialist China's stance in international politics. On the issue of the Sino-Soviet split, the returned overseas Chinese students from the Number 9 High School of Fuzhou raised questions such as these: "The Soviet Union is a revisionist country. But how come a revisionist country could master highly developed science and technology? The Soviet Union sent its astronaut to outer space. We are not a revisionist country. Why can't we do that?"[80] Students from the Nan'an Guoguang High School said: "It makes sense that the Soviet Union criticized us over our economic difficulties. Our people wore sandals made from grass whereas the Soviet people wore leather shoes." Other students criticized the Chinese government for being "shallow": "It's a big mess at home. The motherland does not have sufficient food for its own people. But it insists on supporting other countries."[81]

In the early 1960s, with the rise of civil disobedience among the returnees, the tension between the migrants and CCP cadres managing overseas Chinese farms increased. On the national level, the Overseas Chinese Affairs Commission in Beijing directed its provincial branches to gradually and gently help the returnees adapt to socialism or, in other words, "to give them drizzling showers" (*xia maomao yu*) of socialist education instead of adopting the draconian methods that were usually used against counterrevolutionaries.[82] For instance, the returnees should be granted the freedom to grow their private crops or to cook their own food.[83] Many policy makers at the provincial level and above seemed to believe that, since these migrants had made the decision to return to the motherland, their political loyalty had already been tested and they would ultimately adapt to the new socialist environment. However, at the level of individual counties and farms, lower-ranking Communist Party cadres sometimes had little sympathy for the migrants. Instead of recognizing the returnees' grievances as legitimate reactions to economic difficulties, some regarded the migrants as spoiled by "the capitalist way of life, the good food, and nice clothes" and therefore unable to "understand the unavoidable difficulties of the current stage of socialism in China."[84] The party secretary of the Binlinshan Farm of Hainan Island criticized the migrants for their disdain for manual labor. The party secretary wrote in a report: "They [the returnees] thought they would just sit around and enjoy life once they came back to the motherland."[85]

With the returnees filled with discontent against the government and pressured by grave economic conditions, the anarchic situation that Wang Hanjie had observed in Fujian in 1949 reemerged in the early 1960s on a number of farms. On the Changshan Farm of Fujian Province, some returnees stole produce from the local peasants and thus created communal tension between the long-time residents in the region and the newly arrived migrants from abroad. The local peasants, infuriated, accused the returnees of acting like "bandits."[86] On the Binlinshan Farm of Hainan Island, the Communist Party authority on the farm almost lost control of the situation. In a letter requesting support from the provincial government, the party secretary of the Binlinshan Farm wrote that his authority was compromised and his "self-respect was hurt" by the unlawful behavior of the returnees.[87] Theft was so rampant that the atmosphere on the farm became "harrowing." The party leadership felt powerless to stop the crimes because "both children and adults" stole and they took "everything from everywhere, openly, secretly, collectively, individually" from both the local Hainanese peasants and the supply and marketing cooperatives (gongxiao she). Stolen goods included coconuts, chilis, bananas, and sugar cane. Some returnees even carried out "armed robberies" with sharp knives in which they stole sweet potatoes, vegetables, peanuts, chickens, and ducks. Ten returnees were said to have put out the oil lamp at the cooperative at night and to have then taken away more than five kilograms of oil under the cover of darkness. And they showed no remorse. They openly said: "Hainan is such a damned place! All Hainanese are evil. In the imperialist countries, we used to be able to buy everything. Back in the motherland we can buy nothing. It would be stupid not to steal." A returnee named Rao Zengxi was quoted as saying: "The power of the farm is in our hands: the returned overseas Chinese. We do whatever we want to do." "They are incurable," the party secretary concluded, "we educate them today and they will go off to steal again tomorrow."[88]

As the schism between local Communist Party authorities and the returnees deepened, many returned overseas Chinese regretted their decision to migrate to China. However, since 1952, Beijing had imposed stringent border controls to prevent a mass exodus of people fleeing the land reform.[89] Under this tightened entry-and-exit policy, all migrants from Indonesia, including both Chinese citizens and ethnic Chinese who once took Indonesian citizenship, had to surrender their passports once they landed in the PRC. Yet some returnees refused to do so, while those who had already turned in their passports tried to get their travel documents back. Some even wrote letters to the Indonesian embassy in Beijing seeking political asylum.[90] Students were often among the first to voice their disillusionment and desire to escape socialism. For example, some dissatisfied returned overseas Chinese students from Indonesia at Guoguang Middle School in Nan'an, Fujian Province, openly said: "I would rather become a *becak* [the Indonesian word for tricycle] driver than return to China" and "I would sacrifice everything to go back to Indonesia."[91] In the 1960s, many overseas Chinese students crossed over to Hong Kong with exit permits on the pretext of visiting family members or conducting financial affairs.[92]

In February 1963, on the Binlinshan Overseas Chinese Farm, a group of residents who had collectively migrated from the same village in Bali started killing the chickens and pigs they had raised for a farewell party. Through letter exchanges with the Balinese rajas, police chief, and military officers, the leader of this group, Li Yulong, had formulated an exit strategy for his fellow disgruntled returnees. In preparation for departure, Li had collected travel document processing fees and identity pictures from those who were interested in joining him. But the plan failed due to the intervention of the provincial government. A team dispatched from the provincial Overseas Chinese Affairs Commission investigated the Binlinshan farm and concluded that the returnees had suffered from cultural and linguistic estrangement and from the rampant corruption of local CCP cadres on the farm. These migrants, who were described by local officials as reckless hooligans, turned out to be merely peranakan and believers in Hinduism with a limited command of Mandarin Chinese. In their own words, "China is our mother, Indonesia is our father."[93] The local officials, on the other hand, "stayed up late playing cards," "never participated in manual labor," and "feasted on chickens from the public canteen." The investigative team decided that theft committed by the returnees was triggered by food scarcity and was disproportionately punished by local officials.[94] By the end, the team called a meeting on the farm at which the CCP cadres were publicly reprimanded. Nonetheless, the investigative team was not confident that the returnees were determined to settle permanently.[95]

On June 9, 2013, on Shuangdi Overseas Chinese Farm in Shima County, Longhai City, Fujian Province, I was introduced to "Auntie Meiping," a returnee from Indonesia who is well known in the neighborhood for the Indonesian desserts and snacks she makes. Like Pak Lemper, Auntie Meiping has had her private bakery business since the 1960s. Having migrated to

FIGURE 10.3. A household of returnees from Bali, Xinglong Overseas Farm, Hainan, September 28, 2013. Photo by author.

China in 1961, Meiping and her husband still used bahasa Indonesia every day in their household. Meiping was sixteen years old when she returned and was not given the opportunity to further her education. She remembered crying when she saw the harsh living conditions on the farm for the first time. Meiping's husband, who had once taken Indonesian citizenship, talked at length about his struggles in the socialist system. At the time of my visit, both were retirees of formerly state-owned enterprises, enjoying the benefits of free housing and adequate pensions. Both agreed that, despite the "bitterness" (*pahit*) in the past, their life in postsocialist China was more comfortable than that of those who stayed behind in Indonesia as well as those who chose to migrate to Hong Kong after 1972, when the government changed its previous policy and allowed the returnees to leave. At the end of our meeting, when I thanked the couple for their hospitality, Aunt Meiping smiled and said "kita semua orang Tiongkok" (we are all Chinese) in bahasa Indonesia.[96]

This chapter has reconstructed the processes by which a diasporic sense of belonging among ethnic Chinese like Aunt Meiping transformed into an acceptance of a socialist way of life after their migration and resettlement in

Mainland China. Mostly well-versed in trade and commerce, the returnees had to get used to manual labor, navigate their way through the planned economy, and build a new political vocabulary through waves of ideological campaigns. As Glen Peterson points out, the term "return" in the context of the relocation of the overseas Chinese back to China means not merely a reverse movement.[97] It implies a redefinition of oneself from being "Chinese" in terms of cultural identity to being a "socialist subject" in terms of political allegiance, civic responsibilities, and obedience to state authority.[98] Although the state seemed to wield overwhelming power over individual migrants, it also had its limitations. While New China had achieved a certain degree of success in using the resources of the diasporic communities to overcome a US-led embargo and speed up economic construction, it seemed underprepared for the challenges of managing the oftentimes "disobedient" domestic overseas Chinese.[99] The returnees carried with them the daily practices of capitalism and connections to the circulation of capital in the wider world. Under the leadership of Deng Xiaoping, China began to adopt market principles and embrace international trade. The returnees became an important medium through which the Chinese government attracted overseas Chinese investment and expanded its trade networks. Coastal South China, where the returnees had been resettled, was at the forefront of China's economic reform and opening up to the world in the late 1970s.

Conclusion

"The Motherland Is a Distant Dream"

In June 1955, on the Dutch ocean liner traveling from Jakarta to Hong Kong, Liang Yingming's expectations for a new future in new China kept his nostalgia for his days in Indonesia at bay. The ship was overcrowded with Indonesian-born Chinese youth like Liang. At night, they had to lie down next to one another on the deck. After arriving in Hong Kong, Liang immediately boarded a northbound train to Shenzhen, a dormant fishing village at the mouth of the Pearl River delta. The British authorities in Hong Kong were wary of these young Chinese who were presumed to be leftist. Liang remembers being confined inside the train car, where Gurkha soldiers guarded the entrances. He peered curiously out of the window for a glimpse of Hong Kong.

Liang made the final stretch of his journey on foot. After the train stopped at the border between Hong Kong and Shenzhen, all the passengers had to disembark and walk across the Lo Wu Bridge, which marked the border between the capitalist British colony and socialist China. On the bridge, Liang cried when he caught sight of the Five-Star Red Flag. He did not shed tears when he waved goodbye to his father at the Tanjung Priok harbor, but he felt overwhelmed when he physically set foot on his ancestral homeland. "It was as if I were a son who had been wandering around far away from home. Now, I had finally returned to my mother, who had always been waiting for me," Liang recalled.[1]

Almost twelve years later, on May 6, 1967, seventeen-year-old Huang Huilan boarded the ship *Guanghua* in Medan bound for Guangzhou. The departure brought long-awaited relief to many who had witnessed the mass violence in 1965 and 1966. At the harbor of Medan, Huang bade farewell to her friends on the shore, saying "See you in the motherland!" The atmosphere was heavy with conflicting emotions: the excitement of homecoming, sadness over separation, fear of uncertainties, and anxiety about the Cultural Revolution in China. As a former student at the pro-Beijing Medan Overseas Chinese High School, Huang was familiar with Cultural Revolution propaganda texts, art, and music. She knew the famous song, "Sailing the Seas Depends on the Helmsman," which was translated into Indonesian and widely circulated:

Berlayar perlu juru mudi	Sailing the seas depends on the helmsman
semua hidup oleh mata hari	The growth of everything depends on the sun
segar segar karena embun	The plants were nurtured by the dew
revolusi bersenjata mentari Mao Zedong	And revolution depends on the thought of Mao Zedong[2]

"Political education" dominated Huang's five-day-and-six-night journey on the sea. Huang and her fellow passengers were required to memorize "the three short essays written by Mao Zedong before the PRC was established" (*lao san pian*) as well as *Quotations from Chairman Mao Zedong*. Despite her preparation on the *Guanghua* and her engagement with China-oriented politics in Indonesia, when Huang arrived at the Huangpu Port in Guangzhou, she was astonished by the sight of countless propaganda posters and the collective chanting of slogans such as "Down with Liu Shaoqi, Deng Xiaoping, and Tao Zhu!" The intensity of political campaigns in the Cultural Revolution far exceeded what she had imagined.[3]

Liang arrived in China at a promising moment in the mid-1950s when Beijing and Jakarta had successfully rallied support among the newly independent countries. But by the time of Huang's repatriation, the Afro-Asian movement was already in decline. The tale of these two countries is not merely bilateral. Many key events in the evolution of Sino-Indonesian relations were of great importance in the broader formerly colonized world. At the Bandung Conference of 1955, previously voiceless Third World countries demanded autonomy in the Cold War. But the abortive second Afro-Asian Conference ten years later showed increasing isolation faced by both China and Indonesia. The near-parallel radicalization of their domestic politics was the catalyst for the two countries' transformation from reasonable campaigners for Afro-Asian solidarity to fierce rebels against the international system. By 1965 not only were the two countries unable to bring unity to a diverse group of Afro-Asian nations but the alliance between the two had also become fragile despite hyperbolic rhetoric.

The ebb and flow of diplomatic relations affected the lives of ordinary overseas Chinese in three ways. Overall, the Chinese, loathed for their perceived dominance in commerce, became easy targets for violence during times of political instability and economic downturn. First, discord in bilateral relations usually amplified antagonism toward the ethnic Chinese. During the Indonesian National Revolution, the Chinese Nationalist government's unwillingness to grant diplomatic recognition to the Republic of Indonesia and to treat it as an equal partner aggravated pribumi aggression toward the Chinese. The September Thirtieth Movement changed the fate of many ethnic Chinese in Indonesia. This book substantiates the conjecture in earlier works that the Special Bureau within the PKI—headed by its chairman, D. N. Aidit—orchestrated the movement. In its aftermath, pribumi right-wing youth ransacked the PRC diplomatic mission in Indonesia and the Red Guards in Beijing launched counterattacks against the Indonesian embassy. Despite Beijing's lack of direct involvement, these conflicts created an image of an interventionist Communist power and gave the anti-Communists in Indonesia an excuse for instigating violence against the ethnic Chinese. Second, anti-Chinese riots persisted even when bilateral relations were cordial. During the Sino-Indonesian honeymoon between 1963 and 1965, the two countries' mutual ambition to redefine the terms of the Cold War and their perception of shared security threats failed to offset the "Chinese problem." Indonesia's turn toward the left and its close collaboration with Beijing created a more explosive environment in which anti-Communist forces could exploit stereotypes of the ethnic Chinese as alien capitalists, financial backers of the PKI, and the fifth column of Communist China. Third, diplomatic frictions implicated both Indonesian citizens of Chinese descent and Chinese nationals living in Indonesia. Although some anti-Chinese regulations issued by the Indonesian government, such as Presidential Decree No. 10, made a legal distinction between citizen and noncitizen Chinese, in reality the Chinese fell victim to government-led discrimination and grassroots violence regardless of their national allegiance.

Notwithstanding the changing status of diplomatic relations, there had always been pribumi groups that accused all ethnic Chinese of being pawns of a foreign power irrespective of their citizenship status and ideological inclination. Stemming from long-standing social, economic, and political

circumstances in Indonesia, this prejudice was also influenced by the way
the Chinese Nationalist and Communist governments conducted diplomacy
in Indonesia. Both governments instrumentalized the overseas Chinese to
advance their respective foreign policy objectives. In the 1930s and 1940s, the
Chinese Nationalist Party had penetrated deeply into the diasporic society.
After Indonesia switched its diplomatic recognition to the Chinese Communist government in 1950, Taipei was still able to intervene in Indonesian politics through the extensive networks it had established earlier. Meanwhile, in
the 1940s, CCP underground cadres arrived in Indonesia and worked closely
with left-wing ethnic Chinese youth. Some of these young people later
migrated to the PRC and became the first generation of Indonesia experts
who oversaw the day-to-day management of bilateral relations. Those who
remained in Indonesia zealously joined in PRC-oriented activities in the
1950s. Although Beijing had attempted to distance itself from diasporic politics in the 1950s and early 1960s, its diplomatic mission and the diasporic society remained entangled. For instance, PRC diplomats in Indonesia recruited
pro-PRC ethnic Chinese to provide logistical support and security for the
PRC delegation to the Bandung Conference in 1955. To restrain the Indonesian government's anti-Chinese measures in 1960, the PRC embassy encouraged ethnic Chinese traders to stage strikes.

Throughout the 1950s, the pro-Beijing and pro-Taipei factions vied
for hegemony in the Chinese-language press, schools, and civic associations. Their rivalry deepened the gulf between the Chinese minority and
the pribumi. The competition left the Indonesian general public with the
impression that the ethnic Chinese were primarily concerned with the politics of their ancestral homeland and were apathetic about Indonesia's destiny. Many pribumi elites regarded the Chinese as a monolithic minority,
conflating the two opposing political camps of "Red" and "Blue." Right-
wing forces in Indonesia retaliated against the entire Chinese community
when provoked by Taipei's support for separatist movements in 1958 and by
Beijing's relentless condemnation of Suharto after the September Thirtieth
Movement.

Average ethnic Chinese in Indonesia influenced international relations
through their everyday social and political practices as well as their ideological beliefs and economic ties. The tension between states and individual
overseas Chinese was constant as the migrants navigated Cold War politics
on their own terms. During the Indonesian National Revolution, some ethnic Chinese criticized the Chinese Nationalist government's insistence on
the right of blood principle for citizenship and advocated instead for Chinese
integration into the newborn Republic of Indonesia. The Red-versus-Blue

struggle had its roots in the Chinese Civil War, but points of contention were particular to diasporic societies. Taipei's sometimes blind eagerness to claim legitimacy was used by opportunistic individuals for personal gain. Meanwhile, although the PRC aimed to achieve domination vis-à-vis the ROC in the overseas Chinese community, the intensity of intracommunal conflict far exceeded what Beijing had deemed to be beneficial to its foreign policy goals. Ultimately, the political passion of the pro-Beijing Chinese spiraled out of control, unraveling the Sino-Indonesian alliance.

In the mid-1960s, while the PRC did not export a Communist revolution to Indonesia, over 160,000 repatriated overseas Chinese brought back a capitalistic outlook and behavior. Experienced in entrepreneurship, many migrants circumvented the planned economy by engaging in black market trade or running informal small businesses. In the late 1970s, the commercial links between coastal South China and Southeast Asia revived, creating investment opportunities and paving the way for China's reform and opening to the world. Today, the Indonesian culture of the Xinglong Overseas Chinese Farm in Hainan has become a resource for developing the tourist industry. The growth of tropical products such as coffee, pepper, and coconuts, whose seeds were smuggled by the migrants during the US-led embargo against the PRC, became an important part of the ecological landscape and agricultural economy of Hainan Island. To a certain degree, the collective market-oriented actions of these migrants subverted the socialist system and transcended the Cold War.

While this book ends in 1967, the dynamics it describes have continued. Accusing China of intervening in the September Thirtieth Movement, the Suharto regime not only froze its diplomatic ties with the country but also developed a discourse that portrayed the PRC as a historically aggressive foreign power. This narrative was taught in schools and reiterated in a number of books produced during the Suharto era.[4] Under the influence of this state propaganda, the pribumi majority came to regard links with China as politically "dirty."[5] Meanwhile, the Suharto-era policy of forced assimilation deprived the generation born after the 1960s of the opportunity to receive Chinese-language education or partake in Chinese cultural or civic activities. Although business tycoons like Liem Sioe Liong maintained influential networks abroad, the majority of the ethnic Chinese in Indonesia lost their institutional and cultural ties to the PRC.[6] While the ethnic Chinese became increasingly distant from their ancestral homeland, it was difficult for them to argue that they "belonged" in Indonesia because of their marginal position under Suharto's rule.[7] Suharto took advantage of the financial resources and business skills of the ethnic Chinese, but he created a cycle where this minority had to purchase security from those in power in order to continue their economic activities.[8] As a result, the ethnic Chinese remained at risk in times of political and economic stress, as is exemplified by the mass violence against the ethnic Chinese in May 1998, which accompanied the fall of Suharto.

China's rapid economic development since the 1980s has altered Indonesian policy makers' attitudes toward the country. The business opportunities presented by China's rise motivated Suharto to normalize relations with Beijing. Sino-Indonesian relations formally resumed in 1990 and proceeded relatively smoothly for the remainder of the 1990s. For example, Beijing expressed concern but refrained from taking action during the anti-Chinese riots in 1998. The Chinese leaders were aware that the victims were almost all Indonesian citizens of Chinese descent rather than PRC nationals.[9] The rapprochement between the PRC and Indonesia was a blow to Taipei. The PRC's increasing economic clout and geopolitical influence mean that it is no longer possible for Taipei to contest Beijing's legitimacy as forcefully as it did in the 1950s.

In the comparatively liberal atmosphere of the post-Suharto era, the increase in economic cooperation between the PRC and Indonesia has incentivized some diaspora Chinese to reclaim their Chinese identity.[10] Since the 2000s, public celebrations of Chinese festivals have reemerged with official support from the Indonesian government, while the Chinese-language press and civic associations have mushroomed. Mandarin Chinese–language courses have not only revived with government approval but have also become immensely popular.[11] The growth of commercial ties between China and Indonesia in the 2010s has added extra impetus to this resurgence of Chinese culture in Indonesia. In 2013, during a state visit to Indonesia, the Chinese president Xi Jiping unveiled the Twenty-First Century Maritime Silk Road Initiative, which is often referred to in combination with the Silk Road Economic Belt Initiative as the Belt and Road Initiative. The plan is to reinvigorate and expand the ancient Silk Road through investment in infrastructure across the Asia-Pacific, Europe, and East Africa. The Maritime Silk Road initiative pays special attention to Southeast Asia and the region's largest economy: Indonesia. China is Indonesia's largest trade partner. Chinese investment plays a key role in the execution of the infrastructure and maritime projects outlined in the Indonesian president Joko Widodo's blueprint for developing Indonesia into a global "maritime fulcrum."[12] In 2015 China won the bid for the Jakarta-Bandung High Speed Railway, which is expected to boost the tourism, manufacturing, logistics, and property sectors in an envisioned Jakarta-Bandung megapolitan area.[13]

Hoping to harvest personal benefits from these booming bilateral trade and investment schemes, some ethnic Chinese in Indonesia, particularly the pre-1965 generation of totoks who have a good command of Mandarin Chinese, have strategically positioned themselves as intermediaries between the two countries. They have actively reestablished ties with China by facilitating visits to Indonesia by PRC business elites and officials and cultivating relations with the PRC diplomatic mission.[14] Echoing the situation of the 1950s, some totok elders' renewed affinity for China has led to division within the Chinese community and pribumi suspicion. The younger generation, the majority of whom are peranakans, feel excluded. At the same time, pribumi groups from the political Right still view the ethnic Chinese as "perpetual foreigners." They launch attacks in the Indonesian media accusing Chinese Indonesian businessmen of being the PRC's puppets.[15]

As in the past, Chinese ethnicity and an association with China remain politically dangerous in Indonesia. The former Jakarta governor Basuki Tjahaja Purnama, better known by his nickname "Ahok," an ethnic Chinese Christian, was controversially incarcerated for insulting Islam. President Joko Widodo, an ally of Ahok whose friendly policy toward the PRC has aroused discontent, was accused of being ethnic Chinese in a smear campaign during the 2014 presidential race.[16] In 2015 rumors spread in the Indonesian social media that ten million migrant workers from the PRC had entered the country. *Tempo*, an influential news weekly in Jakarta, published a special investigation accompanied by a caricature of President Joko wearing overalls like a Chinese worker and wielding a hammer. The magazine expressed concern that Chinese investment projects had failed to live up to their promise of creating employment opportunities for the locals.[17] In this new socioeconomic environment, old fears persist. In the eyes of some right-wing or Islamist groups, China is penetrating Indonesia not with its Communist ideology but with capital and migrant workers. The ethnic Chinese, no longer potential Communist agitators, are now suspected of colluding with the PRC to exploit Indonesia's natural resources and invade the nation's vast market. Overall, China's economic achievements and growing presence in Indonesia have been met with both admiration and apprehension among the general public. The connection between China and the ethnic Chinese in the archipelago continues to be a source of pribumi misgivings and anxiety.[18]

What was it like to be a youth in search of an ancestral homeland that one had never set foot on, or an economic refugee whose expertise in private business became undesirable in one's new home in the socialist state? What ideological beliefs or practical calculations motivated individuals to commit to one particular nationality while forsaking another? This book has demonstrated that these microlevel questions about ordinary migrants are crucial to a deeper understanding of the macrolevel dynamics of governmental interactions. The general thrust of the book has been a reinterpretation of diasporic politics, ethnic conflicts, and international relations in an integrated and interactive framework. Through this method, I have sought to bridge the fields of diplomatic history and migration studies and to reconstruct the experiences of China and Indonesia in the Cold War as part of a cross-Asian transnational social history.

The PRC ambassador Ba Ren personifies the intertwined histories of China and Indonesia and the entanglement of diplomacy and migration. In his long poem *The Song of Indonesia*, which was composed in the Sumatran jungle in 1945, Ba Ren wrote that, to the overseas Chinese, "the motherland is a distant dream."[19] Yet Indonesia became a distant dream for Ba Ren after his return to China. During the Cultural Revolution, he was persecuted and sent to his ancestral village for reeducation. There is no information on his reaction to the September Thirtieth Movement. But the collapse of the Sino-Indonesian strategic alignment and the Chinese suffering in 1965–66 stymied any possibility for the multiethnic alliance of the working class that he had envisioned and promoted. Perhaps in search of solace from this cruel reality as well as from the torture of the Cultural Revolution and his mental illness, Ba Ren spent most of his free time during the late 1960s and early 1970s drafting his *History of Pre-Modern Indonesia* and *History of Modern Indonesia* and revising the play he wrote during the Indonesian National Revolution: *The Temple of Five Ancestors*. Ba Ren renamed the play *The Proletariat Who First Lit the Torch* and added new characters who were ethnic Chinese Red Guards on a plantation in North Sumatra. He also included long sections from *Quotations from Chairman Mao Zedong* and a new ending in which the ethnic Chinese Red Guards, the Indian laborers, and the Malay, Gayo, and Batak villagers all join hands to burn down the plantation.[20] In 1972, in rural Zhejiang Province, Ba Ren passed away in destitution. In his will, he asked his family to bury half of his ashes in his native place and to scatter the rest at sea, so that the ocean waves would carry his spirit back to Indonesia.[21]

NOTES

Introduction

1. Franklin B. Weinstein, *Indonesian Foreign Policy and the Dilemma of Dependence* (Ithaca, NY: Cornell University Press, 1976), 118.

2. Liang Yingming, interview by author, Beijing, July 21, 2013.

3. "Bacheng" is the Chinese transliteration of Batavia, the colonial capital of the Dutch East Indies and present-day Jakarta.

4. The "September Thirtieth Movement" is the name of the group that carried out the abduction and murder of six senior anticommunist generals in the early morning hours of October 1, 1965. In this book, following scholars such as John Roosa, I use the term "the movement" principally to refer to the event itself instead of the actors within it. See John Roosa, *Pretext for Mass Murder: The September 30th Movement and Suharto's Coup d'Etat in Indonesia* (Madison: University of Wisconsin Press, 2006).

5. For relevant literature, see Stephen Fitzgerald, *China and the Overseas Chinese: A Study of Peking's Changing Policy, 1949–1970* (Cambridge: Cambridge University Press, 1980); and Hong Liu, "An Emerging China and Diasporic Chinese: History, State and International Relations," *Journal of Contemporary China* 20, no. 72 (2011): 813–832. Fitzgerald's study is seminal but dated. Liu's research focuses on the post–Cold War era.

6. This definition is inspired by Wang Gungwu's work, although he deliberately avoids the term "overseas Chinese," which, according to him, only refers to "Chinese sojourners, subjects or nationals temporarily residing abroad." He prefers to use "Chinese overseas" to refer to all Chinese living abroad. See Wang Gungwu, "Greater China and the Chinese Overseas," *China Quarterly* 136 (1993): 926–948.

7. The term "diaspora" is rejected by some researchers in the field of Chinese migration studies for its association with Jewish history. But a new generation of scholars advocates that the term could be a useful paradigm for analysis. See Shelly Chan, "The Case for Diaspora: A Temporal Approach to the Chinese Experience," *Journal of Asian Studies* 74, no. 1 (2015): 107–128.

8. G. William Skinner, "The Chinese Minority," in *Indonesia*, ed. Ruth T. McVey (New Haven, CT: Yale University Southeast Asian Studies, 1963), 97.

9. Departement van Landbouw, Nijverheid en Handel, Dutch East Indies, *Volkstelling 1930* (Batavia: Batavia Centrum, 1931), 7:22.

10. Skinner, "Chinese Minority," 97.

11. "Yindunixiya de jiben qingkuang he dongxiang" [The basic situation and tendencies of Indonesia], February 25, 1956, no. 102-00055-02, Chinese Foreign Ministry Archives, Beijing (CFMA); "Yinni huaqiao guoji wenti zhi xin yanbian" [The new

changes in the overseas Chinese issue in Indonesia], September 21, 1953, from the file "Yinni huaqiao guoji wenti" [The nationality issue of the overseas Chinese], July 18, 1951–December 11, 1954, no. 020-010807-0026, Academia Historica, Taipei.

12. Wu Shihuang, *Yindunixiya* [Indonesia] (Beijing: Shijie zhishi chubanshe, 1956), cited in Huang Kunzhang, *Yinni huaqiao huaren shi* [A history of ethnic Chinese and overseas Chinese citizens in Indonesia] (Guangzhou: Guangdong gaodeng jiaoyu chubanshe, 2005), 10.

13. For the generation born before World War II, the medium of communication was *bahasa Melayu Tionghoa* (Chinese Malay). The basic structure of this language was Malay, although Hokkien and Dutch terms were extensively used. See Leo Suryadinata, *Pribumi Indonesian, the Chinese Minority, and China*, 3rd ed. (Singapore: Heinemann Asia, 1992), 87.

14. Suryadinata, *Pribumi Indonesian, the Chinese Minority, and China*, 95.

15. "Interview with Mr. Hsieh Shan-ts'ai, CNA correspondent," Jakarta, November 7, 1950, box 2, ser. 2, G. William Skinner Papers, Division of Rare and Manuscript Collections, Cornell University Library.

16. Chen Zhongde (Chan Chung Tak), interview by author, Hong Kong, September 18, 2013.

17. Skinner, "Chinese Minority," 99.

18. Ibid., 101.

19. In this book, "Outer Islands" refers to the Indonesian islands other than Java and Madura.

20. Information Office, the Overseas Chinese Affairs Committee of the PRC, ed., *Zhongguo Yinni shuangchong guoji tiaoyue wenti ziliao* [Materials on the dual nationality treaty between China and Indonesia] (Beijing: Zhongqiaowei ziliaoshi, 1960), 1–2.

21. In bahasa Indonesia, there are two terms to refer to the ethnic Chinese: *Tionghoa* and *Cina*. Many ethnic Chinese in Indonesia consider Cina to be derogative and prefer Tionghoa instead. However, in 1966 the emerging Suharto regime officially adopted Cina to "remove the feeling of superiority" on the part of the Chinese. See Charles A. Coppel and Leo Suryadinata, "The Use of the Terms 'Tjina' and 'Tionghoa' in Indonesia: A Historical Survey," *Papers in Far Eastern History* 2 (1970): 97–118.

22. Pribumi's equivalents in bahasa Indonesia include *asli* (native) or *bumiputera* (sons of the soil). These terms refer to those who were considered to be the native inhabitants of the Indonesian archipelago.

23. Skinner, "Chinese Minority," 112.

24. J. A. C. Mackie and Charles A. Coppel, "A Preliminary Survey," in *The Chinese in Indonesia: Five Essays*, ed. J. A. C. Mackie (Honolulu: University Press of Hawai'i, 1976), 12.

25. J. A. C. Mackie, "Anti-Chinese Outbreaks in Indonesia 1959–68," in *Chinese in Indonesia*, 129.

26. Charles A. Coppel, *Indonesian Chinese in Crisis* (Kuala Lumpur: Oxford University Press, 1983), 12–15.

27. "Surat-surat bulan Agustus 1947–Agustus 1948 tentang penduduk Tionghoa di Indonesia," November 3 and 12, 1947, no. 213, Djodja Documenten, Arsip Nasional Republik Indonesia (ANRI). Originally in English.

28. Hong Liu identifies the "three pillars" in his 1998 article. See Hong Liu, "Old Linkages, New Networks: The Globalization of Overseas Chinese Voluntary Associations and Its Implications," *China Quarterly*, no. 155 (September 1998): 582.

29. Suryadinata, *Pribumi Indonesian, the Chinese Minority, and China*, 170.

30. "John W. Henderson, Consul for Political Affairs, US Embassy, Jakarta, to the Department of State Washington D.C.," April 6, 1959, no. 020-010809-0001, Academia Historica, Taipei. Originally in English.

31. "Surat dari Kejaksaan Agung kepada Presiden RI mengenai kegiatan politik dan kebudayaan orang Tionghoa sejak adanya Kedutaan Agung RRT di Indonesia," August 15, 1950, no. 1977, Inventaris Arsip Sekretariat Negara Kabinet Perdana Menteri Tahun 1950–1959, ANRI.

32. Chen Erli, "Jinian Sishui xinhuazhongxue jianxiao liushiba zhounian" [Celebrating the sixty-eighth anniversary of the Xinhua High School of Surabaya], in *Jinian Sishui xinhuazhongxue jianxiao liushiba zhounian tekan* [Special issue celebrating the sixty-eighth anniversary of the Xinhua Middle School of Surabaya] (Hong Kong: Alumni Society of Xinhua High School, 2006), 37–40; Hong Yuanyuan, *Hong Yuanyuan zizhuan* [The autobiography of Hong Yuanyuan], trans. Liang Yingming (Beijing: Zhongguo huaqiao chuban gongsi, 1989), 204–206.

33. For a theoretical discussion of the rituals of national commemoration and nationalism focused on modern India, see Sripura Roy, "Marching in Time: Republic Day Parades and the Ritual Practices of the Nation-State," in *Beyond Belief: India and the Politics of Postcolonial Nationalism* (Durham, NC: Duke University Press, 2007), chap. 2, Kindle.

34. For an overview of the September Thirtieth Movement and the massacres that followed, see Robert Cribb, "The Indonesian Massacres," in *Century of Genocide: Critical Essays and Eyewitness Accounts*, ed. Samuel Totten, William S. Parsons, and Israel W. Charny, 2nd ed. (London: Routledge, 2004), 233–262. For different interpretations of the movement in English-language scholarship, see, for example, Arnold Brackman, *Communist Collapse in Indonesia* (New York: W. W. Norton, 1969); W. F. Wertheim, "Suharto and the Untung Coup—The Missing Link," *Journal of Contemporary Asia* 1 (1970): 50–57; Benedict Richard O'Gorman Anderson and Ruth T. McVey, *A Preliminary Analysis of the October 1, 1965, Coup in Indonesia* (Ithaca, NY: Cornell University Southeast Asia Program Publications, 1971); Harold Crouch, *The Army and Politics in Indonesia* (Ithaca, NY: Cornell University Press, 1978); and Roosa, *Pretext for Mass Murder*.

35. "Mao Zhuxi jiejian Aidi shuailing de Yinnigong daibiaotuan tanhua jilu" [Chairman Mao receives the delegation of the PKI led by Aidit], August 5, 1965, Chinese Communist Party Central Archives, Beijing.

36. See Victor M. Fic, *Anatomy of the Jakarta Coup, October 1, 1965* (New Delhi: Abhinav Publications, 2004); Jung Chang and Jon Halliday, *Mao: The Unknown Story* (New York: Anchor Books, 2005), 487–489.

37. Anderson and McVey, *Preliminary Analysis*.

38. Roosa, *Pretext for Mass Murder*.

39. Madeline Y. Hsu, *The Good Immigrants: How the Yellow Peril Became the Model Minority* (Princeton, NJ: Princeton University Press, 2017); Meredith Oyen, *The Diplomacy of Migration: Transnational Lives and the Making of U.S.-Chinese Relations in the Cold War* (Ithaca, NY: Cornell University Press, 2015).

40. Oyen, *Diplomacy of Migration*, 5.

41. For representative works, see Shen Zhihua and Li Danhui, *After Leaning to One Side: China and Its Allies in the Cold War* (Stanford, CA: Stanford University Press, 2011); Lorenz M. Luthi, *The Sino-Soviet Split, 1956–1966: Cold War in the Communist*

World (Princeton, NJ: Princeton University Press, 2008); Sergey Radchenko, *Two Suns in the Heavens: The Sino-Soviet Struggle for Supremacy, 1962–1967* (Stanford, CA: Stanford University Press, 2009); and Chen Jian, *Mao's China and the Cold War* (Chapel Hill: University of North Carolina Press, 2001).

42. See Gregg A. Brazinsky, *Winning the Third World: Sino-American Rivalry during the Cold War* (Chapel Hill: University of North Carolina Press, 2017); and Jeremy Friedman, *Shadow Cold War: The Sino-Soviet Competition for the Third World* (Chapel Hill: University of North Carolina Press, 2015).

43. See, for example, Hajimu Masuda, *Cold War Crucible: The Korean Conflict and the Postwar World* (Cambridge, MA: Harvard University Press, 2015); Michael Szonyi, *The Cold War Island: Quemoy on the Front Line* (Cambridge: Cambridge University Press, 2008); Sulmaan Wasif Khan, *Muslim, Trader, Nomad, Spy: China's Cold War and the People of the Tibetan Borderlands* (Chapel Hill: University of North Carolina Press, 2015); and Hong Liu, *China and the Shaping of Indonesia, 1949–1965* (Singapore: National University of Singapore Press, 2011).

44. For early scholarship on the overseas Chinese, see, for example, Yen Ching Hwang, *The Overseas Chinese and the 1911 Revolution: With Special Reference to Singapore and Malaya* (Kuala Lumpur: Oxford University Press, 1976); and Victor Purcell, *The Chinese in Modern Malaya* (Singapore: Eastern Universities Press, 1960). For more recent research, see Wang Gungwu, *Don't Leave Home: Migration and the Chinese* (Singapore: Times Academic Press, 2001); Philip A. Kuhn, *Chinese among Others: Emigration in Modern Times* (Singapore: National University of Singapore Press, 2008); and Leo Suryadinata, ed., *Ethnic Chinese as Southeast Asians* (Singapore: Institute of Southeast Asian Studies, 1997).

45. On the transnational turn, see C. A. Bayly et al., "AHR Conversation: On Transnational History," *American Historical Review* 111, no. 5 (2006): 1441–1464. For representative works that adopt a transnational approach to Chinese migration, see Adam McKeown, *Chinese Migrant Networks and Cultural Change: Peru, Chicago, Hawaii, 1900–1936* (Chicago: University of Chicago Press, 2001); Eric Tagliacozzo and Wen-Chin Chang, eds., *Chinese Circulations: Capital, Commodities, and Networks in Southeast Asia* (Durham, NC: Duke University Press, 2011); Madeline Y. Hsu, *Dreaming of Gold, Dreaming of Home: Transnationalism and Migration between the United States and South China, 1882–1943* (Stanford, CA: Stanford University Press, 2000); Glen Peterson, *Overseas Chinese in the People's Republic of China* (London: Routledge, 2012); and Shelly Chan, *Diaspora's Homeland: Modern China in the Age of Global Migration* (Durham, NC: Duke University Press, 2018).

46. Fujio Hara, *Malayan Chinese and China: Conversion in Identity Consciousness, 1945–1957* (Singapore: National University of Singapore Press, 2003); Fredy Gonzalez, *Paisanos Chinos: Transpacific Politics among Chinese Immigrants in Mexico* (Berkeley: University of California Press, 2017); Charlotte Brooks, *Between Mao and McCarthy: Chinese American Politics in the Cold War Years* (Chicago: University of Chicago Press, 2015); and Oyen, *Diplomacy of Migration*.

47. "Ba Ren" is the pen name of Wang Renshu. He was best known by this pen name in Indonesia, or as "Pak Barhen [*sic*]" (Uncle Ba Ren).

48. For methodological discussions of the use of oral history in the Southeast Asian context and particularly in research on Indonesia in the 1960s, see Eric Tagliacozzo, "Amphora, Whisper, Text: Ways of Writing Southeast Asian History," *Crossroads:*

An Interdisciplinary Journal of Southeast Asian Studies 16, no. 1 (2002): 128–158; and Vannessa Hearman, "Under Duress: Suppressing and Recovering Memories of the Indonesian Sixties," *Social Transformation* 1, no. 1 (2013): 5–25.

1. The Chinese Nationalist Party and the Overseas Chinese

1. "Telegram masalah Cina mengenai resolusi di Chung Hwa Chung Hwee di Jambi," May 28, 1948, no. 208, Inventaris Arsip Kementerian Penerangan RI 1945–1949, ANRI.

2. "Laporan dari Sekretariat Perdana Menteri bagian Kepolisian Jogja yang diterima dari Kementerian Penerangan mengenai kiriman-kiriman surat dari 'Hantu malam' yang ditujukan pada segenap bangsa Tionghoa," July 26, 1948, no. 145, Inventaris Kabinet Perdana Menteri RI Jogyakarta 1949–1950, ANRI.

3. Mary Somers Heidhues, "Anti-Chinese Violence in Java during the Indonesian Revolution, 1945–49," *Journal of Genocide Research* 14, nos. 3–4 (2012): 381.

4. "Jiang Jiadong zonglingshi qianze gongheguo jiaotu zhengce" [Consul General Jiang Jiadong condemns the scorched-earth policy of the Republican forces], *Da Gong Bao*, July 27, 1947, no. 0582, clipping collections at the Center for Southeast Asian Studies of Xiamen University (CSASXU). A patriotic song calls Bandung a "sea of fire" during this battle. For details, see John Smail, *Bandung in the Early Revolution, 1945–1946: A Study in the Social History of the Indonesian Revolution* (Ithaca, NY: Cornell University Modern Indonesia Project, 1964).

5. "Interview with Dr. Tan Eng Oen, accountant," November 1, 1950, box 2, ser. 2, Skinner Papers.

6. Heidhues, "Anti-Chinese Violence," 391.

7. Ibid., 386.

8. After the Japanese surrender, the Netherlands was critically weakened in Europe by World War II and did not return as a significant military force until early 1946. The British Commonwealth troops were responsible for restoring order after the Japanese surrender, while the Dutch were preparing to reclaim the sovereignty of Indonesia.

9. Heidhues, "Anti-Chinese Violence," 397–398n2.

10. "Naskah Pidato Kementerian Pertahanan tanggal August 5, 1947 tentang kedudukan golongan asing terdiri dari Tionghoa, Arab dan India yang bukan WNI di Indonesia," August 5,1947, no. 65, Inventaris Arsip Kementerian Pertahanan RI, ANRI.

11. "Sudao Jugang huaqiao wugu canzao shahai" [Innocent Overseas Chinese in Palembang, Sumatra, were brutally killed], *Fujian Shibao*, February 22, 1947, no. 0582, CSASXU.

12. Heidhues, "Anti-Chinese Violence," 387.

13. "Surat-surat bulan Agustus 1947–Agustus 1948 tentang penduduk Tionghoa di Indonesia," November 3 and 12, 1947, no. 213, Djodja Documenten, ANRI. Originally in English.

14. Heidhues, "Anti-Chinese Violence," 391.

15. Box 19, Niels A. Douwes Dekker Papers, 1944–1946, Division of Rare and Manuscript Collections, Cornell University Library. There is no exact information, unfortunately, attached to this or to the other two pictures, probably due to the chaos

of war and the need to transfer this sensitive material out of Indonesia near the end of the Dutch-Indonesian conflict. Dekker himself explained: "I took thousands of pictures and made the arrangements for the taking of tens of thousands more. The Pacific War blew away 90% and the chaos of the revolution blew away the remnants of official and private collections. The end of 1949 was characterized by a nervousness rising to panic due to a fear that the nationalists would persecute fellow Indonesians who had been cooperative with the Dutch. This led to a general action to wipe out all possible traces that could be considered compromising. My Indonesian and Indochinese personnel informed me that they wanted to get rid of the pictorial material by burning. I was compelled to accept boxes of unsorted and mostly uncaptioned materials as personal belongings." See Anne L. Schiller, "The Niels Alexander Douwes Dekker Collection," *Documentation Newsletter* 14, no. 2 (1988): 1–8.

16. "Kronologi mengenai golongan Tionghoa di Jawa Barat, Jawa Tengah dan Jawa Timur," May 25,1948, Inventaris Arsip Kementerian Penerangan RI 1945–1949, no. 205, ANRI.

17. "Kepolisian Negara Bagian PAM: Laporan tentang golongan Tionghoa, Indo Belanda, India dll.," August 18, 1948, no. 741, Inventaris Arsip Kepolisian Negara RI 1947–1949, ANRI.

18. Ibid. On Chung Hwa Tsung Hwee and its role during the Indonesian National Revolution, see Mary Somers Heidhues, "Citizenship and Identity: Ethnic Chinese and the Indonesian Revolution," in *Changing Identities of the Southeast Asian Chinese since World War II*, ed. Jennifer W. Cushman and Wang Gungwu (Hong Kong: Hong Kong University Press, 1988), 115–139.

19. Heidhues, "Anti-Chinese Violence," 382.

20. Skinner, "Chinese Minority," 97–98.

21. Mackie and Coppel, "Preliminary Survey," 8.

22. Takashi Shiraishi, *An Age in Motion: Popular Radicalism in Java, 1912–1926* (Ithaca, NY: Cornell University Press, 1990), 45–46.

23. Twang Peck Yang, *The Chinese Business Élite in Indonesia and the Transition to Independence, 1940–1950* (Kuala Lumpur: Oxford University Press, 1998), 122–127.

24. Mackie and Coppel, "Preliminary Survey," 8.

25. Zhuang Guotu, *Huaren huaqiao yu Zhongguo de guanxi* [The relations between overseas Chinese and China] (Guangzhou: Guangdong gaode jiaoyu chubanshe, 2001), 216.

26. Kuhn, *Chinese among Others*, 247.

27. Ibid., 60–61.

28. Ibid., 76–77. See also Mona Lohanda, *The Kapitan Cina of Batavia, 1837–1942: A History of Chinese Establishment in Colonial Society* (Jakarta: Djambatan, 1996).

29. Lea E. Williams, *Overseas Chinese Nationalism: The Genesis of the Pan-Chinese Movement in Indonesia, 1900–1916* (Glencoe, IL: Free Press, 1960), 57.

30. Oiyan Liu, "The Educational Movement in Early 20th Century Batavia and Its Connections with Singapore and China," *BiblioAsia* 6, no. 3 (October 2010): 22.

31. Liang, Yingming. "Cong zhonghua xuetang dao sanyu xuexiao—lun Yindunixiya xiandai huawen xuexiao de fazhan yu yanbian" [From Tiong Hoa Hak Tong to trilingual schools—on the development and evolution of Chinese medium education in modern Indonesia], *Huaqiao huaren lishi yanjiu* 2 (2013): 1–13.

32. Leo Suryadinata, "Indonesian Chinese Education: Past and Present," *Indonesia* 14 (1972): 63.

33. Chang Yau Hoon, " 'A Hundred Flowers Bloom': The Re-Emergence of the Chinese Press in Post-Suharto Indonesia," in *Media and the Chinese Diaspora: Community, Communications and Commerce*, ed. Sun Wanning (London: Routledge, 2006), 93.

34. Ibid., 94–95.

35. "Lin Chuan, Wu Lixin jiashu qingxu" [Petitions from the families of Lin Chuan and Wu Lixin], July 16, 1946–October 12, 1947, no. 020000000249, Academia Historica, Taipei.

36. Ibid.

37. For instance, see Jianli Huang, "Umbilical Ties: The Framing of the Overseas Chinese as the Mother of the Revolution," *Frontiers of History in China* 6, no. 2 (2011): 183–228.

38. Kuhn, *Chinese among Others*, 267.

39. Peterson, *Overseas Chinese in the People's Republic of China*, 16.

40. Kuhn, *Chinese among Others*, 267–268.

41. Fitzgerald, *China and the Overseas Chinese*, 8.

42. Peterson, *Overseas Chinese in the People's Republic of China*, 16.

43. Li Yinghui, *Huaqiao zhengce yu haiwai minzuzhuyi, 1912–1949* [Overseas Chinese policies and overseas Chinese nationalism, 1912–1949] (Taipei: Guoshiguan, 1997), 501–505.

44. Peterson, *Overseas Chinese in the People's Republic of China*, 17.

45. For details, see Yoji Akashi, *The Nanyang National Salvation Movement, 1937–1941* (Lawrence: Center for East Asian Studies, University of Kansas, 1970).

46. Heidhues, "Anti-Chinese Violence," 394.

47. Donald E. Willmott, *The National Status of the Chinese in Indonesia, 1900–1958* (Singapore: Equinox, 2009), 43.

48. "Shou Yinni guoji fa yingxiang huaqiao guoji cheng wenti" [Influenced by the Indonesian Nationality Law, the nationality of overseas Chinese has become a problem], *Min Zhu Bao*, June 6, 1946, no. 0581, CSASXU.

49. "Dongyin qiaobao yichang zhuyi" [Special attention, our fellow countrymen in the Dutch East Indies], *Zhongyang Ribao*, April 19, 1947, no. 0582, CSASXU.

50. "Surat-surat bulan Agustus 1947–Agustus 1948."

51. Ibid., 41.

52. "Laporan dari Sekretariat Perdana Menteri bagian Kepolisian Jogja."

53. Ibid., 391.

54. "Chen Kewen cheng Waijiaobu Yinni shicha baogao" [A report submitted by Chen Kewen to the Foreign Ministry on his recent survey in Indonesia], June 1952, from file "Yinni zajuan" [Miscellaneous dossier on Indonesia], January 20, 1952–January 29, 1958, no. 020-010899-0036, Academia Historica, Taipei. As will be explained in the next chapter, Chen was a special envoy of the ROC government in Taiwan to make contacts with Indonesia to establish informal relations. He noted in his report that "because of the belated recognition of the Republic of Indonesia by our government, the Indonesian government was resentful and usually vented their dissatisfaction toward the overseas Chinese." See also "Naskah Pidato Kementerian Pertahanan tanggal 5 August 1947."

55. "Zhuawa qiaobao reng dai yuanjiu" [The overseas Chinese in Java are still waiting for rescue], *Qiaosheng Bao*, July 24, 1946, no. 0581, CSASXU.

56. "Heshu Sudong huaqiao jinkuang" [The recent conditions of the overseas Chinese in Dutch East Sumatra], *Jiangsheng Bao*, September 13,1946, no. 0581, CSASXU.

57. "Zhonghua minguo zhu Bacheng zonglingshi Jiang Jiadong wuyan zaijian qiaobao" [The ROC consul general to Batavia, Jiang Jiadong, is too ashamed to face the overseas Chinese again], *Qiaosheng Bao*, July 30, 1946, no. 0581, CSASXU.

58. "Heshu Sudong huaqiao jinkuang" [The recent conditions of the overseas Chinese in Dutch East Sumatra], *Jiangsheng Bao*, September 14,1946, no. 0581, CSASXU.

59. Ibid.

60. "Surat-surat bulan Agustus 1947–Agustus 1948."

61. "Huaqiao yu Yinni duli" [The overseas Chinese and Indonesia's independence], *Nanqiao Ribao*, August 23, 1947, no. 333, CSASXU.

62. "Jiang Jiadong zonglingshi qianze gongheguo jiaotu zhengce."

63. "Surat-surat bulan Agustus 1947–Agustus 1948."

64. Heidhues, "Anti-Chinese Violence," 394–395.

65. Anne van der Veer, "The Pao An Tui in Medan: A Chinese Security Force in Dutch Occupied Indonesia, 1945–1948" (Master's thesis, Utrecht University, 2013), 3.

66. Ibid.

67. "Kepolisian Negara: Laporan, 20 April 1948 tentang pembunuhan seorang bangsa Tionghoa oleh Barisan Gerilya yang dipimpin oleh Sukemi; disertai lampiran," April 20, 1948, Delegasi Indonesia no. 486, ANRI.

68. "Surat-surat bulan Agustus 1947–Agustus 1948."

69. "Nanjing zhengfu waijiao cizhang zhuzhang Heyin huaqiao zuzhi Bao An Dui" [Deputy foreign minister of the Nanjing government supports the Pao An Tui organized by the overseas Chinese in the Dutch East Indies], *Da Gong Bao*, November 2, 1947, no. 334, CSASXU.

70. van der Veer, "Pao An Tui in Medan," 36.

71. Ibid., 44.

72. "Yinni huaqiao de xuezhai" [The blood debt of the Chinese in Indonesia], *Da Gong Bao*, February 21, 1949, no. 334, CSASXU.

73. "Kronologi mengenai golongan Tionghoa di Jawa Barat, Jawa Tengah dan Jawa Timur."

74. Ibid.

75. "Surat-surat bulan Agustus 1947–Agustus 1948."

76. Ibid.

77. Heidhues, "Anti-Chinese Violence," 384–385.

78. Willmott, *National Status of the Chinese*, 36–37.

79. Heidhues, "Anti-Chinese Violence," 384.

80. "Dongyin huaqiao kun chu wei jing, zhengfu jing shushiwudu" [The overseas Chinese in the Dutch East Indies in jeopardy, the government is merely standing by], *Qiaosheng Bao*, July 21, 1946, no. 0581, CSASXU.

81. "Zhonghua minguo zhu Bacheng zonglingshi."

82. Ibid.

83. Ibid. The ROC allowed formal overseas Chinese representation in its government. A 1912 law governing the National Assembly required that 6 of the 274 senators be elected by an electoral college composed of representatives of Chinese Chambers of Commerce abroad. See Peterson, *Overseas Chinese in the People's Republic of China*, 16.

84. "Huaqiao yu Yinni duli" [The overseas Chinese and Indonesia's independence], *Nanqiao Ribao*, August 23, 1947, no. 333, CSASXU.

85. Ibid.

86. "Yinni huaqiao zuzhi Bao An Dui jiashen huaqiao de eyun" [The Pao An Tui organized by the overseas Chinese in Indonesia made the misfortune of these Chinese even worse], *Haibin Ribao*, September 13, 1947, no. 334, CSASXU. "Barbarians" here refers to the pribumi.

87. "Huaqiao zai Sumendala" [The overseas Chinese in Sumatra], *Qiaosheng Bao*, October 9, 1946, no. 334, CSASXU.

88. "Huaqiao Bao An Dui buneng wanquan zhongli" [The Pao An Tui organized by the overseas Chinese cannot stay completely neutral], *Da Gong Bao*, August 24, 1947, no. 334, CSASXU.

89. "Dukungan terhadap republik Sekretariat Delegasi Indonesia dari Kementerian Penerangan: Resolusi Golongan Tionghoa, 3 Pebruari 1948 tentang dukungan terhadap Pemerintah Republik; disertai surat pengantar," February 3, 1948, no. 360, Delegasi Indonesia 1957–1951, ANRI.

90. Heidhues, "Anti-Chinese Violence," 384–385.

91. "Hasil percakapan Tony Wen dengan Letnan Kolonel Ratcliff tanggal 13 September 1947 mengenai pendapat penduduk Tionghoa terhadap situasi politik dan militer," September 13, 1947, no. 272, Djogdja Documenten 1945–1949, ANRI.

92. Melani Budianta, "Malang Mignon: Cultural Expressions of the Chinese, 1940–1960," in *Heirs to World Culture: Being Indonesian, 1950–1965*, ed. Jennifer Lindsay and Maya H. T. Liem (Leiden: KITLV Press, 2012), 261–262.

93. "Hasil percakapan Tony Wen dengan Letnan Kolonel Ratcliff."

94. Liao Zhangran, interview by author, Medan, January 9, 2013.

95. Ba Ren, "Zai waiguo jianlao li" [In the foreign prison], in *Ba Ren wen ji huiyilu juan* [Collected Works of Ba Ren: Memoirs], ed. Editing Committee of *Collected Works of Ba Ren*, Zhejiang Academy of Social Sciences (Ningbo: Ningbo chubanshe, 1997), 424–425.

2. The Chinese Communist Party and the Overseas Chinese

1. Ba Ren, "Zai Silabaye cun" [In Village Surabeia], in Editing Committee of *Collected Works of Ba Ren, Ba Ren wen ji huiyilu juan*, 406.

2. Ba Ren, "Yindunixiya zhi ge" [Song of Indonesia], in *Ba Ren wen ji shige xuba juan* [Collected works of Ba Ren: Poems, prefaces, and postscripts], ed. Editing Committee of *Collected Works of Ba Ren*, Zhejiang Academy of Social Sciences (Ningbo: Ningbo chubanshe, 1997), 346.

3. Fitzgerald, *China and the Overseas Chinese*, x.

4. Peterson, *Overseas Chinese in the People's Republic of China*, 22.

5. Ba Ren, "Yindunixiya zhi ge," 320.

6. Ba Ren, "Yindunixiya geming guangan" [Observations and opinions on the Indonesian Revolution], in *Ba Ren yu Yindunixiya—jinian Ba Ren (Wang Renshu) danchen 100 zhounian* [Ba Ren and Indonesia—in memory of the 100th birthday of Ba Ren a.k.a. Wang Renshu], ed. Zhou Nanjing (Hong Kong: Nandao chubanshe, 2001), 258.

7. Peterson, *Overseas Chinese in the People's Republic of China*, 17–18; Ren Guixiang and Zhao Hongying, *Huaqiao huaren yu guogong guanxi* [Overseas Chinese and

the relations between the Communist and Nationalist Parties] (Wuhan: Wuhan chubanshe, 1999), 93.

8. Xu Xiaosheng, *Huaqiao yu diyici guogong hezuo* [Overseas Chinese and the first United Front between the Communist and Nationalist Parties] (Guangzhou: Jinan daxue chubanshe, 1993), 74–76.

9. Huang Weici, "Dui huaqiao he gang'ao tongbao de tongzhan gongzuo" [United Front work on overseas Chinese and fellow countrymen in Hong Kong and Macau], in *Nanfangju dangshi ziliao: tongzhan gongzuo* [Historical materials of the Southern Bureau: On the United Front], ed. Editing Group of the Historical Materials of the Southern Bureau of the CCP (Chongqing: Chongqing chubanshe, 1990), 374–387.

10. Elizabeth Sinn, "Moving Bones: Hong Kong's Role as an 'In-Between Place' in the Chinese Diaspora," in *Cities in Motion: Interior, Coast and Diaspora in Transnational China*, ed. David Strand and Sherman Cochran (Berkeley: University of California Press, 2007), 248–249.

11. For a historical survey on this propaganda war and the US policy of containment, see Meredith Oyen, "Communism, Containment and the Chinese Overseas," in *The Cold War in Asia: The Battle for Hearts and Minds*, ed. Yangwen Zheng, Hong Liu, and Michael Szonyi (Leiden: Brill, 2010), 59–93.

12. Hu Yuzhi, "Wo zai kangzhan shiqi de jingli" [My experience during the war of resistance against the Japanese], in Editing Group of the Historical Materials of the Southern Bureau of the CCP, *Nanfangju dangshi ziliao*, 183–190.

13. Ba Ren, "Zizhuan" [Autobiography], in Editing Committee of *Collected Works of Ba Ren, Ba Ren wen ji huiyilu juan*, 491–492.

14. Lei was a faithful Communist and a women's rights activist. In Indonesia, she also adopted an alias, Liu Yan. Ba Ren and Lei Derong pretended to be husband and wife when they first arrived in Sumatra, but later fell in love and became a real couple.

15. A more complete list of left-wing intellectuals who traveled to Sumatra during World War II includes Ba Ren, Shen Zijiu, Yang Sao, Zheng Chuyun, Wang Jiyuan, Gao Yunlan, Wang Jinding, and Shao Zonghan.

16. Wang Qianyu, *Zai chidao xian shang* [On the equator] (Hong Kong: Dadao chubanshe, 2008), 157.

17. Mackie and Coppel, "Preliminary Survey," 7.

18. Ba Ren, "Rensheng jiqi zhouwei de yiqun" [Rensheng and those around him], in Editing Committee of *Collected Works of Ba Ren, Ba Ren wen ji huiyilu juan*, 131–198.

19. Ibid., 131.

20. During his years in Indonesia, Yu Dafu assisted the Malaya Communist Party (MCP) through his social network in Payakumbuh. When it was discovered that he was one of the few locals in the area who could speak Japanese, Yu Dafu was forced to help the Japanese military police, *Kempeitai*, as an interpreter. In 1945, when his true identity was exposed, he was arrested and executed by the Kempeitai. Yu left behind him a peranakan Chinese wife who was pregnant with their daughter, Yu Meilan. Yu Meilan, interview by author, Xiamen, October 24 and 25, 2013. See also Xia Yan, "Yi Dafu" [In memory of Dafu], September 20, 1985, *Renmin Ribao*; and Hu Yuzhi, "Wo zai kangzhan shiqi de jingli," in Editing Group of the Historical Materials of the Southern Bureau of the CCP, *Nanfangju dangshi ziliao*, 183–190.

21. Huang Shuhai, "Yinni Subei huaqiao kangri douzheng gai lue" [Brief history of anti-Japanese struggles among the overseas Chinese in North Sumatra in Indonesia], in *Wang buliao de suiyue* [Times that cannot be forgotten], ed. Huang Shuhai (Beijing: Shijie zhishi chubanshe, 2003), 2–10. The editor, Huang, was a left-wing youth from Siantar who later became a PRC diplomat.

22. Ba Ren, "Zai faxisi lianyu zhi huo zhong xinsheng" [Rebirth in the inferno of fascism], in Zhou Nanjing, *Ba Ren yu Yindunixiya*, 204–250.

23. Ba Ren, "Yindunixiya geming," 257.

24. Ibid., 222.

25. Ibid.

26. Mary Somers Heidhues reports that, after the Japanese occupation, Ba Ren became close to Abdul Karim, a PKI leader. See Heidhues, "Citizenship and Identity," 125.

27. Ba Ren, "Yindunixiya geming," 222.

28. A youth group targeting women organized by Lei. See Huang Fulian, "Yi Liu Yan yu Xianda jiazheng dushuhui" [In memory of Liu Yan and the household management reading group in Siantar], in Huang Shuhai, *Wang buliao de suiyue*, 89–91.

29. This left-wing group appeared publicly in the name of a Chinese youth basketball team. See Xiao Fei, "Huiyi Xianda jianshen dushuhui de huodong pianduan" [In memory of the activities at the fitness and book club in Siantar], in Huang Shuhai, *Wang buliao de suiyue*, 87.

30. Ibid.

31. Xiao Fei, "Yi Ba Ren Liu Yan zai Xianda de liuwang he zhandou shenghuo" [In memory of the life of exile and struggle of Ba Ren and Liu Yan in Siantar], in Huang Shuhai, *Wang buliao de suiyue*, 78.

32. Ba Ren, "Zai faxisi lianyu zhi huo," 228–229.

33. Lin Jian, "Yi Fanmeng jiaotong lianluo zhan de jianli jiqi fazhan guocheng" [In memory of the establishment and development of the transportation network of the People's Antifascist Alliance in Sumatra], in Huang Shuhai, *Wang buliao de suiyue*, 68–76.

34. Ibid., 76.

35. Ba Ren, "Yindunixiya geming," 258.

36. Ba Ren, "Linren men" [Neighbors], in Editing Committee of *Collected Works of Ba Ren*, *Ba Ren wen ji huiyilu juan*, 310.

37. Lin Kesheng, "Huainian Ba Ren tongzhi" [In memory of Comrade Ba Ren], in Zhou Nanjing, *Ba Ren yu Yindunixiya*, 457–462.

38. Ba Ren, "Yindunixiya geming," 258.

39. Ba Ren, "Linren Men," 333.

40. Ba Ren, "Yindunixiya zhi ge," 287–288.

41. Ba Ren, "Yindunixiya geming," 258.

42. Ba Ren, "Yindunixiya zhi ge," 362, 369, 320.

43. Ibid., 355.

44. In this context, "bapak" and "nyonya" have a similar meaning as Mr. and Mrs., though the terms have a stronger connotation of respect.

45. Ba Ren, "Linren Men," 365–366.

46. Ba Ren, interview by Muhammad Radjab, Siantar, Sumatra, July 14, 1947, in *Tjatatan di Sumatera*, by Muhammad Radjab (Jakarta: Balai Pustaka, 1949), 66.

47. Lin Kesheng, "Huainian Ba Ren," 457–462.

48. See Milton Sacks, "The Strategy of Communism in Southeast Asia," *Pacific Affairs* 23, no. 3 (1950): 228.

49. Wang Qianyu, *Zai chidao xian shang*, 3–21.

50. Ba Ren, "Zai waiguo jianlao li," 422.

51. Ibid., 423.

52. Ba Ren, "Yindunixiya geming," 253–254.

53. By "fraternal ethnic groups," Ba Ren was referring to the pribumi. It is a term commonly used among ethnic Chinese in Indonesia to express goodwill toward the pribumi.

54. Ibid., 254.

55. Ba Ren, interview by Muhammad Radjab, Siantar, Sumatra, July 14, 1947.

56. Wang Qianyu, *Zai chidao xian shang*, 44, 61.

57. Ba Ren, "Wu Zu Miao" [Temple of Five Ancestors], in Editing Committee of *Collected Works of Ba Ren, Ba Ren wen ji xiju juan*, 245–246.

58. Ba Ren, "Wu Zu Miao," 244–245.

59. Ba Ren, "Wu Zu Miao," 300.

60. Ba Ren, "Wu ge bei diaosi de kuli" [Five coolie laborers who were hanged], in Zhou Nanjing, *Ba Ren yu Yindunixiya*, 120.

61. Ibid., 256, 257.

62. Ibid., 264, 271, 359.

63. Ibid., 355.

64. Xu Anru, "Wang Renshu jiqi Wu Zu Miao" [Wang Renshu and his Temple of Five Ancestors], in Zhou Nanjing, *Ba Ren yu Yindunixiya*, 484–492. The author used to be the editor of the *Democratic Daily* and was one of the people in charge of the "New China Drama Club."

65. Wang Qianyu, *Zai chidao xian shang*, 89–90.

66. Ming Lun, "Zao Helan daibu de Ba Ren" [Ba Ren under arrest by the Dutch], in Zhou Nanjing, *Ba Ren yu Yindunixiya*, 494.

67. Ba Ren, "Zai waiguo jianlao li," 424–425.

68. "Waijiaobu: Wang Renshu deng bei Malaiya quzhu chujing" [Foreign Ministry: Wang Renshu and several others expelled by Malaya], August 25, 1947–December 6, 1948, no. 020-010607-0025, Academia Historica, Taipei.

69. Ba Ren, "Zai waiguo jianlao li," 465–466.

70. Ba Ren, "Yindunixiya geming," 256.

71. Ibid., 314–315, 262–263.

72. See Wang Qianyu, *Zai chidao xian shang*; Huang Shuhai, *Xianda zhaopian* [Pictures from Siantar] (Beijing: Hongwen jijinhui, 2008); Huang Shuhai, interviews by author, Beijing, July 17, 2009; and Wen Liu, interview by author, Xiamen, October 23, 2013.

3. The Diplomatic Battle between the Two Chinas

1. "Tangshan" (Tang Mountain) refers to China. This is a common term for China among the global South Chinese diaspora.

2. Ba Ren, "Rensheng jiqi zhouwei de yiqun xiaohou ji" [Afterword to *Rensheng and Those around Him*], in *Ba Ren wen ji shige xuba juan*, 487–489.

3. Qiu Zheng'ou, *Sujianuo shidai Yinni paihua shishi* [Historical facts of the anti-Chinese movements during the Sukarno era] (Taipei: Institute of Modern History, Academia Sinica, 1995), 5.

4. "Berkas tentang permintaan bekas Konsul di Tiongkok Nasionalis Tuan New Shu Chun tetap tinggal di Jogjakarta," May 6, 1950, no. 1962, Kabinet Perdana Menteri Tahun 1950–1959, ANRI.

5. Wen Guangyi, Cai Renlong, Liu Aihua, and Luo Mingqing, *Yindunixiya huaqiao shi* [History of overseas Chinese in Indonesia] (Beijing: Haiyang chubanshe, 1985), 433; Huaqiao Zhi Editorial Board, *Yinni huaqiao zhi* [General records of the overseas Chinese in Indonesia] (Taipei: Huaqiao Zhi Editorial Board, 1961), 161.

6. Xu Zhengzheng, "Yindunixiya huaren zhong de qin Taiwan qunti: jingyu yu yingdui [The pro-Taiwan Chinese communities in Indonesia: Challenges and responses]" (PhD diss., Xiamen University, 2008), 46.

7. "The Party's core mission in 1950," January 11, 1951, in *Zhongguo Guomindang dangwu fazhan shiliao—zhongyang gaizao weiyuanhui ziliao huibian* [Historical documents of the development of the Chinese Nationalist Party—a collection of materials of the Central Committee for Reform], ed. Party History Committee of the Chinese Nationalist Party (Taipei: Jindai zhongguo chubanshe, 2000), 1:337–338.

8. Oyen, "Communism, Containment and the Chinese Overseas," 67–68.

9. G. William Skinner, "Communism and Chinese Culture in Indonesia: The Political Dynamics of the Chinese Youth" (unpublished manuscript, August 1962), typescript available at Kroch Asia Library, Cornell University, 18.

10. "Molifen Zhonghua Zonghui zhi waijiaobu xinhan" [Chinese General Association in Madiun to the Foreign Ministry of the ROC], July 18, 1951, from file "Yinni huaqiao guoji wenti" [The nationality issue of the overseas Chinese in Indonesia], July 18, 1951–December 11, 1954, no. 020-010807-0026, Academia Historica, Taipei.

11. Zheng Yanfen to Ye Gongchao, September 20, 1951, and Ye Gongchao to Zheng Yanfen, September 28, 1951, from file "Yinni zhuanjuan" [Special dossier on Indonesia], June 15, 1949–August 25, 1953, no. 020-010801-0018, Academia Historica, Taipei.

12. Ibid.

13. "Man'gu Zhu Changdong baogao zai Yinni mimi xiaozu jingguo qingxing" [Report from Zhu Changdong, who is based in Bangkok, about the process of forming a secret group in Indonesia], September 28, 1951, from file "Yinni zhuanjuan," no. 020-010899-0036, Academia Historica, Taipei.

14. The names of the committee members are Wu Shenji, Chen Xingyan, Wen Juming, Guo Meicheng, Qiu Yuanrong, Liang Xiyou, Zhang Xunyi, Ma Shuli or Mah Soo Lay, and Zhu Changdong. Zhu recorded the following information about the founding of the organization Liu Dexian in his report to Taipei: "We remember that when the Communist bandits established diplomatic relations with Indonesia, around ten patriotic [pro-Taiwan] leaders of the Chinese society secretly got together to discuss the local political situation, as well as how to gain control of the Chinese associations and schools and to prevent these organizations from being used by the Communist bandits. The central Nationalist Party branch in Jakarta coordinated with branches in other parts of Indonesia, and they collaborated with the Chinese business and retail associations to reinforce anti-Communist propaganda and to conduct civil diplomacy." See "Man'gu Zhu Changdong baogao."

15. "Man'gu Zhu Changdong baogao."

16. Herbert Feith, *The Decline of Consitutional Democracy in Indonesia* (Jakarta: Equinox, 2007), 188.

17. Cai Renlong, *Chidaoxian shang de jiaoyin* [Footprints on the equator] (Hong Kong: Xianggang shenghuo wenhua jijinhui, 2014), 380–385. The author is professor emeritus at the Research School for Southeast Asian Studies, Xiamen University. He was born in West Kalimantan and used to be a pro-Beijing student activist in Jakarta before returning to China in 1953. Yang Xinrong is his father-in law.

18. "Man'gu Zhu Changdong baogao."

19. Lawrence Kessler, "Reconstructing Zhou Enlai's Escape from Shanghai in 1931: A Research Note," *Twentieth Century China* 34, no. 2 (2008): 112–131.

20. Tang Liangli to Chen Kewen, January 25, 1952, from file "Yinni zajuan" [Miscellaneous dossier on Indonesia], no. 020-010899-0036, Academia Historica, Taipei. It is unclear what Tang meant by "real Chinese nationals." Most likely he was referring to the Chinese residing in Indonesia who had already rejected or intended to reject Indonesian citizenship.

21. "Agreed minutes of the conversation," December 1, 1951, from file "Yinni zajuan" [Miscellaneous dossier on Indonesia], January 20, 1952–January 29, 1958, no. 020-010899-0036, Academia Historica, Taipei.

22. Tang Liangli to Chen Kewen, January 25, 1952.

23. Xue Shouheng to Chen Kewen, February 20, 1952, from file "Yinni zajuan," no. 020-010899-0036, Academia Historica, Taipei.

24. Chen Fong-ching, ed., *Chen Kewen riji 1937–1952* [Diary of Chen Kewen, 1937–1952] (Taipei: Institute of Modern History, Academia Sinica, 2012), 2:1315–1316.

25. "Surat dari Kejaksaan Agung kepada Presiden RI mengenai kegiatan politik dan kebudayaan orang Tionghoa sejak adanya Kedutaan Agung RRT di Indonesia," August 15, 1950, no. 1977, Inventaris Arsip Sekretariat Negara Kabinet Perdana Menteri Tahun 1950–1959, ANRI.

26. Ibid.

27. In mid-September 1948, violence broke out between pro-Communist troops and government forces in Madiun, East Java. Without the knowledge of the top leadership of the PKI, army commanders with Communist leanings decided to publicly proclaim the beginning of a revolution. Presented with this fait accompli, the PKI central leadership tried to transform a localized conflict into a full-scale rebellion against the authority of the Republic of Indonesia. But, within two weeks, most of the PKI leaders were arrested or killed by Republican forces. After the Madiun Affair, the PKI became "tainted forever with treachery against the Revolution." See M. C Ricklefs, *A History of Modern Indonesia since c. 1300*, 2nd ed. (Stanford, CA: Stanford University Press, 1993), 229.

28. "Kejaksaan Agung kepada Presiden RI: surat-surat tanggal 6 Januari, 1953 tentang China Demokratie League dan Perkumpulan Shaw Nien Erh T'ung Hui," January 6, 1953, no. 1852, Inventaris Arsip Kabinet Presiden RI 1950–1959, ANRI.

29. Shi Zhe, *Zai lishi juren de shenbian* [Standing beside a historical giant] (Beijing: Zhongyang wenxian chubanshe, 1991), 412.

30. Liu Shaoqi, "Zai Ya'ao gonghui huiyi shang de kaimuci" [Opening remarks at the Trade Union Conference of Asian and Australasian Countries], November 16, 1949, in *Jianguo yilai Liu Shaoqi wengao* [Liu Shaoqi's manuscripts since the founding

of the PRC], ed. CCP Central Documentary Research Department (Beijing: Zhong-yang wenxian chubanshe, 1998), 134–135.

31. "Surat dari Jaksa Agung kepada Perdana Menteri mengenai pelarangan utu-san dari Indonesia ke Konferensi Panitia Perdamaian Dunia karena dianggap pro komunis," November 9, 1951, no. 2028, Inventaris Arsip Sekretariat Negara Kabinet Perdana Menteri Tahun 1950–1959, ANRI.

32. Ibid.

33. "Surat dari Kejaksaan Agung kepada Presiden RI mengenai kegiatan politik dan kebudayaan orang Tionghoa."

34. Ibid.

35. "Berkas mengenai permohonan dan perjinan kepada Duta Besar RRT untuk membuka konsulat-konsulat di Indonesia oleh beberapa organisasi kemasyarakatan Tionghoa di Sumatera Utara, Sumatera Timur dan Aceh," January 27, 1951, no. 1970, Kabinet Perdana Menteri Tahun 1950–1959, ANRI.

36. "Surat dari Kejaksaan Agung kepada Presiden RI mengenai kegiatan politik dan kebudayaan orang Tionghoa."

37. Ba Ren, "Ziwo zongjie [Summary of one's own work]" (unpublished hand-written manuscript, 1952), courtesy of Wang Keping.

38. Zheng Junyi, *Guiqiao Peng Guanghan de wangshi jinshi* [The past of returned overseas Chinese Peng Guanhan] (Hong Kong: Xiangang shehui kexue chubanshe, 2005), 291.

39. Ibid., 292.

40. Ibid., 297.

41. "Mao Zedong jiejian Taiguo jingji wenhua daibiaotuan de tanhua" [Minutes of Mao Zedong's meeting with an economic and cultural delegation from Thai-land], December 21, 1955, in *Jingwai Huaren guoji wenti taolunji* [Discussions outside of China on the citizenship issue of the overseas Chinese], ed. Zhou Nanjing (Hong Kong: Hong Kong Social Science Press, 2005), 9.

42. "Mao Zedong di'erci jiejian Xihanuke de tanhua" [Mao Zedong's second meeting with Sihanouk], August 16, 1958, in Zhou Nanjing, *Jingwai Huaren guoji wenti taolunji*, 10.

43. "Zhou Enali guanyu huaqiao shuangchong guoji wenti zai Yinni Yajiada dui huaqiao de jianghua jielu" [Excerpt of Zhou Enlai's speech on the dual nationality issue of the overseas Chinese delivered to the ethnic Chinese in Jakarta, Indonesia], June 4, 1956, in Zhou Nanjing, *Jingwai Huaren guoji wenti taolunji*, 18–20.

44. "Yinni yu Zhonggong miuding guoji tiaoyue" [Indonesia and the Chinese Communists signed the ridiculous dual nationality treaty], *Xingdao Ribao*, May 2, 1955, Overseas Chinese Clippings Collection, Hong Kong Baptist University (OCCCHKBU).

45. Ibid.

46. Ibid.

47. "Record of [Jiang Tingfu's] Conversation with Donald Gilpatrick," July 24, 1951, from file "Yinni huaqiao guoji wenti" [The nationality issue of the overseas Chinese in Indonesia], no. 020-010807-0026, Academia Historica, Taipei. Originally in English.

48. Qiu Zheng'ou, *Huaqiao wenti yanjiu* [A study of the overseas Chinese issue] (Taipei: Institute of the Department of Defense, 1965), 8. Qiu later became a scholar

of overseas Chinese studies after being deported from Indonesia and relocating to Taiwan.

49. "Zhongguo Guomindang zhongyang gaizao weiyuanhui disanzu dai dian" [Telegram from Team Three, Central Committee for Party Reform, Chinese Nationalist Party], January 30, 1951, from file "Yinni huaqiao guoji wenti," no. 020-010807-0026, Academia Historica, Taipei.

50. Overseas Chinese Research Association, ed., *Yafei diqu huaqiao qingkuang jieshao* [An introduction to the overseas Chinese in Asia and Africa] (Beijing: Huaqiao wenti yanjiuhui bianyin, 1955), 65–66.

51. "Man'gu Zhu Changdong baogao."

52. *Harian Rakyat*, October 7, 1954, cited in Overseas Chinese Research Association, *Yafei diqu huaqiao*, 68.

53. Ibid.

54. Wu Shihuang, *Yindunixiya* [Indonesia], 56.

55. "Fu Zhang Xunyi deng bei qianfan shi" [Response to the expulsion of Zhang Xunyi and others], October 14, 1954, no. 118-00271-01, CFMA; and "Dui Yinni zhengfu daibu Jiangfei shi de taidu" [Our attitude toward the Indonesian government's decision to arrest the Chiang bandits], October 29, 1954, no. 118-00271-01, CFMA.

56. "Fu Zhang Xunyi deng bei qianfan shi." As will be explained in Chapter 4, the PRC refers to the pro-Beijing overseas Chinese as "patriotic."

57. "Waijiao bu yingjiu Yinni qiaoling Zhang Xunyi deng bei Yinni quzhu chujing jiesong dalu an" [Foreign Ministry reporting on the case of rescuing Zhang Xunyi and several other leaders of the overseas Chinese communities in Indonesia who were expelled and about to be sent to the mainland], October 17, 1954, no. 020-010807-0069, Academia Historica, Taipei.

58. "Qingshi shifou fagei Zhang Xunyi rujing qianzheng" [On issuing an entry visa to Zhang Xunyi], October 9, 1954, no. 118-00271-011, CFMA.

59. Ibid.

60. "Fu Zhang Xunyi deng bei qianfan shi."

61. Ibid.

62. For discussions of the Taiwan Strait Crisis of 1954–1955, see Chen Jian, *Mao's China and the Cold War*, 167–170; and Gordon H. Chang and He Di, "The Absence of War in the U.S.-China Confrontation over Quemoy and Matsu in 1954–1955: Contingency, Luck, Deterrence?," *American Historical Review* 98 (1993): 1500–1524.

63. Chang and He, "Absence of War," 1520.

64. Chen Jian, "Bridging Revolution and Decolonization: The 'Bandung Discourse' in China's Early Cold War Experience," *Chinese Historical Review* 15, no. 2 (2008): 216–17.

65. "Yindunixiya de jiben qingkuang he dongxiang" [The basic situation and tendencies of Indonesia], February 25, 1956, no. 102-00055-02, CFMA.

66. See Chen Jian, "Bridging Revolution and Decolonization"; and Shu Guang Zhang, "Constructing 'Peaceful Coexistence': China's Diplomacy toward the Geneva and Bandung Conferences, 1954–55," *Cold War History* 7, no. 4 (2007): 509–528.

67. The Five Principles or "Pancasila" include (1) mutual respect for sovereignty and territorial integrity, (2) nonaggression, (3) noninterference in other country's internal affairs, (4) equal and mutual benefit, and (5) peaceful coexistence.

68. Chen Jian, "Bridging Revolution and Decolonization," 232.

69. Steve Tsang, "Target Zhou Enlai: The 'Kashmir Princess' Incident of 1955," *China Quarterly* 139 (1994): 766–782.

70. Zhu Yi, *Wanlong jiaoxiangqu—jinian yafei huiyi wushi zhounian* [Symphony at Bandung: Celebrating the fiftieth anniversary of the Bandung Conference] (Shenyang: Liaoning renmin chubanshe, 2005), 18. The Iron and Blood Group was initially founded in 1912 as the Republic of China's Iron and Blood Group for the Northern Expedition (zhonghua minguo beifa tiexue tuan). Later, this organization merged with the other troops in the Northern Expedition. It expanded into Chinese societies in Southeast Asia during World War II. For information on its development in Thailand, see Li Enhan, *Dongnanya huaren shi* [A history of overseas Chinese in Southeast Asia] (Taipei: Wunan tushu, 2003), 411–412.

71. Chen Yushan and Chen Shaojing, *Yuan Geng zhi mi* [The myth of Yuan Geng] (Guangzhou: Huacheng chubanshe, 2005), 89. Yuan Geng was appointed as the consul general of the PRC in Jakarta in 1953. He oversaw intelligence work before, during, and after the Afro-Asian Conference of 1955.

72. "Zhou Enlai zongli yu Yindunixiya zongli Ali dierci huitan jiyao" [The second meeting between Premier Zhou Enlai and the Indonesian premier Ali Sastroamidjojo], May 28, 1955, no. 204-00014-03, CFMA.

73. Ibid.

74. West Irian is the western half of the island of New Guinea, which used to be under the colonial control of the Netherlands. Dutch and Indonesian leaders failed to reach an agreement about the sovereignty of West Irian at the Roundtable Conference in 1949. During the 1950s, the Dutch government began to prepare West Irian for full independence. Indonesian leaders regarded this as a blatant assault on their sovereignty.

75. Benedict Richard O'Gorman Anderson, *Imagined Communities* (London: Verso, 1991), 176–177.

76. "Zhou Enlai zongli yu Yindunixiya zongli."

77. Ibid.

78. "Premier Chou En-lai's answers to questions put by Indonesian correspondents," June 2, 1955, no. 204-00014-05, CFMA. Originally in English.

79. "Sujianuo zongtong chuguo fangwen chengjiu juda, Yindunixiya baozhi relie zanyang" [President Sukarno's foreign visit was extremely fruitful and was warmly praised by Indonesian newspapers], *Renmin Ribao*, October 19, 1956; "Sujianuo zongtong dui Zhongguo renmin de guangbo yanshuo" [President Sukarno delivered a speech to the Chinese people on the radio], *Renmin Ribao*, October 16, 1956.

80. Hong Liu, *China and the Shaping of Indonesia*, 205–230.

81. "Zhongguo he Yindunixiya de youyi zhi qiao" [The bridge of friendship between China and Indonesia], *Renmin Ribao*, October 15, 1956.

82. For details, see chapter 7 in Chen Jian, *Mao's China and the Cold War*; and chapter 6 in Thomas J. Christensen, *Useful Adversaries: Grand Strategy, Domestic Mobilization, and Sino-American Conflict, 1947–1958* (Princeton, NJ: Princeton University Press, 1996).

83. This is based on the Indonesian ambassador to China Soekardjo Wiriopranoto's explanation of the background of the regional autonomy movements to Chen Yi. See "Chen Yi buzhang tong Yindunixiya Sujiazuo jiu Yinni panluan he goumi deng

wenti de tanhua jilu" [Minutes of discussion between Foreign Minister Chen Yi and the Indonesian ambassador Soekardjo on regional rebellions in Indonesia, rice purchase, etc.], March 2, 1958, no. 105-00366-02, CFMA. For more details, see Audrey R. Kahin and George McT. Kahin, *Subversion as Foreign Policy: The Secret Eisenhower and Dulles Debacle in Indonesia* (New York: New Press, 1995), 54–65.

84. "Chen Yi buzhang tong Yindunixiya Sujiazuo."

85. Kahin and Kahin, *Subversion as Foreign* Policy, 1.

86. "Zhang fubuzhang jiejian Yinni Sujiazuo dashi de tanhua jilu" [Minutes of Vice Foreign Minister Zhang and the Indonesian ambassador Soekardjo], April 29, 1958, no. 105-00366-01, CFMA.

87. "Chinese statement on U.S. intervention in Indonesia," issued on May 15, 1958, reprinted in *Peking Review*, May 20, 1958, 20–21.

88. "Guanyu Yindunixiya zongtong Sujianuo jing Yinnigong lingdaoren Aidi yaoqiu Zhongguo zhengfu fabiao shengming jinggao Xifang guojia ganshe Yinni neizheng shi" [Indonesian President Sukarno requested the Chinese government to issue a warning against Western intervention in the domestic affairs of Indonesia via Aidit, the leader of the PKI], February 24–April 12, 1958, no. 105-00363-01, CFMA.

89. Ibid.

90. "Geguo dui woguo zhengfu fabiao shengming chize waiguo ganshe Yindunixiya neizheng de fanying" [Different countries' responses to our government's public announcement against foreign intervention in the domestic affairs of Indonesia], May 19–June 6, 1958, no. 105-00363-07, CFMA. Mozingo made similar speculations based on his interviews with Indonesian foreign policy makers; see David Mozingo, *Chinese Policy toward Indonesia, 1949–1967* (Ithaca, NY: Cornell University Press, 1976), 146.

91. "Geguo dui woguo zhengfu."

92. "Chen Yi buzhang tong Yindunixiya Sujiazuo."

93. "Zhang fubuzhang jiejian Yinni Sujiazuo."

94. Fan Zhonghui, *Jiangjun, waijiao jia, yishu jia—Huang Zhen zhuan* [General, diplomat, and artist—a biography of Huang Zhen] (Beijing: Zhongyang wenxian chubanshe, 2007), 377.

95. "Zhang fubuzhang jiejian Yinni Sujiazuo."

96. "Telegram from the Embassy in the Republic of China to the Department of State," May 22, 1958, U.S. Department of State, *Foreign Relations of the United States (FRUS)*, 1958–1960, 17:194.

97. "Guofangbu gongbao yingwen yigao" [English translation of the announcement of the Ministry of Defense], May 23, 1958, no. 020-010899-0043, Academia Historica, Taipei.

98. Kahin and Kahin, *Subversion as Foreign Policy*, 174–184.

99. Barbara Sillars Harvey, *Permesta: Half a Rebellion* (Ithaca, NY: Cornell Modern Indonesia Project, 1977), 150–152.

100. "Kuomingtang" translates to "the Chinese Nationalist Party."

101. "Uncle Barhen," *Time*, January 22, 1951, 34. "Wang Jen-shu" is a different spelling of Ba Ren's official name "Wang Renshu." "Soekarno" is a different spelling of "Sukarno."

102. Zheng Junyi, *Guiqiao Peng Guanghan*, 294.

4. The Communal Battle between the Red and the Blue

1. Weng Xihui, "Yinni aiguo qiaoling Weng Fulin Zhuanji" [Biography of the patriotic leader of the overseas Chinese in Indonesia, Weng Fulin], in Qian Ren and Liang Junxiang, *Sheng Huo Bao de huiyi*, 238.

2. Referring to the Indonesian national flag.

3. Hei Ying, *Hong Bai Qi Xia* [Underneath the Red-and-White flag] (Hong Kong: Chidao chubanshe, 1950), 1–3.

4. "Yindunixiya huaren renkou, fenbu, guoji deng qingkuang de shuzi tongji" [Statistics on the population, demographic distributions, and nationality status of the ethnic Chinese in Indonesia], June 1, 1958, no. 105-00978-06, CFMA. This number corroborates earlier studies by Mely G. Tan and Donald Willmott. See Mely G. Tan, "The Ethnic Chinese in Indonesia: Issues of Identity," in *Ethnic Chinese as Southeast Asians*, ed. Leo Suryadinata (Singapore: Institute of Southeast Asian Studies, 1997), 35; and Willmott, *National Status of the Chinese*, 91.

5. "Berkas mengenai perjanjian antara RI dengan RRC tentang Dwi Kewarganegaraan beserta pengantar," July 3, 1956, no. 2144, Kabinet Perdana Menteri Tahun 1950–1959, ANRI.

6. "Huaqiao xuanze guoji wenti" [Overseas Chinese making their decisions on nationality], *Sheng Huo Bao*, May 18, 1950.

7. Wang Gungwu, "Chinese Politics in Malaya," *China Quarterly* 43 (1970): 4–5.

8. Overseas Chinese Research Association, *Yafei diqu huaqiao*, 55.

9. Skinner, "Communism and Chinese Culture in Indonesia," 18.

10. "Yecheng huaqiao zhengban tuoji" [The overseas Chinese in Jakarta rushed to renounce (Indonesian) citizenship], *Xin Bao*, December 10, 1951, no. 0329, CSASXU.

11. "Sishui qiaosheng tuoji de duo" [Many overseas Chinese students in Surabaya renounce (Indonesian) citizenship], *Xin Bao*, December 3, 1951, no. 0329, CSASXU.

12. "Guanyu guoji wenti" [On the nationality issue], May 10, 1950, *Sishui Da Gong Shang Bao*, in *Yindunixiya huaqiao wenti ziliao* [Materials on the issue of overseas Chinese in Indonesia], ed. Overseas Chinese Research Institute (Beijing: Xinhua shudian, 1951), 50.

13. Ibid.

14. Leo Suryadinata, *Eminent Indonesian Chinese: Biographical Sketches*, 4th ed. (Singapore: Institute of Southeast Asian Studies, 2015), 151–152. Liem was opposed to Japanese imperialism. He was detained when the Japanese occupied Java but was soon released. After Indonesia gained its independence, Liem was appointed as a member of the Indonesian Central National Committee (1946) and a member of the Indonesian Delegation to the Renville Conference (1947). As time passed, he became more interested in the Communist movement in China. He translated Gunther Stein's book *The Challenge of Red China* and published it in June 1949, predicting the victory of the Communists over the Chinese Nationalist Party. In 1950 he reestablished a multiracial political party, the Persatuan Tenaga Indonesia (New PTI), which advocated for Indonesian nationalism. A year later, in 1952, he died in Medan and was identified as a businessman who had held Chinese citizenship.

15. "Lin Qunxian weishenme tuoji" [Liem Koen Hian on why he repudiated Indonesian citizenship], *Xin Bao*, December 17, 1951, no. 0329, CSASXU.

16. Mackie and Coppel, "Preliminary Survey," 11–12.

17. "Yindunixiya huaren renkou, fenbu, guoji.".

18. "Problem of Chinese Residents in Indonesia," 1951, in "Yinni zajuan" [Miscellaneous dossier on Indonesia], no. 020-010899-0036, Academia Historica, Taipei. Originally in English. The statistics from Beijing and Taipei are further corroborated by Mozingo's estimation based on information from the Indonesian Department of Justice. See Mozingo, *Chinese Policy toward Indonesia*, 95, 105.

19. "Berkas mengenai perjanjian antara RI dengan RRC."

20. Overseas Chinese Research Association, *Yafei diqu huaqiao*, 53.

21. "Berkas mengenai perjanjian antara RI dengan RRC."

22. Overseas Chinese Research Association, *Yafei diqu huaqiao*, 53.

23. Mackie and Coppel, "Preliminary Survey," 10.

24. Suryadinata, *Pribumi Indonesian, the Chinese Minority, and China*, 170.

25. "Berkas mengenai perjanjian antara RI dengan RRC."

26. Ibid.

27. "Kasus Tjhia Ay Ay," no. 079/KKWN/IKI/VII/2009, Institut Kewarganegaraan Indonesia.

28. Eddy Setiawan (head of Institut Kewarganegaraan Indonesia), interview by author, Jakarta, March 20, 2013.

29. Zheng Junyi, *Guiqiao Peng Guanghan de wangshi jinshi*, 300, 302.

30. "Zuoqing gongshang renshi zhi mingyun" [The destiny of left-leaning businessmen and industralists], *Tian Sheng Ri Bao*, June 27, 1952.

31. Alumni Society of the Overseas Chinese School of Jimei and the Overseas Chinese University of Jimei, eds., *Mianhuai yu jingyang: jinian Jimei qiaoxiao Yang Xinrong laoxiaozhang danchen yibai zhounian* [Celebrating the one hundredth birthday of Yang Xinrong, the president of the Jimei Overseas Chinese Continuation School] (Xiamen, 2007), 8.

32. Yang Qiusheng, "Tuanjie Zhuawa aiguo minzhu renshi de dazhong maoyi youxian gongsi" [The Big China Trade Company that united the patriotic and democratic overseas Chinese in Java], in Qian Ren and Liang Junxiang, *Sheng Huo Bao de huiyi*, 61–65.

33. Ibid.

34. Wang Yifan, "Pushi wuhua de shengshuo, xuanliduocai de rensheng—ji Yinni zhiming qiaoling, jinrongjia, wenhuajiaoyu jie zhimingrenshi Wang Dajun xiansheng he ta de Wang shi jiazu" [Humble life, colorful life—renowned leader of the Chinese community in Indonesia, banker and renowned figure in culture and education, Wang Dajun and his family], in Qian Ren and Liang Junxiang, *Sheng Huo Bao de huiyi*, 309–313.

35. Weng Xihui, "Yinni aiguo qiaoling," 242.

36. Ibid.

37. "Interview with Mr. Kwee Kek Beng, Peranakan Businessman," Jakarta, November 10, 1950, box 2, ser. 2, Skinner Papers, Cornell University Library.

38. Ibid.

39. "Interview with Mr. Ang Jan Goan, editor of *Sin Po*," Jakarta, November 9, 1950, box 2, ser. 2, Skinner Papers, Cornell University Library.

40. Zheng Chuyun, "Lun huaqiao aiguo fandi tongyi zhanxian" [On the overseas Chinese patriotic, anti-imperialist united front], *Sheng Huo Bao*, January 1, 1951, in

Zheng Chuyun wenji [Collected works of Zheng Chuyun], ed. Zheng Binbin (Guang-zhou: Shijie tushu chuban Guangdong youxian gongsi, 2013), 56.

41. Ibid.

42. "Yindunixiya de jiben qingkuang he dongxiang," February 25, 1956, no. 102-00055-02, CFMA.

43. Leo Suryadinata, "Yinni huawen baokanshi yu guojia rentong" [A history of Chinese-language newspapers in Indonesia and national identification], in *Sheng Huo Bao jinian congshu shoufa yantaohui wenjian huibian* [Collection of papers presented at the conference on *Sheng Huo Bao*], ed. *Sheng Huo Bao* Collection Editorial Board (Xia-men: Shenghuowenhua jijinhui, October 2013), 21–29.

44. Leo Suryadinata, *Yinni huaren: wenhua yu shehui* [Chinese in Indone-sia: Culture and society] (Singapore: Singapore Society of Asian Studies, 1993), 126–127.

45. "Interview with Mr. Hsieh Shan-ts'ai, CNA correspondent," Jakarta, Novem-ber 7, 1950, box 2, ser. 2, Skinner Papers, Cornell University Library; Huang Kun-zhang, *Yinni huaqiao huaren shi*, 116.

46. "Huaqiao yingyou de renshi" [The recognition that the overseas Chinese should obtain], *Tian Sheng Ri Bao*, November 6, 1950, in *Tian Sheng Ri Bao shelun xuanji* [Collected editorials from *Tian Sheng Ri Bao*] (Jakarta: Harian Thien Sung Yit Po, 1951), 106–108.

47. Qiu Zheng'ou, *Huaqiao wenti lunji* [Collection of works on the overseas Chi-nese issue] (Taipei: Huagang, 1978), 172–173.

48. "Huaqiao yingyou de renshi."

49. "Huaqiao shi zhonggong qingsuan de duixiang" [The overseas Chinese are the target of the Chinese Communists' political cleansing], *Tian Sheng Ri Bao*, June 26, 1951, in *Tian Sheng Ri Bao shelun xuanji*, 134–136.

50. "Huaqiao yingyou de renshi."

51. "Lun suowei gongzuo weiyuanhui" [On the so-called working committee], *Tian Sheng Ri Bao*, September 16, 1950, in *Tian Sheng Ri Bao shelun xuanji*, 100–101.

52. "Kan Mayao yu Jiabidan de youling de huoyue" [The haunting ghosts of Majoor and Kapiten], *Tian Sheng Ri Bao*, September 16, 1950, in *Tian Sheng Ri Bao shelun xuanji*, 102–106.

53. Ibid.

54. Overseas Chinese Research Association, *Yafei diqu huaqiao*, 55.

55. "Kan Mayao."

56. Wang Jiyuan, "Dangqian huaqiao baoren de renwu" [The responsibilities of ethnic Chinese journalists at present], in *Wang Jiyuan wenxuan* [Collected works of Wang Jiyuan], ed. Wang Xiya (Guangzhou: Shijie tushu chuban Guangdong youxian gongsi, 2013), 88.

57. Zheng Chuyun, "Lun huaqiao aiguo fandi tongyi zhanxian."

58. Weng Xihui, "Yinni aiguo qiaoling," 232–234.

59. "Interview with Mr. Hsieh Shan-ts'ai, CNA correspondent," Jakarta, Novem-ber 7, 1950, box 2, ser. 2, Skinner Papers, Cornell University Library.

60. "Lun Yinni jianguo" [On the establishment of the Republic of Indonesia], *Sheng Huo Bao*, August 4, 1949.

61. Liang Yingming, "Yindunixiya *Sheng Huo Bao* de lishi gongji" [The historical significance of *Sheng Huo Bao* from Indonesia], in *Sheng Huo Bao* Collection Editorial Board, *Sheng Huo Bao jinian congshu*, 11.

62. See a series of editorials in *Sheng Huo Bao*: "Heping jianshe zhinian" [A year of peaceful construction], January 4, 1950; "Tufeimengjin de zuguo jingji jianshe" [The rapidly developing economic construction of the motherland], April 12, 1950; "Zouxiang xinsheng fanrong de zuguo jingji" [The economy of the motherland marching toward prosperity], June 21, 1950; "Wo quanguo shichang huoyue jingji fanrong" [The lively markets all over our country and the prosperous economy], August 7, 1952; "Zhongguo renmin yiding neng zhansheng ziran zaihai" [The Chinese people can combat natural disaster], August 11, 1954; "Woguo shehui zhuyi gaizao gongzuo de shengli" [The victory of socialist reform], January 17, 1956; and "Women de zuguo qiancheng sijin" [Our motherland has a bright future], July 5, 1957.

63. "Woguo jianshe shehuizhuyi zongluxian de weida shengli" [The great victory of the policy line of our socialist construction], *Sheng Huo Bao*, December 19, 1958.

64. "Woguo nongye shengchan dayuejin de daoli" [The reasons behind the Great Leap Forward in our country's agricultural production], *Sheng Huo Bao*, August 7, 1958.

65. See a series of editorials in *Sheng Huo Bao*: "You gangtie chanliang de tigao kan woguo de jinbu" [The progress of our country evidenced by the increase of steel production], September 3, 1958; "Xiangzhe quanmin xingfu zhitu maijin" [Marching toward the happiness of all our countrymen], August 20, 1958; "Huanxin guwu hua gongshe" [Cheerfully discussing the People's Commune], November 19, 1958; and "Canjia gongshe ji shi zouxiang xingfu de daolu" [Joining the People's Commune means taking the road to happiness], December 11, 1958.

66. Zheng Chuyun, "Lun huaqiao aiguo fandi tongyi zhanxian."

67. Qian Ren, "Bu zai kan Meidi dianying le" [I will never watch the movies made by the American imperialists], in *Qian Ren zaoqi shiwenxuan* [Collected works on the earlier poems and essays of Qian Ren], ed. Qian Ren (Guangzhou: Shijie tushu chuban Guangdong youxian gongsi, 2013), 35.

68. Lin Shangzhi and Lin Shangyi, interview by author, Fuzhou, Fujian Province, May 26, 2013; Zhang Meiping and Chen Yongji, interview by author, Shuangdi Overseas Chinese Farm, Shima County, Longhai City, Fujian Province, June 9, 2013.

69. Liang Yingming, "Yindunixiya *Sheng Huo Bao* de lishi gongji."

70. Weng Xihui, "Yinni aiguo qiaoling," 242.

71. Ibid.

72. *Warung* (translated as *yanong* in Chinese) is a type of small family-owned business in Indonesia; they were often casual shops, modest restaurants, or cafés.

73. Wang Jiyuan, "Lun Zhonghua zonghui" [On the Chinese General Association], in Wang Yixia, *Wang Jiyuan wenxuan*, 9–11.

74. Li Xuemin, "Ba qingchun fengxiangei zuguo he huaqiao zhengyi jinbu shiye—Zheng Manru xiansheng qingnian he zhuangnian shidai shiji shulue" [Mr. Zheng Manru devoted his youth to the motherland and the progressive and righteous affairs among the overseas Chinese], in Qian Ren and Liang Junxiang, *Sheng Huo Bao de huiyi*, 295–308.

75. Ibid.

76. Ding Jian and Xiaowen, *Qiandao zhi guo yue canghai: qiaoling He Longchao zhuan* [Watching the tides of history on the Indonesian archipelago: A biography of a leader of the overseas Chinese community, He Longchao] (Beijing: Zhongguo huaqiao chubanshe, 2004), 121–122.

77. Li Xuemin, "Ba qingchun fengxiangei zuguo."

78. Zheng Manru, "Longchuan Xin You She chengli qizhounian jinian gongyan teji" [Speech at the ceremony celebrating the seventh anniversary of the establishment of the Xin You Society of Semarang], in *Zheng Manru wenji* [Collected works of Zheng Manru], ed. Zheng Binbin (Guangzhou: Shijie tushu chuban Guangdong youxian gongsi, 2013), 64–65.

79. Huang Kunzhang, *Yinni huaqiao huaren shi*, 50–51.

80. "Zhu Yinni shiguan guanyu Yinni huaqiao gaikuang de baogao" [Report on the status of the overseas Chinese from our embassy in Indonesia], September 3, 1950, no. 118-00356-03, CFMA.

81. "Baobu aiguo qiaoling fenfen yaoqiu buchengren wei Zhonghua Zonghui" [Report to the Foreign Ministry: Patriotic leaders of the overseas Chinese communities asked our government not to recognize the illegitimate Chinese General Association], April 23, 1952, no. 118-00163-01, CFMA.

82. Ibid.

83. "Fu Yinni Zhong (Qingfa) yaoqiu wo buchengren wei Zhonghua Zonghui" [Reply to the proposal of Zhong (Qingfa) of Indonesia not to recognize the illegitimate Chinese General Association], May 16, 1952, no. 118-00163-01, CFMA.

84. Hong, *Hong Yuanyuan zizhuan*, 204.

85. "Lun suowei gongzuo weiyuanhui."

86. "Kan Mayao."

87. Huang Kunzhang, *Yinni huaqiao huaren shi*, 49.

88. Cai, *Chidaoxian shang de jiaoyin*, 115.

89. "Yinni Longchuan huaqiao xuexiao jiaoshi bajiao, fandui wangu xiaozhang wuli jiepin jiaoshi" [Teachers at the Chinese-language schools of Semarang on strike, opposing the principal's decision to dismiss teachers without proper reason], *Sheng Huo Bao*, October 15, 1950, no. 05239, CSASXU.

90. Li Xuemin, "Ba qingchun fengxiangei zuguo."

91. Ibid.

92. "Yinni Longchuan huaqiao xuexiao."

93. "Jugang aiguo qiaoxiao chi guoqi canjia youxing; jing zao Jiang feite lantu oushang shisheng duoren" [The patriotic Chinese school students in Palembang participated in the National Day parade holding the national flag; they were attacked by the Chiang bandits and several were injured], *Qiao Xun*, October 24, 1952, no. 05239, CSASXU.

94. Skinner, "Communism and Chinese Culture in Indonesia," 62.

95. "Dangpai tuichu xuexiao" [Chinese-language schools should be free from party politics], *Tian Sheng Ri Bao*, April 21, 1950, in *Tian Sheng Ri Bao shelun xuanji*, 97.

96. Ibid., 55.

97. Lin Shangzhi and Lin Shangyi, interview by author, Fuzhou, Fujian Province, May 26, 2013.

98. Skinner, "Communism and Chinese Culture in Indonesia," 4.

99. "Zhu Yinni shiguan guanyu Yinni huaqiao gaikuang de baogao."

100. Huang Kunzhang, *Yinni huaqiao huaren shi*, 76.

101. China News Agency, ed., *Yindunixiya huaqiao he Yindunixiya jiben qingkuang (neibu cankao ziliao)* [Basic information on Indonesia and the overseas Chinese residing in the country (for internal reference)] (Beijing: Zhongguo xinwenshe, 1959), 4.

102. Liang Yingming, interview by author, Beijing, July 21, 2013.

103. Huang Shuhai, interview by author, Beijing, July 17, 2009; Wen Liu, interview by author, Xiamen, October 23, 2013.

104. Liang Yingming, interview by author, Beijing, July 21, 2013.

105. "Zhu Yinni shiguan guanyu Yinni huaqiao gaikuang de baogao."

106. *Xin Bao*, August 4, 1950, cited in Twang Peck-yang, "Political Attitudes and Allegiances in the *Totok* Business Community, 1950–1954," *Indonesia* 28 (1979): 78.

107. "Interview with Mr. Ang Jan Goan, editor of *Sin Po*," Jakarta, November 9, 1950, box 2, ser. 2, Skinner Papers, Cornell University Library.

108. Liang Yingming, interview by author, Beijing, July 21, 2013.

109. Li Xuemin, "Ba qingchun fengxiangei zuguo."

110. Hong, *Hong Yuanyuan zizhuan*, 204–206.

5. *Pribumi* Perceptions of the "Chinese Problem"

1. "Surat dari Kejaksaan Agung kepada Presiden RI mengenai kegiatan politik dan kebudayaan orang Tionghoa sejak adanya Kedutaan Agung RRT di Indonesia," August 15, 1950, no. 1977, Inventaris Arsip Sekretariat Negara Kabinet Perdana Menteri Tahun 1950–1959, ANRI.

2. "Kabinet Presiden RI: surat-surat tanggal 26 Maret 1952 tentang kegiatan orang-orang Cina di Indonesia," March 26, 1952, no. 1806, Inventaris Arsip Kabinet Presiden RI 1950–1959, ANRI.

3. A. J. Muaja, *The Chinese Problem in Indonesia* (Djakarta: New Nusantara, 1958).

4. Suryadinata, *Pribumi Indonesian, the Chinese Minority, and China*, 191.

5. "Surat dari Mahkamah Agung kepada Perdana Menteri mengenai kedudukan sosial-ekonomi orang Tionghoa dalam RI pada saat ini," October 23, 1958, no. 2342, Inventaris Arsip Sekretariat Negara Kabinet Perdana Menteri Tahun 1950–1959, ANRI.

6. Ibid.

7. Mackie and Coppel, "Preliminary Survey," 7–8.

8. "Kejaksaan Agung kepada Perdana Menteri RI: surat tanggal 18 Pebruari 1953 tentang keributan dan serangan yang dilakukan oleh petani-petani Cina Tionghoa di Bindjei," February 18, 1953, no. 1860, Inventaris Arsip Kabinet Presiden RI 1950–1959, ANRI.

9. "Kejaksaan Agung kepada Perdana Menteri RI: surat tanggal 18 Pebruari 1953."

10. Ibid.

11. "Surat dari Kejaksaan Agung kepada Presiden RI."

12. "Kejaksaan Agung kepada Presiden RI: surat-surat tanggal 6 Januari, 1953 tentang China Demokratie League dan Perkumpulan Shaw Nien Erh T'ung Hui," January 6, 1953, no. 1852, Inventaris Arsip Kabinet Presiden RI 1950–1959, ANRI.

13. "Surat dari Kejaksaan Agung kepada Presiden RI."

14. Ibid.

15. "Surat dari Kejaksaan Agung kpd Menteri PP&K mengenai aksi politik yang tdk diinginkan di sekolah-sekolah Tionghoa di Singkawang 10 April–12 Mei 1952," April 10–May 12, 1952, no. 2057, Inventaris Arsip Sekretariat Negara Kabinet Perdana Menteri Tahun 1950–1959, ANRI.

16. Ibid.

17. "Menteri PP & K: Surat keputusan-Surat Keputusan tanggal 24 Maret 1952–28 Pebruari 1957 tentang larangan terhadap penggunaan terbitan-terbitan berbahasa Cina dan mengajar di sekolah-sekolah Cina," March 24 1952–February 28, 1957, no. 1805, Inventaris Arsip Kabinet Presiden RI 1950–1959, ANRI.

18. "Surat dari Kejaksaan Agung kepada Presiden RI."

19. "Kejaksaan Agung kepada Presiden RI: surat-surat tanggal 6 Januari, 1953."

20. Ibid.

21. Ibid.

22. Cai, *Chidaoxian shang de jiaoyin*, 115.

23. "Surat dari Kejaksaan Agung kepada Presiden RI."

24. "Yinni zuigao jianchaguan xialing kongsu Yechehng sanjia huawen baozhi" [Indonesian attorney general started prosecution against three Chinese newspapers in Jakarta], December 27, 1951, no. 118-00163-09, CFMA.

25. Ibid.

26. "Jaksa Agung pada Mahkamah Agung Indonesia: Kegiatan orang orang Tionghoa di Kalimantan Barat," January 29,1953, no. 1860, Inventaris Arsip Kabinet Presiden RI 1950–1959, ANRI.

27. Ibid.

28. J. A. C. Mackie, *Konfrontasi: The Indonesia-Malaysia Dispute, 1963–1966* (Kuala Lumpur: Oxford University Press, 1974), 347.

29. Ibid., 344.

30. Ibid.

31. See Mary Somers Heidhues, *Golddiggers, Farmers, and Traders in the "Chinese Districts" of West Kalimantan* (Ithaca, NY: Southeast Asia Program Publications, Cornell University, 2003).

32. Mackie and Coppel, "Preliminary Survey," 7.

33. "Jaksa Agung pada Mahkamah Agung Indonesia: Kegiatan orang orang Tionghoa."

34. Ibid.

35. Seng Guo Quan, "The Origins of the Socialist Revolution in Sarawak (1945–1963)," (master's thesis, National University of Singapore, 2008), 20.

36. Mackie, *Konfrontasi*, 64.

37. Fujio Hara, "The North Kalimantan Communist Party and the People's Republic of China," *Developing Economies* 43, no. 4 (2005): 490.

38. Mackie, *Konfrontasi*, 61, 347.

39. "Jaksa Agung pada Mahkamah Agung Indonesia: Kegiatan orang orang Tionghoa."

40. Seng, "Origins of the Socialist Revolution in Sarawak," 40–45.

41. "Laporan dari Jawatan Kepolisian mengenai imigran etnis Tionghoa yang masuk ke Indonesia secara ilegal," January 10, 1952, no. 2404, Inventaris Arsip Sekretariat Negara Kabinet Perdana Menteri Tahun 1950–1959, ANRI.

42. "Jaksa Agung pada Mahkamah Agung Indonesia: Kegiatan orang orang Tionghoa."

43. Ibid.

44. Ibid.

45. Seng, "Origins of the Socialist Revolution in Sarawak," 47–48.

46. "Jaksa Agung pada Mahkamah Agung Indonesia: Kegiatan orang orang Tionghoa."

47. Ibid.

48. "Laporan dari Jawatan Kepolisian mengenai imigran etnis Tionghoa."

49. Ibid.

50. "Kejaksaan Agung kepada Perdana Menteri RI: surat tanggal 18 Pebruari 1953."

51. "Kejaksaan Agung kepada Presiden RI: surat-surat tanggal 6 Januari, 1953."

52. "Surat dari Kejaksaan Agung kepada Presiden RI."

53. "Kejaksaan Agung kepada Presiden RI: surat-surat tanggal 6 Januari, 1953."

54. Ibid.

55. Ibid.

56. "Kejaksaan Agung kepada Perdana Menteri RI: surat tanggal 18 Pebruari 1953."

57. Ibid.

58. "Laporan S.I.: Laporan tentang organisasi Tionghoa 'Shin Sheng Shih,'" December 1, 1953, no. 511, Arsip Marzuki, SE 1945–1984, ANRI.

59. "Surat dari Jaksa Agung kepada Perdana Menteri mengenai pelarangan utusan dari Indonesia ke Konferensi Panitia Perdamaian Dunia karena dianggap pro komunis," November 9, 1951, no. 2028, Inventaris Arsip Sekretariat Negara Kabinet Perdana Menteri Tahun 1950–1959, ANRI.

60. For a biographical account of Sneevliet, see Michael Williams, "Sneevliet and the Birth of Asian Communism," *New Left Review* 123 (1980): 82–90. See also Tony Saich, *Origins of the First United Front in China: The Role of Sneevliet (alias Maring)* (Boston, MA: Brill, 1991).

61. Alimin bin Prawirodirdjo, "My biography," folder 84, "Indonesian Exiles of the Left" Collection, Institute of International Social History (ISSH), Amsterdam.

62. Liang Yingming, interview by author, Beijing, July 21, 2013.

63. Ibid.

64. China Democratic League Central Literary and History Committee, ed., *Zhongguo minzhu tongmeng lishi wenxian, 1949–1988* [Historical sources on the China Democratic League, 1949–1988] (Beijing: Wenwu chubanshe, 1991), 99.

65. Ibid., 94.

66. "Kejaksaan Agung kepada Perdana Menteri RI: surat tanggal 18 Pebruari 1953."

67. Ibid.

68. "Mianlan tejing qiangsha hua Yin nongmin de shiqing" [The truth about how the special police force in Medan shot the Chinese and Indonesian peasants with guns], *Xing Zhou Ri Bao*, April 29, 1953, no. 04105, CSASXU.

69. "Kejaksaan Agung kepada Perdana Menteri RI: surat tanggal 18 Pebruari 1953."

70. Ibid.

71. "Usul pengeluaran dari Indonesia agitator agitator dan redaktur redaktur harian buruh Tionghoa 'Kung Sheng' di Biliton," May 5, 1953, no. 1866, Inventaris Arsip Kabinet Presiden RI 1950–1959, ANRI.

72. Lai Yumei, "Yi xianfu Zou Fangjin" [Remembering my late husband Zou Fangjin], in *Zou Fangjin Wenji* [Collected works of Zou Fangjin], ed. Zou Jianyun (Guangzhou: Shijie tushu chuban Guangdong youxian gongsi, 2013), 2; Zou Fangjin, "Guanyu yuanhou susong" [About the monkey litigation], *Sheng Huo Bao*, July 25, 1952, in Zou Jianyun, *Zou Fangjin Wenji*, 27.

73. Ibid.

74. "Usul pengeluaran daň Indonesia agitator."

75. "He Xiangning guoqingjie guangbo: Zuguo chengjiu weida weixin yi tigao, qiaobao ying wei aiguo datuanjie fendou" [He Xiangning's radio speech on the national day. The motherland has made great achievements and its reputation has increased. The overseas Chinese should be united for the love of the nation], *Sheng Huo Bao*, October 3, 1951.

76. John O. Sutter, *Indonesianisasi: Politics in a Changing Economy, 1940–1955* (Ithaca, NY: Cornell University Southeast Asia Program Data Paper, 1959), 3:1017.

77. Suryadinata, *Pribumi Indonesian, the Chinese Minority, and China*, 130–133.

78. Overseas Chinese Research Association, *Yafei diqu huaqiao*, 55.

79. Suryadinata, *Pribumi Indonesian, the Chinese Minority, and China*, 133.

80. Ibid.

81. Ibid.

82. V. Hanssens, "The Campaign against Nationalist Chinese in Indonesia," in *Indonesia's Struggle, 1957–1958*, ed. B. H. M. Vlekke (The Hague: Netherland's Institute of International Affairs, 1959), 69–70.

83. Assaat Datuk Mudo, "The Chinese Grip on Our Economy," in *Indonesian Political Thinking*, ed. Herbert Feith and Lance Castles (Jakarta: Equinox, 2007), 346.

84. "Surat dari Mahkamah Agung kepada Perdana Menteri."

85. "Guanyu Yinni zousi maoyi wenti" [On smuggling and trade with Indonesia], August 30, 1958, no. 129-1-11, Bao'an District Archives, Shenzhen, Guangdong Province, PRC.

86. Ibid.

87. Heidhues, "Anti-Chinese Violence," 385.

88. "Surat dari Kejaksaan Agung kepada Presiden RI."

89. Ibid.

90. "Surat dari Jaksa Agung Muda kepada Perdana Menteri mengenai sidang dari *Chinese Communist Political Bureau* di Peking," September 17, 1959, no. 2372, Inventaris Arsip Sekretariat Negara Kabinet Perdana Menteri Tahun 1950–1959, ANRI.

91. Ibid.

92. Ibid.

93. "Surat dari Mahkamah Agung kepada Perdana Menteri."

94. "Surat kaleng tanggal 21 Desember 1951 tentang minta penjelasan mengenai status Republik Indonesia, dengan lampiran. N.B.: Bahasa Tiongkok dan terjemahan," December 21, 1951, no. 1289, Kabinet Presiden RI, ANRI.

95. Mozingo, *Chinese Policy toward Indonesia*, 159.

96. Zhou Nanjing and Kong Zhiyuan, eds., *Sujianuo zhongguo Yindunixiya huaren* [Sukarno, China, and the Chinese minority in Indonesia] (Hong Kong: Xianggang shehui kexue chubanshe, 2003), 58.

6. The 1959–1960 Anti-Chinese Crisis

1. "Yinni jinzhi waiqiao xiaoshangfan yingye" [Indonesia banned business by petty traders of foreign nationalities], *Cankao Xiaoxi*, August 12, 1959.

2. "Fan paihua douzheng qingkuang fanying" [Progress of the struggle against the anti-Chinese actions], in file "Benwei guanyu jiedai anzhi Yinni guiqiao gongzuo jianbao" [The Overseas Chinese Committee of Fujian Province: Draft of the report on the resettlement of the returnees from Indonesia], January 26, 1960, no. 0148-002-1105-0001, Fujian Provincial Archives (FJPA).

3. "Geng Biao fubuzhang jiejian Yindunixiya linshi daiban Suleiman tan Gang-guo jushi he Laowo wenti" [Conversations between Deputy Foreign Minister Geng Biao and Indonesian chargé d'affaires ad interim on the situations in Congo and Laos], November 29, 1960, no. 105-00703-01, CFMA.

4. "Mijian: Lianggeyue lai guanche 'duo che shao liu' fangzhen qingkuang jian-bao" [Secret document: A brief report on the implementation of the "less repatriated more stay" guideline in the past two months], October 18, 1960, no. 105-00708-02, CFMA.

5. "Chen Yi fuzongli jiejian zhuhua dashi Sujiazuo Weiyuepulanuotuo tanhua jilu" [Minutes of the meetings between Vice Premier Chen Yi and the Indonesian ambassador Soekardjo Wiriopranoto], December 9, 1959, no. 105-00389-03, CFMA.

6. Suryadinata, *Pribumi Indonesian, the Chinese Minority, and China*, 136.

7. My argument confirms the conclusions of earlier studies; see, for example, Suryadinata, *Pribumi Indonesian, the Chinese Minority, and China*; Coppel, *Indonesian Chinese in Crisis*; and Mozingo, *Chinese Policy toward Indonesia*.

8. "Chen Yi fuzongli jian waizhang jiejian Yinni xinren zhuhua dashi Sukani Katuodiweiyue tanhua jilu" [Minutes of the meeting between Vice Premier and Foreign Minister Chen Yi and the new Indonesian ambassador Sukarni Kartodiwirjo], September 27, 1960, no. 105-00416-04 (1), CFMA.

9. Ibid.

10. Wu Lengxi, *Shinian lunzhan* [A decade of debate] (Beijing: Zhongyang wenxian chubanshe, 1999), 1:234.

11. Mao Zedong, "Talk with the American Correspondent Anna Louise Strong," in *Selected Readings from the Works of Mao Tse-tung* (Beijing: Foreign Languages Press, 1971), 348.

12. "Guanyu Zhongguo he Yindunixiya zhijian de huaqiao wenti" [On the problem of overseas Chinese between China and Indonesia], August 1, 1960, no. 105-00978-03, CFMA.

13. "Chen Yi fuzongli tong Yinni fuzongli Subandeliyue huitan jilu" [Conversation between Vice Premier Chen Yi and Indonesian deputy prime minister Suban-drio], January 24, 1965, no. 105-01910-05, CFMA.

14. "Chen Yi fuzongli jian waizhang jiejian Yinni xinren zhuhua dashi."

15. "Liu Shaoqi zhuxi, Chen Yi fuzongli he Zhang Hanfu fuwaizhang fenbie jiejian Yindunixiya dashi (jiang liren) Sujiazuo jiu huaqiao wenti he Zhongyin guanxi de tanhua jilu" [Minutes of separate meetings of Chairman Liu Shaoqi, Vice Premier Chen Yi, and Deputy Foreign Minister Zhang Hanfu with the Indonesian ambassador Soekardjo Wiriopranoto (departing) on the overseas Chinese issue and Sino-Indonesian relations], January 25–February 20, 1960, no. 105-00416-02, CFMA.

Soekardjo's term was cut short due to the frictions between the two countries over the anti-Chinese crisis.

16. "Liu Zhuxi zai Yinni zhuhua dashi Sukani chengjiao guoshu hou jiejian Sukani de tanhua jilu" [Minutes of the meeting between Chairman Liu and the Indonesian ambassador to China, Sukarni, after the presentation of credentials], September 23, 1960, no. 105-00416-04 (1), CFMA.

17. "Liu Shaoqi zhuxi, Chen Yi fuzongli he Zhang Hanfu fuwaizhang."

18. "Chen Yi fuzongli jiejian zhuhua dashi Sujiazuo."

19. "Buchong tongbao Chen Yi fuzongli yu Yindunixiya waijiao buzhang de huitan qingkuang" [Additional notice on the meeting between Vice Premier Chen Yi and the Indonesian foreign minister], October 24, 1959, no. 105-00387-06, CFMA.

20. "Liu Shaoqi zhuxi, Chen Yi fuzongli he Zhang Hanfu fuwaizhang."

21. "Zhongguo yu Yindunixiya zai huaqiao wenti shang de maodun ji wo duice" [Conflicts between China and Indonesia on the overseas Chinese and our countermeasures], June 6–August 10, 1959, no. 105-00610-02, CFMA.

22. Mozingo, *Chinese Policy toward Indonesia*, 154.

23. Studies on Indonesian politics during this period include Daniel S. Lev, *The Transition to Guided Democracy, 1957–1959* (Jakarta: Equinox, 2009); J. D. Legge, *Sukarno: A Political Biography* (New York: Praeger, 1972); and Herbert Feith, "Dynamics of Guided Democracy," in McVey, *Indonesia*, 309–355.

24. "Gefang dui Chen Yi waizhang 12 yue 9 ri Subandeliyue de xin de fanying" [Responses from various political blocs in Indonesia to Foreign Minister Chen Yi's reply to Subandrio's letter on December 9], December 11, 1959, no. 105-00914-01, CFMA.

25. "Zhongguo yu Yindunixiya zai huaqiao wenti."

26. "Yindunixiya gongchandang dongtai di yi qi" [Activities of the Communist Party of Indonesia, issue 1], January 1960, no. 105-00980-01, CFMA.

27. Suryadinata, *Pribumi Indonesian, the Chinese Minority, and China*, 37–38.

28. "Yindunixiya gongchandang dongtai di san qi" [Activities of the Communist Party of Indonesia, issue 3], April 1960, no. 105-00980-03, CFMA.

29. See, for example, "Yi Yindunixiya Zhongguo youhao de jingshen he xingdong lai jiejue huaqiao wenti Yindunixiya gongchandang zhongyang zhengzhiju ershier ri de sheng ming" [The PKI's declaration on November 22 called for a resolution of the overseas Chinese issue based on the spirit of friendship], *Renmin Ribao*, November 25, 1959; "Yindunixiya gongchandang dier fuzhuxi Yueduo zuo baogao Meiguo jieli shanqi fanhua yundong yanshi qinlue zhengce wangtu fenlie yafei tuanjie pohuai yafei minzu duli" [The second deputy secretary general of the PKI, Njoto, gave a talk on how the US fueled anti-Chinese sentiments to cover its aggressive policies of eroding Afro-Asian unity and independence], *Renmin Ribao*, November 26, 1959; "Yindunixiya gongchandang zhuxi Aidi tan huaqiao wenti burong pohuai Yindunixiya Zhongguo youyi" [The secretary general of the PKI, Aidit, talked about the overseas Chinese issue and announced that his party would not allow any damage to the Indonesia-China friendship], *Renmin Ribao*, November 27, 1959; and "Yindunixiya gongchandang fuzhuxi Lukeman fabiao shengming qianze youpai baokan yong paihuai wenti shandong fangong" [The deputy secretary general of the PKI, Lukman,

condemned the right-wing newspapers' attack on Communism by using the ethnic Chinese issue], *Renmin Ribao*, December 3, 1959.

30. "Yindunixiya gongchandang dongtai di san qi."

31. "Guanyu Zhongguo he Yindunixiya zhijian de huaqiao wenti."

32. *Harian Rakjat*, November 25, 1959, quoted in Suryadinata, *Pribumi Indonesian, the Chinese Minority, and China*, 37.

33. "Chen Yi fuzongli jiejian zhuhua dashi Sujiazuo."

34. Ibid.

35. "Guanyu Zhongguo he Yindunixiya zhijian de huaqiao wenti."

36. Ibid.

37. Ibid.

38. "Liu Shaoqi zhuxi, Chen Yi fuzongli he Zhang Hanfu fuwaizhang."

39. Ibid.

40. "Chen Yi fuzongli jian waizhang jiejian Yinni xinren zhuhua dashi."

41. "Chen Yi fuzongli jiejian Yindunixiya Antala tongxunshe jizhe Suweiduo" [Meeting between Vice Premier Chen Yi and Suwito, journalist from Antara News Agency of Indonesia], December 28, 1960, no. 105-00416-06, CFMA.

42. Ibid.

43. "Chen Yi fuzongli jian waizhang jiejian Yinni xinren zhuhua dashi."

44. "Guanyu Zhongguo he Yindunixiya zhijian de huaqiao wenti."

45. Ibid.

46. "Yinni jinzhi waiqiao xiaoshangfan yingye."

47. "Zhao Zhenkui lingshi fu Wulidong Bangjia zhidao qiaotuan banli cheqiao qingkuang baogao" [Report by Consul Zhao Zhenkui on his trip to Bangka-Belitung for assistance with repatriation], August 15, 1960, no. 118-832-01, CFMA.

48. "Guanyu Huang Zhen dashi jiu qianfan huaqiao, shuangchong guoji, Jiang Yan, Liu Qingyou liang lingshi shi yu Yindunixiya waizhang Subandeliyue de jiaoshe qingkuang" [Ambassador Huang Zhen's negotiations with the Indonesian foreign minister Subandrio on issues regarding repatriation of the overseas Chinese, dual nationality, and Consuls Jiang Yan and Liu Qingyou], November 12–December 20, 1960, no. 105-00418-04, CFMA.

49. "Fan paihua douzheng qingkuang fanying."

50. "Bao Zhang Yu tongzhi qu Gubang jieqiao gongzuo qingkuang" [Report on Comrade Zhang Yu's work in repatriation of overseas Chinese in Kupang], November 15, 1960, no. 118-832-01, CFMA.

51. "Xianggang Da Gong Bao jielu Yinni dangju zai xi Zhuawa dangju wuli biqian huaqiao exing" [*Da Gong Bao* of Hong Kong exposed the atrocities committed by the Indonesian authorities of their forceful relocation program targeting the ethnic Chinese in West Java], November 25, 1959, in China News Agency, *Yindunixiya huaqiao he Yindunixiya jiben qingkuang*, 2–4.

52. "Xizhuawa junshi dangju hengbao xialing daibu huaqiao" [The military authority in West Java arbitrarily ordered the arrest of overseas Chinese], December 4, 1959, in China News Agency, *Yindunixiya huaqiao he Yindunixiya jiben qingkuang*, 8.

53. "Chen Yi fuzongli jiejian zhuhua dashi Sujiazuo."

54. Ibid.

55. Ibid.
56. Ibid.
57. "Zhaigao Zhou Enlai zongli jiejian Yinni zhuhua dashi Sukani tanhua jilu" [Reports on Premier Zhou Enlai's meeting with the Indonesian ambassador to China, Sukarni], December 25, 1961, no. 105-01768-01, CFMA; and "Liu Shaoqi zhuxi, Chen Yi fuzongli he Zhang Hanfu fuwaizhang."
58. "Chen Yi fuzongli jiejian Yindunixiya Antala."
59. "Zhongguo yu Yindunixiya zai huaqiao wenti."
60. Ibid.
61. "Sanbaolong junfang jing mingling jinzhi huaqiao tong wo shiguan renyuan jiechu" [The military authorities in Semarang forbade local people from contacting our embassy staff], November 7, 1959, in China News Agency, *Yindunixiya huaqiao he Yindunixiya jiben qingkuang*, 7.
62. "Xiang geshilingguan tongbao Chen Yi fuzongli jiu Yinni waizhang de fuxin zhong suo sheji de huaqiao wenti jiejian Yinni dashi de tanhua zhaiyao" [A summary of Vice Premier Chen Yi's meeting with the Indonesian ambassador on the Indonesian foreign minister's letter in response to the overseas Chinese issue], December 21, 1959, no. 105-00390-03, CFMA.
63. "1959 nian Zhongguo yu Yindunixiya guanxi dashiji" [A record of major events in the relations between China and Indonesia in 1959], January 1–December 31, 1959, no. 105-01714-01, CFMA.
64. "Chen Yi fuzongli jiejian zhuhua dashi Sujiazuo."
65. "Yindunixiya difang junshi dangju paihua shouduan riyi yeman; Xi Zhuawa huaqiao shengming caichan shoudao yanzhong weixie" [Local military authorities in Indonesia use increasingly cruel measures against the Chinese; the lives and property of the overseas Chinese in West Java are severely threatened], *Renmin Ribao*, July 4, 1960; "Zai Yindunixiya youshili jituan de cedong he zhichi xia Xi Zhuawa junshi dangju zhizao tusha huaqiao can'an" [The military authorities in West Java slaughtered overseas Chinese in Cimahi with the support and instigation of powerful political cliques], *Renmin Ribao*, July 5, 1960.
66. "Yindunixiya zhengfu jiu Zhimaxu can'an fu wo kangyi zhaohui" [Indonesian foreign ministry's diplomatic note in reply to our protests against the tragedy in Cimahi], July 25, 1960, no. 105-00432-02, CFMA.
67. Ibid.
68. "Yindunixiya Mianlan qiaobao peihe Zhimaxu can'an huodong qingkuang ji Yinni junren pohai huaqiao qingkuang he wo dui ci wenti de jiancha zongjie" [The Medan Chinese's response to the tragedy in Cimahi, the Indonesian military's oppression of the ethnic Chinese, and our reflections on this issue], July 14–August 8, 1960, no. 105-00695-02, CFMA.
69. "Chen Yi fuzongli jiejian zhuhua dashi Sujiazuo."
70. Ibid.
71. "Liu Shaoqi zhuxi, Chen Yi fuzongli he Zhang Hanfu fuwaizhang."
72. "Zhu Yinni shilingguan guanyu zuzhi cheqiao de qingkuang baogao" [Our embassy in Indonesia's report on the repatriation of overseas Chinese], August 23–October 18, 1960, no. 118-832-01, CFMA.
73. Ibid.

74. "Chen Yi fuzongli jiejian zhuhua dashi Sujiazuo."

75. "Guanyu Huang Zhen dashi jiu qianfan huaqiao."

76. "Mijian."

77. Ibid.

78. Ibid.

79. Zhang Xiaoxin, "Jiusanling shijian hou Zhongguo dui Yinni guinanqiao jiuji anzhi gongzuo lunxi" [China's resettlement and relief work for refugee returnees after the September Thirtieth Movement in Indonesia], *Huaren huaqiao lishi yanjiu* [Overseas Chinese history studies], no. 2 (June 2011): 55.

80. "Guanghua lun zhengzhi sixiang gongzuo sishitiao" [Forty principles for ideological and political work on the ship *Guanghua*], January 11, 1964, no. 291-1-112-146-153, Guangdong Provincial Archives (GDPA).

81. "Huang Zhen dashi yu Yindunixiya waizhang Subandeliyue guanyu jiejue huaqiao wenti huitan qingkuang" [Ambassador Huang Zhen's meeting with the Indonesian foreign minister Subandrio on the resolution of the overseas Chinese issue], July 13–18, 1960, no. 105-00418-03, CFMA.

82. "Zhongguo yu Yindunixiya zai huaqiao wenti."

83. "Huang Zhen dashi yu Yindunixiya waizhang."

84. "Yindunixiya Mianlan qiaobao."

85. "Chen Yi fuzongli jiejian Yindunixiya Antala."

86. "Sujianuo zongtong tan huaqiao wenti Yindunixiya he Zhongguo zhijian youxie xiao kunnan yikao liangguo de shanyi zhexie kunnan nenggou jiejue" [President Sukarno remarks on the overseas Chinese issue: small difficulties between Indonesia and China can be overcome with goodwill], *Renmin Ribao*, August 24, 1960.

87. "Liu Shaoqi zhuxi, Chen Yi fuzongli he Zhang Hanfu fuwaizhang."

88. "Chen Yi fuzongli jiejian Yindunixiya Antala."

89. "Yindunixiya zhengfu jiu Zhimaxu can'an fu wo kangyi zhaohui"; "Guanyu Huang Zhen dashi jiu qianfan huaqiao."

90. *Like an Angel That Strikes from the Skies: The March of Our Revolution* (Djakarta: Ministry of Information, 1960), 30, quoted in Mozingo, *Chinese Policy toward Indonesia*, 179.

91. "Yindunixiya xinren dashi Sukani fanguo shuzhiqian yu Chen Yi fuzongli jiu shuangchong guoji wenti shishi banfa, qianzi he daikuan wenti ji Chen Yi fuzongli huifang deng de tanhua jilu" [Minutes of the meeting between the new Indonesian ambassador Sukarni and Vice Premier Chen Yi before Sukarni returns to Indonesia to report on his work, on the issues of the implementation of the Dual Nationality Treaty, China's loan to Indonesia, and Vice Premier Chen Yi's visit to Indonesia], November 8–10, 1960, no. 105-00416-05, CFMA; see also "Geng Biao fubuzhang jiejian Yindunixiya linshi daiban."

92. "Zhou Zongli jiejian Yinni xinren zhuhua dashi Sukani tanhua jilu" [Minutes of the meeting between Premier Zhou Enlai and the new Indonesian ambassador Sukarni], September 27, 1960, no. 105-00416-04 (1), CFMA.

93. "Mao Zedong zhuxi jiejian Yinni zongtong Sujianuo tanhua jilu" [Conversation between Chairman Mao and Indonesian president Sukarno], June 13, 1961, no. 204-01469-02, CFMA.

94. "Huang Zhen dashi yu Yindunixiya waizhang."

7. The Ambivalent Alliance between Beijing and Jakarta

1. "Guanyu Guanghua lun jiesong canjia xinsheng liliang yundonghui yundongyuan renwu de baowei cuoshi de baogao" [Report on the ship *Guanghua*'s security measures for its mission to transport the athletes participating in GANEFO], October 14, 1963, no. 291-1-43-115-118, GDPA.

2. "Zhou Enali zongli zhihan Yinni zongtong Sujianuo zhichi Yinni tuichu guoji Aolinpike weiyuanhui" [Premier Zhou Enlai's letter to President Sukarno in support of Indonesia's decision to quit the International Olympic Committee], February 20, 1963, no. 105-01833-01, CFMA. For the ideological origin of GANEFO, see Stefan Huebner, *Pan-Asian Sports and the Emergence of Modern Asia, 1913–1974* (Singapore: National University of Singapore Press, 2016), 186–187.

3. Ibid.

4. Amanda Shuman, "Elite Competitive Sport in the People's Republic of China, 1958–1966: The Games of New Emerging Forces (GANEFO)," *Journal of Sport History* 40, no. 2 (2013): 260.

5. Theodore Friend, *Indonesian Destinies* (Cambridge, MA: Belknap Press of Harvard University Press, 2003), 89.

6. "Zhou Enlai zongli jiejian Yinni zongtong junshi guwen Suliyadama jiqi furen de tanhua jilu" [Minutes of meeting between Premier Zhou Enlai and the military advisor of the Indonesian president], October 2, 1964, no. 105-01240-03, CFMA.

7. J. A. C. Mackie, "Anti-Chinese Outbreaks in Indonesia, 1959–1968," in Mackie, *Chinese in Indonesia*, 97–98.

8. "Tuidong huaqiao biaotai zhichi Yinni tuichu lianheguo deng shi" [On promoting the overseas Chinese's support for Indonesia's exit from the United Nations, etc.], January 21–22, 1965, no. 105-01913-03, CFMA.

9. Greg Poulgrain, *The Genesis of Konfrontasi: Malaysia, Brunei, Indonesia, 1945–1965* (London: C. Hurst, 1998), 185.

10. "Geng Biao fuwaizhang jiejian Yinni zhuhua dashi Sukani tanhua jilu" [Minutes of meetings between Deputy Foreign Minister Geng Biao and the Indonesian ambassador to China, Sukarni], January 24–February 20, 1963, no. 105-01160-01, CFMA.

11. "Yingguo yu Yindu, Malaixiya guanxi wenti" [British relations with India and Malaysia], January 31, 1964, no. 110-01696-03, CFMA.

12. Niu Jun, "1962: The Eve of the Left Turn in China's Foreign Policy," *Cold War International History Project Working Paper* no. 48 (Washington, DC: Woodrow Wilson Center, 2005), 29–36, https://www.wilsoncenter.org/sites/default/files/NiuJunWP481.pdf.

13. "Mao Zhuxi jiejian Yinni hezuo guohui yizhang Aluqi tanhua jilu" [Minutes of the meeting between Chairman Mao and the chairman of the Indonesian People's Consultative Assembly], June 9, 1964, no. 105-01336-02, CFMA.

14. "Big Unity Plan," *Straits Times*, May 28, 1961.

15. For background see, for example, Matthew Jones, *Conflict and Confrontation in South East Asia, 1961–1965: Britain, the United States, Indonesia and the Creation of Malaysia* (Cambridge: Cambridge University Press, 2001); Mackie, *Konfrontasi*.

16. "Sujianuo biaoshi fandui 'Malaixiya' zhichu 'Malaixiya' shi dui Yindunixiya geming de duikang" [Sukarno announces confrontation against "Malaysia," which

opposes and threatens Indonesia's revolution], *Renmin Ribao*, July 13, 1963; "Liu Shaoqi zhuxi tong Yinni zongtong Sujianuo de huitan jilu" [Minutes of the meeting between Chairman Liu Shaoqi and the Indonesian president Sukarno], April 18, 1963, no. 105-01167-02, CFMA.

17. "Geng Biao fuwaizhang jiejian Yinni zhuhua dashi Sukani tanhua jilu."

18. Joseph Chinyong Liow, "Tunku Abdul Rahman and Malaya's Relations with Indonesia, 1957–60," *Journal of Southeast Asian Studies* 36, no. 1 (2005): 96–98.

19. "Liu Shaoqi zhuxi tong Yinni zongtong Sujianuo de huitan jilu."

20. Liow, "Tunku Abdul Rahman and Malaya's Relations with Indonesia," 96–98.

21. "Yinni youpai qitu zuzhi 'Sumendalaguo' ji Yinni zhengfu pohuo liangqi junshi panluan shijian" [Right-wing groups in Indonesia attempted to organize a "State of Sumatra"; two cases of military rebellions suppressed by the Indonesian government], July 16, 1964, no. 105-01233-01, CFMA.

22. Ibid.

23. "Xinjiapo zongli Li Guang Yao zai Xianggang yu wo jiechu tan 'Malaixiya jihua,' Xinjiapo he Malaixiya hebing, Xinjiapo daibiaotuan fangwen Zhongguo deng wenti" [Lee Kuan Yew, the Singaporean prime minister, contacted us in Hong Kong for discussions on "the plan for the formation of Malaysia," Singapore's merger with Malaya, and Singaporean delegations visiting China], May 23, 1962, no. 105-01795-01, CFMA.

24. Ibid.

25. Ibid.

26. Ibid.

27. "Liu Shaoqi zhuxi tong Yinni zongtong Sujianuo de huitan jilu."

28. "Deng Xiaoping daizongli jiejian Yinni zhuhua dashi Sukani tanhua jilu" [Minutes of Acting Premier Deng Xiaoping's meeting with the Indonesian ambassador Sukarni], March 12, 1964, no. 105-01869-07, CFMA.

29. "Guanyu Taiwan dangju zai Malaixiya she lingshiguan wenti" [On the issue of Taiwan authority's establishment of consulate in Malaysia], December 1–2, 1964, no. 105-01243-02, CFMA.

30. "Premier Chou En-lai's Speech at the banquet in honor of the Indonesian mission," January 24, 1965, no. 201-01062-03, CFMA. Originally in English.

31. "Mao Zhuxi jiejian Yinni hezuo guohui."

32. "Premier Chou En-lai's Speech."

33. "Guanyu Yinni zhengfu yao wo zhichi qi fan Malaixiya shi" [On the Indonesian government's request to us to support their konfrontasi against Malaysia], March 23, 1964, no. 105-01871-03, CFMA.

34. "Wei Yindunixiya diyi fuzongli jian waizhang Subandeliyue fanghua bianxie de cankaoziliao" [Reference materials prepared for the forthcoming visit of the Indonesian first deputy prime minister and foreign minister Subandrio], January 20, 1965, no. 204-01344-02, CFMA.

35. "Zhou zongli, Chen Yi fuzongli jiejian Yinni zhuhua dashi Sukani tanhua jilu" [Minutes of the meeting between Premier Zhou Enlai, Vice Premier Chen Yi, and the Indonesian ambassador to China Sukarni], March 19, 1964, no. 105-01869-06, CFMA.

36. "Zhou Enlai zongli he Chen Yi fuzongli tong Yinni fuzongli Subandeliyue dierci huitan jilu" [The second meeting between Premier Zhou Enlai, Vice Premier

Chen Yi, and the Indonesian first deputy prime minister Subandrio], January 25, 1965, no. 105-01910-02, CFMA.

37. "Guanyu Yinni zhengfu yao wo zhichi."

38. Ibid.

39. "Chen Yi fuzongli tong Yinni fuzongli Subandeliyue huitan jilu" [Minutes of the meeting between Vice Premier Chen Yi and the Indonesian first deputy prime minister Subandrio], January 24, 1965, no. 105-01910-05, CFMA.

40. "Zhou Enlai zongli he Chen Yi fuzongli tong Yinni fuzongli Subandeliyue dierci huitan jilu"; "Chen Yi fuzongli tong Yinni fuzongli Subandeliyue huitan jilu."

41. "Chen Yi fuzongli tong Yinni fuzongli Subandeliyue huitan jilu."

42. "Guanyu Yinni zhengfu yao wo zhichi."

43. "He Long fuzongli tong Yinni waizhang Subandeliyue huitan qingkuang" [Vice Premier He Long's meeting with the Indonesian foreign minister Subandrio], November 11–23, 1963, no. 105-01835-01, CFMA.

44. "Guanyu xiang Yinni tigong wu qian wan mei yuan daikuan shi" [On the issue of providing 50 million USD loan to Indonesia], December 8–9, 1964, no. 105-01872-01, CFMA.

45. "Jiedai Yinni fu shouxi buzhang Subandeliyue fanghua jianbao" [Briefing on the Indonesian first deputy prime minister Subandrio's visit to China], January 2–7, 1963, no. 204-01504-01, CFMA.

46. "Luo Ruiqing zongcanmouzhang, Peng Zheng fuweiyuanzhang jiejian Yinni zhiyuan renyuan daibiaotuan tanhua jilu" [Minutes of the meetings between the chief of the PLA General Staff Luo Ruiqing, the vice chairman of the National People's Congress Peng Zhen, and the delegation of Indonesian volunteers], June 29,1965, no. 105-01689-02, CFMA.

47. Ibid.

48. Mackie, *Konfrontasi*, 138.

49. Mackie, "Anti-Chinese Outbreaks in Indonesia," 107.

50. "Tuidong huaqiao biaotai zhichi."

51. Ibid.

52. "Guanyu Yinni zhengfu yao wo zhichi."

53. Ibid.

54. "Xinjiapo zongli Li Guang Yao."

55. "Transcript of a Press Conference Given by the Prime Minister of Singapore, Mr. Lee Kuan Yew, at Broadcasting House, Singapore, at 1200 hours, on Monday, August 9, 1965," National Archives of Singapore, http://www.nas.gov.sg/archivesonline/data/pdfdoc/lky19650809b.pdf.

56. For background, see Wen-Qing Ngoei, "The Best Hope," chap. 4 in *The Arc of Containment: Britain, the United States, and Anticommunism in Southeast Asia, 1941–1976* (Ithaca, NY: Cornell University Press, 2019).

57. "Xinjiapo zongli Li Guang Yao."

58. Ibid.

59. "Chen Yi fuzongli zai Yinni fangwen qingkuang ji tong Yinni zongtong Sujianuo deng huitan deng wenti" [Vice Premier Chen Yi's visit to Indonesia and his meeting with the Indonesian president Sukarno], August 14–22, 1965, no. 105-01324-03, CFMA.

60. "Chen Yi fuzongli yu Yinni gongchandang zhuxi Aidi tanhua jilu" [Minutes of Vice Premier Chen Yi's meeting with the Indonesian Communist Party chairman Aidit], August 15, 1965, no. 105-01912-04, CFMA.

61. Ibid.

62. Hara, "North Kalimantan Communist Party and the People's Republic of China," 508. Wen stayed in China after September 1965 and never returned to Sarawak.

63. Justus M. van der Kroef, "The Sarawak-Indonesian Border Insurgency," *Modern Asian Studies* 2, no. 3 (1968): 250; Mackie, *Konfrontasi*, 215.

64. Jamie S. Davidson and Douglas Kammen, "Indonesia's Unknown War and the Lineages of Violence in West Kalimantan," *Indonesia* 73 (2002): 57.

65. Ibid.

66. "Geng Biao fuwaizhang jiejian Yinni zhuhua dashi Sukani tanhua jilu."

67. "Guanyu Yinni zhengfu yao wo zhichi."

68. "Zhou zongli, Chen Yi fuzongli jiejian Yinni zhuhua dashi Sukani tanhua jilu."

69. "Qian zhiyuanjun zhengzhi weiyuan Li Zhimin jiejian Yinni dang dier zhuxi Weiduoyue tanhua jilu" [Minutes of the meeting between the former commander-in-chief of the People's Volunteer Army, Li Zhimin, and the chairman of *Partai Indonesia*, Wardojo], May 27, 1964, no. 105-01241-02, CFMA.

70. "Zhou Enlai zongli he Chen Yi fuzongli tong Yinni fuzongli Subandeliyue dierci huitan jilu."

71. "Yingguo yu Yindu, Malaixiya guanxi wenti."

72. Ibid.

73. Ibid.

74. "Geng Biao fubuzhang jiejian Yindunixiya linshi daiban Suleiman tan Gangguo jushi he Laowo wenti" [Conversations between Deputy Foreign Minister Geng Biao and the Indonesian chargé d'affaires ad interim on the situations in Congo and Laos], November 29, 1960, no. 105-00703-01, CFMA.

75. "Liu Shaoqi zhuxi tong Yinni zongtong Sujianuo de huitan jilu."

76. "Guanyu zhaokai dierci Yafei huiyi shi" [On the second Afro-Asian Conference], September 18–October 31, 1962, no. 105-01789-08, CFMA.

77. "Zhou Enlai zongli tong Yinni fuzongli Subandeliyue huitan qingkuang" [The meeting between Premier Zhou Enlai and the First Vice Premier Subandrio], January 24–25, 1965, no. 105-01319-01, CFMA.

78. "Guanyu zhaokai dierci Yafei huiyi shi."

79. "Yindunixiya zongli Zhu An Da fangwen Nansilafu, Tietuo fangwen Yindunixiya" [Indonesian Prime Minister Djuanda Kartawidjaja's visit to Yugoslavia and Tito's visit to Indonesia], October 11–December 31, 1958, no. 105-00866-08, CFMA.

80. Ibid.

81. Ibid.

82. "Bujiemeng guojia huiyi qingkuang ji Yinni zai bujiemeng huiyi shang de biaoxian" [Reports on the Conference of Non-Aligned Countries and Indonesia's activities at the conference], September 3–November 7, 1961, no. 105-01043-02, CFMA.

83. Ibid.

NOTES TO PAGES 147-149

NOTES TO PAGES 147–149   255

84. "Mao Zedong zhuxi jiejian Yinni zongtong Sujianuo tanhua jilu" [Conversation between Chairman Mao and the Indonesian president Sukarno], June 13, 1961, no. 204-01469-02, CFMA.

85. "Liu Shaoqi zhuxi tong Yinni zongtong Sujianuo de huitan jilu."

86. "Yinni zhengfu wei zhaokai dierci Yafei huiyi choubei qingkuang" [The Indonesian government's preparations for the second Afro-Asian Conference], September 6–October 4, 1962, no. 105-01089-04, CFMA.

87. Ibid.

88. "Deng Xiaoping daizongli."

89. "Indonesian President Sukarno's speech on the non-aligned movement summit (on colonialism, peaceful co-existence, international peace and security)," October 6, 1964, no. 105-01236-05, CFMA. Originally in English.

90. "Deng Xiaoping daizongli."

91. "Yinni waizhang Subandeliyue tan fan Malaixiya xin celue" [The Indonesian foreign minister Subandrio talks about new strategies for konfrontasi], February 2, 1964, no. 105-01871-02, CFMA.

92. "Zhu Yinni shiguan dui Yinni zongtong Sujianuo 'Ba yi qi' yanshuo de kanfa" [Our embassy in Indonesia analyses the Indonesian president Sukarno's "August 17 speech"], August 24, 1964, no. 105-01233-02, CFMA.

93. "Yinni youguan renshi dui bujiemeng guojia huiyi wenti de fanying" [Responses to the conference of non-aligned movements among related parties in Indonesia], October 10, 1964, no. 105-01236-06, CFMA.

94. "Yindunixiya gongchandang zhongyang shuji Aidi deng lingdao tan Sulian gongchandang di 22 ci dahui" [The PKI Central Committee secretary Aidit and other leaders talked about the 22nd Congress of the Communist Party of the Soviet Union], November 26, 1961, no. 109-03044-06, CFMA.

95. "Deng Xiaoping daizongli."

96. Li Qianyu, "Shilun Zhongguo dui dierci Yafei huiyi zhengce de yanbian" [China's policy toward the second Afro-Asian Conference], *Guoji zhengzhi yanjiu* [*Journal of International Studies*] 4 (2010): 118.

97. Marshal Green, *Indonesia: Crisis and Transformation, 1965–1968* (Washington, DC: Compass Press, 1990), 36.

98. "1965 nian di yi sheng chunlei" [The first spring thunder that wakens the world in the year of 1965], *Shijie Zhishi* 2 (1965): 1.

99. "Keyi ling jian yige geming de lianheguo" [An alternative UN can be set up], *Shijie Zhishi* 3 (1965): 1.

100. "Yinni zongtong Sujianuo jiejian geguo dang daibiaotuan de tanhua jilu" [Minutes of the meeting between the Indonesian president Sukarno and Communist Party delegations from various countries], May 26, 1965, no. 105-01915-11, CFMA.

101. "Zhongguo zhengfu he Yinni zhengfu guanyu jianshe xinxing liliang huiyi dasha de yidingshu" [Protocol between the Chinese and Indonesian governments on the construction of the CONEFO building], November 13, 1965, no. 105-01673-04, CFMA.

102. "Deng Xiaoping daizongli."

103. "Yinni zongtong Sujianuo jiejian geguo dang."

104. Research Centre for Diplomatic History at the PRC Ministry of Foreign Affairs, *Zhou Enlai waijiao huodong dashiji* [The chronology of Zhou Enlai's activities in foreign affairs] (Beijing: Zhongyang wenxian chubanshe, 1993), 434.

105. Ibid., 466.

106. "Chen Yi fuzongli zai Yinni fangwen."

107. Eric Gettig, "'Trouble Ahead in Afro-Asia': The United States, the Second Bandung Conference, and the Struggle for the Third World, 1964–1965," *Diplomatic History* 39, no. 1 (2015): 155.

108. "Sujianuo zongtong zai Liu Shaoqi fangwen Yinni juxing de gaobie yanhui shang de jianghua" [President Sukarno's speech at the farewell ceremony for President Liu Shaoqi], *Renmin Ribao*, April 19, 1963.

109. For background on the Afro-Asian movement, see Vijay Prashad, *The Darker Nations: A People's History of the Third World* (New York: New Press, 2007).

110. "Guanyu Yinni zongtong Sujianuo yuejian Yao Zhongming dashi tan Yinni tuichu lianheguo deng shi" [The Indonesian president Sukarno invites Ambassador Yao Zhongming for discussions on Indonesia's withdrawal from the UN and other issues], January 17, 1965, no. 105-01909-02, CFMA.

8. China and the September Thirtieth Movement

1. "262 Putjuk Sendjata Dapat Dirampas," *Duta Masyarakat*, October 11, 1965. According to this report, among the 262 pieces of weaponry confiscated in the army's first week of operations against the PKI in the aftermath of the movement, 150 pieces were Tjung rifles produced in China.

2. "Kisah Gagalanja Coup Gestapu Jang Dimasak di Peking, I: Rezim Peking perintahkan bunuh 7 Djenderal & semua Perwira 'Reaksioner'; RRT sanggupi pengiriman sendjata & perlangkapan untuk 30,000 orang," *Angkatan Bersendjata*, April 25, 1966. The American consul general in Hong Kong reported to the US embassy in Jakarta that this report was an "almost word for word reproduction" of an article that had appeared in a Hong Kong–based Chinese-language periodical that was written to "ridicule the Peking regime." See "Telegram 222 from American consul general Hong Kong to American embassy Jakarta, limited official use," April 27, 1966, document no. 28, in *U.S. Embassy Tracked Indonesia Mass Murder 1965*, ed. Bradley R. Simpson. https://nsarchive.gwu.edu/briefing-book/indonesia/2017-10-17/indonesia-mass-murder-1965-us-embassy-files.

3. *Pengkhianatan G30S/PKI*, directed by Arifin C. Noer, 1984.

4. Jemma Purdey, *Anti-Chinese Violence in Indonesia, 1996–1999* (Singapore: National University of Singapore Press, 2005), 13–14.

5. Mackie, "Anti-Chinese Outbreaks in Indonesia," 111.

6. Fic, *Anatomy of the Jakarta Coup*; Chang and Halliday, *Mao*, 487–89.

7. "Yinni fuzongli Subandeliyue daibiaotuan laifang he shuangbian huitan qingkuang" [Indonesian first deputy prime minister Subandrio's visit and bilateral negotiations], February 2, 1965, no. 105-01318-05, CFMA.

8. Feith, "Dynamics of Guided Democracy," 323.

9. "Yindunixiya Shibao jizhe Nasudewen he Renmin Ribao jizhe Punuoguihua fanghua jianbao" [Reports on the visit of Indonesian journalists from *Tempo* and *Harian Rakyat*], August 1–23, 1960, no. 105-00985-03, CFMA.

10. Rex Mortimer, *Indonesian Communism under Sukarno: Ideology and Politics, 1959–1965* (Ithaca, NY: Cornell University Press, 1974), 19.

11. Ibid., 332.

12. "Yindunixiya gongchandang dongxiang" [Activities of the Communist Party of Indonesia], May 11, 1959, no. 105-00919-01, CFMA.

13. Yang Kuisong, *Mao Zedong yu Mosike de enenyuanyuan* [Amity and enmity between Mao Zedong and Moscow] (Nanchang: Jiangxi renmin chubanshe, 1999), 536–539.

14. "Yindunixiya gongchandang dongtai di er qi" [Activities of the Communist Party of Indonesia, issue 2], March 1960, no. 105-00980-02, CFMA.

15. "Conversations between comrade Mao Zedong and General Secretary of the PKI Aidit," November 17, 1961, quoted in Yang Kuisong, *Mao Zedong yu Mosike*, 551.

16. "Zai huanying Yindunixiya gongchandang daibiaotuan de hui shang, Aidi tongzhi tan Sugong ershier da" [Comrade Aidit commented on the twenty-second CPSU congress at the welcoming reception for the returning PKI delegation], *Renmin Ribao*, December 1, 1961.

17. *Harian Rakjat*, October 4, 1963. Cited in Mortimer, *Indonesian Communism under Sukarno*, 356–357.

18. "Yingyao zai zhonggong zhongyang gaoji dangxiao zuo zhengzhi baogao, Aidi tongzhi chanshu Yindunixiya geming jiben wenti" [Comrade Aidit invited to deliver a political report to CCP Central Party School on the basic issues of the Indonesian Revolution], *Renmin Ribao*, September 3, 1963.

19. D. N. Aidit, *Set Afire the Banteng Spirit! Ever Forward, No Retreat!* (Beijing: Foreign Languages Press, 1964); Lin Biao, *Long Live the Victory of the People's War! In Commemoration of the 20th Anniversary of Victory in the Chinese People's War of Resistance against Japan* (Beijing: Foreign Languages Press, 1965).

20. "Yingyao zai zhonggong zhongyang gaoji dangxiao."

21. "Yinni zhengfu wei zhaokai dierci Yafei huiyi choubei qingkuang" [The Indonesian government's preparations for the Second Afro-Asian Conference], September 6–October 4, 1962, no. 105-01089-04, CFMA.

22. Ibid.

23. Tong Xiaopeng, *Fengyu sishinian* [Forty years in all weather] (Beijing: Zhongyang wenxian chubanshe, 1996), 2:219.

24. Ibid.

25. "Jiedai Yinni fu shouxi buzhang Subandeliyue fanghua jianbao" [Briefing on Indonesian first deputy prime minister Subandrio's visit to China], January 2–7, 1963, no. 204-01504-01, CFMA.

26. Ibid.

27. "Luo zongzhang yu Yindunixiya daibiaotuan jundui chengyuan huitan jilu" [Minutes of the meetings between the chief of the PLA General Staff Luo Ruiqing and the military personnel from the Indonesian delegation], January 24, 1965, no. 105-01910-07, CFMA.

28. "Guanyu Zhong Yinni junshi wanglai wenti" [On the military interactions between China and Indonesia], June 9, 1965, no. 105-01694-01, CFMA.

29. *Harian Rakjat*, January 15, 1965. Aidit said that there were ten million peasants and five million workers ready to be armed. Cited in Harold Crouch, *The Army and Politics in Indonesia* (Ithaca, NY: Cornell University Press, 1978), 87.

30. *Harian Rakjat*, May 19, 1965, cited in Crouch, *Army and Politics in Indonesia*, 87.

31. "Yinni fuzongli Subandeliyue daibiaotuan laifang."

32. "Luo Ruiqing zongcanmouzhang, Peng Zheng fuweiyuanzhang jiejian Yinni zhiyuan renyuan daibiaotuan tanhua jilu" [Minutes of the meetings between the chief of the PLA General Staff Luo Ruiqing, the vice chairman of the National People's Congress Peng Zhen, and the delegation of Indonesian volunteers], June 29,1965, no. 105-01689-02, CFMA.

33. "Zhou Enlai zongli jiejian Yinni zhiyuan renyuan daibiaotuan tanhua jilu" [Minutes of the meeting between Prime Minister Zhou Enlai and the delegation of Indonesian volunteers], July 11, 1965, no. 105-01689-03, CFMA.

34. "Wo zhu Yinni dashi Yao Zhongming yuejian Yinni fuzongli Subandeliyue qingkuang" [Briefings on the meeting between our ambassador to Indonesia Yao Zhongming and Indonesian first deputy prime minister Subandrio], February 11, 1965, no. 105-01319-05, CFMA.

35. "Guanyu Yinni kongjun yao wo tigong wuqi zhuangbei jidi zhouwei renmin shi" [On the Indonesian air force's request for weapons to arm the people living in the areas surrounding the base], July 2, 1965, no. 105-01697-02, CFMA. A circle around Halim with a diameter of fifty kilometers covers a large area. The air force was probably not planning on arming the people in the immediate vicinity of Halim Air Force Base to protect the airfield. Andoko was most likely just justifying the air force's request for a large number of arms.

36. Ibid.

37. "Guanyu jiedai Yindunixiya kongjun siling, Bajisitan kongjun renyuan juti anpai de qingshi ji Ba kongjun daibiaotuan renyuan mingdan" [Plans for receiving the commander of the Indonesian air force, staff from the Pakistani air force, and the name list of the delegation of the Pakistani air force], September 16, 1965, no. 204-01123-02, CFMA.

38. "Jiedai Yinni kongjun siling jihua qingshi" [Request for instruction on plans for receiving the commander of the Indonesian air force], September 15, 1965, no. 204-01174-01, CFMA.

39. "Wo zhu Yinni shiguan dui Yinni zhichi Bajisitan fandui Yindu qinlue lichang de kanfa" [Analysis by our embassy in Indonesia on Indonesia's position of supporting Pakistan while opposing Indian aggression], September 25, 1965, no. 105-01679-04, CFMA.

40. Omar Dani, *Berkas perkara Omar Dani, ex laksamana madya udara dalam peristiwa Gerakan 30 September* (Djakarta: Mahkamah Militer Luar Biasa, 1966), 17.

41. Djali Ahimsa, interview by author, Jakarta, April 18, 2013. Djali Ahimsa could not recall the exact date of this meeting, but the earliest possible date is September 22, 1965.

42. See Anderson and McVey, *Preliminary Analysis*, 21; and Roosa, *Pretext for Mass Murder*, 45–46.

43. Ragna Boden, "The 'Gestapu' Events of 1965 in Indonesia: New Evidence from Russian and German Archives," *Bijdragen tot de Taal-, Land- en Volkenkunde* (BKI) 163, no. 4 (2007): 511.

44. "Fei yu Yinni guanxi" [The bandits' relations with Indonesia, 1965], October 1–December 31, 1965, no. 020-0000-1910A, Academia Historica, Taipei. "Bandits"

was the standard term used by the Chinese Nationalist regime in Taiwan to refer to the Communist regime in Mainland China. This is part of a Japanese intelligence report that was shared with Taipei and translated into Mandarin by the Taiwanese consulate in Osaka.

45. "Indonesian Army Attitudes towards Communism," November 22, 1965, U.S. Department of State, *FRUS, 1964–68*, 26:178.

46. Bradley R. Simpson, *Economists with Guns: Authoritarian Development and U.S.-Indonesian Relations, 1960–1968* (Stanford, CA: Stanford University Press, 2010).

47. Mortimer, *Indonesian Communism under Sukarno*, 37.

48. Zhang Haitao, *Disanci baise kongbu* [The third white terror] (Beijing: Huaxia chubanshe, 1988), 1.

49. "Guanyu Yinni huaqiao zai baoluan zhong de ziwei zijiu wenti ji wo zhu Yinni shiguan duiying cuoshi de bushu deng" [On self-defense and self-protection during the anti-Chinese riots in Indonesia, and the deployment of contingency measures by our embassy in Indonesia], June 23, 1963, no. 105-01826-03, CFMA.

50. "You guan Yinni keneng fasheng zhengbian deng wenti" [On a possible coup in Indonesia], October 30–December 20, 1964, no. 105-01233-06, CFMA.

51. "Yinni zongtong Sujianuo de bingqing ji wo yiliaozu wei qi zhiliao qingkuang" [President Sukarno's illness and our medical team's treatment for him], August 5, 1965, no. 105-01330-01, CFMA.

52. "Mao Zhuxi jiejian Aidi shuailing de Yinnigong daibiaotuan tanhua jilu" [Chairman Mao receives the delegation of the PKI led by Aidit], August 5, 1965, Chinese Communist Party Central Archives.

53. Roosa, *Pretext for Mass Murder*.

54. "Zhou zongli jiejian Yinni linshi renmin xieshang huiyi daibiaotuan diyici tanhua jilu" [Minutes of Prime Minister Zhou Enlai's first meeting with the delegation of the Temporary People's Consultative Assembly of Indonesia], September 30, 1965, no. 105-01917-03, CFMA.

55. "Enclosure 1: A-666, Djakarta," April 27, 1966, Document no. 29, in Simpson, *U.S. Embassy Tracked Indonesia Mass Murder 1965*. This report analyses an article entitled "The Peking Regime Ordered the Murder of the Seven Generals and All Reactionary Officers. The CPR Promised to Supply Arms and Munitions, etc. for 30,000 people," published in *Angkatan Bersendjata* on April 25–26, 1966.

56. "Mao Zedong zhuxi, Liu Shaoqi zhuxi jiejian Yinni daibiaotuan tanhua jilu" [Minutes of Chairman Mao Zedong and Chairman Liu Shaoqi's meeting with the Indonesian delegation], September 30, 1965, no. 105-01917-02, CFMA.

57. I have discussed the potential transfer of nuclear technology and material from China and Indonesia in detail elsewhere. See Taomo Zhou, "China and the Thirtieth of September Movement," *Indonesia* 98 (October 2014): 29–58.

58. "Jiedai Yinni jingji daibiaotuan de yuanzineng xiaozu jianbao" [Briefings on receiving the atomic energy group of the Indonesian economic delegation], September 21–28, 1965, no. 105-01323-02, CFMA.

59. "Zhou Enlai zongli jiejian Yinni kongjun canmou xueyuan kaochatuan tanhua jilu" [Minutes of the meeting with Prime Minister Zhou Enlai and the delegation of the staff college of the Indonesian air force], October 3, 1965, no. 105-01687-02, CFMA. Zhou told the delegation of the staff college of the Indonesian air force: "We sent a telegram to our embassy in Jakarta the day before yesterday, but we have not

received a reply yet." Yet, in his talk with Chairul Saleh, he said that some telegrams went through on October 2, 1965. See "Zhou Enlai zongli jiejian Yinni linshi renmin xieshang huiyi daibiaotuan di er san ci tanhua jilu."

60. "Zhou Enlai zongli jiejian Yinni linshi renmin xieshang huiyi daibiaotuan di er san ci tanhua jilu" [Minutes of Prime Minister Zhou Enlai's second and third meetings with the delegation of the Temporary People's Consultative Assembly of Indonesia], October 1 and 4, 1965, no. 105-01917-01, CFMA.

61. "Zhou Enlai zongli, Chen Yi fuzongli tong Chaoxian Li Zhouyuan fushouxiang dierci huitan jilu" [Prime Minister Zhou Enlai and Vice Prime Minister Chen Yi's second meeting with the vice prime minister of North Korea Ri Ju-yeon], November 11, 1965, no. 106-01476-06, CFMA.

62. "Youguan Yinni jiusanling shijian" [On the September Thirtieth Movement in Indonesia], October 2, 1965, no. 204-01389-04, CFMA.

63. "Zhou Enlai zongli jiejian Yinni kongjun canmou xueyuan kaochatuan tanhua jilu."

64. "Zhou Enlai zongli jiejian Yinni linshi renmin xieshang huiyi daibiaotuan di er san ci tanhua jilu."

65. "Zhongguo zhengfu xiang Yindunixiya zhengfu tichu qianglie kangyi" [The Chinese government strongly protests against the Indonesian government], *Renmin Ribao*, October 19, 1965.

66. "Zhou Enlai zongli, Chen Yi fuzongli tong Chaoxian Li Zhouyuan fushouxiang dierci huitan jilu."

67. Ibid.

68. Ibid.

69. Ibid.

70. Ibid.

71. Mao Zedong. "Pusuanzi dao guoji gongchanzhuyi zhanshi aidi tongzhi" [In memory of Comrade Aidit, an international Communist fighter], December 1965, http://cpc.people.com.cn/GB/69112/70190/70199/4763391.html.

72. Ibarruri has written about her experience in China in Ibarruri Putri Alam, *Roman biografis Putri Alam, anak sulung D. N. Aidit* (Jakarta: Hasta Mitra, 2006). For analysis on this book, see David T. Hill, "Writing Lives in Exile: Autobiographies of the Indonesian Left Abroad," in *Locating Life Stories: Beyond East-West Binaries in (Auto)Biographical Studies*, ed. Maureen Perkins (Honolulu: University of Hawai'i Press, 2012), 215–236.

73. Utuy Tatang Sontani, *Di Bawah Langit Tak Terbintang* (Jakarta: Pustaka Jaya, 2001), 77–104. The sanatorium in South China that Sontani mentioned might be the guesthouse for Southeast Asian Communist exiles located in Nanchang, Jiangxi Province. Suar Suroso, interview by author, Nanchang, Oct. 9, 2013. Suar Suroso, the former secretary of the West Java branch of the PKI's youth organization Pemuda Rakyat, arrived in Beijing from Moscow in 1967. The international liaison office of the CCP made arrangements for Suar Suroso and his family to settle in Nanchang.

74. Adam Wong (Wang Jinming), interview by author, Hong Kong, September 16, 2013. Mr. Wong was one of the "41 young ethnic Chinese heroes" who were engaged in conflicts with the army and local police in Medan. In early 1967, he and other "heroes" gave talks all around China, including the Nanjing Military Academy. Soerjono, a *Harian Rakyat* journalist stationed in Beijing, suggested that the Nanjing

program once had a reputation as "the gateway for resisting the Suharto regime" among the exiles. Soerjono Papers, "Indonesian Exiles of the Left Collection," IISH.

75. Sontani, *Di Bawah Langit Tak Terbintang*, 91–97. Sontani did not mention the name "Nanjing Military Academy" explicitly, but he wrote that the city was known as the fireplace or "tungku" of China (a common nickname for Nanjing among the Chinese). The place was guarded by the Chinese military, and almost all Indonesian exiles were dressed in Chinese military uniforms.

76. Ibarruri Putri Alam, *Roman biografis Putri Alam*, 152–175.

77. Suar Suroso, interview by author, Nanchang, China, October 10 and 12, 2013. After the Cultural Revolution ended in 1976, Suar Suroso was assigned to teach at a local university, and his wife, who was trained in medicine, to work at a local hospital.

78. Qian Qichen, *Ten Episodes in China's Diplomacy* (New York: Harper Collins, 2005), 93–94.

79. Roosa, *Pretext for Mass Murder*.

80. "Telegram A-673 from American Embassy to Department of State, Confidential. 'Example of Anti-Chinese Propaganda,'" March 4, 1966, Document 30; and "Telegram 222 from American Consul General Hong Kong to American Embassy Jakarta, Limited Official Use," April 27, 1966, Document 28; both in Simpson, *U.S. Embassy Tracked Indonesia Mass Murder 1965*.

81. Geoffrey B. Robinson, *The Killing Season: A History of the Indonesian Massacres, 1965–1966* (Princeton, NJ: Princeton University Press, 2018), 190, Kindle.

82. "Guoqing Yinni shangjiang Nasudi'an zhi woguo guoqing hedian chuli qingkuang" [Dealing with Indonesian general Nasution's congratulatory telegram on the sixteenth anniversary of the founding of the PRC], October 7, 1965, no. 117-01220-01, CFMA.

9. Beijing, Taipei, and the Emerging Suharto Regime

1. Kong Zhiyuan, "Zai qiandao zhiguo si yanyuan" [A tribute to my alma mater from the Indonesian archipelago] (unpublished handwritten manuscript, January 12, 1988). Courtesy of Kong Zhiyuan.

2. Kong Zhiyuan, interview by author, Beijing, July 18, 2013.

3. "Guanyu Yinni jushi biaotai he Yinni dui wo shiguan huodong xianzhi de duice" [Request for advice on our response to the situation in Indonesia and to restrictions imposed on the activities of our embassy by the Indonesian government], November 3, 1965, no. 117-01469-02, CFMA. According to a telegram sent by the Chinese embassy in Jakarta to the Foreign Ministry in Beijing on November 3, 1965, "On November 2, the Indonesian Foreign Ministry issued a diplomatic note to all the diplomatic missions, imposing a ban on traveling outside of Jakarta upon all diplomatic personnel either for business or for personal reasons. Although, on the surface, the note was issued to everyone, in substance only our embassy was targeted. In response, we plan to break our confinement by issuing the Indonesian side a diplomatic note, claiming that our embassy staff will travel to the Outer Islands as diplomatic messengers. We will engage in oral reasoning and struggle if necessary. Afterwards we will issue a note of protest. . . . The Indonesian Foreign Ministry demanded that all diplomatic missions should update their permits to carry weapons." According to Kong, only the PRC military attaché owned a pistol.

4. Kong Zhiyuan, interview by author, Beijing, July 18, 2013.

5. "Fu Yinni gongzuo jingguo yu suohuo chengguo baogaoshu Xu Juqing" [Report on achievements in Indonesia by Xu Juqing], November 4, 1967, no. 020-010899-0004-0010X, Academia Historica, Taipei.

6. Ibid.

7. "Zai Yinni dui fei douzheng celue (xiugai cao'an)" [Strategies for our struggle against the bandits in Indonesia (revised draft)], August 28, 1968–March 14, 1969, no. 0202-010899-0006-0209X, Academia Historica, Taipei.

8. Robert Cribb and Charles A. Coppel, "A Genocide That Never Was: Explaining the Myth of Anti-Chinese Massacres in Indonesia, 1965–66," *Journal of Genocide Research* 11, no. 4 (2009): 447–465.

9. Purdey, *Anti-Chinese Violence in Indonesia*, 14–15.

10. "Yindunixiya youpai zuzhi baotu xiji wo zhu Mianlan lingshiguan" [Mobs from right-wing political organizations in Indonesia attacked our consulate in Medan], *Remin Ribao*, November 6, 1965.

11. "Yindunixiya baotu xiji woguo lingshiguan de jingguo chongfen biaoming shi Mianlan junzheng dangju zuzhi he zhishi de" [Evidence showing that the Indonesian mob's attack on our consulate was instigated by the military authority in Medan], *Remin Ribao*, November 6, 1965.

12. "Zhongguo zhengfu xiang Yindunixiya zhengfu tichu qianglie kangyi" [The Chinese government strongly protests against the Indonesian government], *Renmin Ribao*, October 19, 1965.

13. Ibid.

14. "Yindunixiya youpai zhizao shiduan pohuai liangguo youhao guanxi shiying meidi xuyao zhixing fanhua fangong fanrenmin de zhengce" [The Indonesian right wing attempts to destroy the friendly relations between the two countries; to cater to the needs of the American imperialists, they are carrying out campaigns against China, against Communism, and against the people], *Renmin Ribao*, October 21, 1965.

15. "Guanyu Yinni jushi biaotai."

16. "Guanyu wo jianzhu zhuanjia zhudi bei jiancha deng wenti" [Issues relating to the Indonesian army's search of our construction site and our experts], November 20, 1965, no. 105-01673-05, CFMA.

17. "Wo shiguan renyuan Zhao Xiaoshou tongzhi guangrong fushang yingyong baohu guoqi bushou Yinni baotu wuru" [Staff at our embassy, Comrade Zhao Xiaoshou, was injured when trying to protect the national flag. He refused to be humiliated by the Indonesian mobs], *Renmin Ribao*, April 17, 1966.

18. Reports on Zhao were later compiled into a book: Renmin chubanshe, ed., *Yong xianxue baowei wuxinghongqi xiang Mao Zedong shidai de waijiao zhanshi Zhao Xiaoshou tongzhi xuexi* [Defending the Five-Star-Red-Flag with blood: Learning from Comrade Zhao Xiaoshou, a diplomatic fighter of the Mao Zedong era] (Beijing: Renmin chubanshe, 1966).

19. Renmin chubanshe, *Yong xianxue baowei wuxinghongqi*, 2.

20. "Xiang waijiao zhanxian shang de yingxiong zhanshi zhijing" [A salute to our hero on the battlefield of foreign affairs], *Shijie zhishi* 9 (1966): 6.

21. "Awas Neo-imperialisme Kuning," *Angkatan Bersendjata*, April 25, 1965.

22. "Woguo zhengfu yanchi Yinni zhengfu zaoyao wumie" [Our Foreign Ministry harshly rebuked the slanders by the Indonesian government], *Renmin Ribao*, June 11, 1966.

23. The PRC embassy in Jakarta could only communicate with the Foreign Ministry in Beijing via the Vietnamese and Romanian embassies in Jakarta and via the Chinese embassies in Vietnam and Romania.

24. "Bixu fensui Yinni fandongpai fanhua paihua de xinyinmou" [We have to debunk the new anti-China conspiracy of the Indonesian reactionaries], *Renmin Ribao*, July 29, 1967.

25. "Hongse waijiao zhanshi Yao Dengshan, Xu Ren fennu qianze Yinni fandongpai fengkuang fanhua paihua taotian zuixing" [Red diplomatic fighters Yao Dengshan, Xu Ren, furiously condemned the horrifying crimes against China and the Chinese in Indonesia by the reactionary government], *Renmin Ribao*, May 14, 1967.

26. Kong Zhiyuan, interview by author, Beijing, July 18, 2013.

27. "Mao zhuxi de hongse waijiao zhanshi cong Yinni huijing" [Chairman Mao's red diplomatic fighters returned to Beijing from Indonesia], *Renmin Ribao*, May 1, 1967.

28. "Mao zhuxi Lin Biao tongzhi jiejian cong Yinni huiguo de hongse waijiao zhanshi" [Chairman Mao and Comrade Lin Biao received the red diplomatic fighters from Indonesia], *Renmin Ribao*, May 2, 1967.

29. Niu Jun, *Zhonghua renmin gongheguo duiwai guanxi shi gailun* [History of the foreign relations of the PRC] (Beijing: Peking University Press, 2010), 204.

30. Ibid.

31. Yao Dengshan and Zhao Xiaoshou, "Zai guoji shang tuixing touxiangzhuyi de huo chouju—chi fandong jilu yingpian *Fangwen Yindunixiya*" [An ugly farce that promotes surrenderism internationally—critiques on the counterrevolutionary documentary *Visit to Indonesia*], *Renmin Ribao*, July 30, 1967.

32. "Zhuanti baodao: Yindunixiya 'shi yi' zhengbian yu huaqiao de chujing" [Special report: Indonesia's 'October 1' Coup and the situation of the overseas Chinese], April 1,1966, no. 11-EAP-02713, Academia Historica, Taipei.

33. Ibid.

34. "Dui Yinni qiaowu chuyi" [A preliminary view on the overseas Chinese affairs in Indonesia], August 28, 1968–May 14, 1969, no. 0202-010899-0005-0022X, Academia Historica, Taipei.

35. "Dangqian Yinni gongzuo chubu jihua zhaiyao cao'an" [A summary of the preliminary draft for our work plan in Indonesia], January 1966–March 1967, no. 11-EAP-02736, Academia Historica, Taipei.

36. Ibid.

37. "Yu Yinni xin zhengfu jiechu jingguo jielue" [A summary of the process of contacting the new government in Indonesia], January 1966–March 1967, no. 11-EAP-02736, Academia Historica, Taipei.

38. Ibid.

39. Ibid.

40. "Fujian san" [Attachment no. 3], May 15, 1969, no. 0202-010899-0006-0037A, Academia Historica, Taipei.

41. Ibid.

42. Yuan Houchun, *Yigecanyu zhizao lishi de huaren—Situ Meisheng chuanqi* [The legends of Situ Meisheng—an overseas Chinese who participated in the making of history] (Beijing: Renminwenxue chubanshe, 2006), 189–198.

43. "Dangqian Yinni gongzuo chubu jihua zhaiyao cao'an."

44. "Zai Yinni dui fei douzheng."

45. Ibid.

46. "Fujian san."

47. Ibid.

48. Ibid.

49. Ibid.

50. Weng Deyong, interview by author, May 11, 2013, Surabaya.

51. Jess Melvin's study shows that the houses of pro-Beijing ethnic Chinese in Banda Aceh were also marked out, but with signs in red paint made by unknown militia, probably with support from the pro-Taipei group. Jess Melvin, *The Army and the Indonesian Genocide: Mechanics of Mass Murder* (London: Routledge, 2018), 258.

52. Li Peinan, interview by author, June 6, 2017, Quanshang Overseas Chinese Farm, Fujian Province, PRC.

53. See, for example, Jess Melvin, "Why Not Genocide?: Anti-Chinese Violence in Aceh, 1965–1966," *Journal of Current Southeast Asian Affairs* 32, no. 3 (2013): 63–91; Yen-ling Tsai and Douglas Kammen, "Anti-Communist Violence and the Ethnic Chinese in Medan, North Sumatra," in Kammen and McGregor, *Contours of Mass Violence in Indonesia*, 131–155; and Taufik Ahmad, "South Sulawesi: The Military, Prison Camps and Forced Labour," in Kammen and McGregor, *Contours of Mass Violence in Indonesia*, 157–181.

54. Purdey, *Anti-Chinese Violence in Indonesia*, 14–15; Melvin, "Why Not Genocide?," 73.

55. Melvin, "Why Not Genocide?," 73.

56. Tan Swie Ling, interview by author, May 12, 2013, Jakarta. Tan Swie Ling is a human rights activist and a former political prisoner. He was a student at Universitas Res Republik in 1965. See Tan Swie Ling, *G30S 1965, Perang Dingin & Kehancuran Nasionalisme: Pemikiran Cina Jelata Korban Orba* (Depok: Komunitas Bambu bekerja sama dengan Lembaga Kajian Sinergi Indonesia, 2010).

57. Melvin, *Army and the Indonesian Genocide*, 246.

58. Ibid., 246–249.

59. Melvin, *Army and the Indonesian Genocide*, 246.

60. Coppel, *Indonesian Chinese in Crisis*, 69.

61. Liao Yiping, interview by author, June 6, 2017, Quanshang Overseas Chinese Farm, Fujian Province, PRC.

62. Coppel, *Indonesian Chinese in Crisis*, 67.

63. Purdey, *Anti-Chinese Violence in Indonesia*, 18–19.

64. "Wushi yuren jiang jing Gang fan dalu Yinni huaqiao bukan huishou lvju yixiang yuanyi jimo nankan gengnakan tuzhu chenji pohai" [More than fifty people returning to the mainland via Hong Kong; their lonely sojourning life became unbearable when the natives seized a chance to persecute them], *Xianggang Xinsheng Wanbao*, March 28, 1966, OCCCHKBU.

65. Mackie, "Anti-Chinese Outbreaks in Indonesia," 126.

66. Ibid.

67. Hui Yew-Foong, *Strangers at Home: History and Subjectivity among the Chinese Communities of West Kalimantan, Indonesia* (Boston, MA: Brill, 2011), 120–121; Purdey, *Anti-Chinese Violence in Indonesia*, 19–20.

68. Jamie S. Davidson, *From Rebellion to Riots: Collective Violence on Indonesian Borneo* (Madison: University of Wisconsin Press, 2008), 56–84.

69. "Zhuanti baodao."

70. Ibid.

71. "Zai Yinni dui fei douzheng."

72. "Yinni xinwaijiao zhengce ji wo yu Yinni xiuhao zhi zhanwang" [Indonesia's new foreign policy and the outlook of a rapprochement between Indonesia and our country], 1969, no. 0202-010899-0006-0161X, Academia Historica, Taipei.

73. Ibid.

74. "Wo Guanghua lun jieyun disipi Yinni huaqiao shengli fanhang" [The fourth batch of overseas Chinese refugees who rode on the ship *Guanghua* arrived home victoriously], *Renmin Ribao*, May 10, 1967.

75. Ibid.

76. Melvin, *Army and the Indonesian Genocide*, 257, 259.

77. "Woguo zhengfu yanchi Yinni zhengfu."

78. Ibid.

79. The Japanese scholar Kimihiko Baba has interviewed the ethnic Chinese from Indonesia who immigrated to Taiwan. See Kimihiko Baba, "The Hostility of China and Taiwan on the Relationship between Indonesia after the September 30th Incident," *Journal of Asia-Pacific Studies* 26 (2016): 81–97.

80. "Huaqiao shiwu weiyuanhui fuzeren xiang Xinhua she jizhe fabiao tanhua qianglie qianze Yinni zhengfu pohuai wo jieqiao gongzuo" [In an interview with NCNA reporters, the leader of the Overseas Chinese Affairs Commission strongly condemned the Indonesian government's obstruction of the transportation of overseas Chinese refugees to our country], *Renmin Ribao*, March 30, 1967.

81. For instance, ethnic Chinese in North Aceh organized a "repatriation committee" (*fanguo weiyuanhui*), which, according to the NCNA, sent telegrams to the Chinese embassy in Indonesia six times in July and August 1966, "expressing the urgent need of around 2,500 victimized overseas Chinese" for transportation "back to the motherland as soon as possible." See "Wo zhu Yinni dashiguan zhichi shou pohai huaqiao de fanguo yaoqiu" [Our embassy in Indonesia supports the requests from persecuted overseas Chinese for repatriation], *Renmin Ribao*, August 26, 1966.

82. "1966 nian *Guanghua* lun jieqiao baowei gongzuo" [Security and safety work for the ship *Guanghua*'s mission to transport the overseas Chinese in 1966], 1966, no. 291-1-95-163-166, GDPA.

83. Zhang Xiaoxin, "Jiusanling shijian hou," 55.

84. "Yinni fandong zhengfu zunao Zhongguo zhengfu jieyun shouhai huaqiao de yinmou youyici zaodao kechi shibai" [The Indonesian reactionary government's obstruction of the transportation of overseas Chinese refugees to our country encountered another shameful failure], China News Agency, May 11, 1967, OCCCH-KBU.

85. "Yinni renmin buwei qiangbao tingshen erchu baohu huaqiao" [Indonesian people courageously came forward to protect the overseas Chinese], *Renmin Ribao*, February 20, 1967.

86. Ibid.

87. "Wo disanpi nanqiao tuoli Yinni fandongpai mozhua" [A third batch of overseas Chinese refugees escaped from the evil claws of the Indonesian reactionaries], *Renmin Ribao*, February 1, 1967.

88. "1966 nian Guanghua lun."

89. Huang Huilan, interview by author, Yingde Overseas Chinese Farm, Guangdong Province, August 17 and 18, 2013. Huang was aboard the *Guanghua* in May 1967.

90. "Wo disanpi nanqiao tuoli Yinni."

91. "Disipi guiguo nanqiao canguan nongmin yundong jiangxisuo juexin yongyuan gen Mao zhuxi gan geming" [The fourth batch of overseas Chinese refugees visited the Peasant Movement Training Center and expressed their determination to follow Chairman Mao forever and actively participate in the revolution], China News Agency, May 23, 1967, OCCCHKBU.

92. "Disanpi cheng *Guanghua* lun huiguo de nanqiao jihui kongsu Yinni fandongpai fanhua paihua de xin zuixing" [A third batch of overseas Chinese refugees who were aboard the ship *Guanghua* congregated to condemn the anti-China, anti-Chinese crimes committed by the Indonesian reactionaries], NCNA, February 9, 1967, OCCCHKBU.

93. Adam Wong, interview by author, Hong Kong, September 16, 2013.

94. Yu Yazhou's diary entry on May 10, 1966, in *Forty-One Red Hearts Are with Chairman Mao Forever* (Beijing: Foreign Languages Press, 1967), 54. Originally in English.

95. Adam Wong, interview by author, Hong Kong, September 16, 2013.

96. *Forty-One Red Hearts*, 7.

97. "Paean to Mao Zedong Thought from Overseas," *Remin Ribao*, December 9, 1966, in *Forty-One Red Hearts*, 46.

98. "Xiang yong Mao Zedong sixiang wuzhuang de sishiyiming huaqiao qingshaonian xuexi" [Learn from the forty-one overseas Chinese youth who are armed with the weapon of Mao Zedong's thought], *Renmin Ribao*, December 30, 1966.

99. "Sishiyi ming huaqiao qingshaonian yong qinshen jingli tongchi dangnei touhao zou zibenzhuyidaolu dangquanpai de fangeming xiuzhengzhuyi luxian" [Based on their firsthand experience, the forty-one overseas Chinese youth harshly condemned the biggest capitalist roader inside the party's counterrevolutionary revisionist policy], China News Agency, April 17, 1967, OCCCHKBU.

100. "Yichang jilie de guoji jieji douzheng" [A fierce international class struggle], *Xin Nankai*, May 22, 1967, OCCCHKBU.

101. Huang Huilan, interview by author, Ying de Overseas Chinese Farm, August, 18, 2013.

102. "Wo Guanghua lun jieyun disipi Yinni huaqiao."

103. "Yinni xinwaijiao zhengce."

104. "Fujian san."

10. The Overseas Chinese "Returning" to the People's Republic

1. Charles A. Coppel, *Studying Ethnic Chinese in Indonesia* (Singapore: Singapore Society of Asian Studies, 2002), 337.

2. Suryadinata, *Pribumi Indonesian, the Chinese Minority, and China*, 136.

3. "Jiedai diyipi Yinni guiqiao zongjie baogao" [Report on receiving the first batch of returned overseas Chinese from Indonesia], April 20, 1960, no. 0148-002-1111-0061, FJPA.

4. "Lemper" means sticky rice cake in bahasa Indonesia. "Pak Lemper," interview by author, Yingde Overseas Chinese Farm, Guangdong Province, August 17 and 18, 2013.

5. "Guanyu qiaohui wenti de chubu diaochao yijian" [Preliminary results of our research on the remittance issue], December 21, 1949, no. 0101-001-0039, FJPA.

6. "Fujian sheng qiaowu weiyuanhui zuzhi gangyao cao'an ji huaqiao gongzuo tigang cao'an" [Proposal and outline for future work in overseas Chinese affairs by the Overseas Chinese Commission of Fujian Province], 1949, no. 0101-001-0038, FJPA.

7. "Jinjiang xian qiaoqu zaoshou Jiangji saorao qingkuang baogao" [The harassment by fighter jets of the Chiang bandits in Jinjiang district], September 14, 1954, no. 0148-002-0527, FJPA.

8. "Guanyu qiaohui wenti." *Shuike* can also be translated as "couriers."

9. Ibid.

10. "Zeng Jingbing tongzhi zai shengwei diyici huaqiao gongzuo huiyi shang de kaimuci" [Opening speech at the first working meeting of the Overseas Chinese Commission of Fujian Province by Comrade Zeng Jingbing], March 5, 1953, no. 0101-001-0262, FJPA.

11. "Zeng Jingbing tongzhi."

12. Ibid.

13. Peterson, *Overseas Chinese in the People's Republic of China*, 14–15.

14. On the local/global dynamics of the Chinese migrant networks, see McKeown, *Chinese Migrant Networks and Cultural Change*.

15. "Zeng Jingbing tongzhi."

16. For more details, see Shu Guang Zhang, *Economic Cold War: America's Embargo against China and the Sino-Soviet Alliance, 1949–1963* (Stanford, CA: Stanford University Press, 2002).

17. "Yinni zhengfu reng buxu huaqiao huikuan jieji guonei jiashu; liangming huaqiao beikong jingying 'mimi yinhang' zoulou waihui" [The Indonesian government does not allow the overseas Chinese to send remittances back to their family in China; two ethnic Chinese were charged with running a "secret bank"], *Sheng Huo Bao*, July 5, 1952, no. 04105, CSASXU.

18. "Quandao qiaojuan shoudao Yinni qiaohui wuhuixin" [Please stop the families of the overseas Chinese from replying after receiving remittances from Indonesia], January 21, 1955, no. 204-1-350-009, GDPA.

19. "Yinni huaren antan lesuo qiaopiju, qiaopiyuan" [Undercover Chinese Indonesian detectives blackmailed overseas Chinese remittance firms and agents], September 7, 1956, *Haiwai qiaoqing* 18, no. 74-2-46, Hainan Provincial Archives (HNPA).

20. "Zeng Jingbing tongzhi."

21. "Chaozhuan Yajiada lingshiguan baogao youguan Yinni dixia qiaohui qingkuang" [A copy of the report from the consulate in Jakarta on underground remittance], April 16, 1956, no. 148-2-616, FJPA.

22. "Quandao qiaojuan."

23. "Chaozhuan Yajiada."

24. "Huaqiao guxiang de jiefang" [The liberation of the native places of the overseas Chinese], *Sheng Huo Bao*, August 25, 1949.

25. Ibid.

26. "Zeng Jingbing tongzhi."

27. See, for example, "Zhaodai huaqiao huiguo guanguangtuan gongzuo jihua" [Plans for receiving overseas Chinese sightseeing groups], September 25, 1954, no. 235-1-115-007, GDPA; "Yinni huaqiao guanguangtuan Miandian huaqiao lvxingtuan jiedai gongzuo yijian" [Suggestions on receiving overseas Chinese sightseeing groups from Indonesia and Burma], April 20, 1957, no. 148-2-881, FJPA; and "Di si jie Yinni Miandian huaqiao huiguo guanguangtuan lai Minsheng xingqin de qingkuang huibao" [Report on the visit to Fujian of the fourth batch of overseas Chinese sightseeing groups from Indonesia and Burma], February 21, 1955, no. 148-1-65, FJPA.

28. Peterson, *Overseas Chinese in the People's Republic of China*, chapter 4.

29. "Nanyang Pak" refers to Chinese compatriots from Southeast Asia.

30. "Guanyu Yinni huaqiao Huang Jie zhu xiansheng huiguo touzi gongye wenti" [Mr. Huang Jie and other ethnic Chinese from Indonesia plan to invest in industries in collaboration with the government], July 12, 1951, no. 206-1-132-140, GDPA.

31. Weng Xihui, "Yinni aiguo qiaoling," 245.

32. "Huanan caiwei diaoyun weiyuanhui diwuci yewu huiyi jilu Yinni yiban gongzuo baogao" [Report on the fifth meeting of the Committee of Transport and Commodity Circulation under the South China Ministry of Finance related to Indonesia], July 25, 1951, no. 206-1-21-115-121, GDPA.

33. Ibid.

34. Fang Qingyi, "Jiemi xiaobubao zhimi" [Revealing the secrets behind the mysterious cloth parcels], in *Xinglong Huaqiao Nongchang* [Xinglong Overseas Chinese Farm], ed. Wu Shuxiang (Haikou: Hainan chubanshe, 2011), 78–80.

35. Peterson, *Overseas Chinese in the People's Republic of China*, 86–94.

36. "Zeng Jingbing tongzhi."

37. Ibid.

38. Ibid.

39. Ibid.

40. Peterson, *Overseas Chinese in the People's Republic of China*, 23–24.

41. "Zhonghua renmin gongheguo huaqiao shiwuweiyuanhui Fang Fang fuzhuren dui dangqian qiaowu gongzuo de zhishi jianghua" [Speech by Fang Fang, the deputy director of the Overseas Chinese Affairs Commission of the PRC, on the future direction of overseas Chinese affairs], February 10, 1958, no. 74-3-61, HNPA.

42. Ibid.

43. "Fujian sheng qiaoqu huaqiao tugai yiliu wenti he muqian chuli qingkuang" [Summary of the remaining problems with land reform in the native places of the overseas Chinese], May 18–June 14, 1953, no. 0148-001-0028, FJPA.

44. "Jinjiang zhuanqu guanche zongluxian zhong guiqiao qiaojuan de yixie hutu sixiang" [Some confused thoughts of the returned overseas Chinese and families of the overseas Chinese in Jinjiang district during the implementation of the policy line], February 26, 1954, no. 0148-002-0527, FJPA.

45. "Guyi, Gu'er dadui tiqian gaibian chengfen de huaqiao difuhu qingkuang diaocha" [An investigative report on the early change of class statuses among the

landlord families of the overseas Chinese in production teams Gu'yi and Gu'er],
August 25, 1963, no. 217-1-748-22-23, GDPA.

46. Ibid.

47. "Di shiba hangci zongjie" [Summary of the eighteenth voyage], August 21,
1964, no. 291-1-112-89-97, GDPA.

48. Zhang Liukun, "Huiguo ji" [On my journey back to the motherland], in Wu
Shuxiang, *Xinglong Huaqiao Nongchang*, 185–192.

49. "Jieqiaochuan shang xuanchuan gongzuo jingyan jiaoliu zongjie huiyi jianbao" [Summary of the propaganda work on the ships dispatched to take the overseas
Chinese back to the motherland], June 22, 1960, no. 74-4-81, HNPA.

50. Zhang Liukun, "Huiguo ji," 185–192.

51. Ibid.

52. For a detailed discussion of the returned overseas Chinese students, see Shelly
Chan, "The Disobedient Diaspora: Overseas Chinese Students in Mao's China, 1958–
1966," *Journal of Chinese Overseas* 10 (2014): 220–238.

53. For instance, Tang Juniang, a nurse who had a letter of introduction from
Sukarno's private doctor, was appointed as the head nurse of the Ophthalmology
Department at the hospital attached to the Sun Yat-sen Medical School. See "Anpai
Yinni guiqiao Tang Juniang de gongzuo wenti" [On the work assignment of a returned
overseas Chinese from Indonesia, Tang Juniang], April 23, 1963, no. 216-1-355-59-61,
GDPA. An interesting case is that of Li Jinhan, a former Chinese Nationalist Party
sympathizer who witnessed the murder of Wu Lixin, the Indonesian-born Chinese
Nationalist intelligence agent whose story appeared in Chapter 1. He was given a
position as a governmental consultant because the Chinese embassy in Jakarta considered him an important figure among the politically "backward" returnees. See
"Anpai Yinni guiqiao Li Jinhan wei Shengcan yanjiuyuan" [On appointing Li Jinhan
as a researcher at the Guangdong Provincial Consultative Institute], November 21,
1960, no. 216-1-228-70, GDPA.

54. Chan, "Disobedient Diaspora," 228–229.

55. "Fujiansheng qiaowuweiyuanhui guanyu Changshan huaqiao nongchang de
diaocha baogao" [Report on Changshan Overseas Chinese Farm by the Overseas
Chinese Affairs Commission of Fujian Province], August 6, 1960, no. 0148-001-0156,
FJPA.

56. Chinese diplomats in Indonesia reported a case where a returnee wrote to
an Indonesian military officer from the Xinglong Overseas Chinese Farm on Hainan
Island to ask for salted fish. "Mijian: Lianggeyue lai guanche 'shao che duo liu' fangzhen de qingkuang jianbao" [Secret document: A brief report on the implementation
of the 'less repatriated more stay' guideline in the past two months], October 18,
1960, no. 105-00708-02, CFMA.

57. "Guanyu dangqian guiqiao gongzuo de baogao" [Report on the current status of our work on the returned overseas Chinese], January 15, 1961, no. 74-4-85,
HNPA.

58. "Fujiansheng qiaowuweiyuanhui guanyu Changshan."

59. "Piglets" refers to the Chinese coolies who were either forced or deceptively
coerced into indentured labor in the early nineteenth century.

60. "Fujiansheng qiaowuweiyuanhui guanyu Changshan."

61. "Guanyu Shuangdi huaqiao nongchang xinguiqiao naoshi qingkuang diaocha baogao" [Report on riots staged by newly returned overseas Chinese on the Shuangdi Overseas Chinese Farm], August 10, 1960, no. 0148-001-0156, FJPA.

62. "Wulidong pinku qiaogong jiedai anzhi gongzuo zongjie" [Summary of the resettlement of the poor returned overseas Chinese laborers from Belitung], August 19, 1959, no. 74-3-72, HNPA.

63. Ibid.

64. Zhang Liukun, "Liushi niandai chu Xinglong huaqiao nongchang Yinni guiqiao de shenghuo" [The life of the returned overseas Chinese from Indonesia on the Xinglong Overseas Chinese Farm in the early 1960s], in Wu Shuxiang, *Xinglong Huaqiao Nongchang*, 202.

65. "Qiaoqing fanying Yongchun xian huaqiao shiwuju bian" [Conditions of the returned overseas Chinese, edited by the Overseas Chinese Affairs Office of Yongchun County], June 15, 1963, no. 0148-003-2805-0001, FJPA.

66. Ibid.

67. "Guanyu Shuangdi."

68. "Guoying Binlinshan huaqiao nongchang Rao Huihuang gei Liao zhuren de xin" [Letter from Rao Huihuang from state-owned Binlinshan Overseas Chinese Farm to Director Liao], November 2, 1960, no. 74-4-79, HNPA.

69. "Guanyu Shuangdi."

70. "Guanyu dangqian guiqiao gongzuo de baogao."

71. "Fujian sheng Nan'an Guoguang zhongxue guanyu woxiao qiaosheng muqian zhengzhi sixiang qingkuang diaocha baogao" [Report on the political thoughts of the students in our school by Guoguang High School, Nan'an, Fujian], 1963, no. 0148-003-2805-0001, FJPA.

72. "Guangzhou guiqiao xuesheng zhongdeng buxi xuexiao dui xinqiaosheng jinxing aiguozhuyi jiaoyu de qingkuang" [The conditions of patriotic education among the newly arrived returned overseas Chinese students at the continuation schools in Guangzhou], May 3, 1961, no. 232-1-51-40-52, GDPA.

73. Ibid.

74. "Guangdongsheng Lufeng Huaxian liangge huaqiao nongchang de guiguo huaqiao qingnian qingkuang" [Conditions of returned overseas Chinese youth on Lu Feng and Hua Xian Overseas Chinese Farms], May 1, 1961, no. 232-1-51-25-39, GDPA.

75. Chen Zhende, interview by author, Yingde Overseas Chinese Farm, Guangdong Province, August 17 and 18, 2013.

76. "Guangzhou guiqiao xuesheng zhongdeng buxi xuexiao."

77. "Guanyu chuanda guanche 'guiguo huaqiao xuesheng jiaoyu gongzuo fangzhen zhengce ruogan wenti de gongzuo jihua' lianhe tongzhi" [Announcement on "The Principles of Educating the Returned Overseas Chinese Students"], March 31, 1958, no. 232-2-177-16-20, GDPA.

78. "Huaqiao Daxue xuesheng xialingying huodong xiaojie" [Summary on the summer activities of the students at the Overseas Chinese University], August 20, 1963, no. 0133-001-0701, FJPA.

79. "Fujian sheng Nan'an Guoguang zhongxue."

80. "Fujiansheng Fuzhou dijiu zhongxue baogao" [Report from the Number 9 High School of Fuzhou, Fujian Province], June 12, 1963, no. 0148-003-2805-0001, FJPA.

81. "Fujian sheng Nan'an Guoguang."
82. "Fujiansheng qiaowuweiyuanhui guanyu Changshan."
83. "Jiedai diyipi Yinni guiqiao zongjie baogao."
84. "Guanyu dangqian guiqiao gongzuo de baogao."
85. Ibid.
86. "Fujiansheng qiaowuweiyuanhui guanyu Changshan."
87. "Guanyu dangqian guiqiao gongzuo de baogao."
88. Ibid.
89. Peterson, *Overseas Chinese in the People's Republic of China*, 135.
90. "Fujiansheng qiaowuweiyuanhui guanyu Changshan."
91. "Fujiansheng Fuzhou dijiu zhongxue baogao."
92. Peterson, *Overseas Chinese in the People's Republic of China*, 136.
93. "Guoying Binlinshan huaqiao nongchang bufen Yinni Bali guiqiao yunniang chuguo qingkuang de diaocha baogao" [Report on some of the Balinese returnees' plan to leave the country on state-owned Binlinshan Overseas Chinese Farm], March 23, 1963, no. 74-6-129, HNPA.
94. Ibid. The report noted that a woman who stole 2.5 kilograms of fox nuts was fined five kilograms of rice. The subsidies for the entire returnee community were also cut down by 10 percent, which "caused confusion among the residents of the farm."
95. Ibid.
96. Zhang Meiping and Chen Yongji, interview by author, Shuangdi Overseas Chinese Farm, Fujian Province, June 9, 2013.
97. Peterson, *Overseas Chinese in the People's Republic of China*, 132.
98. Ibid.
99. Chan, "Disobedient Diaspora," 221.

Conclusion

1. Liang Yingming, interview by author, Beijing, July 21, 2013.
2. Huang Huilan, interview by author, Yingde Overseas Chinese Farm, Guangdong Province, August 17 and 18, 2013.
3. Ibid.
4. Rizal Sukma, *Indonesia and China: The Politics of a Troubled Relationship* (London: Routledge, 1999), 44–45, 52.
5. Charlotte Setijadi, "'A Beautiful Bridge': Chinese Indonesian Associations, Social Capital and Strategic Identification in a New Era of China-Indonesia Relations," *Journal of Contemporary China* 25, no. 102 (2016): 825; Johannes Herlijanto, "Emulating China: Representation of China and the Contemporary Critique of Indonesia" (PhD diss., Vrije Universiteit Amsterdam, 2013), 4.
6. For discussions on the powerful ethnic Chinese business leaders and the transnational business networks during the Suharto era, see Hong Liu, "Old Linkages, New Networks."
7. Purdey, *Anti-Chinese Violence in Indonesia*, 21.
8. Ibid.
9. Purdey, *Anti-Chinese Violence in Indonesia*, 165–167; Leo Suryadinata, *The Rise of China and the Overseas Chinese* (Singapore: ISEAS, 2017), 63–65.
10. Setijadi, "'Beautiful Bridge,'" 822–835.

11. Chang-Yau Hoon, "More Than a Cultural Celebration: The Politics of Chinese New Year in Post-Suharto Indonesia," *Chinese Southern Diaspora Studies* 3 (2009): 90–105; Hoon, "'Hundred Flowers Bloom,'" 91–118; Charlotte Setijadi, "Being Chinese Again: Learning Mandarin in Post-Suharto Indonesia," in *Multilingualism in the Chinese Diaspora Worldwide: Transnational Connections and Local Social Realities*, ed. Wei Li (London: Routledge, 2015), 141–160.

12. Charlotte Setijadi, "Ethnic Chinese in Contemporary Indonesia: Changing Identity Politics and the Paradox of Sinification," *ISEAS Perspective*, 2016, no. 12, March 17, 2016, https://www.iseas.edu.sg/images/pdf/ISEAS_Perspective_2016_12.pdf.

13. "Japan Loses Indonesian High-Speed Railway Contract to China," *Japan Times*, September 30, 2015.

14. Setijadi, "Beautiful Bridge,'" 827–828.

15. Ibid., 834.

16. Setijadi, "Ethnic Chinese in Contemporary Indonesia."

17. Leo Suryadinata, "Anti-China Campaign in Jokowi's Indonesia," *Straits Times*, January 10, 2017.

18. Johannes Herlijanto, "Public Perceptions of China in Indonesia: The Indonesia National Survey," *ISEAS Perspective*, 2017, no. 89, December 4, 2017, https://www.iseas.edu.sg/images/pdf/ISEAS_Perspective_2017_89.pdf.

19. Ba Ren, "Yindunixiya zhi ge" [Song of Indonesia], 346.

20. Wang Keping, "Ba Ren yu Wu Zu Miao" [Ba Ren and the *Temple of Five Ancestors*], *Xin wenxue shiliao* 4 (2005): 144–147.

21. Ibid.

GLOSSARY

PINYIN	OTHER ROMANIZATIONS	CHINESE CHARACTERS
Ai Siqi		艾思奇
Ba Jin		巴金
Ba Ren	also known as "Wang Renshu"	巴人（王任叔）
Bacheng / Badaweiya	Batavia	吧城 / 巴达维亚
Bai Chongxi		白崇禧
Bao An Dui	Pao An Tui	保安队
Bayanyabi	Bagansiapiapi	峇眼亚比
Binlinshan huaqiao nongchang		彬林山华侨农场
Changshan huaqiao nongchang		常山华侨农场
Chen Jiageng	Tan Kah Kee	陈嘉庚
Chen Kewen		陈克文
Chen Linru	Tan Ling Djie	陈粦如
Chen Xingyan	Tan Hin Hie	陈兴砚
Chen Yi		陈毅
Da Gong Shang Bao	*Tay Kong Siang Po*	大公商报
Deng Xiaoping		邓小平
Fang Fang		方方
Guo Keming	Kwee Kek Beng	郭克明
He Xiangning		何香凝
Hong Yuanyuan	Ang Jan Goan	洪渊源
Huang Zhen		黄镇
Huang Zhougui		黄周规
Huaqiao Zonghui	Hua Ch'iao Chung Hui	华侨总会
Jiang Jiadong	Tsiang Chia Tung	蒋家栋
Jiang Jieshi	Chiang Kai-shek	蒋介石
Jiang Tingfu	Tsiang Tinfu	蒋廷黻
Jimei huaqiao xuesheng buxi xuexiao		集美华侨学生补习学校
Jing Bao	*Keng Po*	竞报
Jingliwen	Cirebon	井里汶
Jugang	Palembang	巨港
Kuanglu Ribao		匡庐日报
Kundian	Pontianak	坤甸
Lei Derong	also known as Liu Yan	雷德容（刘岩）

PINYIN	OTHER ROMANIZATIONS	CHINESE CHARACTERS
Li Guangyao	Lee Kuan Yew	李光耀
Liang Xiyou		梁锡佑
Liao Chengzhi		廖承志
Lin Biao		林彪
Lin Chuan		林川
Lin Qunxian	Liem Koen Hian	林群贤
Liu Shaoqi		刘少奇
Luo Ruiqing		罗瑞卿
Ma Lin (Maring)	Hendricus Sneevliet	马林
Mao Dun		茅盾
Mao Xinyu		毛欣禹
Mao Zedong	Mao Tse-tung	毛泽东
Maowu	Bogor	茂物
Mianlan	Medan	棉兰
Molifen	Madiun	茉莉芬
Niu Shu Chun	New Shu Chun	纽树春
Peng Pai		彭湃
Qiaosheng Bao		侨声报
Qingguang Ribao	*Tsing Kwang Yit Po*	青光日报
Qiu Yuanrong	Hioe Njan Yoeng	丘元荣
Qiu Zheng'ou		邱正欧
Quanshang huaqiao nongchang		泉上华侨农场
Sanbaolong / Longchuan	Semarang	三宝垄 / 垄川
Shankouyang	Singkawang	山口洋
Shao Zonghan		邵宗汉
Shen Yiping		沈一平
Shenghuo Bao	*Seng Hwo Pao*	生活报
Shuangdi huaqiao nongchang		双第华侨农场
Sijiaoba	Pulau Halang	四角芭
Sijili	Segiri	司吉利
Simawei	Lhokseumawe	司马委
Sishui	Surabaya	泗水
Situ Meisheng	Soeto Meisen	司徒眉生
Song Qingling	Soong Ching-ling	宋庆龄
Sun Zhongshan	Sun Yat-sen	孙中山
Tang Liangli	Thung Liang Lee or Tubagus Pranata Tirtawidjaya	汤良礼
Tao Zhu		陶铸
Tian Sheng Ri Bao	*Thien Sung Yit Po*	天声日报
Wang Dajun		汪大均
Wang Guangmei		王光美
Wang Hanjie		王汗杰

PINYIN	OTHER ROMANIZATIONS	CHINESE CHARACTERS
Wang Jiaxiang		王稼祥
Wang Jingwei		汪精卫
Wang Jiyuan		王纪元
Wang Yalu	Suwandi Hamid, Ong Ah Lok	王亚禄
Wang Yongli	Ong Eng Die	王永利
Wangjiaxi	Makassar	望加锡
Wanlong	Bandung	万隆
Wen Jingduo	Tony Wen	温敬多
Wen Mingquan	Wen Ming Chyuan	文铭权
Wendeng	Tangerang	文登
Weng Fulin		翁福林
Wu Lixin		吴立信
Wu Qinming		吴钦明
Wu Shihuang		吴世璜
Wu Tiecheng		吴铁城
Wu Zu Miao		五祖庙
Wulidong	Belitung	勿里洞
Xia Yan		夏衍
Xianda	Siantar	先达
Xiao Yucan	Siauw Giok Tjhan	萧玉灿
Xin Bao	*Sin Po*	新报
Xin you she		新友社
Xinglong huaqiao nongchang		兴隆华侨农场
Xingzhong Ribao		兴中日报
Xingzhou Ribao	*Sin Chew Jit Poh*	星洲日报
Xu Juqing		徐琚清
Xu Ren		徐仁
Xu Suhun		许甦魂
Yajiada / Yecheng	Jakarta	雅加达 / 耶城
Yan Jiakan	Yen Chia-kan	嚴家淦
Yang Xinrong		杨新容
Ya'nong	Warung	亚弄
Yao Dengshan		姚登山
Yao Zhongming		姚仲明
Ye Gongchao	George Kung-chao Yeh	叶公超
Ye Yidong		叶贻东
Yingde huaqiao nongchang		英德华侨农场
Yu Dafu		郁达夫
Zeng Jingbing		曾镜冰
Zhang Guoji		张国基
Zhang Xunyi		章勋义

PINYIN	OTHER ROMANIZATIONS	CHINESE CHARACTERS
Zhao Xiaoshou		赵小寿
Zheng Chuyun		郑楚耘
Zheng Jiemin		郑介民
Zheng Manru		郑曼如
Zheng Yanfen	Cheng Yen-fen	郑彦棻
Zhige	Tegal	直葛
Zhonghua huiguan	Tiong Hoa Hwee Koan (THHK)	中华会馆
Zhonghua xuetang	Tiong Hoa Hak Tong	中华学堂
Zhonghua zonghui	Chung Hwa Tsung Hwee / Chung Hua Tsung Hui	中华总会
Zhou Enlai	Chou En-lai	周恩来
Zhu Changdong		朱昌东
Zou Fangjin		邹访今

Bibliography

Archives

Academia Historica, Taipei

Bao'an District Archives, Shenzhen, Guangdong Province, PRC

Chinese Foreign Ministry Archives, Beijing (CFMA)

Niels A. Douwes Dekker Papers, Division of Rare and Manuscript Collections, Cornell University Library, Ithaca, New York

Fujian Provincial Archives, Fuzhou (FJPA)

Guangdong Provincial Archives, Guangzhou (GDPA)

Hainan Provincial Archives, Haikou (HNPA)

"Indonesian Exiles of the Left" Collection, Institute of International Social History (IISH), Amsterdam

Institut Kewarganegaraan Indonesia, Jakarta

"Minutes of Meetings between Chairman Mao and Leaders of Various Communist Parties," Chinese Communist Party Central Archives, Beijing

National Archives of the Republic of Indonesia (Arsip Nasional Republik Indonesia), Jakarta (ANRI)

G. William Skinner Papers, Division of Rare and Manuscript Collections, Cornell University Library, Ithaca, New York

Online Primary Sources

Mao Zedong. "Pusuanzi dao guoji gongchanzhuyi zhanshi Aidi tongzhi" [In memory of comrade Aidit, an international communist fighter]. December 1965. http://cpc.people.com.cn/GB/69112/70190/70199/4763391.html.

National Archives of Singapore. "Transcript of a Press Conference Given by the prime minister of Singapore, Mr. Lee Kuan Yew, at Broadcasting House, Singapore, at 1200 hours, on Monday, August 9, 1965." http://www.nas.gov.sg/archivesonline/data/pdfdoc/lky19650809b.pdf.

Simpson, Bradley R., ed. *U.S. Embassy Tracked Indonesia Mass Murder 1965*. https://nsarchive.gwu.edu/briefing-book/indonesia/2017-10-17/indonesia-mass-murder-1965-us-embassy-files.

Published Primary Sources

Aidit, Dipa Nusantara. *Set Afire the Banteng Spirit! Ever Forward, No Retreat!* Beijing: Foreign Languages Press, 1964.

Alumni Society of the Overseas Chinese School of Jimei and the Overseas Chinese University of Jimei, eds. *Mianhuai yu jingyang: jinian Jimei qiaoxiao Yang Xinrong laoxiaozhang danchen yibai zhounian* [Celebrating the one hundredth birthday of Yang Xinrong, the president of the Jimei Overseas Chinese Continuation School]. Xiamen, 2007.

Assaat, Datuk Mudo. "The Chinese Grip on Our Economy." In *Indonesian Political Thinking*, edited by Herbert Feith and Lance Castles, 343–346. Jakarta: Equinox, 2007.

Ba Ren. "Linren men" [Neighbors]. In Editing Committee of *Collected Works of Ba Ren, Ba Ren wen ji huiyilu juan*, 251–334.

——. "Rensheng jiqi zhouwei de yiqun" [Rensheng and those around him]. In Editing Committee of *Collected Works of Ba Ren, Ba Ren wen ji huiyilu juan*, 131–198.

——. "Rensheng jiqi zhouwei de yiqun xiaohou ji" [Afterword to "Rensheng and those around him"]. In Editing Committee of *Collected Works of Ba Ren, Ba Ren wen ji shige xuba juan*, 487–489.

——. "Wu ge bei diaosi de kuli" [Five coolie laborers who were hanged]. In Zhou Nanjing, *Ba Ren yu Yindunixiya*, 117–203.

——. "Wu Zu Miao" [Temple of Five Ancestors]. In Editing Committee of *Collected Works of Ba Ren, Ba Ren wen ji xiju juan*, 237–377.

——. "Yindunixiya geming guangan" [Observations and opinions on the Indonesian Revolution]. In Zhou Nanjing, *Ba Ren yu Yindunixiya*, 251–329.

——. "Yindunixiya zhi ge" [Song of Indonesia]. In Editing Committee of *Collected Works of Ba Ren, Ba Ren wen ji shige xuba juan*, 238–397.

——. "Zai faxisi lianyu zhi huo zhong xinsheng" [Rebirth in the inferno of Fascism]. In Zhou Nanjing, *Ba Ren yu Yindunixiya*, 204–250.

——. "Zai Silabaye cun" [In Village Surabeia]. In Editing Committee of *Collected Works of Ba Ren, Ba Ren wen ji huiyilu juan*, 335–418.

——. "Zai waiguo jianlao li" [In the foreign prison]. In Editing Committee of *Collected Works of Ba Ren, Ba Ren wen ji huiyilu juan*, 419–466.

——. "Ziwo zongjie" [Summary of one's own work]. Unpublished handwritten manuscript, 1952.

——. "Zizhuan" [Autobiography]. In Editing Committee of *Collected Works of Ba Ren, Ba Ren wen ji huiyilu juan*, 469–500.

Cai Renlong. *Chidaoxian shang de jiaoyin* [Footprints on the equator]. Hong Kong: Xianggang shenghuo wenhua jijinhui, 2014.

CCP Central Documentary Research Department, ed. *Jianguo yilai Liu Shaoqi wengao* [Liu Shaoqi's manuscripts since the founding of the PRC]. Beijing: Zhongyang wenxian chubanshe, 1998.

Chen Erli. "Jinian Sishui xinhuazhongxue jianxiao liushiba zhounian" [Celebrating the 68th anniversary of the Xinhua High School of Surabaya]. In *Jinian Sishui xinhuazhongxue jianxiao liushiba zhounian tekan* [Special issue celebrating the 68th anniversary of the Xinhua Middle School of Surabaya], 37–40. Hong Kong: Alumni Society of Xinhua High School, 2006.

Chen Fong-ching, ed. *Chen Kewen riji 1937–1952* [Diary of Chen Kewen, 1937–1952]. Vol. 2. Taipei: Institute of Modern History, Academia Sinica, 2012.

China Democratic League Central Literary and History Committee, ed. *Zhongguo minzhu tongmeng lishi wenxian, 1949–1988* [Historical sources on the China Democratic League, 1949–1988]. Beijing: Wenwu chubanshe, 1991.

China News Agency, ed. *Yindunixiya huaqiao he Yindunixiya jiben qingkuang (neibu cankao ziliao)* [Basic information on Indonesia and the overseas Chinese residing in the country (for internal reference)]. Beijing: Zhongguo xinwenshe, 1959.

Dani, Omar. *Berkas perkara Omar Dani, ex laksamana madya udara dalam peristiwa Gerakan 30 September*. Djakarta: Mahkamah Militer Luar Biasa, 1966.

Departement van Landbouw, Nijverheid en Handel, Dutch East Indies. *Volkstelling 1930*. Vol. 7. Batavia: Batavia Centrum, 1931.

Editing Committee of the *Collected Works of Ba Ren*, Zhejiang Academy of Social Sciences, ed. *Ba Ren wen ji huiyilu juan* [Collected works of Ba Ren: Memoirs]. Ningbo: Ningbo chubanshe, 1997.

——, ed. *Ba Ren wen ji shige xuba juan* [Collected works of Ba Ren: Poems, prefaces, and postscripts]. Ningbo: Ningbo chubanshe, 1997.

——, ed. *Ba Ren wen xiju juan* [Collected works of Ba Ren: Plays]. Ningbo: Ningbo chubanshe, 1997.

Editing Group of the Historical Materials of the Southern Bureau of the CCP, ed. *Nanfangju dangshi ziliao: tongzhan gongzuo* [Historical materials of the Southern Bureau: On the United Front]. Chongqing: Chongqing chubanshe, 1990.

Forty-One Red Hearts Are with Chairman Mao Forever. Beijing: Foreign Languages Press, 1967.

Green, Marshal. *Indonesia: Crisis and Transformation, 1965–1968*. Washington, DC: Compass Press, 1990.

Hong Yuanyuan. *Hong Yuanyuan zizhuan* [The autobiography of Hong Yuanyuan]. Translated by Liang Yingming. Beijing: Zhongguo huaqiao chuban gongsi, 1989.

Hu Yuzhi. "Wo zai kangzhan shiqi de jingli" [My experience during the war of resistance against the Japanese]. In Editing Group of the Historical Materials of the Southern Bureau of the CCP, *Nanfangju dangshi ziliao*, 183–190.

Huang Fulian. "Yi Liu Yan yu Xianda jiazheng dushuhui" [In memory of Liu Yan and the household management reading group in Siantar]. In Huang Shuhai, *Wang buliao de suiyue*, 89–91.

Huang Shuhai, ed. *Wang buliao de suiyue* [Times that cannot be forgotten]. Beijing: Shijie zhishi chubanshe, 2003.

—— "Yinni Subei huaqiao kangri douzheng gai lue" [Brief history of anti-Japanese struggles among the overseas Chinese in North Sumatra in Indonesia]. In Huang Shuhai, *Wang buliao de suiyue*, 1–15.

——. *Xianda zhaopian* [Pictures from Siantar]. Beijing: Hongwen jijinhui, 2008.

Huang Weici. "Dui huaqiao he gang'ao tongbao de tongzhan gongzuo" [United Front work on overseas Chinese and fellow countrymen in Hong Kong and Macau]. In Editing Group of the Historical Materials of the Southern Bureau of the CCP, *Nanfangju dangshi ziliao*, 374–387.

Ibarruri Putri Alam. *Roman biografis Putri Alam, anak sulung D. N. Aidit*. Jakarta: Hasta Mitra, 2006.

Information Office, the Overseas Chinese Affairs Commission of the PRC, ed. *Zhongguo Yinni shuangchong guoji tiaoyue wenti ziliao* [Materials on the dual nationality treaty between China and Indonesia]. Beijing: Zhongqiaowei ziliaoshi, 1960.

Kong Zhiyuan. "Zai qiandao zhiguo si yanyuan" [A tribute to my alma mater from the Indonesian archipelago]. Unpublished handwritten manuscript, January 12, 1988. Courtesy of Kong Zhiyuan.

Lai Yumei. "Yi xianfu Zou Fangjin" [Remembering my late husband Zou Fangjin]. In Zou Jianyun, *Zou Fangjin Wenji*, 1–4.

Li Xuemin. "Ba qingchun fengxiangei zuguo he huaqiao zhengyi jinbu shiye—Zheng Manru xiansheng qingnian he zhuangnian shidai shiji shulue" [Mr. Zheng Manru devoted his youth to the motherland and the progressive and righteous affairs among the overseas Chinese]. In Qian Ren and Liang Junxiang, *Sheng Huo Bao de huiyi*, 295–308.

Lin Biao. *Long Live the Victory of the People's War! In Commemoration of the 20th Anniversary of Victory in the Chinese People's War of Resistance against Japan*. Beijing: Foreign Languages Press, 1965.

Lin Jian. "Yi Fanmeng jiaotong lianluo zhan de jianli jiqi fazhan guocheng" [In memory of the establishment and development of the transportation network of the People's Antifascist Alliance in Sumatra]. In Huang Shuhai, *Wang buliao de suiyue*, 68–76.

Lin Kesheng. "Huainian Ba Ren tongzhi" [In memory of Comrade Ba Ren]. In Zhou Nanjing, *Ba Ren yu Yindunixiya*, 457–462.

Mao Zedong. "Talk with the American Correspondent Anna Louise Strong." In *Selected Readings from the Works of Mao Tse-tung*, 345–351. Beijing: Foreign Languages Press, 1971.

Ming Lun. "Zao Helan daibu de Ba Ren" [Ba Ren under arrest by the Dutch]. In Zhou Nanjing, *Ba Ren yu Yindunixiya*, 493–495.

Muaja, A. J. *The Chinese Problem in Indonesia*. Djakarta: New Nusantara, 1958.

Overseas Chinese Research Association, ed. *Yafei diqu huaqiao qingkuang jieshao* [An introduction to the overseas Chinese in Asia and Africa]. Beijing: Huaqiao wenti yanjiuhui bianyin, 1955.

——. *Yindunixiya huaqiao wenti ziliao* [Materials on the issue of the overseas Chinese in Indonesia]. Beijing: Xinhua shudian, 1951.

Party History Committee of the Chinese Nationalist Party, ed. *Zhongguo Guomindang dangwu fazhan shiliao—zhongyang gaizao weiyuanhui ziliao huibian* [Historical documents of the development of the Chinese Nationalist Party—a collection of materials of the Central Committee for Reform]. Vol. 1. Taipei: Jindai zhongguo chubanshe, 2000.

Qian Qichen. *Ten Episodes in China's Diplomacy*. New York: Harper Collins, 2005.

Qian Ren. "Bu zai kan Meidi dianying le" [I will never watch the movies made by the American imperialists]. In *Qian Ren zaoqi shiwenxuan* [Collected works on the earlier poems and essays of Qian Ren], edited by Qian Ren, 35–36. Guangzhou: Shijie tushu chuban Guangdong youxian gongsi, 2013.

Qian Ren, and Liang Junxiang, eds. *Sheng Huo Bao de huiyi* [Memories of Sheng Huo Bao]. Guangzhou: Shijie tushu chuban Guangdong youxian gongsi, 2013.

Radjab, Muhammad. *Tjatatan di Sumatera*. Jakarta: Balai Pustaka, 1949.

Renmin chubanshe, ed. *Yong xianxue baowei wuxinghongqi xiang Mao Zedong shidai de waijiao zhanshi Zhao Xiaoshou tongzhi xuexi* [Defending the Five-Star Red Flag with blood: Learning from Comrade Zhao Xiaoshou, a diplomatic fighter of the Mao Zedong era]. Beijing: Renmin chubanshe, 1966.

Research Centre for Diplomatic History at the PRC Ministry of Foreign Affairs. *Zhou Enlai waijiao huodong dashiji* [The chronology of Zhou Enlai's activities in foreign affairs]. Beijing: Zhongyang wenxian chubanshe, 1993.

Shi Zhe. *Zai lishi juren de shenbian* [Standing beside a historical giant]. Beijing: Zhongyang wenxian chubanshe, 1991.

Sontani, Utuy Tatang. *Di Bawah Langit Tak Terbintang*. Jakarta: Pustaka Jaya, 2001.

Tong Xiaopeng. *Fengyu sishinian* [Forty years in all weather]. Vol. 2. Beijing: Zhong-yang wenxian chubanshe, 1996.

U.S. Department of State. *Foreign Relations of the United States [FRUS]*. Washington, DC: Government Printing Office, 1862–.

Wang Jiyuan. "Dangqian huaqiao baoren de renwu" [The responsibilities of ethnic Chinese journalists at present]. In Wang Yixia, *Wang Jiyuan wenxuan*, 88.

——. "Lun Zhonghua zonghui" [On the Chinese General Association]. In Wang Yixia, *Wang Jiyuan wenxuan*, 9–11.

——. "Zhankai fanfengjian de dadao" [Fly the flag of antifeudalism]. In Wang Yixia, *Wang Jiyuan wenxuan*, 6–8.

Wang Qianyu. *Zai chidao xian shang* [On the equator]. Hong Kong: Dadao chuban-she, 2008.

Wang Yifan. "Pushi wuhua de shengshuo, xuanliduocai de rensheng—ji Yinni zhim-ing qiaoling, jinrongjia, wenhuajiaoyu jie zhimingrenshi Wang Dajun xiansh-eng he ta de Wang shi jiazu" [Humble life, colorful life—renowned leader of the Chinese community in Indonesia, banker and renowned figure in culture and education, Wang Dajun and his family]. In Qian Ren and Liang Junxiang, *Sheng Huo Bao de huiyi*, 309–313.

Wang Yixia, ed. *Wang Jiyuan wenxuan* [Collected works of Wang Jiyuan]. Guang-zhou: Shijie tushu chuban Guangdong youxian gongsi, 2013.

Weng Xihui. "Yinni aiguo qiaoling Weng Fulin Zhuanji [Biography of the patriotic leader of the overseas Chinese in Indonesia, Weng Fulin]. In Qian Ren and Liang Junxiang, *Sheng Huo Bao de huiyi*, 227–250.

Wu Lengxi. *Shinian lunzhan* [A decade of debate]. Vol. 1. Beijing: Zhongyang wenx-ian Chubanshe, 1999.

Xiao Fei. "Huiyi Xianda jianshen dushuhui de huodong pianduan" [In memory of the activities at the fitness and book club in Siantar]. In Huang Shuhai, *Wang buliao de suiyue*, 86–88.

——. "Yi Ba Ren Liu Yan zai Xianda de liuwang he zhandou shenghuo" [In memory of the life of exile and struggle of Ba Ren and Liu Yan in Siantar]. In Huang Shuhai, *Wang buliao de suiyue*, 77–82.

Xu Anru. "Wang Renshu jiqi Wu Zu Miao" [Wang Renshu and his Temple of Five Ancestors]. In Zhou Nanjing, *Ba Ren yu Yindunixiya*, 484–492.

Yang Qiusheng. "Tuanjie Zhuawa aiguo minzhu renshi de dazhong maoyi youxian gongsi" [The Big China Trade Company that united the patriotic and demo-cratic overseas Chinese in Java]. In Qian Ren and Liang Junxiang, *Sheng Huo Bao de huiyi*, 61–65.

Zhang Haitao. *Disanci baise kongbu* [The third white terror]. Beijing: Huaxia chuban-she, 1988.

Zheng Chuyun. "Lun huaqiao aiguo fandi tongyi zhanxian" [On the overseas Chi-nese patriotic, anti-imperialist United Front]. *Sheng Huo Bao*, January 1, 1951. In *Zheng Chuyun wenji* [Collected works of Zheng Chuyun], edited by Zheng Binbin, 51–56. Guangzhou: Shijie tushu chuban Guangdong youxian gongsi, 2013.

Zheng Manru. "Longchuan Xin You She chengli qizhounian jinian gongyan teji" [Spe-ech at the ceremony celebrating the seventh anniversary of the establishment of the Xin You society of Semarang]. In *Zheng Manru wenji* [Collected works of Zheng Manru], edited by Zheng Binbin, 64–65. Guangzhou: Shijie tushu chuban Guangdong youxian gongsi, 2013.

Zhou Nanjing, ed. *Ba Ren yu Yudunixiya—jinian Ba Ren (Wang Renshu) danchen 100 zhounian* [Ba Ren and Indonesia—in memory of the 100th birthday of Ba Ren a.k.a. Wang Renshu]. Hong Kong: Nandao chubanshe, 2001.

———, ed. *Jingwai Huaren guoji wenti taolunji* [Discussions outside of China on the citizenship issue of the overseas Chinese]. Hong Kong: Hong Kong Social Science Press, 2005.

Zhu Yi. *Wanlong jiaoxiangqu—jinian yafei huiyi wushi zhounian* [Symphony at Bandung: Celebrating the fiftieth anniversary of the Bandung Conference]. Shenyang: Liaoning renmin chubanshe, 2005.

Zou Jianyun, ed. *Zou Fangjin Wenji* [Collected works of Zou Fangjin]. Guangzhou: Shijie tushu chuban Guangdong youxian gongsi, 2013.

Periodicals

Angkatan Bersendjata (Jakarta)

Cankao Xiaoxi (Beijing)

China Pictorial (Beijing)

Clipping collections at the Center for Southeast Asian Studies of Xiamen University (CSASXU)

Da Gong Bao (Hong Kong)

Duta Masyarakat (Jakarta)

Fujian Shibao (Fuzhou)

Harian Rakyat (Jakarta)

Japan Times (Tokyo)

Jiangsheng Bao (Xiamen)

Nanqiao Ribao (Singapore)

Overseas Chinese Clippings Collection, Hong Kong Baptist University (OCCCH-KBU)

Peking Review (Beijing)

Qiaosheng Bao (Shanghai)

Qiaoxun (Beijing)

Renmin Ribao (Beijing)

Sheng Huo Bao (Jakarta)

Shijie Zhishi (Beijing)

Sishui Da Gong Shang Bao (Surabaya)

Straits Times (Singapore)

Tian Sheng Ri Bao shelun xuanji [Collected editorials from *Tian Sheng Ri Bao*]. Jakarta: Harian Thien Sung Yit Po, 1951.

Time (New York)

Xianggang Xinsheng Wanbao (Hong Kong)

Xin Bao (Jakarta)

Xingdao Ribao (Hong Kong)

Oral History Interviews

Chen Yongji, Shuangdi Overseas Chinese Farm, Fujian Province, June 9, 2013

Chen Zhende, Yingde Overseas Chinese Farm, Guangdong Province, August 17 and 18, 2013

Chen Zhongde (Chan Chung Tak), Hong Kong, September 18, 2013

Djali Ahimsa, Jakarta, April 18, 2013

Huang Huilan, Yingde Overseas Chinese Farm, Guangdong Province, August 17 and 18, 2013

Huang Shuhai, Beijing, July 17, 2009

Kong Zhiyuan, Beijing, July 18, 2013

Li Peinan, Quanshang Overseas Chinese Farm, Fujian Province, June 6, 2017

Liao Yiping, Quanshang Overseas Chinese Farm, Fujian Province, June 6, 2017

Liao Zhangran, Medan, January 9, 2013

Liang Yingming, Beijing, July 21, 2013

Lin Shangyi, Fuzhou, Fujian Province, May 26, 2013

Lin Shangzhi, Fuzhou, Fujian Province, May 26, 2013

Eddy Setiawan, Jakarta, March 20, 2013

Suar Suroso, Nanchang, October 9, 10, and 12, 2013

Tan Swie Ling, Jakarta, May 12, 2013

Wen Liu, Xiamen, October 23, 2013

Weng Deyong, Surabaya, May 11, 2013

Adam Wong (Wang Jinming), Hong Kong, September 16, 2013

Yu Meilan, Xiamen, October 24 and 25, 2013

Zhang Meiping, Shuangdi Overseas Chinese Farm, Fujian Province, June 9, 2013

Secondary Sources

Ahmad, Taufik. "South Sulawesi: The Military, Prison Camps and Forced Labour." In Kammen and McGregor, *Contours of Mass Violence in Indonesia*, 157–181.

Akashi, Yoji. *The Nanyang National Salvation Movement, 1937–1941.* Lawrence: Center for East Asian Studies, University of Kansas, 1970.

Anderson, Benedict Richard O'Gorman. *Imagined Communities.* London: Verso, 1991.

Anderson, Benedict Richard O'Gorman, and Ruth T. McVey. *A Preliminary Analysis of the October 1, 1965, Coup in Indonesia.* Ithaca, NY: Cornell University Southeast Asia Program Publications, 1971.

Baba, Kimihiko. "The Hostility of China and Taiwan on the Relationship between Indonesia after the September 30th Incident." *Journal of Asia-Pacific Studies* 26 (2016): 81–97.

Bayly, C. A., Sven Beckert, Matthew Connelly, Isabel Hofmeyer, Wendy Kozol, and Patricia See. "AHR Conversation: On Transnational History." *American Historical Review* 111, no. 5 (2006): 1441–1464.

Boden, Ragna. "The 'Gestapu' Events of 1965 in Indonesia: New Evidence from Russian and German Archives." *Bijdragen tot de Taal-, Land- en Volkenkunde* (BKI) 163, no. 4 (2007): 507–528.

Brackman, Arnold C. *Communist Collapse in Indonesia.* New York: W. W. Norton, 1969.

Brazinsky, Gregg A. *Winning the Third World: Sino-American Rivalry during the Cold War.* Chapel Hill: University of North Carolina Press, 2017.

Brooks, Charlotte. *Between Mao and McCarthy: Chinese American Politics in the Cold War Years.* Chicago: University of Chicago Press, 2015.

Budianta, Melani. "Malang Mignon: Cultural Expressions of the Chinese, 1940–1960." In *Heirs to World Culture: Being Indonesian, 1950–1965*, edited by Jennifer Lindsay and Maya H. T. Liem, 000–000. Leiden: KITLV Press, 2012.

Chan, Shelly. "The Case for Diaspora: A Temporal Approach to the Chinese Experience." *Journal of Asian Studies* 74, no. 1 (2015): 107–128.

——. *Diaspora's Homeland: Modern China in the Age of Global Migration*. Durham, NC: Duke University Press, 2018.

——. "The Disobedient Diaspora: Overseas Chinese Students in Mao's China, 1958–1966." *Journal of Chinese Overseas* 10 (2014): 220–238.

Chang, Gordon H., and He Di. "The Absence of War in the U.S.-China Confrontation over Quemoy and Matsu in 1954–1955: Contingency, Luck, Deterrence?" *American Historical Review* 98 (1993): 1500–1524.

Chang, Jung, and Jon Halliday. *Mao: The Unknown Story*. New York: Anchor Books, 2005.

Chen, Jian. "Bridging Revolution and Decolonization: The 'Bandung Discourse' in China's Early Cold War Experience." *Chinese Historical Review* 15, no. 2 (2008): 207–241.

——. *Mao's China and the Cold War*. Chapel Hill: University of North Carolina Press, 2001.

Chen Yushan, and Chen Shaojing. *Yuan Geng zhi mi* [The myth of Yuan Geng]. Guangzhou: Huacheng chubanshe, 2005.

Christensen, Thomas J. *Useful Adversaries: Grand Strategy, Domestic Mobilization, and Sino-American Conflict, 1947–1958*. Princeton, NJ: Princeton University Press, 1996.

Coppel, Charles A. *Indonesian Chinese in Crisis*. Kuala Lumpur: Oxford University Press, 1983.

——. *Studying Ethnic Chinese in Indonesia*. Singapore: Singapore Society of Asian Studies, 2002.

Coppel, Charles A., and Leo Suryadinata. "The Use of the Terms 'Tjina' and 'Tionghoa' in Indonesia: A Historical Survey." *Papers in Far Eastern History* 2 (1970): 97–118.

Cribb, Robert. "The Indonesian Massacres." In *Century of Genocide: Critical Essays and Eyewitness Accounts*, edited by Samuel Totten, William S. Parsons, and Israel W. Charny, 233–262. 2nd ed. New York: Routledge, 2004.

Cribb, Robert, and Charles A. Coppel. "A Genocide That Never Was: Explaining the Myth of Anti-Chinese Massacres in Indonesia, 1965–66." *Journal of Genocide Research* 11, no. 4 (2009): 447–465.

Crouch, Harold. *The Army and Politics in Indonesia*. Ithaca, NY: Cornell University Press, 1978.

Davidson, Jamie S. *From Rebellion to Riots: Collective Violence on Indonesian Borneo*. Madison: University of Wisconsin Press, 2008.

Davidson, Jamie S., and Douglas Kammen. "Indonesia's Unknown War and the Lineages of Violence in West Kalimantan." *Indonesia* 73 (2002): 53–87.

Ding Jian, and Xiaowen. *Qiandao zhi guo yue canghai: qiaoling He Longchao zhuan* [Watching the tides of history on the Indonesian archipelago: A biography of a leader of the overseas Chinese community, He Longchao]. Beijing: Zhong-guo huaqiao chubanshe, 2004.

Fan Zhonghui. *Jiangjun, waijiao jia, yishu jia—Huang Zhen zhuan* [General, diplomat, and artist—a biography of Huang Zhen]. Beijing: Zhongyang wenxian chu-banshe, 2007.

Fang Qingyi. "Jiemi xiaobubao zhimi" [Revealing the secrets behind the mysterious cloth parcels]. In Wu Shuxiang, *Xinglong Huaqiao Nongchang*, 78–80.

Feith, Herbert. *The Decline of Constitutional Democracy in Indonesia.* Jakarta: Equinox Publishing, 2007.

——. "Dynamics of Guided Democracy." In McVey, *Indonesia*, 309–355.

Fic, Victor M. *Anatomy of the Jakarta Coup, October 1, 1965.* New Delhi: Abhinav Pub-lications, 2004.

Fitzgerald, Stephen. *China and the Overseas Chinese: A Study of Peking's Changing Policy, 1949–1970.* Cambridge: Cambridge University Press, 1980.

Friedman, Jeremy. *Shadow Cold War: The Sino-Soviet Competition for the Third World.* Chapel Hill: University of North Carolina Press, 2015.

Friend, Theodore. *Indonesian Destinies.* Cambridge, MA: Belknap Press of Harvard University Press, 2003.

Gettig, Eric. "'Trouble Ahead in Afro-Asia': The United States, the Second Bandung Conference, and the Struggle for the Third World, 1964–1965." *Diplomatic His-tory* 39, no. 1 (2015): 125–156.

Gonzalez, Fredy. *Paisanos Chinos: Transpacific Politics among Chinese Immigrants in Mexico.* Berkeley: University of California Press, 2017.

Hanssens, V. "The Campaign against Nationalist Chinese in Indonesia." In *Indonesia's Struggle, 1957–1958*, edited by B. H. M. Vlekke, 56–76. The Hague: Nether-land's Institute of International Affairs, 1959.

Hara, Fujio. *Malayan Chinese and China: Conversion in Identity Consciousness, 1945–1957.* Singapore: National University of Singapore Press, 2003.

——. "The North Kalimantan Communist Party and the People's Republic of China." *Developing Economies* 43, no. 4 (2005): 489–513.

Harvey, Barbara Sillars. *Permesta: Half a Rebellion.* Ithaca, NY: Cornell Modern Indo-nesia Project, 1977.

Hearman, Vannessa. "Under Duress: Suppressing and Recovering Memories of the Indonesian Sixties." *Social Transformation* 1, no. 1 (2013): 5–25.

Hei Ying. *Hong Bai Qi Xia* [Underneath the Red-and-White flag]. Hong Kong: Chidao chubanshe, 1950.

Heidhues, Mary Somers. "Anti-Chinese Violence in Java during the Indonesia Revolu-tion, 1945–49." *Journal of Genocide Research* 14, nos. 3–4 (2012): 381–401.

——. "Citizenship and Identity: Ethnic Chinese and the Indonesian Revolution." In *Changing Identities of the Southeast Asian Chinese since World War II*, edited by Jennifer W. Cushman and Wang Gungwu, 115–139. Hong Kong: Hong Kong University Press, 1988.

——. *Golddiggers, Farmers, and Traders in the "Chinese Districts" of West Kalimantan.* Ithaca, NY: Southeast Asia Program Publications, Cornell University, 2003.

Herlijanto, Johannes. "Emulating China: Representation of China and the Contem-porary Critique of Indonesia." PhD diss., Vrije Universiteit Amsterdam, 2013.

——. "Public Perceptions of China in Indonesia: The Indonesia National Survey." *ISEAS Perspective*, 2017, no. 89, December 4, 2017. https://www.iseas.edu.sg/images/pdf/ISEAS_Perspective_2017_89.pdf.

Hill, David T. "Writing Lives in Exile: Autobiographies of the Indonesian Left Abroad." In *Locating Life Stories: Beyond East-West Binaries in (Auto)Biographical Studies*, edited by Maureen Perkins, 215–236. Honolulu: University of Hawai'i Press, 2012.

Hoon, Chang Yau. " 'A Hundred Flowers Bloom': The Re-Emergence of the Chinese Press in Post-Suharto Indonesia." In *Media and the Chinese Diaspora: Community, Communications and Commerce*, edited by Sun Wanning, 91–118. London: Routledge, 2006.

——. "More Than a Cultural Celebration: The Politics of Chinese New Year in Post-Suharto Indonesia." *Chinese Southern Diaspora Studies* 3 (2009): 90–105.

Hsu, Madeline Y. *Dreaming of Gold, Dreaming of Home: Transnationalism and Migration between the United States and South China, 1882–1943*. Stanford, CA: Stanford University Press, 2000.

——. *The Good Immigrants: How the Yellow Peril Became the Model Minority*. Princeton, NJ: Princeton University Press, 2017.

Huang, Jianli. "Umbilical Ties: The Framing of the Overseas Chinese as the Mother of the Revolution." *Frontiers of History in China* 6, no. 2 (2011): 183–228.

Huang Kunzhang. *Yinni huaqiao huaren shi* [A history of the ethnic Chinese and overseas Chinese citizens in Indonesia]. Guangzhou: Guangdong gaodeng jiaoyu chubanshe, 2005.

Huaqiao Zhi Editorial Board. *Yinni huaqiao zhi* [General records of the overseas Chinese in Indonesia]. Taipei: Huaqiao Zhi Editorial Board, 1961.

Huebner, Stefan. *Pan-Asian Sports and the Emergence of Modern Asia, 1913–1974*. Singapore: National University of Singapore Press, 2016.

Hui, Yew-Foong. *Strangers at Home: History and Subjectivity among the Chinese Communities of West Kalimantan, Indonesia*. Boston, MA: Brill, 2011.

Jones, Matthew. *Conflict and Confrontation in South East Asia, 1961–1965: Britain, the United States, Indonesia and the Creation of Malaysia*. Cambridge: Cambridge University Press, 2001.

Kahin, Audrey R., and George McT. Kahin. *Subversion as Foreign Policy: The Secret Eisenhower and Dulles Debacle in Indonesia*. New York: New Press, 1995.

Kammen, Douglas, and Katherine McGregor, eds. *Contours of Mass Violence in Indonesia: 1965–1968*. Singapore: National University of Singapore Press, 2012.

Kessler, Lawrence. "Reconstructing Zhou Enlai's Escape from Shanghai in 1931: A Research Note." *Twentieth Century China* 34, no. 2 (April 2008): 112–131.

Khan, Sulmaan Wasif. *Muslim, Trader, Nomad, Spy: China's Cold War and the People of the Tibetan Borderlands*. Chapel Hill: University of North Carolina Press, 2015.

Kuhn, Philip A. *Chinese among Others: Emigration in Modern Times*. Singapore: National University of Singapore Press, 2008.

Legge, J. D. *Sukarno: A Political Biography*. New York: Praeger, 1972.

Lev, Daniel S. *The Transition to Guided Democracy, 1957–1959*. Jakarta: Equinox, 2009.

Li Enhan. *Dongnanya huaren shi* [A history of the overseas Chinese in Southeast Asia]. Taipei: Wunan tushu, 2003.

Li Qianyu. "Shilun Zhongguo dui dierci Yafei huiyi zhengce de yanbian" [China's policy toward the second Afro-Asian Conference]. *Guoji zhengzhi yanjiu* [Journal of International Studies] 4 (2010): 115–133.

Li Yinghui. *Huaqiao zhengce yu haiwai minzuzhuyi, 1912–1949* [Overseas Chinese policies and overseas Chinese nationalism, 1912–1949]. Taipei: Guoshiguan, 1997.

Liang Yingming. "Cong zhonghua xuetang dao sanyu xuexiao—lun Yindunixiya xiandai huawen xuexiao de fazhan yu yanbian" [From Tiong Hoa Hak Tong to trilingual schools—on the development and evolution of Chinese medium education in modern Indonesia]. *Huaqiao huaren lishi yanjiu* 2 (2013): 1–13.

——. "Yindunixiya *Sheng Huo Bao* de lishi gongji" [The historical significance of *Sheng Huo Bao* from Indonesia]. In *Sheng Huo Bao* Collection Editorial Board, *Sheng Huo Bao jinian congshu shoufa yantaohui wenjian huibian*, 6–16.

Liow, Joseph Chinyong. "Tunku Abdul Rahman and Malaya's Relations with Indonesia, 1957–60." *Journal of Southeast Asian Studies* 36, no. 1 (2005): 87–109.

Liu, Hong. *China and the Shaping of Indonesia, 1949–1965.* Singapore: National University of Singapore Press, 2011.

——. "An Emerging China and Diasporic Chinese: History, State and International Relations." *Journal of Contemporary China* 20, no. 72 (2011): 813–832.

——. "Old Linkages, New Networks: The Globalization of Overseas Chinese Voluntary Associations and Its Implications." *China Quarterly*, no. 155 (September 1998): 582–609.

Liu, Oiyan. "The Educational Movement in Early 20th Century Batavia and Its Connections with Singapore and China." *BiblioAsia* 6, no. 3 (October 2010): 22–26.

Lohanda, Mona. *The Kapitan Cina of Batavia, 1837–1942: A History of Chinese Establishment in Colonial Society.* Jakarta: Djambatan, 1996.

Luthi, Lorenz M. *The Sino-Soviet Split, 1956–1966: Cold War in the Communist World.* Princeton, NJ: Princeton University Press, 2008.

Mackie, J. A. C. "Anti-Chinese Outbreaks in Indonesia, 1959–1968." In Mackie, *Chinese in Indonesia*, 77–138.

——, ed. *The Chinese in Indonesia: Five Essays.* Honolulu: University Press of Hawai'i, 1976.

——. *Konfrontasi: The Indonesia-Malaysia Dispute, 1963–1966.* Kuala Lumpur: Oxford University Press, 1974.

Mackie, J. A. C., and Charles A. Coppel. "A Preliminary Survey." In Mackie, *Chinese in Indonesia*, 1–18.

Masuda, Hajimu. *Cold War Crucible: The Korean Conflict and the Postwar World.* Cambridge, MA: Harvard University Press, 2015.

McKeown, Adam. *Chinese Migrant Networks and Cultural Change: Peru, Chicago, Hawaii, 1900–1936.* Chicago: University of Chicago Press, 2001.

McVey, Ruth T., ed. *Indonesia.* New Haven, CT: Yale University Southeast Asian Studies, 1963.

Melvin, Jess. *The Army and the Indonesian Genocide: Mechanics of Mass Murder.* London: Routledge, 2018.

——. "Why Not Genocide?: Anti-Chinese Violence in Aceh, 1965–1966." *Journal of Current Southeast Asian Affairs* 32, no. 3 (2013): 63–91.

Mortimer, Rex. *Indonesian Communism under Sukarno: Ideology and Politics, 1959–1965.* Ithaca, NY: Cornell University Press, 1974.

Mozingo, David. *Chinese Policy toward Indonesia, 1949–1967.* Ithaca, NY: Cornell University Press, 1976.

Ngoei, Wen-Qing. *The Arc of Containment: Britain, the United States, and Anticommunism in Southeast Asia, 1941–1976.* Ithaca, NY: Cornell University Press, 2019.

Niu, Jun. "1962: The Eve of the Left Turn in China's Foreign Policy." *Cold War International History Project Working Paper* no. 48. Washington, DC: Woodrow Wilson Center, 2005. https://www.wilsoncenter.org/sites/default/files/NiuJunWP481.pdf.

——. *Zhonghua renmin gongheguo duiwai guanxi shi gailun* [History of the foreign relations of the PRC]. Beijing: Peking University Press, 2010.

Oyen, Meredith. "Communism, Containment and the Chinese Overseas." In *The Cold War in Asia: The Battle for Hearts and Minds*, edited by Yangwen Zheng, Liu Hong, and Michael Szonyi, 59–93. Leiden: Brill, 2010.

——. *The Diplomacy of Migration: Transnational Lives and the Making of U.S.-Chinese Relations in the Cold War.* Ithaca, NY: Cornell University Press, 2015.

Peterson, Glen. *Overseas Chinese in the People's Republic of China.* London: Routledge, 2012.

Poulgrain, Greg. *The Genesis of Konfrontasi: Malaysia, Brunei, Indonesia, 1945–1965.* London: C. Hurst, 1998.

Prashad, Vijay. *The Darker Nations: A People's History of the Third World.* New York: New Press, 2007.

Purcell, Victor. *The Chinese in Modern Malaya.* Singapore: Eastern Universities Press, 1960.

Purdey, Jemma. *Anti-Chinese Violence in Indonesia, 1996–1999.* Singapore: National University of Singapore Press, 2005.

Qiu Zheng'ou. *Huaqiao wenti lunji* [Collection of works on the overseas Chinese issue]. Taipei: Huagang, 1978.

——. *Huaqiao wenti yanjiu* [A study of the overseas Chinese issue]. Taipei: Institute of the Department of Defense, 1965.

——. *Sujianuo shidai Yinni paihua shishi* [Historical facts of the anti-Chinese movements during the Sukarno era]. Taipei: Institute of Modern History, Academia Sinica, 1995.

Radchenko, Sergey. *Two Suns in the Heavens: The Sino-Soviet Struggle for Supremacy, 1962–1967.* Stanford, CA: Stanford University Press, 2009.

Ren Guixiang, and Zhao Hongying. *Huaqiao huaren yu guogong guanxi* [Overseas Chinese and the relations between the Communist and Nationalist Parties]. Wuhan: Wuhan chubanshe, 1999.

Ricklefs, M. C. *A History of Modern Indonesia since c. 1300.* 2nd ed. Stanford, CA: Stanford University Press, 1993.

Robinson, Geoffrey B. *The Killing Season: A History of the Indonesian Massacres, 1965–1966.* Princeton, NJ: Princeton University Press, 2018. Kindle.

Roosa, John. *Pretext for Mass Murder: The September 30th Movement and Suharto's Coup d'Etat in Indonesia.* Madison: University of Wisconsin Press, 2006.

Roy, Sripura. *Beyond Belief: India and the Politics of Postcolonial Nationalism.* Durham, NC: Duke University Press, 2007. Kindle.

Sacks, Milton. "The Strategy of Communism in Southeast Asia." *Pacific Affairs* 23, no. 3 (1950): 227–247.

Saich, Tony. *Origins of the First United Front in China: The Role of Sneevliet (alias Maring).* Boston, MA: Brill, 1991.

Schiller, Anne L. "The Niels Alexander Douwes Dekker Collection." *Documentation Newsletter* 14, no. 2 (1988): 1–8.

Seng, Guo Quan. "The Origins of the Socialist Revolution in Sarawak (1945–1963)." Master's thesis, National University of Singapore, 2008.

Setijadi, Charlotte. "'A Beautiful Bridge': Chinese Indonesian Associations, Social Capital and Strategic Identification in a New Era of China-Indonesia Relations." *Journal of Contemporary China* 25, no. 102 (2016): 822–835.

——. "Being Chinese Again: Learning Mandarin in Post-Suharto Indonesia." In *Multilingualism in the Chinese Diaspora Worldwide: Transnational Connections and Local Social Realities*, edited by Wei Li, 141–160. London: Routledge, 2015.

——. "Ethnic Chinese in Contemporary Indonesia: Changing Identity Politics and the Paradox of Sinification." *ISEAS Perspective*, 2016, no. 12, March 17, 2016. https://www.iseas.edu.sg/images/pdf/ISEAS_Perspective_2016_12.pdf.

Shen Zhihua, and Li Danhui. *After Leaning to One Side: China and Its Allies in the Cold War*. Stanford, CA: Stanford University Press, 2011.

Sheng Huo Bao Collection Editorial Board, ed. *Sheng Huo Bao jinian congshu shoufa yantaohui wenjian huibian* [Collection of papers presented at the conference on *Sheng Huo Bao*]. Xiamen: Shenghuowenhua jijinhui, October 2013.

Shiraishi, Takashi. *An Age in Motion: Popular Radicalism in Java, 1912–1926*. Ithaca, NY: Cornell University Press, 1990.

Shuman, Amanda. "Elite Competitive Sport in the People's Republic of China, 1958–1966: The Games of New Emerging Forces (GANEFO)." *Journal of Sport History* 40, no. 2 (2013): 258–83.

Simpson, Bradley R. *Economists with Guns: Authoritarian Development and U.S.-Indonesian Relations, 1960–1968*. Stanford, CA: Stanford University Press, 2010.

Sinn, Elizabeth. "Moving Bones: Hong Kong's Role as an 'In-Between Place' in the Chinese Diaspora." In *Cities in Motion: Interior, Coast and Diaspora in Transnational China*, edited by David Strand and Sherman Cochran, 247–271. Berkeley: University of California Press, 2007.

Skinner, G. William. "The Chinese Minority." In McVey, *Indonesia*, 97–117.

——. "Communism and Chinese Culture in Indonesia: The Political Dynamics of the Chinese Youth." Unpublished manuscript, August 1962. Typescript available at Kroch Asia Library, Cornell University.

Smail, John. *Bandung in the Early Revolution, 1945–1946: A Study in the Social History of the Indonesian Revolution*. Ithaca, NY: Cornell University Modern Indonesia Project, 1964.

Sukma, Rizal. *Indonesia and China: The Politics of a Troubled Relationship*. London: Routledge, 1999.

Suryadinata, Leo. *Eminent Indonesian Chinese: Biographical Sketches*. 4th ed. Singapore: Institute of Southeast Asian Studies, 2015.

——, ed. *Ethnic Chinese as Southeast Asians*. Singapore: Institute of Southeast Asian Studies, 1997.

——. "Indonesian Chinese Education: Past and Present." *Indonesia* 14 (1972): 49–71.

——. *Pribumi Indonesian, the Chinese Minority, and China*. 3rd ed. Singapore: Heinemann Asia, 1992.

——. *The Rise of China and the Overseas Chinese*. Singapore: ISEAS, 2017.

——. *Yinni huaren: wenhua yu shehui* [Chinese in Indonesia: Culture and society]. Singapore: Singapore Society of Asian Studies, 1993.

——. "Yinni huawen baokanshi yu guojia rentong" [A history of Chinese-language newspapers in Indonesia and national identification]. In *Sheng Huo Bao* Collection Editorial Board, *Sheng Huo Bao jinian congshu shoufa yantaohui wenjian huibian*, 21–29.

Sutter, John O. *Indonesianisasi: Politics in a Changing Economy, 1940–1955.* Vol. 3. Ithaca, NY: Cornell University Southeast Asia Program Data Paper, 1959.

Szonyi, Michael. *The Cold War Island: Quemoy on the Front Line.* Cambridge: Cambridge University Press, 2008.

Tagliacozzo, Eric. "Amphora, Whisper, Text: Ways of Writing Southeast Asian History." *Crossroads: An Interdisciplinary Journal of Southeast Asian Studies* 16, no. 1 (2002): 128–158.

Tagliacozzo, Eric, and Wen-Chin Chang, eds. *Chinese Circulations: Capital, Commodities, and Networks in Southeast Asia.* Durham, NC: Duke University Press, 2011.

Tan, Mely G. "The Ethnic Chinese in Indonesia: Issues of Identity." In *Ethnic Chinese as Southeast Asians*, edited by Leo Suryadinata, 33–65. Singapore: Institute of Southeast Asian Studies, 1997.

Tan Swie Ling. *G30S 1965, Perang Dingin & Kehancuran Nasionalisme: Pemikiran Cina Jelata Korban Orba.* Depok: Komunitas Bambu bekerja sama dengan Lembaga Kajian Sinergi Indonesia, 2010.

Tsai, Yen-ling, and Douglas Kammen. "Anti-Communist Violence and the Ethnic Chinese in Medan, North Sumatra." In Kammen and McGregor, *Contours of Mass Violence in Indonesia*, 131–155.

Tsang, Steve. "Target Zhou Enlai: The 'Kashmir Princess' Incident of 1955." *China Quarterly* 139 (1994): 766–782.

Twang, Peck Yang. *The Chinese Business Élite in Indonesia and the Transition to Independence, 1940–1950.* Kuala Lumpur: Oxford University Press, 1998.

——. "Political Attitudes and Allegiances in the Totok Business Community, 1950–1954." *Indonesia* 28 (1979): 65–83.

van der Kroef, Justus M. "The Sarawak-Indonesian Border Insurgency." *Modern Asian Studies* 2, no. 3 (1968): 245–65.

van der Veer, Anne. "The Pao An Tui in Medan: A Chinese Security Force in Dutch Occupied Indonesia, 1945–1948." Master's thesis, Utrecht University, 2013.

Wang, Gungwu. "Chinese Politics in Malaya." *China Quarterly* 43 (1970): 1–30.

——. *Don't Leave Home: Migration and the Chinese.* Singapore: Times Academic Press, 2001.

——. "Greater China and the Chinese Overseas." *China Quarterly* 136 (1993): 926–948.

Wang Keping. "Ba Ren yu Wu Zu Miao" [Ba Ren and the *Temple of Five Ancestors*]. *Xin wenxue shiliao* 4 (2005): 144–147.

Weinstein, Franklin B. *Indonesian Foreign Policy and the Dilemma of Dependence.* Ithaca, NY: Cornell University Press, 1976.

Wen Guangyi, Cai Renlong, Liu Aihua, and Luo Mingqing. *Yindunixiya huaqiao shi* [History of overseas Chinese in Indonesia]. Beijing: Haiyang chubanshe, 1985.

Wertheim, W. F. "Suharto and the Untung Coup—The Missing Link." *Journal of Contemporary Asia* 1 (1970): 50–57.

Williams, Lea E. *Overseas Chinese Nationalism: The Genesis of the Pan-Chinese Movement in Indonesia, 1900–1916.* Glencoe, IL: Free Press, 1960.

Williams, Michael. "Sneevliet and the Birth of Asian Communism." *New Left Review* 123 (1980): 82–90.

Willmott, Donald E. *The National Status of the Chinese in Indonesia, 1900–1958*. Singapore: Equinox, 2009.

Wu Shihuang. *Yindunixiya* [Indonesia]. Beijing: Shijie zhishi chubanshe, 1956.

Wu Shuxiang, ed. *Xinglong Huaqiao Nongchang* [Xinglong Overseas Chinese Farm]. Haikou: Hainan chubanshe, 2011.

Xu Xiaosheng. *Huaqiao yu diyici guogong hezuo* [Overseas Chinese and the first United Front between the Communist and Nationalist Parties]. Guangzhou: Jinan daxue chubanshe, 1993.

Xu Zhengzheng. "Yindunixiya huaren zhong de qin Taiwan qunti: jingyu yu yingdui" [The pro-Taiwan Chinese communities in Indonesia: Challenges and responses]. PhD diss., Xiamen University, 2008.

Yang Kuisong. *Mao Zedong yu Mosike de enenyuanyuan* [Amity and enmity between Mao Zedong and Moscow]. Nanchang: Jiangxi renmin chubanshe, 1999.

Yen Ching Hwang. *The Overseas Chinese and the 1911 Revolution: With Special Reference to Singapore and Malaya*. Kuala Lumpur: Oxford University Press, 1976.

Yuan Houchun. *Yigecanyu zhizao lishi de huaren—Situ Meisheng chuanqi* [The legends of Situ Meisheng—an overseas Chinese who participated in the making of history]. Beijing: Renminwenxue chubanshe, 2006.

Zhang Liukun. "Huiguo ji" [On my journey back to the motherland]. In Wu Shuxiang, *Xinglong Huaqiao Nongchang*, 185–192.

——. "Liushi niandai chu Xinglong huaqiao nongchang Yinni guiqiao de shenghuo" [The life of the returned overseas Chinese from Indonesia on the Xinglong Overseas Chinese Farm in the early 1960s]. In Wu Shuxiang, *Xinglong Huaqiao Nongchang*, 198–204.

Zhang, Shu Guang. *Economic Cold War: America's Embargo against China and the Sino-Soviet Alliance, 1949–1963*. Stanford, CA: Stanford University Press, 2002.

——. "Constructing 'Peaceful Coexistence': China's Diplomacy toward the Geneva and Bandung Conferences, 1954–55." *Cold War History* 7, no. 4 (2007): 509–528.

Zhang Xiaoxin. "Jiusanling shijian hou Zhongguo dui Yinni guinanqiao jiuji anzhi gongzuo lunxi" [China's resettlement and relief work of refugee returnees after the September Thirtieth Movement in Indonesia]. *Huaren huaqiao lishi yanjiu* [Overseas Chinese history studies], no. 2 (June 2011): 51–60.

Zheng Junyi. *Guiqiao Peng Guanghan de wangshi jinshi* [The past of returned overseas Chinese Peng Guanhan]. Hong Kong: Xiangang shehui kexue chubanshe, 2005.

Zhou Nanjing, ed. *Ba Ren yu Yudunixiya—jinian Ba Ren (Wang Renshu) danchen 100 zhounian* [Ba Ren and Indonesia—in memory of the 100th birthday of Ba Ren a.k.a. Wang Renshu]. Hong Kong: Nandao chubanshe, 2001.

Zhou Nanjing, and Kong Zhiyuan, eds. *Sujianuo Zhongguo Yindunixiya huaren* [Sukarno, China, and the Chinese minority in Indonesia]. Hong Kong: Xianggang shehui kexue chubanshe, 2003.

Zhou, Taomo. "China and the Thirtieth of September Movement." *Indonesia* 98 (October 2014): 29–58.

Zhuang Guotu. *Huaren huaqiao yu Zhongguo de guanxi* [The relations between overseas Chinese and China]. Guangzhou: Guangdong gaode jiaoyu chubanshe, 2001.

INDEX

Aceh, 101, 183–84, 186, 188
Adjitorop, Jusuf, 160, 162, 168
Afro-Asian Conference. *See* Bandung
    Conference
Ahmed Ben Bella, 149–50
Aidit, Dipa Nusantara, 10, 13, 108, 120,
    140, 147, 152, 154–55, 157–58, 160–63,
    167–70, 180, 213
Aidit, Ibarruri, 168–69
Aidit, Sobron, 168
Aidit, Tanti, 160, 162
Albania, 155
Algeria, 149–50
All Indonesia Center of Labor
    Organizations (SOBSI), 106, 108
Allied Forces, 23, 25–26, 29, 32–33, 46, 118
Ang Jan Goan, 3, 78–79, 81, 95–96
Angkatan Bersendjata, 152–53, 163, 180
Antara News Agency, 123, 129
Antifascist Alliance of the Chinese in
    Sumatra, 39–40. *See also* People's
    Antifascist Alliance in Sumatra
Asian Games, 132
Assaat Datuk Mudo, 111, 130
Association of East Sumatran Chinese
    Workers and Peasants, 45
Association of East Sumatran Chinese
    Youth and Women, 45
Awakening of Religious Scholars (NU), 119,
    157, 160
Azahari, A. M., 136, 142–44

Ba Hua High School, 22
Ba Ren
    antifascist propaganda efforts,
        37, 40–41
    China Democratic League leadership,
        45, 107
    Chinese Communist Party (CCP)
        involvement, 33–35, 37–41
    Comintern agent rumors, 106
    consulate establishments, 57–58

    death, 218
    Dutch arrest, 33, 49
    Indonesian National Revolution support,
        33, 44–51
    Japanese invasion escape, 33, 38, 41–42
    League of Left-Wing Writers leadership,
        37
    Nationalist Party infiltration, 37
    Pao An Tui opposition, 45–46
    PRC ambassadorship, 33, 51–52, 57–59, 82
    pribumi dialogue attempts, 35–36, 42, 46
    Proletariat Who First Lit the Torch
        publication, 218
    public speeches, 44–45, 57–58
    Singapore, 37
    The Song of Indonesia poem, 34, 42–43, 218
    Sumatra refuge, 13, 33, 38–42, 106–7, 218
    Temple of Five Ancestors play, 47–49, 218
    typhoid infection, 34, 42
    underground resistance efforts against
        the Japanese, 33, 37–44
    writings, 13, 33–34, 38, 42–43, 46–48, 52,
        57, 218
    youth mobilization skills, 35–36, 39–41,
        45, 101
Bagansiapiapi, 18, 28, 107
Bai Chongxi, 29
Bali, 122, 126, 146, 203, 208–9
Bandung, 18, 26, 60, 91–92, 101, 175, 216
Bandung Conference, 2, 9, 53, 64–67, 89,
    117, 212
Bangka-Belitung Islands, 7, 98, 106, 109–10,
    122, 126, 191, 202
Banjarmasin, 175
Banteng Council, 67–68
Baperki, 76, 81, 95, 183
Basuki Tjahaja Purnama, 217
Batavia, 23, 30, 54, 80
Belawan, 107, 186–87
Below the Wind (Feng Xia), 45, 49, 87
Benteng System, 111
Betrayal of the PKI, The, 153

www.ingramcontent.com/pod-product-compliance
Lightning Source LLC
Chambersburg PA
CBHW020459270326
41926CB00008B/667